BUSINESS, GOVERNMENT, AND THE PUBLIC

BUSINESS, GOVERNMENT, AND THE PUBLIC

MURRAY L. WEIDENBAUM

Director, Center for the
Study of American Business
Washington University

Prentice-Hall, Inc., Englewood Cliffs, New Jersey 07632

Library of Congress Cataloging in Publication Data

Weidenbaum, Murray L
   Business, government, and the public.

   Bibliography: p.
   1. Industry and state—United States. I. Title.
HD3616.U46W44   322'.3'0973   76-23088
ISBN 0-13-099317-4

Printed in the United States of America

10   9   8   7   6

Prentice-Hall International, Inc., *London*
Prentice-Hall of Australia, Pty. Ltd., *Sydney*
Prentice-Hall of Canada, Ltd., *Toronto*
Prentice-Hall of India Private Limited, *New Delhi*
Prentice-Hall of Japan, Inc., *Tokyo*
Prentice-Hall of Southeast Asia Pte. Ltd., *Singapore*
Whitehall Books Limited, *Wellington, New Zealand*

Contents

CASE STUDIES

Preface

This book is an attempt to provide a new view of the impact of government and other external influences on the operations of business firms. Traditional books in this area have emphasized antitrust activities and independent regulatory agencies, such as the Interstate Commerce Commission.

Although it is useful insofar as it covers important aspects of business-government relations, the traditional approach ignores the basic types of public concerns and the resultant government activities that have a daily impact on virtually every enterprise in the nation. Hence, this book tries to break some new ground. Rather than being concerned with the specialized part of the public-private relationship, which is primarily the domain of lawyers (and secondarily of economists), it emphasizes the more far-ranging regulatory activities, which impinge on almost every business executive, line or staff, headquarters or divisional, in small companies and large, and in industries that are not ostensibly "regulated," as well as those that are.

This book is not designed to be a comprehensive encyclopedia of the entire gamut of business-government-public activities. Part I deliberately presents a point of view, albeit at times it is an unconventionally critical view of federal intervention. As tested in the author's classroom, it can be effective in stimulating thought and discussion, both pro and con, on the many provocative issues that are raised.

After thus whetting the readers' intellectual appetites, Part II shifts the focus to a more positive approach. It deals with the varied nature of the business responses—passive and active—to an environment increasingly influenced by government and public interest groups, indicating how business can survive and even prosper in the new situation. Part III deals with the interaction of business and the broader social-political environment of which it is a part. Possibilities of reshaping that environment are also considered.

The focus throughout is on improving the understanding of current and future generations of business executives with reference to an increasingly important, but basically neglected, aspect of their job. In the past at least, the failure of many business firms to respond voluntarily to the changing needs of the society has contributed to increased government involvement in internal business decision-making. Also, hopefully, this book will assist government officials and members of various interest groups to appreciate better the various consequences of their actions on the private sector of the economy.

The preparation of this book was supported in part by the Center for the Study of American Business at Washington University. The author is indebted to Linda Rockwood for helpful research and editorial assistance. Emma Williams carefully typed the drafts and final version of the manuscript.

Portions of various chapters have appeared in earlier form in *Business Horizons, Business and Society Review, Journal of Economic Issues, Michigan Business Review, Policy Analysis*, and in the American Enterprise Institute's monograph, *Government-Mandated Price Increases*. In each case, the editors have kindly consented to the use of these materials.

Murray L. Weidenbaum

BUSINESS,
GOVERNMENT,
AND
THE PUBLIC

REGULATION
BY GOVERNMENT

Chapter 1

An Overview
of Government Regulation

The regulatory process is one of the most powerful ways in which government can influence activities in the private sector of the economy. As an alternative to taxing and spending to achieve national objectives, the federal government has come to rely increasingly on mechanisms that operate through directly controlling the actions of institutions and people in the private sector of the society. Over the course of three different presidential administrations—Johnson, Nixon, Ford—we have witnessed a rising tide of involvement by the federal government in the internal decision-making of individual businesses. Government looms increasingly large between business and its customers, its employees, its shareholders, and the public. Thus, we are constantly reminded that the corporation is very much a creature of government.

The development and introduction of technology related to automobile exhaust emissions furnishes a cogent example. Rather than relying on indirect means of encouragement, such as expenditure, tax, or credit subsidies, or waiting for the market to respond on its own, the federal government has established by law and regulation allowable emissions from motor vehicles. Automobile manufacturers are thus made to innovate to bring their products within the performance standards established by law.

This pollution case is no isolated instance. What the typical business manager sees is that the government is influencing, if not controlling, more and more of the basic management decisions of the firm, ranging from choosing new products and processes to setting prices and determining which production methods to use. The government of the modern state thus has become an active partner in the management of business.

LAUNCHING NEW BUSINESSES AND PRODUCTS

The range of governmental regulatory activity has become quite extensive. What is a more basic entrepreneurial function than starting a new enterprise? In numerous cases, the prospective entrepreneur will find that entry into a business is controlled by one or more government agencies. Examples vary from operating airlines (the Civil Aeronautics Board) and railroads (the Interstate Commerce Commission) to managing radio and television stations (the Federal Communications Commission), distilling alcohol (the Treasury), manufacturing ethical drugs (the Food and Drug Administration), or producing nuclear materials (the Nuclear Regulatory Agency). In many other cases, the requirement to obtain a license before commencing operations is merely an annoying method used by state and local governments to raise revenue.

Prior to marketing many new products, a company must obtain government approval or at least demonstrate that the items will be up to federal standards. Clothes, for example, must meet the requirements of the Wool Labeling Act. Drugs, of course, must be approved by the Food and Drug Administration. The Consumer Product Safety Commission has the authority to set safety standards for consumer products and to ban those presenting "undue" risk of injury.

Government contractors are used to operating under a variety of government directives concerning prices and profits. Yet government influence over private pricing decisions is not limited to the military market. The extractive industries and their customers, for example, keenly feel the effects of government influence and control on the price of agricultural, forestry, and mining output. Transportation, communications, and utility companies deal with a host of federal, state, and at times local regulatory agencies in setting price schedules and in making other basic managerial decisions.

DETERMINING INTERNAL WORKING PROCEDURES

A firm is obliged to follow the business accounting methods of the Internal Revenue Service in at least one set of its books and the increasingly detailed requirements of the Securities and Exchange Commission in its public reporting. More recent innovations in federal regulatory activities include Truth-in-Lending (requiring full disclosure of finance charges), the Wholesome Poultry Products Act, the Poison Prevention Packaging Act, and the Clean Air Act.

Government contractors must adhere to the pay and related standards of the Walsh-Healey and Davis-Bacon Acts. But a far wider array of companies is subject to laws governing minimum wages, equal pay, overtime hours, and the entire area of recognizing, bargaining with, and maintaining day-to-day relations with labor unions.

The literature on public administration does not give much emphasis to the role of the government official as inspector. Yet this often uninvited visitor tends to make his or her appearances with increasing frequency and often without prior notice. Inspections and audits are made by all levels of government and a host of departments and agencies. Their coverage varies from sanitation to working conditions to financial records.

Federal inspectors, an increasingly important physical presence in private industry, are concerned with a growing list of responsibilities. In the mid-1970s the Supreme Court ruled that air pollution inspectors do not need search warrants to enter the property of suspected polluters as long as they do not enter areas closed to the public. The unannounced and warrantless inspections were held not to be in violation of constitutional protections against unreasonable search and seizure.[1] Inspectors of the Labor Department's Occupational Safety and Health Administration (OSHA) can go further. They have "no-knock" power to enter the premises of virtually any business in the United States, without a warrant or even prior announcement, to inspect for health and safety violations. Jail terms are provided in the OSHA law for anyone tipping off a "raid."

A U.S. district court, acting on the case of a firm that had refused an inspector entry until the company's attorney was present, ruled that the federal agents did not need search warrants to enter workplaces.[2]

THE NEW REGULATORY PROGRAMS

Table 1–1 lists the major expansions in federal regulatory activities enacted by Congress since 1962. They cover six major areas: consumer products, discrimination in employment, traffic safety, consumer finance, job safety, and environment and resources. The pace of the development of these regulatory activities has varied substantially within each area.

Increasingly stringent consumer product regulation has been a constant theme since 1962, starting with the requirement in the Food and Drug Amendments that drugs be tested for safety and effectiveness prior to marketing. Several statutes have required labeling of cigarettes with official statements concerning health hazards, notably the Cigarette Labeling and Advertising Act of

---

[1] *Air Pollution Variance Board of the State of Colorado* v. *Western Alfalfa Corporation,* 94 S. Ct. 2114 (May 20, 1974).

[2] "Court Upholds 'Free Entry' for OSHA," *Industry Week,* July 15, 1974, p. 9.

Table 1-1

EXTENSION OF GOVERNMENT REGULATION OF BUSINESS, 1962-74

Year of Enactment	Name of Law	Purpose and Function
1962	Food and Drug Amendments	Requires pretesting of drugs for safety and effectiveness and labeling of drugs by generic names
1962	Air Pollution Control Act	Provides first modern ecology statute
1963	Equal Pay Act	Eliminates wage differentials based on sex
1964	Civil Rights Act	Creates Equal Employment Opportunity Commission (EEOC) to investigate charges of job discrimination
1965	Water Quality Act	Extends environmental concern to water
1965	Cigarette Labeling and Advertising Act	Requires labels on hazards of smoking
1966	Fair Packaging and Labeling Act	Requires producers to state what a package contains, how much it contains, and who made the product
1966	Child Protection Act	Bans sale of hazardous toys and articles
1966	Traffic Safety Act	Provides for a coordinated national safety program, including safety standards for motor vehicles
1966	Coal Mine Safety Amendments	Tightens controls on working conditions
1967	Flammable Fabrics Act	Broadens federal authority to set safety standards for inflammable fabrics, including clothing and household products
1967	Wholesome Meat Act	Offers states federal assistance in establishing interstate inspection system and raises quality standards for imported meat
1967	Age Discrimination in Employment Act	Prohibits job discrimination against individuals aged 40 to 65
1968	Consumer Credit Protection Act (Truth-in-Lending)	Requires full disclosure of terms and conditions of finance charges in credit transactions

Table 1-1

EXTENSION OF GOVERNMENT REGULATION OF BUSINESS, 1962–74

Year of Enactment	Name of Law	Purpose and Function
1968	Interstate Land Sales Full Disclosure Act	Provides safeguards against unscrupulous practices in interstate land sales
1968	Wholesome Poultry Products Act	Increases protection against impure poultry
1968	Radiation Control for Health and Safety Act	Provides for mandatory control standards and recall of faulty atomic products
1969	National Environmental Policy Act	Requires environmental impact statements for federal agencies and projects
1970	Public Health Smoking Act	Extends warning about the hazards of cigarette smoking
1970	Amendments to Federal Deposit Insurance Act	Prohibits issuance of unsolicited credit cards. Limits customer's liability in case of loss or theft to $50. Regulates credit bureaus and provides consumers access to files
1970	Securities Investor Protection Act	Provides greater protection for customers of brokers and dealers and members of national securities exchanges. Establishes a Securities Investor Protection Corporation, financed by fees on brokerage houses
1970	Poison Prevention Packaging Act	Authorizes standards for child-resistant packaging of hazardous substances
1970	Clean Air Act Amendments	Provides for setting air quality standards
1970	Occupational Safety and Health Act	Establishes safety and health standards that must be met by employers
1971	Lead-Based Paint Elimination Act	Provides assistance in developing and administering programs to eliminate lead-based paints
1971	Federal Boat Safety Act	Provides for a coordinated national boating safety program
1972	Consumer Product Safety Act	Establishes a commission to set safety standards for consumer products and bans products presenting undue risk of injury

Table 1-1

EXTENSION OF GOVERNMENT REGULATION OF BUSINESS, 1962-74

Year of Enactment	Name of Law	Purpose and Function
1972	Federal Water Pollution Control Act	Declares an end to the discharge of pollutants into navigable waters by 1985 as a national goal
1972	Noise Pollution and Control Act	Regulates noise limits of products and transportation vehicles
1972	Equal Employment Opportunity Act	Gives EEOC the right to sue employers
1973	Emergency Petroleum Allocation Act	Establishes temporary controls over petroleum
1973	Vocational Rehabilitation Act	Requires federal contractors to take affirmative action on hiring the handicapped
1973	Highway Speed Limit Reduction	Limits vehicles to speeds of 55 miles an hour
1973	Safe Drinking Water Act	Requires EPA to set national drinking water regulations
1974	Campaign Finance Amendments	Restricts amounts of political contributions
1974	Federal Energy Administration Act	Provides authority for mandatory energy conservation programs
1974	Employee Retirement Income Security Act	Sets new federal standards for employee pension programs

1966 and the Public Health Smoking Act of 1970. Children's toys received special attention in 1966, as did inflammable products in 1967. The broad-gauged consumer safety legislation was enacted in 1972.

A series of equal employment opportunity laws also was enacted early in this period. The Equal Pay Act of 1963 eliminated wage differentials based on sex. The Equal Employment Opportunity Commission was established in 1964 and was strengthened in 1972. Job discrimination against individuals aged 40 to 65 was outlawed in 1967. Affirmative action on behalf of handicapped workers was included in the Vocational Rehabilitation Act of 1973.

Modern traffic safety regulation commenced in 1966 with the Traffic Safety Act. That law provides for a national safety program, including setting national safety standards for motor vehicles. Consumer finance legislation was later getting started. The landmark statute, the Consumer Credit Protection Act (usually called Truth-in-Lending), was passed in 1968. It requires full disclosure of the terms and conditions of finance charges in credit transactions. The 1970 amendments to the Federal Deposit Insurance Act regulate credit bureaus and give consumers access to files.

Job safety legislation has a long tradition, going back to federal and state workmen's compensation laws. The Occupational Safety and Health Act of 1970 is the major statute in the fairly recent wave of regulatory legislation in this area. It establishes national employee safety and health standards, which must be met by employers. More specialized laws include the Radiation Control for Health and Safety Act of 1968.

The area of government regulation that has received a very substantial amount of public interest relates to the environment. Beginning with the Air Pollution Control Act of 1962, Congress successively has legislated federal controls over water pollution (the Water Quality Act of 1965), required environmental impact statements (the National Environmental Policy Act of 1969), and regulated noise of products and transportation vehicles (the Noise Pollution Act of 1972). In more recent years, the federal government has enacted a series of laws emphasizing the development and conservation of energy resources—some of these statutes have tended to create conflicts with ecology objectives. The latter include the Emergency Petroleum Allocation Act of 1973 and the Federal Energy Administration Act of 1974. As will be shown, the expansion of regulatory activities almost inevitably results in problems of adjusting to their varying objectives and approaches.

Perspective is needed. Thus, although in general the scope of federal influence is expanding, there are limits to this trend. Some controls do end. For example, in January 1974, the federal government terminated the interest equalization tax on American holdings of foreign stocks and bonds and the five-year-old program of controls over direct investments abroad by United States corporations. Simultaneously, the Federal Reserve System ended its guidelines limiting lending and investments overseas by United States banks and other financial institutions.

The general wage and price control system was allowed to expire at the end of April 1974. Restraints on price increases since then have been limited to the area of energy and to regulated industries operating under federal authorizations, such as the airlines and the railroads.

Also, the federal government does not adopt every suggestion for increasing government regulation of the private sector. In April 1974, the Food and Drug Administration (FDA) rejected a petition by 37 members of Congress and nine consumer groups calling for warning labels on all packaged foods that do not list each ingredient. The commissioner of FDA stated that the proposed label would confuse and mislead consumers, and expressed doubt whether most buyers read the relatively simple statement of ingredients that is now available. [3]

[3] "Stricter food labeling is rejected," *St. Louis Globe-Democrat,* April 20, 1974, p. 4D.

Although the precise changes that will occur in the years ahead are basically a matter for conjecture, the overall trend seems to be fairly clear: on balance there is likely to be more and not less government intervention in internal business decision-making. Despite differences in philosophy and outlook, changes in control of the executive branch and in the composition of Congress and the judiciary seem to have little effect in altering that trend.[4] It is interesting that the same phenomenon has been noted in Great Britain. Professor H. Townsend of the University of Lancaster states that both Conservative and Labor governments have found it necessary to have ministers of consumer affairs. A variety of regulatory legislation has been enacted in recent decades. Examples include the Food and Drugs Act of 1955, the Restrictive Trade Practices Act of 1956, the Weights and Measures Act of 1963, the Resale Prices Act of 1964, the Trade Descriptions Acts of 1968 and 1972, the Supply of Good Act of 1973, and the Fair Trading Act of 1973.[5]

[4]See Murray L. Weidenbaum, *Government-Mandated Price Increases* (Washington, D.C.: American Enterprise Institute for Public Policy Research, 1975).

[5]H. Townsend, *Economics of Consumerism,* Inaugural Lecture at the University of Lancaster, May 1, 1974, p. 1.

Chapter 2

The New Wave
of Government Regulation

A massive expansion of government controls over private industry is under way in the United States. Government officials are exercising new roles in such traditional aspects of business decision-making as product development, production, finance, marketing, and personnel. Impetus for this expanded government participation is being provided by a variety of consumer groups, environmental organizations, civil rights advocates, labor unions, and other citizens' institutions. In many cases, the increasing regulation reflects public and congressional concern that traditional federal and state-local programs have not been effective. The wave of regulation is also reenforced by the belief that the private sector itself is responsible for many of the problems facing society—pollution, discrimination in employment, unsafe products, unhealthy working environments, misleading financial reporting, and so forth.

Yet the process is so extensive and pervasive that we almost have come to take it for granted. As an example, let us examine one issue (May 14, 1975) of the *Wall Street Journal*. There were 19 articles that day dealing with one or more aspects of government-business relations. A mere reading of the headlines conveys a feeling of the depth and variety of the trend of government regulation.

"More Regulation by Government Gets 56% Backing in Poll"
"DuPont, Christiana To Defend Merger Plan in U.S. Court Today"
"U.S. Is Seen Ready to Require Firestone To Begin Largest Tire Recall on Record"

"G. D. Searle's Low-Calorie Sweetner Is Delayed Again, for a Health Review"

"Bill to Make Some Banks Give Loan Data To Government Clears House Committee"

"U.S. Official Urges SEC To Slow Loan-Loss Rule"

"Phaseout of Controls On Oil Prices Voted by House Subpanel"

"Senate Votes Funds Requested by Amtrak"

"Honduran Panel Verifies Bribe by United Brands"

"Better Planning of Less"

"Thiokol Gets Order to Run Army Ammunition Facility"

"AT&T Agrees to Boost Efforts on Hiring And Promoting of Women and Minorities"

"EPA Says Auto Makers Haven't Tried to Meet '78 Standard on Nitrogen Oxide"

"Ralston Purina Says Judge Denies Order on Tuna Ads"

"Consumer Unit Debate Is Halted by Senate, 71–27"

"SEC to Sue Ashland for Not Disclosing Payments Made to Gain Oil Concessions"

"Mobil's Advocacy Ads Lead a Growing Trend, Draw Praise, Criticism"

"Futures Panel Sets More Guidelines to Regulate Trades"

"Minnesota Mining Annual Meeting Is Surprisingly Tame—Management Criticism Is Little Despite Earnings Decline and Illegal Political Gifts"

This wave of governmental regulation is not merely an intensification of existing activities. In good measure, it is a new departure. The traditional theory of government regulation of business, which is still in general use and has dominated thinking on the subject, is based on the model of the Interstate Commerce Commission. Under this approach, a federal commission is established to regulate a specific industry, with the related concern of promoting the well-being of that industry. Often the public or consumer interest is viewed as subordinated, or even ignored, as the agency focuses on the needs and concerns of the industry that it is regulating.[1]

In some cases—because of the unique expertise possessed by the members of the industry or its job enticements for regulators who leave government employment—the regulatory commission is alleged to become a captive of the industry it is supposed to regulate. At least, this is a popularly held view of the development of the federal regulatory process. In addition to the ICC, other examples of this development that have been cited from time to time include the Civil Aeronautics Board, the Federal Communications Commission, the Federal Power Commission, and the Federal Maritime Commission. The head of one of

---

[1] See, for example, Manuel F. Cohen and George J. Stigler, *Can Regulatory Agencies Protect Consumers?* (Washington, D.C.: American Enterprise Institute for Public Policy Research, 1971).

these agencies resigned in 1975 in the midst of charges of excessive zeal in promoting the interests of the industry being regulated.[2]

A comprehensive study by Professor Victor H. Kramer of the Georgetown University Law School showed that, from 1960 to 1975, 30 percent of the persons appointed to nine regulatory commissions came from the industry they were to regulate. The definition of "regulated industry" included employment in companies directly involved in the regulated activity and those working in law firms consulting companies to further industry interests. Of the 85 commissioners who left the agencies during that period, 32 had been employed in the regulated industry within five years.[3]

The regulatory agencies do have rules that restrict the private employment of former employees. Federal law forbids any former federal official from participating in a matter in which he or she was involved while in government service for at least one year after leaving the government. Some agencies have more stringent rules.

The Federal Power Commission will not permit a former employee ever to appear in a case before the Commission if he or she participated in the case while working for the FPC. The Federal Trade Commission bars any previous employee from participating in any proceeding pending while that person was employed by the FTC.

Nevertheless, numerous former members of the regulatory commissions and their staffs now hold positions in the industries they had regulated; one former commissioner of the Securities and Exchange Commission serves as chairman of the largest stock exchange. One person who had served as an FCC commissioner is back with his previous employer, an owner of several radio stations. Several former staff members of the Food and Drug Administration work for food manufacturing companies.

THE NEW MODEL OF GOVERNMENT REGULATION

Although the traditional type of federal regulation of business surely continues, the regulatory efforts established by the Congress in recent years—as described in Chapter I—follow, in the main, a fundamentally different pattern. Evaluating the activities of these newer regulatory efforts with the ICC type of model is inappropriate and may lead to undesirable public policy.

The new federal regulatory agencies are broader in the scope of their jurisdiction than the ICC-CAB-FCC-FPC model. Yet simultaneously in important

---

[2] Albert R. Karr, "Helen Bentley Quits Her Position as Head of Maritime Agency," *Wall Street Journal,* June 18, 1975, p. 14.

[3] "Quality of Appointments to 9 U.S. Agencies Scored," *New York Times,* November 7, 1975, p. 14.

aspects they are far more restricted. This anomaly lies at the heart of the problem of relating their efforts to the national interest (see Figure 2–1).

In the cases of the Environmental Protection Agency, the Equal Employment Opportunity Commission, the Consumer Product Safety Commission, the Federal Energy Administration, and the Occupational Safety and Health Administration, the focus of the regulatory agency is not limited to a single industry. With each of these relative newcomers to the federal bureaucracy, its jurisdiction extends to the bulk of the private sector and at times to productive activities in the public sector itself. It is this far-ranging characteristic that makes it impractical for any single industry to dominate these regulatory activities in the manner of the traditional model. What specific industry is going to capture the EEOC or OSHA, or would have the incentive to do so?

Yet in comparison to the older agencies, the newer federal regulators in many important ways operate in a far narrower sphere. That is, they are not usually concerned with the totality of a company or industry, but only or primarily with the one segment of operations that falls under their jurisdiction. The ICC, for example, must pay attention to the basic mission of the trucking industry—to provide transportation services to the public—as part of its supervision of rates and entry into the trucking business. The EPA, on the other hand, is interested almost exclusively in the effect of those trucking operations on the environment. This limitation prevents the newer agency from developing too close a concern with the overall well-being of any company or industry. Rather, it can result in a lack of concern over the effects of its specific actions on a company or industry.

If there is any special interest that may come to dominate such an agency,

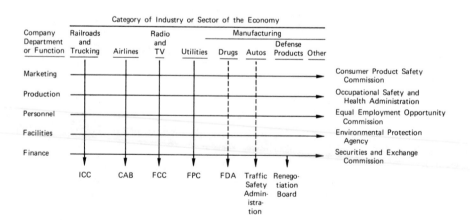

Figure 2-1

VARIATIONS IN FEDERAL REGULATION OF BUSINESS

it is not the industry being regulated, but rather the group that is preoccupied with its specific task—environmental cleanup, elimination of job discrimination, establishment of safer working conditions, reduction of product hazards, and so forth.

Thus, little attention may be given to the basic mission of the industry, to provide goods and services to the public. Also ignored or downplayed are cross-cutting concerns and matters broader than the specific charter of the regulating agency, such as productivity, economic growth, employment, cost to the consumer, effects on overall living standards, and inflationary impacts.

Some important cases may blend the old and the new forms of regulation. The Securities and Exchange Commission is a good example. In one aspect of its activities, it regulates a specific branch of the economy, the securities industry. Yet, as will be brought out in subsequent chapters, its rules also influence the way in which a great many companies prepare their financial statements and reports to shareholders. Economywide regulatory agencies are not entirely a recent creation; the Federal Trade Commission has existed for years. Moreover, a few one-industry agencies continue to be created, notably the Commodity Futures Trading Commission. This commission regulates the financial markets dealing with products of agriculture and other extractive industries.

The results of the new approach to government regulation of business may be the reverse of the traditional situation. Rather than being dominated by a given industry, the newer type of federal regulatory activity is far more likely to utilize the resources of various industries, or to ignore their needs, to further the specific objectives of the agency. Detailed study of the activities of these newer regulatory agencies reveals many negative aspects as well as the intended benefits.

To begin with, we must recognize that it is difficult to criticize the basic mission of these newer regulatory agencies. Only a Scrooge would quarrel with the intent of the new wave of federal regulation—safer working conditions, better products for the consumer, elimination of discrimination in employment, reduction of environmental pollution, and so forth. And we must recognize that the programs were deliberately established by the Congress in response to a surge of rising public expectations about corporate performance. Each of these programs has yielded significant benefits to society as a whole, and at times to business specifically. Some companies have found new outlets for their products in the emerging market for pollution control equipment, and society benefits from the reduction in pollution that results. Opening new employment opportunities for minority groups not only eliminates a basic social inequity but expands the effective labor force that can produce the goods and services desired by the society.

The present trends in federal government regulation in the United States do not represent an abrupt departure from an idealized free market economy, but rather the rapid intensification of the long-term expansion of government influence over the private sector. The new wave of regulation is also reenforced by the widespread belief that many business firms will face these difficult and costly questions only if they are forced to by government edict.

Government regulation at times can be justified as a logical response to what economists call "failures" in the normal market system. Examples of such situations are pollution of the environment, inadequate industrial safety practices, and potential health hazards. Voluntary action to deal with such problems may place a firm under a competitive disadvantage. The specific company attempting to correct the situation would tend to bear the full costs, while the benefits of the improvement would be widely dispersed in the society. "Free riders," who do not make the expensive changes, may nevertheless share in the benefit.

An example of this situation is provided by the regulation of pollution standards in the motor vehicle area. The basic justification for government setting standards for automobiles—particularly in the pollution area where so much of the benefit goes to society as a whole—was clearly stated by John J. Riccardo, president of Chrysler:

> . . . a large part of the public will not voluntarily spend extra money to install emission control systems which will help clean the air. Any manufacturer who installs and charges for such equipment while his competition doesn't soon finds he is losing sales and customers. In cases like this, a Government standard requiring everyone to have such equipment is the only way to protect both the public and the manufacturer.[4]

But no balanced evaluation of the overall practice of government regulation comfortably fits the notion of benign and wise officials always making sensible decisions in society's greater interests. Numerous adverse side effects and other costs are evident, as well as substantial benefits to society. Subsequent chapters will discuss each of these aspects in more detail.

THE DIRECT COST OF GOVERNMENT REGULATION

The number and size of the agencies carrying out federal regulation are expanding—and far more rapidly than the industries they are regulating. Since the mid-1960s, we have seen the formation of the Consumer Product Safety Commission, the Environmental Protection Agency, the Federal Energy Administration, the Cost Accounting Standards Board, the National Bureau of Fire Prevention, the Mining Enforcement and Safety Administration, the National Highway Traffic Safety Administration, and the Occupational Safety and Health Administration, to cite just the better known ones.

[4]John J. Riccardo, "Regulation: A Threat to Prosperity," *New York Times,* July 20, 1975, p. F–12.

The direct costs to the taxpayers are large and growing. As shown in Table 2-1, the operating expenses of the major regulatory agencies came to almost $1.9 billion in the fiscal year 1974. A 48 percent increase was budgeted over the next two years, with the total federal costs of these regulatory activities rising to $2.8 billion in fiscal 1976. It is apparent that the biggest regulatory budgets are not those for the traditional independent regulatory commissions, such as the ICC ($50 million) or the CAB ($85 million). Rather the largest proportion of the funds is devoted to the broader regulatory activities of the Department of Labor ($397 million, mainly for employment standards and job safety) and Agriculture ($381 million, largely for food inspection).

The labor force of inspectors, reviewers, and other regulators maintained by these programs is also growing, from 63,796 in fiscal year 1974 to 72,011 in

Table 2-1

FEDERAL EXPENDITURES FOR BUSINESS REGULATION
(Fiscal years, $ millions)

Agency	1974	1975	1976
Agriculture	330	376	381
Health, Education, and Welfare	145	173	189
Interior	59	74	79
Justice	112	345	383
Labor	232	343	397
Transportation	178	212	234
Treasury	246	306	320
Civil Aeronautics Board	89	85	85
Commodity Futures Trading Commission	—	—	11
Consumer Product Safety Commission	19	43	37
Cost Accounting Standards Board	1	2	2
Council on Wage and Price Stability	—	1	2
Environmental Protection Agency	46	53	54
Equal Employment Opportunity Commission	42	54	60
Federal Communications Commission	38	49	50
Federal Energy Administration	33	127	208
Federal Maritime Commission	6	7	8
Federal Power Commission	27	37	36
Federal Trade Commission	32	41	45
International Trade Commission	7	9	10
Interstate Commerce Commission	38	47	50
National Labor Relations Board	55	63	70
National Transportation Safety Board	8	10	10
Nuclear Regulatory Commission	80	139	198
Occupational Safety and Health Review Commission	5	6	6
Renegotiation Board	5	5	5
Securities and Exchange Commission	35	45	49
Total	1,868	2,652	2,979

Source: Budget of the U.S. Government for the Fiscal Year 1976.

fiscal 1976 (see Table 2–2). Increases are concentrated primarily in the newer agencies such as the Federal Energy Administration, the Occupational Safety and Health Administration, and the Mining Enforcement and Safety Administration. But that represents only the tip of the iceberg. The costs imposed by these agencies on the private sector are larger.

At first blush, government imposition of socially desirable requirements on business appears to be an inexpensive way of achieving national objectives: it seems to cost the government little (aside from the usually overlooked expenses of the regulatory agencies themselves) and therefore is not recognized as much of a burden on the taxpayer. But, on reflection, it can be seen that the public does not escape paying the full cost. For example, every time that the Occupational Safety and Health Administration imposes a more costly, albeit safer, method of production, the cost of the resultant product necessarily will tend to rise. Every time that the Consumer Product Safety Commission imposes a standard which is more costly to attain, some product costs will tend to rise. The same holds true for the activities of the Environmental Protection Agency, the Food and Drug Administration, and so forth.

The point being made should not be misunderstood. What is at issue is not the worthiness of the objectives of these agencies. Rather, it is that the public does not get a "free lunch" by imposing public requirements on private industry.[5] Although the costs of government regulation are not borne by the taxpayer directly, in large measure they show up in higher prices of the goods and services that consumers buy. These higher prices represent the "hidden tax," which is shifted from the taxpayer to the consumer. Moreover, to the extent that government-mandated requirements impose similar costs on all price categories of a given product (say, automobiles), this hidden tax will tend to be more regressive than the federal income tax. That is, the costs may be a higher relative burden on lower income groups than on higher income groups.

THE RANGE OF CONTROLS OVER BUSINESS

Many types of government controls may not be obvious. They may accompany programs that are promotional or supportive activities for an industry or economic sector. For example, the federal government's efforts to assist in the maintenance of a merchant marine consists primarily of direct subsidies to ship builders and ship operators. However, to qualify for the government funds, the ships may incorporate specific national defense and safety features spelled out by the government. These added features raise both acquisition and operating costs.

[5]See Murray L. Weidenbaum, *Government-Mandated Price Increases* (Washington, D.C.: American Enterprise Institute for Public Policy Research, 1975). See also the author's "The High Costs of Government Regulation," *Business Horizons,* August 1975.

Table 2-2

EMPLOYMENT OF FEDERAL REGULATORY AGENCIES

Agency	1974	1975	1976
Agriculture:			
Animal and Plant Health Inspection Service	14,500	14,804	14,844
Commodity Exchange Authority	150	300	—
Packers and Stockyards Administration	188	205	208
Milk Market Orders Assessment Fund	838	838	838
Health, Education, and Welfare:			
Food and Drug Administration	6,128	6,193	6,260
Interior:			
Mining Enforcement and Safety Administration	2,548	2,820	3,068
Justice:			
Antitrust Division	622	682	731
Drug Enforcement Administration	3,703	3,970	4,183
Labor:			
Employment Standards Administration	2,449	2,826	2,788
Occupational Safety and Health Administration	1,613	2,140	2,141
Transportation:			
National Highway Traffic Safety Administration	784	801	844
Federal Railroad Administration	268	343	385
Treasury:			
Bureau of Alcohol, Tobacco, and Firearms	3,684	3,825	3,938
Comptroller of the Currency	2,457	2,760	3,025
Civil Aeronautics Board	688	701	731
Commodity Futures Trading Commission	—	—	497
Consumer Product Safety Commission	836	910	910
Cost Accounting Standards Board	37	39	41
Council on Wage and Price Stability	—	24	41
Environmental Protection Agency	3,889	3,815	4,034
Equal Employment Opportunity Commission	1,870	2,168	2,168
Federal Communications Commission	1,835	1,951	2,010
Federal Deposit Insurance Corporation	2,607	2,632	2,650
Federal Energy Administration	596	3,133	2,283
Federal Maritime Commission	289	303	312
Federal Metal and Nonmetallic Mine Safety Board of Review	2	2	3
Federal Power Commission	1,227	1,310	1,337
Federal Trade Commission	1,555	1,610	1,675
International Trade Commission	325	387	397
Interstate Commerce Commission	1,874	2,045	2,087
National Labor Relations Board	2,428	2,448	2,567
National Transportation Safety Board	277	285	288
Nuclear Regulatory Commission	1,483	1,962	2,329
Occupational Safety and Health Review Commission	161	170	173
Renegotiation Board	194	197	198
Securities and Exchange Commission	1,691	1,955	2,027
Total	63,796	70,554	72,011

Source: Budget of the United States Government for the Fiscal Year 1976, Appendix.

Government procurement contracts spell out not only what goods and services the contractors must provide, but also how they should go about producing them. As shown in detail in Chapter VIII, these requirements range from hiring and training minority groups to adopting federally set wage and hour standards, and to favoring depressed areas and small business firms in subcontracting.

The tax collector also serves as regulator or at least as a source of strong influence. Using the carrot of tax incentives, the federal government is fostering greater social responsibility on the part of business. Specific Internal Revenue Service provisions that have been adopted in recent years include tax credits for hiring certain categories of people (minority groups), tax deferrals for income from exports, and outright tax reductions for investing in capital goods (the investment tax credit). At times there is a direct linkage between taxes and controls. For example, to qualify for rapid tax amortization of pollution control devices, a company's facility must first be certified by both the state involved and the regional office of the Environmental Protection Agency. For the company contributions to qualify as a tax deduction, a pension program must meet detailed requirements spelled out in the Employee Retirement Income Security Act of 1974.

Important distinctions need to be made in evaluating the impacts of government controls over business activity. Many clearly are going to be present, at least in some form, for the foreseeable future. Others may be of an intermittent or short-term nature.

The tax system is the most obvious example of a constant and ongoing control, although even the revenue structure is hardly a static affair. The Congress frequently enacts new or modified provisions in the Internal Revenue Code. The Internal Revenue Service, in turn, regularly reviews and often changes its administrative regulations. Nevertheless, business firms can plan their future activities on the assumption that taxes will continue to be an important form of government intervention in internal business decision-making.

By contrast, wage and price controls have been an on-again, off-again affair. There are many ways in which government intervenes in private wage and price determination (that is, the so-called incomes policies). At one end of the spectrum are generalized government appeals to business and labor to exercise restraint in increasing wages and prices. This practice is often referred to as moral suasion or "jawboning." A more specific step is the government effort to set voluntary standards or "guideposts" for wage and price changes considered to be in the public interest (however that is determined). These nominally voluntary approaches may be supplemented by various forms of government pressure or even coercion, ranging from public chastisement of individual businesses and labor unions to secret threats to cancel government contracts or other benefits. At the compulsory end of the wage and price control spectrum are formal systems that limit increases and absolute freezes that prohibit them for a fixed period of time.

Between the two types of government intervention represented by the durable tax structure and the relatively unpredictable wage and price control actions lies a third area of federal regulation of business. This large and growing intermediate zone consists of evolving programs. The general objective of each of these regulatory programs usually is clear, but the specific means of implementation may be uncertain because changes are made as unexpected problems emerge in the process of applying broad and relatively new policies to operational situations. Environmental and equal employment opportunity programs are perhaps the largest and best known examples of this middle category of federal regulation.

Although specific regulations may be revised repeatedly, the basic federal presence in these areas of business decision-making is likely to prove long lasting. Because government policies are relatively new and volatile, the business response to this sort of government regulation in many cases is not as fully developed as it is for well-established types of government intervention.

The federal government also uses influence in a way that is less direct than controls or regulations. A government agency may monitor a firm's operations, requesting various categories of data and other information; the Treasury Department, for example, monitors financial institutions. In addition to the paper work burden that government requests may place on a company, many business executives are often concerned that the monitoring or disclosure requirements are merely initial steps toward more formal intervention. Although these concerns are occasionally justified, at times use of the information monitoring approach may be a desirable alternative to more direct federal intervention in business decision-making.

Many problems relating to government controls of business result from the fact that these controls all arise out of the political process. Often an extended period of uncertainty predates the congressional mandate for a new regulatory program. In the interim, company decisions on new investments and product lines are often held in limbo. An extra degree of risk is attached to those corporate innovations that do go forward during such periods. In the early 1970s, for example, some petroleum companies were reported to have held off on the construction of new domestic refining facilities partly because of uncertainty about future restrictions on types of gasoline, resulting from increasingly stringent environmental controls.

Other problems may arise when Congress responds to public pressures before the ramifications of the proposed laws—or the possible alternatives to such measures—can be fully considered. Thus, legitimate public concern over the deterioration of the nation's rivers led to a statutory goal of zero discharge of pollutants by 1985, a goal regarded by many economists and industry experts as unattainable. Such quickly enacted legislation also may exacerbate day-to-day business-government relations because executive branch officials find themselves administering policies that are sometimes both unpopular and difficult to carry out. A related problem at times is the lack of knowledge about business operations on the part of many civil servants, whose education and experience is in the field of public administration. Business faces a real challenge in providing pertinent information to these government officials in an open and proper manner.

CONCLUSION

There is little justification for a general attack on all forms of government regulation. Unless you are an anarchist, you believe that the government should set the rules for the society. A society acting through government can and should act to protect consumers against rapacious sellers, individual workers against unscrupulous employers, and future generations against those who would waste the nation's resources. But, as in most things in life, the sensible questions are not matters of either/or, but rather of more or less and how. Thus, we can enthusiastically advocate stringent controls to avoid infant crib deaths without simultaneously supporting a plethora of detailed federal rules and regulations dealing with the color of exit lights and the maintenance of cuspidors. There are serious questions as to what rules to set, how detailed they should be, and how they should be administered. That, of course, is the substance of this book.

Because of the very substantial costs and other adverse side effects that they give rise to, society is beginning to take a new and hard look at the existing array of government controls over business. Efforts are being made to eliminate those controls that generate excessive costs, rather than merely continuing to proliferate government controls over business. In theory, government regulation should be carried to the point where the incremental benefits equal or barely exceed the incremental costs; overregulation (which can be defined as situations where the costs to society exceed the benefits) thus would be avoided.

The frontiers of control are expanding. They are increasing in a geographic sense as local regulation is followed by state or regional regulation, and as federal control is supplemented by international regulatory agencies. The forecast by John Maurice Clark in the 1930s not only has turned out to be accurate, but also to apply to the future outlook:

> Whether one believes government control to be desirable or undesirable, it appears fairly obvious that the increasing interdependence of all parts of the economic system . . . will force more control in the future than has been attempted in normal times in the past.[6]

As corporate managers become more sensitive to evolving social demands, they will consider responding to at least some of the public's expectations as being a normal aspect of conducting business. To the extent that this development occurs voluntarily, businesses themselves will be providing an important constraint on the degree of political pressure that social action interests effectively can exert against them.

[6]John Maurice Clark, "Government Regulation of Industry," *Encyclopedia of the Social Sciences,* III (New York: Macmillan, 1932), 129.

Chapter 3

Consumer Product Regulation

The actions of numerous federal agencies relate to consumer products. Of these, the Consumer Product Safety Commission has the most direct and explicit responsibility. The Consumer Product Safety Act of 1972 created an independent regulatory agency "to protect the public against unreasonable risks of injury associated with consumer products."[1] A five-member Consumer Product Safety Commission sets safety standards for consumer products, bans products presenting undue risk of injury, and in general polices the entire consumer product marketing process from manufacture to final sale.

In creating the Commission, Congress adopted a "no-fault" view of accidental product injuries, involving a complex interaction between the consumer, the product, and the environment. Rather than stressing punitive action against the producers and distributors of unsafe products, the emphasis in the statute is on setting new product standards. Under this approach, products would be redesigned to accommodate to possible consumer misuse and ignorance of proper operation of the product.[2]

Specific functions of the Commission include aiding consumers in the evaluation of product safety, developing uniform product safety standards,

---

[1] Consumer Product Safety Act, Public Law 92–573.

[2] Paul H. Weaver, "The Hazards of Trying to Make Consumer Products Safer," *Fortune*, July 1975, pp. 133–34.

gathering medical data and conducting research on product-related injuries, and coordinating federal, state, and local product safety laws and enforcement. Consumers are assured the right to participate in the Commission's activities, as "any interested person . . . may petition the Commission to commence a proceeding for the issuance, amendment, or revocation of a consumer product safety rule."[3] Safety standards cover product performance, contents, composition, design, construction, finish, packaging, and labeling.

A provision of the Consumer Product Safety Act that became operative in November 1975 gave both business and consumers more power to force the CPSC to accelerate its standard-making process. Under Section 10(e), any private party can bring suit against the Commission if it denies a rule-making petition or if it fails to act on a petition within 120 days. No other federal agency is bound by such a deadline on its decision-making.[4]

Powers of the Commission extend to requiring manufacturers of products found to be hazardous to take corrective actions. These actions include refunds, recalls, public warnings, and reimbursements to consumers for expenses of the recall process. Any product representing an unreasonable risk of personal injury or death may, by court order, be seized and condemned. Under the Consumer Product Safety Act of 1972, the Commission's jurisdiction extends to more than 10,000 products. In addition to banning offending products and requiring expensive recalls and debates, it can charge offending executives with violations that are subject to jail sentences.[5]

THE IMPACT ON CONSUMERS—BENEFITS AND COSTS

Important benefits to the public can be expected from an agency designed to make consumers more aware of product hazards and to require the removal from the market of products likely to cause serious injuries. Simultaneously, it must be noted that such actions also can generate large costs, which will be borne ultimately by the consumer. The consumer's total welfare is therefore maximized by seeking out the most economical and efficient ways of achieving safety objectives. Thus, banning products can be seen as one of a variety of alternatives. These can range from relabeling a product (so that the consumer becomes aware of a previously hidden hazard) to recalling and modifying an existing line of products.

The Stanford Research Institute has estimated that the mandatory safety standards developed by Consumers Union for the Commission would add $250

---

[3]Consumer Product Safety Act, Public Law 92–573.

[4]"Spurring New Action on Product Safety," *Business Week,* November 10, 1975, p. 60.

[5]Consumer Product Safety Act, Public Law 92–573.

million to the price tag for power lawn mowers and put 25 companies out of the business. The Institute estimated that the proposed standards could raise the price of a $100 gasoline-powered rotary mower to as much as $186. Push mowers would increase in price between 30 and 74 percent. The cost of more expensive riding mowers would go up at a slower rate, between 19 and 30 percent. The largest price rises, in the range of 35 to 86 percent, would occur on manual-start push rotary motors.[6]

At times, higher consumer product prices result from the Commission's actions and are brought about by their forcing expensive complexity on the manufacturers of consumer products. Poor, and even middle income, families may thus be priced out of many markets for consumer products. A case in point is the four million electric frying pans for which the Commission has ordered formal hearings to determine if they are hazardous. What is puzzling, however, is that, out of the four million pans, not a single injury has been reported by the Commission.[7]

Professor Max Brunk of Cornell University gets to the heart of the matter: "Consumerism is aimed at the consumer . . . look what it does to the consumer who pays the cost and loses the benefits that a prohibited product or service could have provided."[8] Following this line of reasoning, business can better adjust to these controls than can the consumer, because it can pass on the added costs that result.

Brunk notes that it is interesting to observe that consumer advocates sometimes have as much difficulty convincing the consumer of his or her need for protection as in convincing a regulatory body to provide the protection.[9] The truth-in-lending law is a cogent example. The compulsory requirement to show true interest costs has not slowed down the growth of consumer debt or the rise in interest rates. Since the passage of the act, the ratio of consumer debt to consumer income has reached an all-time high, and interest rates, for many reasons, have risen sharply. The average credit purchaser still seems to be more interested in the absolute amount of the monthly payment than in the rate of interest that is included in it. Similarly, despite the justification for unit pricing as a means of helping low income families to stretch their dollars further, available surveys show that it is the high income, well-educated customers who are most aware of this information.[10]

In the area of product safety, it should be recognized that consumers have unequal tastes for safety as well as other characteristics of product performance.

[6]*Reprints of Selected News Items* (Menlo Park, Cal.: Stanford Research Institute, 1975), p. 8.

[7]"Some Fry Pans and Chain Saws May Be Unsafe," *St. Louis Post-Dispatch*, January 15, 1974, p. 8A.

[8]Max E. Brunk, "Consumerism and Marketing," in *Issues in Business and Society*, ed. George Steiner (New York: Random House, 1972), p. 462.

[9]Ibid., p. 463.

[10]Ibid., p. 465.

Particularly where the safety hazard is minor (the occasional blister on a finger), policy makers need to realize that very large cost increases may merely deprive many consumers of the use of many products. As elsewhere, there is the need to recognize trade-offs between safety and other criteria important to consumers.

For example, a power tool selling for $20 may not have the capability of being in use for more than an hour; the $500 piece of equipment may be safely used for a much longer period. Although the instructions on each tool may be very clear in this respect, some consumers may willingly buy the cheaper model and knowingly take the chance of burning it out. A policy of complete product safety would ban the cheaper item, thereby effectively depriving the low income consumer of buying a power tool.[11]

A vast majority of Americans is concerned over product safety, and this concern has risen steadily since 1971. However, 87 percent of the adult Americans participating in a Harris survey blame consumers themselves for injury from products. Many believe that "most products are safe, but a lot of people do not read the directions or misuse products, so it is unfair to put all the safety blame on manufacturers." In the same survey a distinct opposition was shown to bans on products. Of the consumers surveyed, 73 percent believed that product safety objectives should be accomplished through publicity on product risks and dangers and by health warnings such as those required on cigarettes and drugs.[12]

THE EFFECT ON BUSINESS

The recordkeeping requirements imposed by the Consumer Product Safety Commission's early actions are substantial. In its first major proposed rule in August 1973, it called on every manufacturer, distributor, or retailer—upon learning that a product it sold "creates a substantial risk of injury"—to inform and provide the Commission with a wide array of information including:

1. The number of products that present a hazard or potential hazard.
2. The number of units of each product involved.
3. The number of units of each product in the hands of consumers.
4. Specific dates when the faulty units were manufactured and distributed.
5. An accounting of when and where such products (and the number of units of each) were distributed.
6. The model and serial numbers affected.

---

[11] J. Fred Weston, "Economic Aspects of Consumer Product Safety," in *Issues in Business and Society,* ed. George Steiner (New York: Random House, 1972), p. 499.

[12] Louis Harris, "Concern Over Product Safety," *Washington Post,* June 1, 1975, p. F-2.

7. A list of names and addresses of every distributor, retailer, and producer, if known.
8. A description of the effort made to notify consumers of the defect.
9. Details of corrective tests, quality controls, and engineering changes made or contemplated.[13]

The reporting requirement is not completed until the company submits a final report indicating that the "potential" product hazard has been corrected. Thus, the Commission shifts to the company the responsibility and costs of determining and remedying potential product defects with the possibility of criminal sanctions should the Commission disagree with the company's decisions. Product safety reporting by companies is a necessary input to the Commission's evaluation of potentially dangerous products. The reporting requirements are substantial and, therefore, costly. It is not, however, a question of whether or not companies should report information on product injuries, but of how much detail is needed for decision-making.

An example of prudent action on the part of the Commission was its handling of the alleged hazards involving spray adhesives. In August 1973, the Commission quickly banned these products when informed of findings by a University of Oklahoma scientist suggesting a causal relationship between the adhesives and chromosome breaks leading to birth defects.[14] The following January, however, the Commission announced that the ban was being lifted after in-depth research and independent evaluation reversed the conclusion of the initial study. In this case not only was the Commission quick to impose a ban on a product that it thought might be potentially hazardous, but it also acted expeditiously in conducting confirmatory studies and lifted the ban once evidence negated the original study. (See Appendix at end of this chapter for details of this case.)

The Commission has turned down the most extreme demands of consumer advocates. It rejected the petition of Ralph Nader's Health Research Group, which warned of the "imminent hazard to the public health" represented by lead-wick candles. The petition asserted that small children might chew or swallow the candles, taking lead into their systems, and candlelit suppers would result in "meals literally bathed in lead." In a letter to the Nader group, Commissioner Laurence M. Kushner stated that the petition "was drawn either with abysmal ignorance of elementary physical science, colossal intent to deceive the public, or both. The calculations, in the petition, of possible concentrations of lead in air which might result from burning such candles, were based on assumptions that are physically impossible . . ."[15]

---

[13]*Federal Register,* August 3, 1973, vol. 38, no. 149.

[14]*CPSC Bans Three Spray Adhesives—Asks Manufacturers of Others to Halt Production* (Washington, D.C.: U.S. Consumer Product Safety Commission, August 20, 1973).

[15]"Please Don't Eat the Candles," *Wall Street Journal,* January 16, 1974, p. 12.

THE POWER OF GOVERNMENT REGULATION

In the words of Chairman Arnold Elkind of the National Commission on Product Safety, whose recommendations led to the creation of the Consumer Product Safety Commission:

> It's true that the CPSC may be the most powerful independent regulatory agency ever created ... but it has to be. It has to have a wide choice of weapons to cope with the diverse range of situations it confronts.[16]

The Commission does have an impressive array of powers and at times uses them in a fashion that could seem arbitrary, at least to some people. For example, in promulgating its ban lists, the CPSC appears to have taken the position, perhaps unwittingly, that a company can be guilty until proved innocent. This surprising stand, which contradicts the basic notion of fairness in legal matters, seems implicit in the following statement in an issue of the CPSC's Banned Products List:

> Articles not meeting the requirements of the regulation are to be considered as banned even though they have not yet been reviewed, confirmed as banned, and added to the Banned Products List by the Consumer Product Safety Commission.[17]

Taken literally, the Commission's statement means that the responsibility for treating a product as being banned can fall entirely on the company involved, and in circumstances where the Commission is not even aware of the product's existence, much less of its supposedly hazardous characteristic.

The case of Marlin Toy Products of Horicon, Wisconsin, illustrates the dangers that can arise in the excessive use of the CPSC's great powers. Due to an "editorial error," the Commission put Marlin's major products on its new ban list in 1973. When the error was called to its attention, CPSC refused to issue a prompt retraction. As a result, Marlin was forced out of the toy business. (The appendix to Chapter 13 presents the details of this case.)

Although the Congress has assigned it responsibility for product safety, the Commission members have tried to extend this task to newspapers and magazines. In a session with reporters, the chairman and other members of the Commission stated their belief that publishers should attempt to verify the safety of the products advertised in their publications. Richard O. Simpson, CPSC chair-

---

[16]William H. Miller, "Consumer Product Safety Commission," *Industry Week,* October 29, 1973, p. 41.

[17]U.S. Consumer Product Safety Commission, *Banned Products,* October 1, 1973, p. 1.

man, was quoted as saying that newspapers and magazines who carry advertisements should consider hiring specialists to look over products or should farm out the task to outside consultants.[18] Thus, producers and distributors would have to satisfy not only the federally chartered Consumer Product Safety Commission but also the private safety commissioners appointed by each individual private publication.

Despite having substantial resources at its disposal and after several years of operation, the Commission has been chastized for its slowness in carrying out its principal function—the writing of safety standards for products. As of late 1975, no standards had been completed. In September 1975, the first standards—for swimming pool slides—were proposed.

In addition to difficulties in developing standards, the Commission has encountered problems in determining the boundaries of its own jurisdiction. This was displayed by its involvement in the handgun controversy. In response to a request to ban handgun ammunition as a hazardous substance, the Commission was required by statute to ask for public comments. It received more than 130,000 cards and letters, all on an issue that four of the five commissioners believed they had no business investigating.[19]

The stepped-up pace of regulation by the CPSC is resulting in "reverse distribution"—product recalls—becoming an important part of the marketing function of many companies. In addition to motor vehicles, increasing numbers of manufacturers of television sets, bicycles, ovens, and other nonautomotive products are being involved in recall situations. Product recalls in these cases are frequently justified and may well withstand the test of cost-benefit analysis.

This relatively new activity, however, is requiring a major expansion in record-keeping so that owners of the recalled product can be promptly notified. The Consumer Product Safety Commission ultimately may require manufacturers to keep records of all product complaints and to turn them over to the Commission if it so requests. This information thus could form the basis for additional product recalls. It is, therefore, likely that more of the complaint letters from consumers will be kept in company files—and perhaps acted on.

A particularly costly aspect of the newer product safety regulations is that they often contain retroactive clauses. Should a company discover a product defect several years after it begins selling a product, and if the defect requires a recall, the firm may find that the recall costs exceed the company's net worth.[20]

The cost of recalls varies with the number of products sold, the amount of time and effort required to track down the purchasers, and the percentage of

---

[18]"Consumer Agency Is Critical of Ads," *New York Times*, February 13, 1974, p. 47.

[19]Burt Schoor, "Consumer Product Safety Commission Finds Deep Hazards In Just Getting Itself Rolling," *Wall Street Journal*, May 6, 1975.

[20]E. Patrick McGuire, "The High Cost of Recalls," *New York Times*, March 30, 1975, p. E-1.

products that require repair, replacement, or refund. It cost General Motors $3.5 million for postage alone to notify by certified mail, as required by law, the 6.5 million owners of cars with questionable engine mounts. The cost to Panasonic to recall and repair 280,000 television sets, as ordered by the CPSC because of possible harmful radiation emission, may total $11.2 million—the equal of the company's profits in the United States for the past several years.

Expectations, either for private or public activities, should not be set too high. Considering the importance of the problems confronting the CPSC and the difficulties involved in solving them, perhaps the sympathetic, thoughtful comments of Paul Weaver may provide an appropriate ending note for this section:

> In the end there is no such thing as a perfect safety regulation; in most cases, in fact, even a fairly good one is hard to find. Thus there's nothing surprising or dishonorable about the failure of the Commission to issue perfect regulations in wholesale lots.

> But the environment within which they work—the law, the expectations of Congress, the conflicting pressures from consumerists and industry, the nature of government, the climate of public opinion, the methods and ambitions of the staff, and above all the monumental complexity of the task—makes good judgment difficult. The scarcest ingredient in this marvelously intricate and rational system is the homely virtue of common sense.[21]

LABELS AND LABELING

The CPSC is not the only guardian of the consumer established by Congress. More traditional efforts have centered in the Departments of Agriculture and Health, Education, and Welfare, where they have ranged from controlling the production and distribution of drugs to regulating the sale of pet turtles.

The governmental response to rising consumer pressures now often takes the form of stricter controls over product labeling. Rather than merely attractive coverings, packaging is required increasingly to contain information on the nutritional contents of the product and its usage. One court has held that the standard of clarity applicable to a package label is not what it says to "the reasonable consumer," but rather what it communicates to "the ignorant, the unthinking and credulous . . ."[22] Figure 3–1 contains the old and new approach to labeling a can of green beans.

State and local governments are becoming more active in the area of product labeling. As a greater number of states and localities pass labeling legislation, the likelihood decreases that a nationally marketed product can have a

---

[21]Weaver, "Trying to Make Consumer Products Safer," p. 140.

[22]"Social Issues Briefs," *Business Week,* May 18, 1974, p. 78.

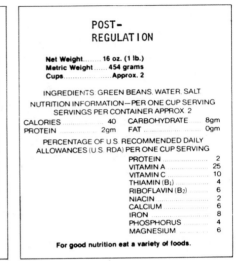

| PRE- | POST- |
| REGULATION | REGULATION |

PRE-REGULATION

Size of Can .. No. 303 / Net Wt. ... 1 lb. / Cups .. Approx. 2

Tender, young Blue Lake green beans, carefully selected for quality and sliced lengthwise to bring out the full delicate flavor of the beans.

SUGGESTIONS FOR SERVING

Pour liquid into saucepan and boil rapidly down to one-half volume; add beans and heat quickly. Do not overcook. If desired, season with salt, pepper, butter or crisply cooked bacon bits. Add minced dill pickle or onion for a zippy flavor. Or serve with a sauce such as: horseradish, mustard, sour cream, tomato.

Nutritional information is available on request

POST-REGULATION

Net Weight......... 16 oz. (1 lb.)
Metric Weight......454 grams
Cups...................Approx. 2

INGREDIENTS. GREEN BEANS. WATER. SALT
NUTRITION INFORMATION—PER ONE CUP SERVING
SERVINGS PER CONTAINER APPROX. 2

CALORIES 40   CARBOHYDRATE 8gm
PROTEIN .... 2gm   FAT 0gm

PERCENTAGE OF U.S. RECOMMENDED DAILY
ALLOWANCES (U.S. RDA) PER ONE CUP SERVING

PROTEIN 2
VITAMIN A 25
VITAMIN C 10
THIAMIN (B_1) 4
RIBOFLAVIN (B_2) 6
NIACIN 2
CALCIUM 6
IRON 8
PHOSPHORUS 4
MAGNESIUM 6

For good nutrition eat a variety of foods.

Figure 3-1

TWO APPROACHES TO LABELING A CAN OF GREEN BEANS

Source: U.S. General Accounting Office.

single label that will meet the requirements of all the jurisdictions in which the company hopes to sell it. The General Foods Corporation reports that it has encountered such a problem in Massachusetts, Oregon, and New York City, which have enacted labeling restrictions in conflict with national regulations as well as the requirements in other local areas. The company has issued the following warning:

> The result of this trend, if it continues unchecked, would be a severe impairment of the ability of food processors to distribute food efficiently and economically . . .[23]

"What's in a name?," asks the U.S. Department of Agriculture. It answers its own question: "Plenty, when a meat or poultry product bears the mark of federal inspection!"[24] The instructions to the producers of beef products are quite extensive. Products labeled "beef with gravy," for example, must contain

[23]*The Impact of Government Regulation on General Foods,* General Foods, January 1975, p. 6.
[24]U.S. Department of Agriculture, *Standards for Meat and Poultry Products,* Animal and Plant Health Inspection Service, 1973, p. 1.

at least 50 percent cooked beef. However, "gravy with beef" requires only 35 percent cooked beef. "Beef and dumplings with gravy" needs only 25 percent beef, as is the case for "Beef and gravy with dumplings." "Beef and pasta in tomato sauce" can get down to as little as 17½ percent beef.

Meeting the poultry requirements, in contrast, is an exercise in straightforward arithmetic. The permutations and combinations are so numerous that they can be best presented in tabular form (see Table 3-1 for the results). To the extent that consumers are unaware of these numerical distinctions, little benefit would seem to result from the imposition of such detailed requirements. Nevertheless, kept within reason, the case for accurate, informative descriptions of food products can be very convincing.

A labeling requirement being considered by the Federal Trade Commission could save consumers substantial sums, albeit that some overtones of "Father knows best" may be present. The Commission believes that the purchase of about $100 million of protein supplements yearly is unnecessary. It cites evidence that strongly indicates that most Americans have ample protein in their diets. The FTC response to this situation is a proposal to require that labels of protein supplements include the following:

> Protein supplements are unnecessary for most Americans. The U.S. Public Health Service has determined that the daily diet of most Americans provides adequate protein.[25]

OUTLOOK

The recent expansion in federal legislation related to consumer interests can be seen in Figure 3-2. Although an upward trend has been visible since the turn of the century, a rapid acceleration in the frequency of new control legislation has occurred since the mid-1960s and shows little signs of diminishing. Not only have more laws been passed in recent times, but, as shown in Chapter 1, the laws are also broader and more far-reaching.

A CONSUMER PROTECTION AGENCY?

Support is mounting in Congress to create a new consumer protection agency within the executive branch, intended to represent consumer interests before other federal agencies and in the courts. As of the fall of 1975, specific legislation to set up an agency for consumer advocacy was being debated in the

---

[25] "Caveats for Protein-Supplement Labels, Advertisements are Proposed by FTC," *Wall Street Journal,* September 5, 1975, p. 10.

Table 3-1

FEDERAL STANDARDS FOR POULTRY

Item	Minimum Required Percent Poultry Meat
Poultry Almondine	50 percent
Poultry Barbecue	40 percent
Poultry Paella	35 percent[a]
Poultry Hash	30 percent
Poultry Chili	28 percent
Poultry Croquettes	25 percent[b]
Poultry Cacciatori	20 percent
Poultry Casserole	18 percent
Poultry Chili With Beans	17 percent
Poultry Tetrazzini	15 percent
Poultry Pies	14 percent
Poultry Brunswick Stew	12 percent[c]
Cabbage Stuffed With Poultry	8 percent
Cannelloni With Poultry	7 percent
Poultry Tamales	6 percent
Poultry Chop Suey	4 percent
Chop Suey With Poultry	2 percent

[a]Or 35 percent poultry meat and other meat (cooked basis); no more than 35 percent cooked rice; must contain seafood.
[b]Or 40 percent with bone.
[c]Must contain corn.
Source: Computed from U.S. Department of Agriculture, *Standards for Meat and Poultry Products,* Animal and Plant Health Inspection Service, 1973.

Congress. Such a new federal agency would be empowered to intervene in decision-making by government regulatory agencies whenever it determined that vital consumer interests were at stake. It would be prohibited from entering the area of labor-management disputes.

APPENDIX: THE AEROSOL SPRAY ADHESIVE CASE[1]

On August 20, 1973, the U.S. Consumer Product Safety Commission banned certain brands of aerosol spray adhesives as an imminent hazard. The Commission's decision was based primarily on the preliminary findings of a chromosome research study by Dr. J. Rodman Seely. Dr. Seely identified pos-

[1]The material in this case is taken from Comptroller General of the United States, *Banning of Two Toys and Certain Aerosol Spray Adhesives,* MWD–75–65. (Washington, D.C.: U.S. General Accounting Office, 1975), pp. 13–30.

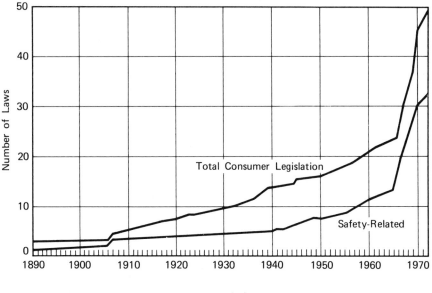

Figure 3-2

FEDERAL CONSUMER PROTECTION LAWS 1890-1972

Source: National Business Council for Consumer Affairs, 1973.

sible links between the use of certain brands of aerosol spray adhesives and chromosome damage and between chromosome damage and birth defects. After more extensive research and review and a medical panel's evaluation of this research, the Commission determined that the ban should not continue, and withdrew it on March 1, 1974.

Background

Dr. Seely is an associate professor of pediatrics, biochemistry, and molecular biology, and cytotechnology at the University of Oklahoma Medical Center. He began his research in March 1973, after being asked to examine a child with multiple birth defects consisting of uncommon or nontypical abnormality patterns. Dr. Seely performed a chromosome analysis and found what he considered to be significant numbers of damaged chromosomes, which he defined as chromosome breaks and gaps. He examined the parents and found damaged chromosome patterns similar to their child's.

The parents participated in a hobby called "foiling" or "foil art"— attaching various designs of multicolored foil paper to posters and other objects, usually with aerosol spray adhesives. The exhibits were usually finished with spray paint. Dr. Seely directed his investigation to determine whether a possible link existed between foilers' use of aerosol spray adhesives and chromosome damage. He discounted the foilers' use of spray paint as a cause factor because it was used for only a short period of time, and chemical agents in spray adhesives were generally more subject to question by the medical community. Aerosol spray adhesives of various formulas have been commercially marketed since 1961.

Dr. Seely examined four other foilers who had been exposed to aerosol spray adhesives and found that their blood cells had chromosome damage similar to that found in the deformed child and parents. Also, in mid-July 1973, Dr. Seely examined another child with uncommon or unusual birth defect characteristics and found that the child and both parents had a high percentage of cells with damaged chromosomes. Both parents were foilers.

In total, Dr. Seely had examined 10 persons with what he considered to be a high percentage (about nine percent) of damaged chromosomes—two deformed children, their four parents, and four other persons.

Medical researchers are not sure what percentage of damaged chromosomes is normal, acceptable, or harmful and have not satisfactorily tied chromosome damage to birth defects. Dr. Seely examined 12 persons who were *not* spray adhesive users for possible chromosome damage. He found that 1.65 percent of the cells sampled showed chromosome damage, compared to 8.99 percent for exposed persons. He considered this 7.34 percent difference—a five-to-one relative difference—statistically significant. These findings reinforced his belief in a possible relationship between aerosol spray adhesives and chromosome damage, and suggested a relationship between chromosome damage and birth defects.

Dr. Seely attempted to identify a chemical agent he thought may have been responsible for the chromosome damage. He contacted the major manufacturer of the sprays the foilers used and obtained its formula. The products did not contain the chemical agent he thought was responsible. Dr. Seely was uncertain of the action to take but believed that a responsible federal agency should look at his preliminary findings and conclusions. On July 25, 1973, he contacted the U.S. Food and Drug Administration (FDA). FDA referred him to the Consumer Product Safety Commission's Bureau of Biomedical Science (BBS), which is responsible for the Commission's laboratory reviews of potential hazards from chemical consumer products.

After the Commission was given some preliminary information on the telephone, BBS and FDA representatives (an FDA researcher was assisting the Commission in reviewing Dr. Seely's study) went to Oklahoma City on August 5, 1973, to meet Dr. Seely, establish his credibility, and review his research findings. At the meeting, the two representatives found Dr. Seely's data to be legitimate and adequately prepared and documented. They concluded that he was a responsbile researcher.

One aspect of the study that they found particularly troubling was the fact that the second child's parents had stopped using aerosol spray adhesives several months before conception, yet both parents and the child had a high percentage of damaged chromosomes. This indicated that aerosol spray adhesives could be a hazard resulting in long-lasting chromosome damage that might remain in a person even after discontinuing the product's use and adversely might affect future generations through heredity. The BBS staff considered this condition critical and believed Dr. Seely's research had identified a link between aerosol spray adhesive use and chromosome damage.

On August 7, 1973, BBS and FDA representatives briefed the Commission chairman and recommended that three brands of aerosol spray adhesives be declared an imminent hazard. Dr. Seely's data had been verbally provided to the Commission because he had not completed his research. The Commission requested the two manufacturers whom Dr. Seely identified in his research—Minnesota Mining and Manufacturing Company (3M) and Borden, Inc.—to submit information on their spray adhesives, including formulas, sales data, and consumer complaints. Both companies complied.

Factors Considered Before The Ban

The commissioners were concerned about Dr. Seely's preliminary research findings. His was the first study suggesting a link between aerosol spray adhesives and genetic problems. The potential severity of this hazard motivated the Commission to act quickly.

On August 15, 1973, the Commission informed 3M and Borden of its concern about the connection between their aerosol spray adhesives and potential health problems, and the possible need for quick regulatory action. Although the companies knew of the Commission's interest in spray adhesives, this was the first indication they had of the possibility of the products being banned as an "imminent hazard" under the Federal Hazardous Substances Act.

The Commission requested the two firms to provide any additional information that could refute Dr. Seely's findings and to discuss any action they planned to take as a result of the anticipated ban. The companies said they had not received Dr. Seely's written report (neither had the Commission at that time) and asked for the opportunity to discuss his findings with him. Commission representatives accompanied 3M and Borden representatives to Oklahoma City on the following day to meet with Dr. Seely.

At that meeting, the Commission received Dr. Seely's report containing his preliminary research findings and conclusions. Although the companies did not receive copies of the report, Dr. Seely read it aloud at the meeting. Company representatives discussed the study's preliminary conclusions and the research methods and laboratory techniques used with Dr. Seely.

The Commission's minutes of the meeting indicate that the company representatives questioned Dr. Seely on the possibility that other foiling materials may have contributed to the high damaged-chromosome readings. Company representatives expressed their concern about the organization of Dr. Seely's information and did not agree that the findings supported his conclusions. Neither company provided the Commission with information substantiating their comments or otherwise refuting the findings. At the completion of these meetings, a BBS representative told the companies that the Commission might ban the products until the study was corroborated or disproved.

Representatives of 3M expressed their concern to the Commission about Dr. Seely's research and conclusions and the short time they were allotted to reply.

The 3M representatives told Dr. Seely and Commission representatives that the company was concerned about possible subjective bias. That is, when analyzing blood samples for chromosome damage, Dr. Seely knew which samples were from exposed and nonexposed persons. They also said Dr. Seely was not fully objective in selecting and analyzing the nonexposed people. They did not believe these methods were consistent with good research techniques.

3M did not question Dr. Seely's data. However, it believed other factors, such as foilers' use of spray paint, could cause or contribute to chromosome damage. Also, 3M did not believe that the data adequately supported identifying its aerosol spray adhesives as the primary cause of chromosome damage and birth defects. It believed that Dr. Seely and the Commission should have contacted medical specialists in mutagenics, genetics, and other related fields to discuss the research results and obtain comments on the preliminary findings and conclusions before taking regulatory action. A 3M toxicologist subsequently told governmental investigators that several such specialists he contacted said damaged chromosomes in the 4- to 8-percent range were common.

3M requested that the Commission wait 1 to 2 weeks before deciding whether to ban the products because Dr. Seely's data were preliminary. This would have permitted the Commission and 3M—working together, as they did after the ban—to look deeper into Dr. Seely's work and obtain the opinions of specialists before taking regulatory action.

Both companies recognized that a significant potential public health problem had been raised and that the Commission had the authority to ban the products immediately as an imminent hazard. They also knew about the general lack of information linking aerosol spray adhesives and chromosome damage and recognized the seriousness of such problem to future generations.

Therefore, knowing of the Commission's intent to declare the products an imminent hazard, both manufacturers voluntarily stopped production and distribution of the aerosol spray adhesives in question on August 17, 1973—the date the Commission announced its intention to ban the sprays.

The Commission banned the aerosol spray adhesives on August 20, 1973, recognizing that certain aspects of Dr. Seely's research justified banning the products and other aspects raised questions about the necessity of a ban. The

Commission did not have documentation showing whether and how it had considered all such factors before the ban. The following information was obtained primarily by interviews subsequently conducted by the U.S. General Accounting Office.

Factors Supporting the Ban. The Consumer Product Safety Commission considered Dr. Seely as credible because of his credentials. He held M.D. and Ph.D. degrees, was a National Institutes of Health (NIH) grant recipient, and was widely published in the medical field. They believed that his research and test techniques showed good organization and investigative methods.

Dr. Seely's study identified two deformed children whose parents had used aerosol spray adhesives. The fact that this association did not have to be extrapolated from animal data added credibility to the research. Also, the fact that the second deformed child's parents had stopped using the products several months before conception illustrated potential long-lasting and hereditary effects of the hazard. The five-to-one ratio between damaged chromosomes in exposed persons and those in nonexposed persons was statistically significant.

Although the Commission knew that little mutagenic testing had been previously performed, its staff believed Dr. Seely's research demonstrated an adverse relationship between aerosol spray adhesive use and chromosome damage and between chromosome damage and birth defects. Neither the Commission nor the manufacturers were able to produce any data assuring the products' safety or refuting Dr. Seely's research.

The Commission's biomedical staff recommended, on the basis of discussions with Dr. Seely and its review of his preliminary research, that the aerosol spray adhesives be declared an imminent hazard. The Commission also believed that enough alternative glue products were being marketed so that consumers would not be overly inconvenienced by the ban.

Factors Raising Questions. Because of the research procedures Dr. Seely used, he knew which blood samples came from exposed and nonexposed persons as he analyzed them. Such analyses are usually made without such knowledge to avoid subjective bias. Commission staff members were aware of such bias in Dr. Seely's research and of the need for additional study and review. However, the Commission considered the percentage difference between damaged chromosomes in the two groups so significant that it did not want to take the time necessary to verify Dr. Seely's research before taking regulatory action.

Although researchers had studied the cause and effect of chromosome damage, its relationship to birth defects was relatively unresearched and little factual data existed at the time. The Commission recognized that Dr. Seely's preliminary research findings were unique and that they addressed a subject not adequately explored by previous research. However, the Commission, relying partly on BBS's review of Dr. Seely's research and laboratory practices, decided that the severity of the potential chromosome damage problem was overriding.

Dr. Seely's contacts with BBS were verbal. No written report was provided the Commission until August 16, 1973, the day before it publicly announced its intention to ban the products. No peer group evaluation of Dr. Seely's research was conducted. Peer group evaluation is a corroboration tool that researchers use to help build confidence and credibility in research findings, especially studies in previously unresearched areas.

Coordinating the Review of Dr. Seely's Study
Before Imposing the Ban

The Commission has no stated policy, regulations, or procedures that provide guidance for coordinating its review of potential hazardous products. Before the banning of aerosol spray adhesives, a Commission representative telephoned the National Library of Medicine and the Environmental Mutagen Information Center to determine if any chromosome damage studies had been performed on selected chemical formulations or aerosol spray adhesives. He was told that there were none.

Also, before the ban the Commission contacted a pediatrician-epidemiologist at NIH to obtain his opinion of Dr. Seely's preliminary findings. The NIH physician did not believe Dr. Seely's preliminary research and findings were correct or that they could be adequately documented and supported. He offered the following comments:

The two deformed children had dissimilar abnormality characteristics, suggesting that the association with aerosol spray adhesives should not be considered seriously without further evaluations. Because of the dissimilarity, there was a good probability that the malformations were not caused by the same chemical agent and aerosol spray adhesives were not the cause.

It is difficult to interpret the meaning of chromosome damage because little is known about causes and effects. An LSD study several years earlier tied chromosome damage to birth defects but was later proven inaccurate.

Because this was the first potential problem identified with aerosol spray adhesives, independent specialists should confirm Dr. Seely's findings by drawing and analyzing new blood samples before any regulatory action.

The Commission should perform chromosome analyses for persons exposed to high concentrations of aerosol spray adhesives—such as industrial users—to ascertain if a problem exists. Industrial users would be affected if the products were hazardous.

BBS discounted these comments because the doctor did not have a report to review and could not be expected to comment on the research's fine points. The NIH doctor provided the names of several specialists the Commission could contact for views on Dr. Seely's preliminary findings. Commission representatives said they did not have time to contact other specialists before taking regulatory action.

Actions in Banning the Adhesives

The Federal Hazardous Substances Act permits the immediate banning of a product considered to be an imminent hazard by publishing a notice in the *Federal Register.* An imminent hazard determination does not require the same due process proceedings as standard regulations, which generally need public hearings and advance notice before their effective date. However, normal regulation proceedings continue after the product is banned as an imminent hazard and a manufacturer has the right to challenge the Commission's determination in court. Neither 3M nor Borden did.

Alerting the Public. The Commission wanted to alert the public immediately to the adhesives' potential danger, but was not prepared to ban the products by publishing the required *Federal Register* notice. Therefore, on the basis of its intention to ban certain aerosol spray adhesives as an imminent hazard under the act, the Commission issued a press release on August 17, 1973.

The press release stated that the Commission was going to use all appropriate means to halt the production and sale of aerosol spray adhesives and was conducting a nationwide investigation to determine the extent of the problem. The Commission believed the seriousness of the potential problem justified warning consumers before the ban. On August 20, 1973, the Commission banned the three aerosol spray adhesive brands as an imminent hazard, with the appropriate notice in the *Federal Register.*

The Commission drew criticism from the medical community because of the contents of the press releases. The Commission's August 17, 1973, press release stated ". . . there is concern about the genetic damage which may cause problems in subsequent offspring . . . ." In an August 27, 1973, announcement, the Commission recommended that adults concerned about aerosol spray adhesive exposure ". . . should consider delaying pregnancies . . ." until further information was available. This announcement also warned pregnant women that the risk for the infant is not known and concern may be increased if both parents have been exposed to aerosol spray adhesives.

Practicing and laboratory medical professionals were concerned about the mental anguish these announcements inflicted on the public, especially pregnant women. Several physicians complained to the Commission that Dr. Seely's findings were based on limited knowledge and were prematurely announced to the public. The Commission's own medical director subsequently stated that because the aerosol spray adhesives case was a medical problem, medical opinions should have been obtained before imposing the ban.

Commission Analysis of Dr. Seely's Research After the Ban

After banning the adhesives, the Commission called on mutagenic and genetic specialists and other researchers to provide additional opinions. The studies were generally completed in about two months and reports transmitted to the Commission in mid-November 1973.

Study A. This study was designed to check the chromosome damage rates of the persons included in Dr. Seely's research. Two researchers reviewed the blood samples Dr. Seely had taken from the patients in the original study. They analyzed different slides than Dr. Seely had analyzed for 12 (6 exposed and 6 nonexposed) of the original 22 persons. These two researchers did not find the same statistical difference between exposed and nonexposed persons that Dr. Seely had found and did not confirm his findings that aerosol spray adhesives adversely affected chromosomes.

Study B. In this study, the doctors that performed Study A reviewed the *same* slides Dr. Seely had analyzed for 6 of the 12 persons examined in their initial study. Their analysis reaffirmed the results of Study A. There was no statistically significant difference in damaged chromosomes between exposed and nonexposed persons. The study did not confirm Dr. Seely's original conclusion of a relationship between aerosol spray adhesives and chromosome damage.

Study C. A medical researcher attempted to corroborate Dr. Seely's findings by analyzing new blood samples from several persons, most of whom were included in Dr. Seely's original study. The researcher studied new blood samples from 10 persons—6 exposed and 4 nonexposed. This study's results conflicted with Dr. Seely's original findings because nonexposed persons showed a higher percentage of damaged chromosomes than did the spray adhesive users. The researcher questioned the objectivity of Dr. Seely's selection of nonexposed people because some worked in the medical field and others were his patients.

Study D. This study was directed at industrial and other heavy users of aerosol spray adhesives (although not necessarily the same brands as those banned). A comparative analysis of 14 aerosol spray adhesive users and 5 nonexposed persons failed to show the same statistically different percentages of damaged chromosomes that Dr. Seely found.

After reviewing the results of the studies, Commission staff believed that continuing the ban was not justified and, in mid-November 1973, recommended that the Commissioners withdraw it. The Commission did not accept the staff recommendation. It did consider the study results adequate to support withdrawing the ban. The Commission prepared a series of questions about the relationships between aerosol spray adhesives and chromosome damage and between chromosome damage and birth defects. It also established an ad hoc committee to review Dr. Seely's and the other studies.

The Ad Hoc Committee. The Commission requested 11 medical researchers in genetics, pediatrics, epidemiology, and toxicology to give their professional opinions on the validity and significance of Dr. Seely's study and the other research performed. The committee members generally responded that Dr. Seely's original conclusions were not corroborated and that the research data failed to establish a relationship between spray adhesive use and chromosome damage.

Most committee members did not believe that the relationship between adhesive use and birth defects was adequately documented. The consensus was that the Commission should withdraw the ban because Dr. Seely's conclusions were not adequately supported by data.

Withdrawing the Ban

The commissioners voted on January 18, 1974, to announce their intent to withdraw the aerosol spray adhesive ban on March 1, 1974. Waiting until March to withdraw the ban would give interested parties time to make other information available or to comment on the proposed action.

In a press release issued on January 25, 1974, the Commission explained that subsequent research did not substantiate Dr. Seely's findings, and it alerted the public to the Commission's intent to withdraw the aerosol spray adhesives ban on March 1, 1974, unless other information was presented affecting the case. The required *Federal Register* notice was published on January 28, 1974.

The Commission received three written responses to its proposed ban withdrawal. A retail store chain said it planned to resume selling aerosol spray adhesives on March 1, 1974. One private citizen supported the Commission's proposal to withdraw the ban. Another suggested that all aerosol sprays be banned. The ban was lifted on March 1, 1974.

The Commission did not publicly announce the ban's withdrawal. A press announcement was not considered necessary because the Commission had issued the earlier press release and published the *Federal Register* notice. The news services did carry stories early in March reporting the ban's withdrawal. The Commission's general counsel sent identical letters to 3M and Borden on March 4, 1974, informing them that the ban had been withdrawn.

Conclusions

The Commission's actions in banning the aerosol spray adhesives were directed at protecting consumers from potentially hazardous products and were within the legal provisions of applicable laws. Although the Commission gave the two manufacturers an opportunity to refute its reasons for banning the products before the ban was effective, provisions for advance notice and public hearings were not applicable because the adhesives were banned as an imminent hazard. The Commission responded in the manner that it believed most appropriate to inform the public of what it considered to be a hazardous product.

In an analysis prepared for the Congress, the General Accounting Office stated that the basis for the Commission's decision could have been strengthened and the controversy surrounding its public announcements minimized if the Commission had coordinated its evaluation of the preliminary research with medical specialists before imposing the ban, and had relied less on undocu-mented verbal evidence and more on documented evaluations in reviewing the preliminary findings and conclusions. If the Commission had documented its review of Dr. Seely's research and checked its evaluation with its own and other medical specialists, the decision and the press announcements could have indicated the limited evidence available and placed the decision in its proper perspective.

The General Accounting Office concluded that the Commission has no formal policy for reviewing possible imminently hazardous products. It urged that a regular procedure be established, including documenting the basis for declaring a product an imminent hazard.

Chapter 4

The Case
of Automobile Production

The most extensive case of the new wave of government regulation of business relates to the production of the passenger automobile. In the words of a former chairman of the board of General Motors, "Government today has something to say about how we design our products, how we build them, how we test them, how we advertise them, how we sell them, how we warrant them, how we repair them, the compensation we pay our employees, and even the prices we may charge our customers."[1]

Regulation of automobile production is an especially interesting case because public policy has proceeded beyond the intitial stages of expanded regulation in response to public concerns. The adverse effects of regulation have been so visible to the consumer—particularly in terms of higher fuel consumption and the increased inconvenience in operating the vehicle—that a dramatic feedback to policy has occurred. The unexpected and unintended side effects of the initial burst of safety and environmental legislation have lead to significant legislative and administrative reductions in the nature and severity of regulation. The most dramatic single change was the congressional reversal in 1975 of the requirement for the "interlock" system of seat belts, shoulder harnesses, and buzzers.

Although a great deal of attention has been given to the inconvenience involved in driving automobiles with federally mandated safety and environ-

[1]General Motors Corporation, *1973 Report on Progress in Areas of Public Concern,* 1973, p. 88.

mental features, much less thought has been devoted to the higher cost of producing these vehicles, and hence the higher prices paid by American motorists. The nuisance or discomfort involved has been depicted graphically. Journalist Vic Gold describes the scene at the National Safety Belt Conference, sponsored by Ralph Nader:

> Three grown men scrambling around, across, and over the front seat of one of those dangerous 1974 model horseless carriages, futilely wrestling with a network of elusive buckles and straps . . . But if I am any judge of my fellow American nonstooges, Big Motherism in the safety belt field has now gone too far.[2]

If Gold's description appears excessively colorful, the same point is made—although unwittingly—in the following excerpt from the Seat Belt System Owner's Guide issued by a major automobile manufacturer:

1. Get in your car.
2. Fasten your lap/shoulder harness.
   A. If you have a front seat passenger, his seat belt must be fastened also, or the car will not start.
   B. If you have a package, handbag, briefcase, etc., weighing 25 lbs. or more, and have space only in the front seat, place the object on the front seat, and then buckle the passenger-side belt.
   C. If you have a dog weighing 25 lbs. or more occupying the passenger seat, buckle the passenger-side belt before attempting to start car.
   D. If the passenger-belt is already buckled when you add the package, dog, or passenger, unbuckle, then rebuckle the belt before attempting to start car.
3. Start your car.
   A. If your car won't start, try unbuckling and rebuckling your belt (and your passenger's) to be sure the buckle was fully fastened.
   B. If that fails, turn the ignition key to "ON," then get out of your car and raise the hood. Press the bypass switch mounted on the fire wall to "START." Close the hood, get back in your car, buckle up, and turn your ignition all the way as in normal starting.
   C. If your car stalls, do not turn the ignition to "OFF" position. That way you can keep trying to start your car as often as necessary without leaving the car.
   D. If you accidentally turn the ignition key to "OFF," turn it back to "ON," unbuckle, get out of the car, open the hood, press the bypass switch again for another "free" start. (Incidentally, if the bypass switch is taped down, the action will be detected in the switch and cancelled.)
4. Drive the car.
   A. If your dog is on the floor when you begin driving the car, and

[2] Quoted in Carl H. Madden, *What's Wrong With Consumerism.* Remarks at the Washington Journalism Center, Washington, D.C., December 10, 1973, p. 8.

then jumps on the seat and the passenger-side belt is unbuckled, a buzzer will sound. Stop the car and buckle the belt.

B. In a somewhat rare situation, when driving over a very rough road, you may be bounced about in your seat. Should your engine be stopped, remain buckled in your seat and restart your car. A "bounce-time" delay (designed primarily to allow you to straighten your clothing after buckling up) also allows a restart in this situation.[3]

Numerous failures were reported in the "interlock" system, which the Federal Motor Vehicle Safety Commission required automotive manufacturers to incorporate into all 1974 cars (this was before the congressional elimination of the requirement). The *New York Times* reported that a check of new car owners around the country showed that the government-mandated safety device was "almost universally disliked," that many owners had the interlock system disconnected, and that malfunctions often kept cars from starting. The owner of a small car rental company in Miami stated that he disconnected all the interlocks on his first 1974 automobiles because of his clients' complaints, and because several cars broke down while in use. An automobile dealer described servicing trouble with the gadget as "fairly frequent."[4] These private costs resulting from government regulation, however, are not separately identified in any available statistics on the economy.

Judging by 1975 congressional legislation eliminating the "interlock" system, Gold's 1973 statement was prescient.

THE EFFECT ON THE CONSUMER

As would be expected, the ever more complicated safety system—as well as federally mandated pollution controls—have increased the price of motor vehicles. Simultaneously, of course, the new safety devices have no doubt contributed to lessened automotive injuries and deaths. Precise measures of benefit are lacking because comprehensive data are lacking on actual seat belt usage. Moreover, to some major but unmeasurable extent, recent declines in motor vehicle accident and death rates can be attributed, at least in part, to the promulgation of lower speed limits in response to the changed energy supply situation.

To comply with the Motor Vehicle Safety Act, nearly 900 items must be tested or checked on the standard full-sized automobile.[5] Table 4–1 shows, for the typical new 1974 passenger automobile, the cost of the successive changes that have been required to meet federal standards. According to these data

[3]Cited in All State advertisement in *Time*, April 15, 1974 (no page number).

[4]"The Interlock System: A 'Devilish Contraption'," *New York Times*, April 7, 1974, Section 1A, p. 20.

[5]Henry L. Duncombe, Jr. and H. Paul Root, "Automobiles, Energy, and Product Planning Risks," *Journal of Contemporary Business*, March 1975, p. 40.

Table 4-1

PRICE INCREASES OF PASSENGER AUTOMOBILES
RESULTING FROM FEDERAL REQUIREMENTS
(Estimated Retail Cost at Time of Introduction)

Model Year	Action	Price Per Car
1968	Seat and shoulder belt installations	$ 11.51
	HEW standards for exhaust emission systems	16.00
1968–1969 combined	Windshield defrosting and defogging systems	.70
	Windshield wiping and washing systems	1.25
	Door latches and hinge systems	.55
	Lamps, reflective devices, and associated equipment	6.30
1969	Head restraints	16.65
1970	Lamps, reflective devices, and associated equipment	4.00
	HEW standards for exhaust emission systems	5.50
1968–1970 combined	Theft protection (steering, transmission, and ignition locking and buzzing system)	7.85
	Occupant protection in interior impact (glove box door remains closed on impact)	.35
1971	Fuel evaporative systems	19.00
1972	Improved exhaust emission standards required by Clean Air Act	6.00
	Warranty changes resulting from federal requirement that all exhaust emission systems be warranted for 5 years or 50,000 miles	1.00
	Voluntarily added safety features in anticipation of future safety requirements	2.00
	Seat belt warning system and locking device on retractors	20.25
1972–1973 combined	Exterior protection (standard #215)	69.90
1973	Location, identification, and illumination of controls improvements	.60
	Reduced flammability of interior materials	5.80
1969–1973 combined	Improved side door strength	15.30
1974	Interlock system and other changes to meet federal safety requirements	107.60
	Improved exhaust emission systems to comply with the Federal Clean Air Act	1.40
	Total	$319.51

Source: U.S. Department of Labor, Bureau of Labor Statistics.

supplied by the Bureau of Labor Statistics of the U.S. Department of Labor, the federally mandated costs averaged \$320 per car.[6] With new car purchases totaling about 9.5 million for the year 1974, American motorists paid approximately \$3 billion extra for meeting governmentally imposed requirements in that one 12-month period.

The automotive industry has presented an even higher estimate. The Ford Motor Company states that the mandatory safety standards alone raised the cost of producing the average 1974 passenger car by \$325.[7]

In addition, the added weight and complication of the mandated features increased the operating costs of the vehicles, particularly for fuel. The added cost of the catalytic converters required on 1975 automobiles is estimated at about \$160 per vehicle.

To an economist, it is not only the magnitude of the resources that are important, but the alternatives to which they can be put—the "opportunity cost." As Paul McCracken has stated the matter:

> ... resources used in one direction are then not available to be used elsewhere. Whether they should be so used, therefore, depends not only on whether the intended use is "good," but on whether it is better than the uses to which the resources would otherwise be put.[8]

The \$3 billion that American motorists paid out in 1974 for the added features mandated by the federal government on new cars had a high "opportunity cost." We as a nation had to forego the opportunity to spend that considerable sum of money for other ways of reducing road accidents. What would a portion of the \$1 billion that was devoted to the "interlock" system have yielded if applied to these alternatives?

1. Identifying and eliminating the serious hazards created by unclear or badly placed road signs, or placing signs where they are needed but now absent.
2. Providing more universal and more intensive driver instruction, including developing and testing simulators for use in training and licensing drivers. Simulators could be used to make driver tests more extensive and demanding. (The appendix to this chapter describes one such effort.)
3. Assessing costs and benefits of more thorough vehicle inspections. Perhaps expanded safety inspections could be combined with checkups on pollution-control equipment and engine operation. This would

---

[6]These costs are underestimated because they utilize BLS data for each year and ignore the inflation that has occurred since. The BLS indices treat these added costs as measures of quality improvement.

[7]U.S. Senate, Committee on Commerce, *Motor Vehicle Safety Oversight* (Washington, D.C.: Government Printing Office, 1974), p. 231.

[8]Paul W. McCracken, "Will There Be An Economics in 2024?," *University of Michigan Business Review,* October 1974, p. 13.

help to meet safety, environment, and energy conservation objectives simultaneously.[9]

Every benefit, to the customer or to the public, has a corresponding cost, and the car buyer ultimately must pay for those costs. In the case of tougher bumpers, for example, any saving in insurance premiums or reduced cost of car repair should be weighed against the additional cost of the bumper and the additional gasoline needed to move the cars made heavier by the new bumpers, supporting frame, and related equipment. In 1971, the average bumper system weighed 104 pounds and cost the consumer approximately $140. The average weight of the bumpers on a 1975 car was 220 pounds and cost the car buyer $278.[10] Like the interlock system and the catalytic converter, bumper standards may be relaxed or even reversed to some degree. The investment in technology and equipment to comply with these standards, however, cannot be recovered.

The extent of the technological investment in research and development in an effort to comply with governmental standards is described by Henry Duncombe and H. Paul Root of General Motors:

To meet the certification requirements for our 1975 models, 284 test cars were driven more than 5 million miles and required that 2,734 separate emission tests be conducted, each taking more than 14 hours to complete. Nearly 500,000 gallons of gasoline were consumed in running these certification tests, and this procedure required the equivalent of 600 persons working an 8-hour day for one full year.[11]

The development of governmental regulation of industry, particularly in the safety area, seems to have at times lost sight of the objective of seeking out the least costly way of achieving the objectives. Professor Roger L. Miller of the University of Miami has described the problem as follows:

Now they seem to be insisting that Detroit should begin producing what amounts to overly expensive tanks without giving much thought to some alternatives that are just as effective, while less costly to society.

Modification or removal of roadside hazards might eliminate as many as one quarter of all motor vehicle fatalities. Another 10 percent or so occur when automobiles collide with bridge abutments, or with pier supports or overpasses.[12]

[9]"The Bureaucrats Belt Us Again," *Fortune,* October 1973, p. 128.

[10]James E. Overbeke, "Washington Bumps Off Tough Bumper Rules," *Industry Week,* January 13, 1975, p. 61.

[11]Duncombe, and Root, "Automobiles, Energy, and Product Planning Risks," p. 42.

[12]Roger L. Miller, *The Nader Files: An Economic Critique.* Paper presented at a Conference on Government and the Consumer at the Center for Government Policy and Business, October 22–28, 1973, p. 3.

According to Miller, most of these hazards could be eliminated by better marking of poorly marked roads and intersections, the installation of breakaway traffic signs and light poles, and the padding of abutments and concrete pillars. The benefit also would go to owners and passengers of old cars, not just those newer models with required safety features.

The driver, not the car, is responsible for four out of every five automobile accidents, according to a study prepared for the Department of Transportation.[13] Moreover, 60 percent of drivers in fatal single car crashes are drunk, as are 50 percent of the drivers at fault in fatal crashes involving two or more cars.

A far less expensive alternative might involve more vigorous legal prosecution of drunken drivers and drunken pedestrians. Decreasing the number of drunks driving or walking may be more efficient than requiring every motorist to invest in expensive safety equipment. Few of the safety devices on automobiles are designed to protect pedestrians. The National Safety Council estimated that 38 percent of the people who died from motor vehicle accidents in 1971— 21,000 out of 54,700—were pedestrians, bicyclists, motorcyclists, and others who could not have been helped by seat restraints of any kind.

Few new car purchasers have been willing to pay for one of the newest safety devices, the air bag. At an additional cost of approximately $300 a car, General Motors offered the air bag as optional equipment on the 1974 model Cadillac and on all full-sized Buicks and Oldsmobiles. But between 1973 and 1975, only 6,000 cars equipped with air bags were sold and most of these were sold to fleet owners.[14] This less than enthusiastic reception led to GM's announcement to terminate the air bag option on 1977 models.

Chrysler Corporation's manager of automobile safety relations, Christopher Kennedy, terms the air bag "nothing more than a $300 shoulder belt useful only for head-on crashes."[15] Apparently, more than half of all fatalities and injuries occur in nonfrontal crashes, and air bags are not designed to inflate under such circumstances. Despite the costs, the lack of testing on small cars, and incomplete data on effectiveness, the Department of Transportation has continued to urge the installation of air bags on new cars.

Professor Donald F. Huelke of the University of Michigan Medical School has criticized federal motor vehicle safety standards as having "been cast in bronze," leaving little room for change, even when research indicates that a standard has become ineffective or unnecessary. Thus, government regulatory activities can become more concerned with complying with the specific stan-

---

[13] Ed Hayward, "Automotive Report," *St. Louis Globe-Democrat*, April 26, 1975, p. D1.

[14] Agis Salpukas, "G.M. Says It Will End Air Bag Option on 1977 Autos," *New York Times*, May 4, 1975, p. 24.

[15] James E. Overbeke, "Air Bags: Delayed, But Still Alive," *Industry Week*, June 2, 1975, p. 57.

dards promulgated by the agency than with attaining the original objectives of decreasing death and injury rates from automobile accidents.[16]

Although further reasonable improvements in automobile safety should not be discarded, it is informative to note that the traffic fatality rate in the United States is far lower than in other industrialized countries and that it had been steadily decreasing prior to the introduction of federally mandated safety requirements (see Figure 4–1).

The upsurge in the number, variety, and extent of government programs to regulate the production of automobiles has revealed various deficiencies in the process of regulation. In April 1974, the Environmental Protection Agency announced a study of the adverse environmental effects of the catalytic converters being put on 1975 model-year automobiles. The study was undertaken after the agency had ordered automobile manufacturers to incorporate that expensive antipollution device. Apparently, both private and governmental researchers had shown that the new "antipollution" equipment could produce harmful amounts of sulphuric acid mists, which can irritate the lungs. In a statement delaying the deadlines for meeting more stringent antipollution standards, Russell Train, head of the Environmental Protection Agency, said, "At some point, catalysts may begin to do more harm by creating sulphuric acid than good through additional control of hydrocarbons and carbon monoxide."[17]

Also, the catalytic converters emit platinum, which, in the words of John B. Moran, director of the EPA's fuel and additive research program, is "really adding a new thing to our environment."[18] Apparently, there is no significant amount of platinum in our air or water at the present time.

Furthermore, EPA subsequently learned that the catalytic converter could be a fire hazard if an automobile's engine is not maintained properly. An improperly functioning engine could heat the converter to as high as 1,200 degrees fahrenheit, substantially increasing the risk of fire. One might ask what the government and public reactions would have been if a private organization had taken an action such as EPA's in requiring catalytic converters without submitting a detailed environmental impact statement and without subjecting itself to the criticisms of the various groups desiring to participate in the review process.

An examination of the costs associated with the catalytic converter contrasts with the increasing doubts as to the net benefits. In addition to the cost of the converters themselves, the automobile manufacturers invested substantial sums in new technology—General Motors alone spent an estimated $100 million. Individual gasoline stations have been required to install nonleaded gas pumps

[16] James E. Overbeke, "Are the Standards 'Cast in Bronze'?" *Industry Week,* June 16, 1975, p. 85.

[17] "Auto Makers Get Delay in Meeting Pollution Rules," *Wall Street Journal,* March 6, 1975, p. 7.

[18] Edmund K. Gravely, Jr., "U.S. to Study Effects on Antipollution Devices," *New York Times,* April 7, 1974, Section 1A, p. 21.

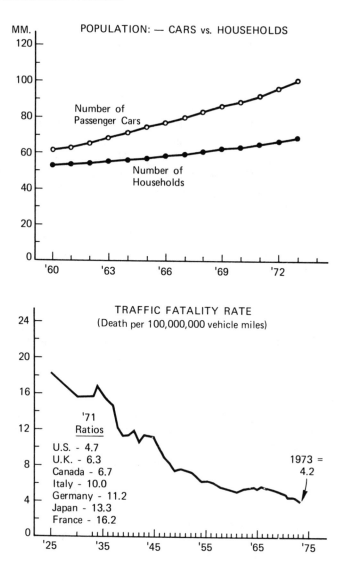

Figure 4-1

AUTOMOBILES AND TRAFFIC SAFETY

Source: James M. Dawson, *The Love Affair With the Automobile,* National City Bank, Cleveland, Ohio, July 5, 1974.

and new gas nozzles to fit the narrower gas spouts of the new automobiles.[19] Yet after the investment of these millions of dollars, EPA chief Russell Train recommended to Congress a plan that would likely eliminate the need for a catalyst by the 1979 model year.[20]

A report sponsored by the National Academy of Sciences and the National Academy of Engineering estimated the annual benefits of the catalytic converters at $5 billion, and the annual cost at $11 billion (assuming that catalytic converters are replaced after 50,000 miles). According to the study, however, if the long-term standards on oxides of nitrogen (NO_x) were relaxed, from 0.4 grams to 2.0 grams per mile, that annual cost would fall to $5 billion. Alternatively, a policy of applying the long-term standards only to automobiles operated principally in seriously polluted or impacted areas—37 percent of the total—also would lower the cost from $11 billion to approximately $5 billion. In either case, the reduction in benefits would not be substantial, and if the NO_x standard were relaxed, changing technology might ultimately render the program's cost negligible.[21]

APPENDIX: DRIVER EDUCATION AS AN ADDITION TO SAFETY REGULATION*

Governmental regulation of the design and production of motor vehicles constitutes one method of attempting to achieve a reduction in road accidents. This appendix describes another method, one that is not necessarily mutually exclusive. Conceivably, improved driver instruction could contribute to more effective use of the automotive safety equipment mandated by the federal government.

This section describes an Advanced Driver Education Program developed at the General Motors Proving Ground. The program was designed around the concept of training drivers to handle specific driving emergencies. It was evaluated by comparing trained and untrained control groups. A large reduction in both numbers of accidents and accident severity was indicated.

[19] M. Stanton Evans, "Is Protection Agency Hazardous to Health?," *St. Louis Globe-Democrat*, April 8, 1975, p. 14A.

[20] "We Told You So," *Wall Street Journal*, March 6, 1975, p. 10.

[21] *Economic Report of the President, February 1975* (Washington, D.C.: U.S. Government Printing Office, 1975), p. 158.

*This section draws on materials in U.S. Senate, Committee on Commerce, *Motor Vehicle Safety Oversight*, (Washington, D.C.: U.S. Government Printing Office, 1975), pp. 383-92.

Background

A formal program of driver education in America was initiated in 1938 when Amos Neyhart developed the first comprehensive curriculum. Driver education has since become an institution in the American school system. At present, the great majority of new drivers receive some formal training prior to licensing.

Introduction

The General Motors Proving Ground has the responsibility of testing the company's automotive products in their environment. An analysis was made of 14 available accident causation studies. The data were then examined to isolate those causation factors primarily related to drivers. It is difficult to isolate any particular factor as the only or primary contributor to an accident. If, however, a careful study of the accident provided a strong possibility that the driver was a significant contributor, it was then tabulated by the probable driver error.

The following driver errors occurred with the greatest frequency: impaired judgment due to alcohol, misinterpretation of the driving task, and improper control of emergency situations.

The effect of alcohol on driving accidents presents a social problem beyond the scope of the project. The driving emergencies identified with a high degree of occurrence were skids, improper evasive maneuvers, improper off-road recovery, and improper braking. Using these specific problem situations and recognizing an obvious need to improve interpretation of the driving task and required driver reaction, a series of training exercises was developed.

Off-road recovery. In normal driving a driver will often either deliberately or inadvertently drop two wheels off the road edge. Due to poor shoulder maintenance on many roads, this edge may be as large as four to six inches. The driver knows he or she should slow down and then return to the road surface. This is undoubtedly a correct approach, but there are several conditions that may prevent the driver from exercising this technique. The shoulder may be blocked by a disabled vehicle or some other obstacle, or the vehicle may be in a stream of high-speed traffic. Whatever the reason, drivers do attempt to return to the road surface and often have problems.

The driver problem occurs because he or she tends to be cautious. The driver scrubs the tire on the road edge, and this requires a very considerable amount of steering to enable the tire to climb the dropoff. When the tire does climb up under such circumstances, the vehicle rapidly crosses the traffic lane, possibly leading to a collision or to a difficult control situation. Exercises were developed to give the student practice in performing the maneuver properly.

This requires a sharp input from a straddle position, with a quick return to the straight-ahead steering position at the moment of tire impact. In this maneuver, the momentum of the vehicle will carry it up on the road and it will still stay within the traffic lane.

Skids. The training of drivers in skid recovery long has been recognized as a desirable feature of advanced driver training programs. The common power skid, where the vehicle has lost rear wheel cornering traction due to overthrottle application on a slippery curve, is the most troublesome type of skid. It is the type the motorist identifies with the word "skid" per se. In the training exercise, this type of skid is simulated by momentarily locking the rear wheels to induce the skid on a wetted skid pad. Students are trained at speeds up to 35 miles an hour, progressing to more severe skids as they become more competent.

Evasive maneuvers. Many cases of a driver either failing to make or improperly performing an evasive maneuver led to the development of an evasive exercise. A major driver deficiency appears to be lack of awareness of the evasive capability of an automobile and overdependence on the brake as an emergency control. In addition, most drivers and many driving instructors are not aware that a locked tire cannot provide steering capability. These reasons led to the development of the evasive maneuver and the controlled braking exercise. In the evasive exercise, the student drives down a cone-marked lane, which is blocked at the end. At a predetermined point, he or she is cued to evade this barricade by making a left or right lane change without braking. Several cueing systems have been used, such as light, plastic curtains that close all but one lane, and vocal command. All appear to be equally effective. The major objective is for the student to become aware of and utilize the evasive capability of the automobile. The student is shown what can be done and then runs through the exercise at increasing speeds as related to his or her progress.

Controlled braking. It is important to brake a vehicle to reduce speed even in an evasive maneuver, but the driver must learn to break without locking the wheels so that he or she can maintain steering control. The controlled braking exercise also requires a lane change evasive maneuver. The student is told that the course is simulating his or her coming over the crest of a hill and, at the cue point, the student has just seen a disabled vehicle in his or her path. The student is to get around this vehicle and then back into his or her road lane because of the possibility of oncoming traffic, and at the same time he or she is to stop the car in the shortest possible distance. The student learns to modulate the brake and detect, as well as react to, wheel lockup. The maximum speed is generally 45 miles an hour for a 50-foot distance between the brake cue and the cone barricade.

Tire blowouts. Tire blowouts are infrequent occurrences today and account for few accidents, but drivers generally have a fear of what will happen if one occurs. The Proving Ground developed a blowout simulator, which is a pneumatic valve that allows the tire to be deflated through the rim in a time comparable to a sudden tire air loss. The device automatically reinflates the tire so that repetitive blowouts can be given on the same tire. (This unit has been licensed and is available to the general public.) Even though tire blowouts are not a major accident causation factor, the fear of a blowout, the ability of giving a driver a simulated emergency, and the similarity of driver control response to other vehicle handling situations make it an effective training exercise. Both front and rear blowouts are given at speeds up to 60 miles an hour while operating in a straight line and on curves.

Serpentine course. Although not directly related to a specific emergency situation, a serpentine course is incorporated to develop proper hand positions, rhythm, and timing of steering inputs, and to increase the driver's ability to perceive the spatial relationship of his or her vehicle with respect to fixed obstacles such as cones.

The six exercises were used as a nucleus of the course with a classroom session consisting of the major topics as outlined below.

I. Explanation of the driving system
   a. Driver
   b. Vehicle
   c. Road
   d. Interrelationships

II. Discussion of driver's role
   a. Driver's role in the driving system
   b. Physical limitations of driver

III. Discussion of importance of vehicle maintenance

IV. Discussion of pretrip driver preparation

V. Basic discussion of vehicle dynamics as related to the particular driving exercises

VI. Discussion of tires as related to vehicle performance with emphasis on tire

VII. Discussion of the elements of defensive driving and how they are used
   a. Sight habits
   b. Concentration
   c. Knowledge
   d. Judgment
   e. Skill

The Program and Its Evaluation

This entire program is designed to be conducted in a single 7½-hour period, with 1½ hours devoted to two classroom sessions and the remaining 6 hours on the driving exercises. Each exercise accommodates three students per car so that the actual behind the wheel time is two hours per person, the remainder being observation time.

Having developed a course in advanced driving techniques, it was important to evaluate achievements of the first objective—does the course reduce accidents? A training program had been conducted using Proving Ground personnel, but the accident experience of this group is so low that no effective evaluation could be made in a reasonable length of time.

A local law enforcement agency, the Oakland County, Michigan, Sheriff's Department, had approached the Proving Ground in regard to a training program for its patrol officers. An experimental program was undertaken. A group of 60 officers was matched to provide two groups of as similar a makeup as possible. Thirty officers were put through the program and 30 were kept as a control group. The officers attended the 7½-hour program in October 1969.

Each officer in the program was evaluated by his instructor for each exercise, using a combined objective-subjective system. The evaluation consisted of such things as hand positions, number of cones knocked down, number of successful passes, speed of each run, lane position, number and types of improper responses, and the instructor's overall opinion of performance, attention, and attitude. At the conclusion of each day's workshop, the evaluation cards were collected, sorted, tabulated, and converted into percentile scores. Upon completion of the workshops, a percentile ranking was made for each exercise and an overall performance percentile ranking was tabulated for the entire trainee control group. The total performance scores ran from a high of 84.3 to a low of 67.8, with a median of 75.2.

Utilizing the evaluation data plus the instructor's personal evaluation of each student, each officer was provided with a private composite analysis of his performance and a listing of his weak and strong areas. As of October 1971, the groups had an accident record of 10 to 5 in favor of the trained group. The trained group showed a 50 percent reduction in accidents as compared to the untrained group. This relates to 13 and 11 accidents respectively for the equal time period preceding October 1969.

It is also useful to examine the severity of the accidents and examine factors relating to a good benefit/cost ratio. A summary is provided below of injuries, days lost, lost wages, and vehicle damage cost as per insurance company payment. This does not include the cost required to replace patrol cars damaged beyond repair or the cost of replacing the man on duty while he was off due to injuries.

These data indicate that the total costs for the untrained group were 10 times those of the trained group. The average cost per accident of the trained group was only 20 percent of that of the untrained group.

Conclusions

Staff of the General Motors Proving Ground drew several conclusions from the study.

Category	Trained group	Untrained group
Number of accidents	5	10
Injuries	0	2
Lost days	0	87
Lost wages	0	$ 3,500.00
Vehicle damage costs	$1,446.50	$11,247.10
Vehicles totaled	0	3
Total cost	$1,446.50	$14,747.10
Average cost/accident	$289.30	$ 1,474.71

1. Prior to this study, it was anticipated that the officers might have a tendency to be more aggressive in their driving since they were trained to handle more severe driving conditions. In fact, observation showed the opposite to be true. The trained group became more cautious in their driving. One could hypothesize that they now have a better understanding of the limits of their capabilities and, therefore, tend to stay within those limits.

2. The group, before the program, did not use restraint systems. Since the program, 29 of the 30 are conscientious restraint device users. From their comments, it was concluded that they use the restraints not because of a fear of injury, but because they are better able to control the car if they are "belted" in the vehicle. This may indicate a more promising method of promoting restraint usage.

3. There appears to be a very rapid rise in the learning curve for this type of training, and a shorter course may be possible. General Motors is not in the position to undertake mass training programs for drivers but hopes to be able to provide assistance to those groups having this responsibility.

Chapter 5

Job Safety Regulation

The Occupational Safety and Health Administration was created in December 1970 "to assure so far as possible every working man and woman in the nation safe and healthful working conditions and to preserve our human resources."[1] Congress outlined several means for OSHA to use in fulfilling this mandate:

1. The encouragement of employers and employees to reduce hazards in the workplace, and to institute and improve existing health and safety programs.
2. The establishment of responsibilities and rights for both employers and employees.
3. The authorization of OSHA to set mandatory occupational safety and health standards.
4. The provision of an effective enforcement program.
5. The encouragement of state responsibility for administering and enforcing their own job safety and health programs, which must be at least as effective as the federal program.
6. The provision of reporting procedures on job injuries, illnesses, and fatalities.[2]

---

[1] Occupational Safety and Health Act, Public Law 91–596.
[2] *All about OSHA*, U.S. Department of Labor, OSHA 2056 (undated), p. 3.

Compliance with OSHA regulations is enforced through inspections. OSHA inspections may be triggered by serious or fatal accidents or employee complaints concerning a specific company or plant, they may be aimed at "target industries" or "target health hazards," or they may be randomly selected workplaces. Target industries are those with injury frequency rates more than double the national average, including longshoring, meat and meat products, roofing and sheet metal, lumber and wood products, and miscellaneous transportation equipment. Target health hazards are associated with the five most hazardous and most commonly used toxic substances: asbestos, carbon monoxide, cotton dust, lead, and silica.

If, upon inspection, an employer is found in violation of one or more OSHA regulations, the violation is to be placed in one of the following categories:[3]

> *De minimis.* A condition having no direct or immediate relation to job health and safety (example: lack of toilet partitions).
>
> *Nonserious violation.* A condition directly related to job safety and health but which is unlikely to cause death or serious physical harm (example: tripping hazard). A penalty of up to $1,000 is optional.
>
> *Serious violation.* A condition in which substantial probability of death or serious physical harm exists, and in which the employer knew or should have known of the hazard (example: absence of point-of-operation guards on punch presses or saws). A penalty of up to $1,000 is mandatory.
>
> *Imminent danger.* A condition where there is reasonable certainty that the hazard can be expected to cause death or serious physical injury immediately or before the hazard can be eliminated through regular procedures. If the employer fails to deal with the violation immediately, OSHA can go directly to a federal district court for legal action as needed.

OSHA requires all employers of eight or more employees to maintain the following records: a log with each reportable job-related accident, injury, or fatality entered on a single line, a supplementary record with details on each case, and an annual summary compiled from the log.[4]

Although the OSHA program is designed to benefit both employers and employees, the bulk of the effort is aimed at the employer. It is the employer's responsibility to assure that safe and healthful conditions exist in the workplace, and to purchase equipment necessary to correct unsafe or unhealthy conditions. It is the employers who must make sure that the employees adhere to safety rules and safe practices. For example, if an employee is instructed to wear a particular piece of personal protective equipment, such as safety-toe footwear, but the employee fails to do so and ultimately sustains an injury as a result of this failure, the OSHA law requires that the citation and the proposed

---

[3]Ibid., pp. 13–14.
[4]Ibid., p. 16.

penalty, if any, be issued against the employer. Investments in safety that result in less lost time due to accidents generate direct benefits to employers as well as to employees.

REACTIONS TO OSHA

The Occupational Safety and Health Act is one of those areas of government activity where the objectives are so worthy that those who question the actual conduct of the effort are put on the defensive to prove that they are not devoid of human compassion. After all, who is not in favor of improving a work environment in which over 14,000 Americans were killed in 1973 in work-related accidents?

Yet criticisms of OSHA have not been infrequent. The Council of the Federation of American Scientists issued the following statement of OSHA:

Regulations are voluminous and complex; the language is convoluted beyond recognition except by a scientist or lawyer.

The Occupational Safety and Health Act, in short, has surfaced at least as many problems as it was designed to solve.[5]

The most severe criticism of the Occupational Safety and Health Administration has come not from business executives or labor but from within the federal government itself, from the chairman of the Occupational Safety and Health Review Commission, the independent agency created to hear appeals from rulings by OSHA inspectors.

Commission Chairman Robert D. Moran has written: ". . . far too many standards are, to paraphrase Winston Churchill, 'riddles wrapped in mysteries inside enigmas.' They don't give the employer even a nebulous suggestion of what he should do to protect his employees from whatever-it-is, also left unexplained, which represents a hazard to their safety and health"[6] After citing one standard, Moran lamented:

What do you think it tells us to do?

I have no idea—and I don't think OSHA could tell you, either, before an inspection, citation, complaint, hearing, and posthearing brief.[7]

Moran concluded, as follows:

[5]"Statement of the Council of the Federation of American Scientists," *FAS Newsletter,* June 1973, p. 1.

[6]Robert D. Moran, "Our Job Safety Law Should Say What It Means," *Nation's Business,* April 1974, p. 23.

[7]Ibid., p. 25.

I submit that there isn't a person on earth who can be certain he is in full compliance with the requirements of this standard at any particular point of time.[8]

A major problem arises when the small employer needs help in interpreting the standards promulgated by a federal regulatory agency such as OSHA. He or she normally cannot afford to employ a staff of experts on the payroll and logically looks to the government to determine his or her obligations. In the case of OSHA, he or she is given a complex pamphlet that takes 24 pages of fine print to list the applicable standards for "general industry." The descriptive material is quite sparse. The section on how to use the guide is quoted below in its entirety:

To be used effectively, this Guide must be considered as a:

1. companion piece to the master document, 29 CFR 1910, Occupational Safety and Health Standards for General Industry.
2. key index to all the standards in 29 CFR 1910 which have been classi-fied under the six categories, and the administrative regulations drawn from Parts 1903, 1904, 1905, 1911, and 1912.

To find the desired information the user should first read the introductory statement to each category. Then, he should analyze the hazard and classify it according to workplace, machines and equipment, materials, the employee, a special process, or a power source. By looking up the applicable category, the location of the applicable standard in 29 CFR can be found. Since hazards may be logically classified in more than one category, look under each category which might apply to your situation.[9]

In the words of the Federation of American Scientists, ". . . businessmen who have no legal or scientific training are unable to understand OSHA regula-tions. Unfortunately, few efforts are being made to translate this information into readable language. . . Equally unnerving to the businesses is the sheer volume of the regulations—thousands of them apply to one small operation."[10] Let us independently attempt to follow the procedure described in the OSHA guide cited above. As we were told, the standards themselves are in something called "29 CFR 1910." Let us assume that we know that this is legalese for the Code of Federal Regulations and that we are to turn to Title 29, which deals with labor, and to Part 1910, Occupational Safety and Health Standards; 29 CFR 1910 contains 455 pages of fine print, including algebraic and trigonometric equations. Let us skip over the obviously technical parts and

---

[8]Ibid.

[9]U.S. Occupational Safety and Health Administration, *Guide for Applying Safety and Health Standards, 29 CFR 1910, General Industry,* 1972, p. 1.

[10]*FAS Newsletter,* June 1973, p. 4. See also Jack R. Nicholas, Jr., "OSHA, Big Government, and Small Business," *MSU Business Topic,* Winter 1973, p. 61.

turn to the section dealing with something supposedly simple—ladders. To begin, we are offered a definition: "A ladder is an appliance usually consisting of two side rails joined at regular intervals by crosspieces called steps, rungs, or cleats, on which a person may step in ascending or descending."[11]

That initiates our education into the subject of ladders. We next have to identify the various types of ladders. The stepladder is, we are informed, "a self-supporting portable ladder, nonadjustable in length, having flat steps and a hinged back. Its size is designated by the overall length of the ladder measured along the front edge of the side rail." We are then led through similar details on the single ladder, the extension ladder, the sectional ladder, the trestle ladder, the extension trestle ladder, the special-purpose ladder, the trolley ladder and the side-rolling ladder.

The next section leads us through an unhelpful definition of "wood characteristics." The reader is informed that "Wood characteristics are distinguishing features which by their extent and number determine the quality of a piece of wood."[12] At this point, the reader's eye may begin to wander. He or she will find that OSHA is prepared for that, for in the next two columns of fine print there are two identical sets of definitions of ladder, each of which is word-for-word similar to those on the previous page, and including identical definitions of stepladder and all the other types of ladders previously enumerated.

The determined reader may then proceed to another section of the OSHA regulations on the subject of ladders. He or she will encounter on page 22118 the following item:

> The angle (a) between the loaded and unloaded rails and the horizontal is to be calculated from the trigonometric equation:
>
> $$\text{Sine } a = \frac{\text{Difference in deflection}}{\text{Ladder width}}$$

Let us assume that, on this first reading, our typical small business executive decides that the subject of ladders is too complicated. Turning pages, he or she comes across something that seems like it would be simpler, "Exit". "Exit" is defined as "that portion of a means of egress which is separated from all other spaces of the building or structure by construction or equipment as required in this subpart to provide a protected way of travel to the exit discharge."[13]

Our business executive realizes that the subject of exit, too, is more complicated than expected. Clearly, he or she must define "a means of egress" as well as the "exit discharge." OSHA provides a definition of each:

[11] *Federal Register,* October 18, 1972, pp. 37, 202, 22105.
[12] Ibid., p. 22106.
[13] Ibid., p. 22130.

A means of egress is a continuous and unobstructed way of exit travel from any point in a building or structure to a public way and consists of three separate and distinct parts: the way of exit access, the exit, and the way of exit discharge. A means of egress comprises the vertical and horizontal ways of travel and shall include intervening room spaces, doorways, hallways, corridors, passageways, balconies, ramps, stairs, enclosures, lobbies, escalators, horizontal exits, courts, and yards.

Exit discharge is that portion of a means of egress between the termination of an exit and a public way.[14]

At this point, it may be informative to turn to the dictionary for a definition of exit. No mention of means of egress or of exit discharges, and no definitions of exit that contain the word exit. Exit is simply—but clearly and accurately—defined as "a passage or way out."[15]

A frequent result of the complexity of OSHA's regulations is to increase the overhead expenses of various companies. Yet some of the most severe impacts may result from its inspection activities. The frustration experienced by small-business executives is exemplified by Irvin H. Dawson, a small businessman who closed his Cleveland operation for a day as a proclamation mourning "the loss of rights of its citizenry under the so-called OSHA."[16] This act of protest was precipitated by an OSHA inspection charging him for nonserious violations such as:

Failing to post a copy of the act (which he never received).

Failure to maintain a separate OSHA folder even though he had all necessary records.

The presence of an "insufficiently" guarded fan, which was dust-covered, its cord wrapped around the base, without brushes, and obviously not in use.

Simultaneously, OSHA has been criticized for various inadequacies in its inspectional activities. With fewer than 800 inspectors in the field to monitor more than five million businesses, the odds are that the average employer will face an OSHA inspection perhaps once in 66 years. On the average, OSHA violations cost an employer only $25 each, and, after three years of operations, only two companies have been convicted of criminal violations.[17] It would seem that the agency has irritated business far out of proportion to the actual scope of its activities.

[14]Ibid.

[15]*The American Heritage Dictionary of the English Language* (Boston: Houghton Mifflin Co., 1969).

[16]Stanley J. Modic, "Are You a Coward?," *Industry Week,* November 4, 1974, p. 5.

[17]Clayton Fritchey, "Foot-Dragging on Occupational Safety," *Washington Post,* November 8, 1975, p. A 27.

COSTS AND BENEFITS OF GOVERNMENT CONTROLS

The potential benefits of occupational safety and health, although important, are often not quantifiable, at least without making numerous assumptions about the value of an arm, of hearing loss, or of life itself. Those assumptions and the subsequent analysis involved are beyond the scope of this book. However, it is useful to try to identify the various types of benefits that can be expected to result from improving occupational health and safety through regulations.

1. The greater productivity of those who would have sustained a job-related injury or illness in the absence of government regulation.
2. The greater enjoyment of life by those who thus avoided work-related disabilities.
3. The resources that would have had to be used in the treatment and rehabilitation of victims of work-related injuries or illnesses which were avoided.
4. The resources that would have had to be used to administer workmen's compensation and insurance, and to train those who would have been needed to replace the sick or disabled.
5. The reduction in the private efforts to increase occupational safety and health, which are replaced or reduced by the government's efforts.
6. The consequent decrease in damage to plant and equipment.
7. The savings that result from less disruption of work routines caused by accidents plus potential improvements in the morale and productivity of the workforce.[18]

The estimates of current expenditures by various industries to meet government safety or other requirements are often no more than reasonable guesses. The results of surveys are not easy to interpret realistically. It is often difficult for a company to distinguish between investment to meet federal requirements and investment in production equipment, which would be purchased in the absence of the governmental restriction. Thus, the data in Table 5–1 should be taken mainly as illustrative of the substantial costs involved in meeting federally mandated requirements. In some cases, safety and health investment is reported to be a significant part of an industry's total capital spending. In 1972, 8 percent of the textile industry's investments and 12 percent of steel's were so related.[19]

---

[18]Russell F. Settle, *Benefits and Costs of the Federal Asbestos Standard.* Paper presented at the Department of Labor Conference on Evaluating the Effects of the Occupational Safety and Health Program. Washington, D.C., March 18, 1975, pp. 3–7.

[19]"The High Price of Job Safety," *Business Week,* May 26, 1973, p. 27.

Table 5-1

ESTIMATED COMPLIANCE COSTS OF OCCUPATIONAL HEALTH AND SAFETY LEGISLATION

Industry	Investments in employee safety and health ($ millions)		
	1972	1973	Percent Change
Manufacturing:			
Stone, clay, and glass	30	87	+190%
Miscellaneous transportation equipment	6	15	+150
Rubber	15	35	+133
Aerospace	14	26	+ 86
Miscellaneous durables	37	66	+ 78
Instruments	12	21	+ 75
Machinery	86	131	+ 52
Petroleum	68	99	+ 46
Fabricated metals	20	29	+ 45
Food and beverages	71	95	+ 34
Chemicals	72	96	+ 33
Paper	50	66	+ 32
Nonferrous metals	37	46	+ 24
Textiles	58	67	+ 16
Electrical machinery	57	64	+ 12
Iron and steel	193	215	+ 11
Miscellaneous nondurables	24	25	+ 4
Autos and trucks	88	74	− 16
Nonmanufacturing:			
Electric utilities	203	370	+ 82
Communications	404	569	+ 41
Mining	84	116	+ 38
Gas utilities	23	26	+ 13
Railroads	31	34	+ 10
Airlines	54	55	+ 2
Miscellaneous transportation	70	66	− 6
Trade	702	663	− 6
Total	2,509	3,156	+ 26

Source: McGraw-Hill Publications Company.

According to the McGraw-Hill Department of Economics, already planned industrial investments in health and safety equipment have been estimated to rise from $2.5 billion in 1972 to $3.4 billion in 1977. These capital outlays can be considered a form of investment in employee productivity, to the extent that they succeed in reducing job-related injuries and illnesses. Some safety efforts can become quite controversial.

The dispute over the regulation of vinyl chloride exemplifies the difficulty that OSHA faces in setting a standard in areas where a chemical is known to be dangerous but is also a critical input to the production process of an entire industry. The dilemma faced by OSHA is inherent in the nature of its activities and essentially involves difficult and often controversial trade-offs among several objectives, each of which is considered worthy in its own right. It has been determined that vinyl chloride causes cancer and other diseases at exposure levels in excess of 50 parts per million. Controversy has arisen over OSHA's attempt to set a new standard for vinyl chloride at "no detectable level." The disagreement arose over how far below the 50 ppm level the danger point lies. The ensuing debate brought out the fact that there is no historical experience with exposure levels below 50 parts per million in most existing plants using or producing vinyl chloride. Thus, if the final standard is set at a level below 50 ppm, as is likely, it will not be based on any firm information as to the actual risk of cancer or other diseases at that exposure level, but rather on educated intuition on where the balance between safety and cost considerations lies.[20]

What is often forgotten amid the emotion of the vinyl chloride debate is that until January 1974 all the information linking vinyl chloride to cancer had been produced by the industry under its own initiative. As Ralph L. Harding Jr., president of the Society of the Plastics Industry, observed, "This is a unique situation. Industry financed the studies, and industry blew the whistle on itself."[21] Concerning the vinyl chloride dilemma, OSHA's basic concern would seem to be to determine the right "trade-offs," to devise regulations in which the increased cost to the plastics industry and society as a whole are related to real increases in benefits in the form of a safer working environment.

An important potential benefit of health and safety regulations has been cited in a study by M.I.T.'s Center for Policy Alternatives. Preliminary findings of the study indicate that in four West European countries and Japan, with health and safety regulations similar to those in the United States, these regulations "tend to encourage technological innovation in firms . . . by forcing firms to implement product or process changes, oftentimes incidentally shocks them out of a rather inflexible production system and thereby provides the catalyst which is necessary for innovation to occur."[22]

The regulation of workplace noise also has been the subject of vigorous debate, not inconsequentially between government agencies. OSHA has proposed a maximum noise level of 90 decibels during an eight-hour day. The cost to industry to attain this standard is estimated at $13 billion. The Environmental Protection Agency, which is responsible for overall federal noise regulation, wants an 85 decibel limit at an estimated cost to industry of approximately $32 billion[23] (see Table 5-2). The Council on Wage and Price Stability asserts that

[20]Paul H. Weaver, "On the Horns Of The Vinyl Chloride Dilemma," *Fortune,* October 1974, p. 203.

[21]Ibid, p. 200.

[22]David Burnham, "U.S. Rules Called Spur to Industry," *New York Times,* June 24, 1975, p. 17.

[23]"Save $32 Billion, Buy Ear Plugs," *St. Louis Globe-Democrat,* April 21, 1975, p. 16A.

Table 5-2

ESTIMATED COMPLIANCE COST OF OSHA NOISE STANDARDS
(in millions of dollars)

Industry	85 dbA (proposed)	90 dbA (existing)
Utilities	$ 6,300	$ 3,200
Nonelectrical machinery	4,200	1,400
Fabricated metal products	3,200	1,100
Transportation equipment	2,900	1,100
Textile mill products	2,700	1,100
Food and kindred products	2,600	590
Electrical machinery	2,300	780
Primary metals	1,900	900
Chemicals and allied products	1,400	1,100
Printing and publishing	1,000	870
Lumber and wood products	650	150
Furniture and fixtures	580	190
Stone, clay, and glass	520	290
Paper and allied products	500	140
Rubber and plastic products	500	302
Petroleum and coal products	260	210
Tobacco	90	48
Apparel and related products	10	0
Leather and leather products	8	0
Total	$31,618	$13,470

Source: Bolt, Beranek and Newman, Inc.

there is no evidence for either standard and that an industry-by-industry system may be more valid.[24]

Another point of contention involves the method of reducing noise levels in the workplace. The agency contends that noise must be "engineered out" of the worker's environment, and has rejected administrative solutions to noise problems such as the use of hearing protectors, the rearranging of work schedules, or the operation of noisy machinery for fewer hours each day. Thus the less expensive approach of providing earmuffs in cases where the costs of eliminating the noise is especially high is not considered to be an acceptable long-term alternative.

The case of the rubber gloves is an example where the costs involved are clearly not commensurate with the benefits achieved. After reading complaints from industry that there was no need for OSHA promulgating a standard for electrical rubber gloves, the author requested details from a knowledgeable Missouri engineer who had worked for a half century in the electrical field. The reply in part follows:

[24] "Workplace Noise Rules Appear Headed for Lengthy Dispute," *Industry Week,* May 12, 1975, p. 13.

During all that period, I have never observed or heard of an accident due to failure of electrical rubber gloves *in service.* One must understand, I believe, the procedures, practices, and daily uses of these gloves to understand this record.

First, each glove is electrically tested by the manufacturer before shipment. Upon receipt of these gloves they are again electrically tested by the utility or a testing laboratory and stamped with a number. Then each lineman is issued at least two pair of gloves—and the numbers recorded. He uses one pair and before using it in his daily work he gives it an "air test," which is done by twirling the cuffs and forcing the entrapped air into the fingers. Obviously—if there is a hole—the air escapes. Meanwhile, his second pair is on test and he changes gloves once every week or two weeks.

After usage—there are of course gloves that fail on test and are replaced. But it is the continual testing that I have described that prevents accidents while gloves are being used.

I hope this information may be of interest to you. I am sure you are aware that a leather protector glove is worn over the rubber gloves when in use.[25]

For many industries the lost time due to illnesses and injuries off the job far exceeds that due to on-the-job hazards. The medical director of Exxon, for example, states that nonoccupational diseases and injuries account for about 96 percent of the time lost due to disability.[26] The OSHA-mandated efforts are thus limited to the remaining four percent of the disability-caused absenteeism in that large company.

Despite the costs, the effectiveness of OSHA, as measured by statistics on job-related injuries and illnesses, is questionable. After OSHA's second full year of operation, the Bureau of Labor Statistics reported that the number of job-related injuries and illnesses increased from 5.6 million in 1972 to 5.9 million in 1973. In addition, the incidence rate for "lost workday" cases in the manufacturing sector rose 7.1 percent during that period.[27]

Without much public attention, the administration of the Occupational Safety and Health Act appears to have shifted responsibility for an individual's actions to safeguard his or her own well-being to the employer. The law makes no provisions for sanctions against employees who violate safety standards, even if they endanger other employees. In one case, the OSHA hearing officer held that merely providing earmuffs to reduce noise levels was not enough. "To avoid violation, the equipment also must be 'used,' and the final responsibility to assure that use rests with the employer."[28] The OSHA regulations shift other responsibilities in a similar way:

[25]Letter to the author, dated June 17, 1974, from Clarence H. LeVee, retired Vice President of Engineering, A. B. Chance Company.

[26]N. J. Roberts, M.D., "Medicine At Work," *The Lamp,* Fall 1974, p. 21.

[27]"Job Injury Rate Shows Little Change," *Industry Week,* January 13, 1975, p. 55.

[28]James C. Hyatt, "Complex Issues Raised by Job Safety Act—Like Earmuff Dispute—Flood Commission," *Wall Street Journal,* January 30, 1973, p. 40.

> Where employees provide their own protective equipment, the employer
> shall be responsible to assure its adequacy, including proper maintenance,
> and sanitation of such equipment.[29]

Another serious problem facing OSHA is the possibility of biased
decision-making. An example relates to the National Institute for Occupational
Safety and Health (NIOSH), the agency that does the basic research underlying
new OSHA regulations. Due to budget limitations, NIOSH signed an agreement
with the Amalgamated Clothing Workers under which an official federal study of
safety and health hazards in the clothing industry is being conducted by a union
employee and financed by the union.

The union agreed to pay the salary of an industrial hygienist, Dr. Peter J.
Nord, to perform the study. In the words of the OSHA publication reporting the
undertaking, "Although Nord will work full time within NIOSH, he is an employee of the union rather than of the federal government... The union will
help obtain the cooperation of plant managers."[30] Consider the reaction of a
company in the textile industry whose premises are being investigated by its
union in behalf of the government.

The agreement does appear to be authorized by existing statute. Section
22 (e) (6) of the Occupational Safety and Health Act provides that NIOSH may
"accept and utilize the services of voluntary and noncompensated personnel."
Perhaps the statute needs to be amended to require NIOSH to use more discretion in its application, although an administrative action to assure impartiality
should suffice.

ANNOUNCEMENT EFFECT

One unmeasurable impact of federal regulation is the announcement
effect. For many years economists have identified what is termed an "announcement effect" of government spending or taxation. That is, potential government
contractors may start preparing to bid on a project before Congress has appro-
priated funds for it. Similarly, consumers may increase their expenditures as
soon as a tax cut is voted on or even while it is being considered.

It now seems that governmental regulatory programs may have somewhat
similar effects. In Illinois, the very rumor of more stringent standards for
migrant worker housing by the Occupational Safety and Health Administration
caused strawberry farmers to reduce their production. Lester Pitchford, the
largest grower in the Centralia area, was quoted as saying, "We don't know if

---

[29]*Federal Register,* October 18, 1972, p. 22230.

[30]"Unique Agreement Signed for Study of Clothing Industry," *Job Safety and
Health,* March 1974, p. 37.

OSHA is coming or not, but when it was even rumored, it put it (strawberry production) out."[31]

By OSHA directive, it is expected that farmers will have to provide 100 square feet of living space for each migrant (the present state standard is 60 square feet), flush toilets and showers in each room, as well as other amenities. Apparently, at least some Illinois strawberry farmers have concluded that the capital investments required cannot be justified for a two-week harvest.

According to James Mills, a sanitary official with the Illinois Department of Public Health, one of the basic problems is the lack of distinction under OSHA regulations between long-term and short-term migratory farm worker housing. Centralia farmers, he was quoted as saying, "just can't compete, and if OSHA puts the pressure on them, they'll get out of the migrant business completely and go strictly U-Pick" (consumers pick the fruit for their own use for a fee).

In the OSHA area the law seems at times to have lost sight of the basic objective—to achieve a safer working environment. The current emphasis is on punishing violations. In a more positive approach, the basic emphasis of the occupational safety and health legislation would be shifted from enumerating specific practices to be followed in a company's operations to focusing on reducing its accident and health hazard rate.

It is doubtful that there is an invariant, unique way of achieving that desirable result. Changes in equipment, variations in work practices, education and training of employees, and leadership on the part of management all may be practical alternatives for achieving the desired ends, at least in some circumstances. An economist would opt for the mix of methods that entails the least loss of productivity and output, and those combinations would probably vary from plant to plant and over time.

OUTLOOK

Congressional interest is mounting in requiring that an "economic impact" statement be published in conjunction with promulgating any new regulatory standard. Several bills have been introduced in both the House of Representatives and the Senate to institute this requirement in the case of the occupational safety and health program. One approach would require OSHA to estimate the total costs incurred by employers in complying with a new regulation. A more vigorous requirement is to determine whether the benefits of the proposed standard justify the cost. These bills also would allow an employer to use equipment

---

[31]Pamela Meyer, "Fear of OSHA Making Farmers Plow Under Strawberry Crops," *St. Louis Post-Dispatch*, June 11, 1974, p. 7C.

and procedures other than those required by a standard where such equipment would afford adequate protection to employees and not create new hazards.

Yet the trend toward more intensive and more expensive job safety and health regulation is likely to continue. OSHA not long ago assigned a social scientist to explore the idea of extending occupational health to management to consider psychological stress among executives.[32]

The immediate future thus appears filled with increased governmental controls over industrial production in the United States. In the longer run, the newer regulatory agencies may undergo some form of "on-the-job" training and adopt procedures that are less disruptive to the companies that they regulate. In contrast to OSHA, the Food and Drug Administration, a much older agency, maintains an inspection program that is not based on surprise visits—the Hazard Analysis of Critical Control Points Program (HACCP). FDA states, "The methods of correction are not the inspector's main interest, as long as they are effective and do not produce new problems. Inspectors are not on the job to punish manufacturers. Instead, they help manufacturers correct any conditions which might lead to violations."[33] FDA's advisory services are used by industry to assist in voluntary compliance.

---

[32]"Boardroom Blues," *Business Week,* June 22, 1974, p. 38.

[33]Harold Hopkins, "A Greater Margin for Food Safety," FDA Consumer, September 1974, p. 3; U.S. Food and Drug Administration, *Inspecting Food Processing Plants,* FDA Fact Sheet (undated), p. 2.

Chapter 6

Managing the Environment

The 1960s brought a new public awareness and often genuine alarm about the deterioration of the nation's physical environment, but concerns expressed were often scattered or focused on merely one aspect of the problem—air pollution, water pollution, pesticides, whatever. With the start of the 1970s, the nation began to understand and deal with these problems as part of the complex relationship of the environment to human health and welfare. The federal government has consolidated most of its various programs relating to air pollution, water pollution, solid waste disposal, pesticide regulation, environmental radiation, and such into one agency—the Environmental Protection Agency (EPA).

As a result of the importance placed on environmental considerations by the public, a massive effort, both in dollars and manpower, was launched to improve environmental quality. The benefits resulting from the billions of dollars expended are difficult to quantify. How much are cleaner air and water worth? With reference to air pollution, EPA contends that its programs withstand the test of cost-benefit analysis. EPA estimates health and property damage at $16.2 billion in 1968, rising to $22.7 billion in 1977. But if $3.9 billion in abatement equipment is added, EPA says damage costs will be reduced by $13.1 billion by 1977.

Disregarding the costs for a moment, the public concern for cleaner air is evident and its attainment is an undeniable benefit. Sulfur oxides were reduced

25 percent between 1970 and 1974, particulates were down 14 percent, and other pollutants have been stabilized or are falling in most areas. Of 20,000 primary sources of air pollution, 15,600 are complying with emission regulations or are on a government-sanctioned abatement schedule.[1] The assaults on water pollution, solid waste, noise, and such are of more recent origin, but similar results may be expected.

Thus, having acknowledged the substantial benefit of a cleaner environment, let us turn to an examination of the government agency assigned this task and to a glimpse of the costs and repercussions of its actions on the business sector.

THE ENVIRONMENTAL PROTECTION AGENCY

The Environmental Protection Agency was established in December 1970, to administer a wide range of environmental protection programs, including air pollution control, water pollution control, solid waste management, and control of pesticides, noise, and radiation. Activities of EPA center around the setting and enforcing of standards relating to these concerns. EPA defines a standard as "the product of fact and theory provided by scientists, and a public value judgment conditioned by the balance of risks against benefits, with a margin of safety on the side of public health and welfare."[2]

EPA has several avenues of enforcement at its disposal. Upon finding a violation, voluntary compliance may be sought. If this approach fails, EPA may order compliance and take court action. Possible penalties for violation of EPA standards include fines and jail sentences. The largest and best-known EPA programs are those dealing with the control of air and water pollution. The Clean Air Act of 1970 provides for a nationwide program of air pollution control, including provisions for setting and enforcing standards. Standards fall into the following categories:

> *Emergency Standards.* EPA defines air pollution levels that pose an imminent and substantial danger to health. When these levels are reached, emergency actions are taken, which can include shutting down industrial polluters.
>
> *National Air Quality Standards.* National air quality standards have been set for the six most common pollutants—sulfur oxides, particulates, carbon monoxide, photochemical oxidants, hydrocarbons, and nitrogen oxides. Regulations come in two parts. A primary standard, aimed at protecting

[1] "The Clean Air Act Will Keep Its Teeth," *Business Week,* July 14, 1975, p. 92.

[2] *Action for Environmental Quality* (Washington, D.C.: Environmental Protection Agency, March 1973), pp. 1–4.

public health, sets a limit on air pollution that is safe for humans. A secondary standard, designed to protect public welfare, establishes a level of pollution that is safe for plants, animals, and property.

National Emission Standards. For hazardous pollutants that "may cause, or contribute to, an increase in mortality or an increase in serious irreversible, or incapacitating reversible, illness," EPA must set national emission standards.

New Plant Standards. EPA is required to set "standards of performance for new stationary sources." The purpose is to require these plants to use the best available technology to control air pollution.

Motor Vehicle Emission Standards. Manufacturers of new or imported cars or engines must have their products certified by EPA that they comply with stated emission levels.

Fuel Standards. EPA can control or prohibit substances in motor vehicles that significantly hinder performance of emission control systems.

Violation of an implementation plan, a new source performance standard, or a hazardous emission standard is punishable by a fine of up to $25,000 a day and one year in prison. Subsequent violations can double both the fine and the jail term. If a manufacturer or dealer sells a car not certified by EPA or disconnects an emission control device, he can be fined up to $10,000 for each offending car or engine. A violation of EPA's motor vehicle fuel standards is punishable by a fine of up to $10,000 a day.

A national effort to fight water pollution was launched under the Water Pollution Control Act of 1972. The law proclaims two major goals: by July 1, 1983, wherever possible, water should be clean enough for swimming and other recreational use, and for the protection of fish and wildlife; and by 1985, no more discharges of pollutants shall be made into the nation's waters. Under the law, EPA issues national effluent limitation regulations and national performance standards for industries and publicly owned waste treatment plants. No discharge of any pollutant into the waters is allowed without a permit.

Violators of the water pollution standards may be fined up to $10,000 a day. Willful or negligent violators can be fined up to $25,000 a day and sentenced to one year in prison; these penalties can be doubled for subsequent violations. EPA may enter and inspect any polluting facility to check its records and monitoring equipment and to test its discharges.

Failure to report the discharge of oil or other hazardous substances into the water can result in a fine of up to $10,000 and one year in jail. Expelling hazardous substances from a vessel can be punished with a fine of up to $5 million; also, clean-up costs of up to $14 million can be assessed to the polluter. Anyone discharging hazardous substances due to willful negligence or misconduct is liable for actual clean-up costs, no matter how high. Both the Clean Air Act and the Water Pollution Control Act empower citizens to bring suit against anyone violating these laws. Citizens can also take court action against EPA itself if it fails to perform any duty required by the two laws.

THE COSTS AND BENEFITS OF A CLEAN ENVIRONMENT

Although, as we have seen, penalties for violation of pollution standards can be substantial, compliance is not inexpensive either. The Council on Environmental Quality (CEQ) reports an estimate of expenditures for pollution control as reaching $80 a year for each citizen in 1976, a figure double the 1973 level. This amount represents over one percent of the average personal income. Approximately $162 billion is expected to be spent by the private sector from 1973 through 1982 for ecological improvements as a result of environmental legislation[3] (see Table 6-1). In this same period, business will spend an additional $50 billion for voluntary environmental improvements over and above what is legally required.

Business expenditures for pollution control and their importance in total investment in plant and equipment are shown in Table 6-2. There is some debate, however, on the relationship between spending for pollution abatement and investment in other plant and equipment. The Georgia-Pacific Corporation asserts that in 1974 a third of the money that would normally have been invested in new plant construction by the pulp and paper industry was devoted to water pollution control; the Department of Commerce put the ratio at 20 percent.[4]

Substantial capital cost increases in the paper industry relating to pollution investments have occurred for two major reasons. First, a higher technological cost is connected with the design of nonpolluting mills and with upgrading existing mills while maintaining an adequate return on this capital, which has a limited economic life. Second, additional costs have emanated from the shortages of capital goods caused by the insufficient capacity to provide all the pollution-free equipment demanded. For example, the foundries that manufacture the parts required for the production of the capital equipment needed to eliminate or control pollution have themselves been affected severely by pollution regulations requiring them to divert funds from investment in increased or even constant capacity. One private study estimates that meeting the pollution standards has cost the economy about 10 percent of its industrial capacity.[5]

The steel industry estimates that it must spend nearly $14 billion through 1983 to comply with air and water pollution control regulations now on the

---

[3]*Environmental Quality* (Washington, D.C.: The Council on Environmental Quality, December 1974), p. 173.

[4]Gladwin Hill, "Environmental Outlays and Inflation: Is There a Link?," *New York Times,* November 9, 1974, p. 28.

[5]Bruce R. Lippke and others, *The Impact of Pollution Standards on Shortages, Inflation, Real Income and Unemployment* (Tacoma, Wash.: Weyerhaeuser Company, 1975), p. 15.

Table 6-1

ESTIMATED PRIVATE SECTOR INCREMENTAL POLLUTION CONTROL EXPENDITURES*
(In billions of 1973 dollars)

Category	1973			1982			Cumulative — 1973–82		
	Operating Costs	Capital Costs	Total Annual Costs	Operating Costs	Capital Costs	Total Annual Costs	Capital Investment	Operating Costs	Total Annual Costs
Air Pollution	2.2	1.2	3.4	12.4	7.2	19.6	47.6	81.1	127.9
Water Pollution	.5	.5	1.0	1.9	1.5	3.3	14.2	14.5	26.6
Noise	NA	.1	NA	NA	1.0–1.4	NA	6.0–8.7	NA	NA
Radiation	NA	NA	NA	<0.05	0.05	0.07	0.3	0.08	0.3
Solid Waste	0.1	<0.05	0.1	0.5	<0.05	0.5	<0.05	2.3	2.3
Land Reclamation	0.3	0	0.3	1.6	0	0.6	0	5.0	5.0
Grand Total**	3.1	1.7	4.8	16.4	10.0	24.1	69.5	103.0	162.1

*Incremental costs are expenditures made pursuant to federal environmental legislation, beyond those that would have been made in the absence of this legislation.

**Excludes noise control.

NA = Not available

Source: Council on Environmental Quality.

Table 6-2

POLLUTION CONTROL OUTLAYS BY BUSINESS, 1975
(millions of dollars)

	Pollution Control			Pollution Control As Percentage Of All Capital Expenditures
	Total	Air	Water	
All Industries	5,900	3,745	2,155	5.1%
Manufacturing	3,942	2,352	1,590	7.9
Durable Goods	1,706	1,162	544	7.4
Primary Metals	843	648	196	15.3
Blast Furnace, Steel Works	289	197	92	11.3
Nonferrous	474	375	100	19.6
Electrical Machinery	182	70	111	6.3
Machinery, except Electrical	85	45	40	1.8
Transportation Equipment	134	66	68	3.8
Motor Vehicles	107	55	52	4.1
Aircraft	24	11	14	3.5
Stone, Clay, and Glass	198	175	23	14.5
Other Durables	265	157	107	5.1
Nondurable Goods	2,236	1,190	1,046	8.3
Food including Beverage	168	66	102	5.3
Textile	31	8	23	4.4
Paper	458	262	196	15.8
Chemical	522	215	306	7.3
Petroleum	965	580	385	9.6
Rubber	68	44	24	4.9
Other Nondurables	25	16	9	1.8
Nonmanufacturing	1,959	1,393	566	2.9
Mining	43	21	21	1.8
Railroad	36	15	21	1.1
Air Transportation	10	7	3	.6
Other Transportation	53	18	36	2.3
Public Utilities	1,618	1,210	408	7.5
Electric	1,568	1,177	391	8.8
Gas and Other	51	33	18	1.4
Communication, Commercial, and Other	199	122	76	.6

Source: Department of Commerce, Bureau of Economic Analysis.

books. As of early 1975, the industry had spent $1.9 billion to meet environmental standards. In addition to the substantial capital requirements, it is estimated that annual operating costs will increase 8 to 10 percent due to pollution standards. Finally, to satisfy all regulations scheduled to be in effect by 1983, the steel industry's consumption of oil products is expected to increase by more than 14 percent.

The E. I. du Pont de Nemours Company is one firm that contends it has trimmed expansion plans as a result of pollution control requirements. Edward R. Kane, Du Pont president, stated in testimony before the Joint Economic Committee in late 1974 that his company's capital investment for pollution control consumes about 13 percent of its capital budget. In 1975 the $175 million that Du Pont scheduled for pollution control facilities could have built a fiber plant employing 2,500 workers and that in turn would have created about 60,000 jobs in "downstream" industries. Although differing markedly from the mainstream of business opinion, Carl Gerstacker, chairman of the Dow Chemical Company, states that his firm has been making a profit from pollution control investments.

Although the costs of complying with pollution standards are substantial, the benefits also can be significant. In the area of air pollution alone, it was estimated that the nation would incur $24.9 billion in damages in 1977 in the absence of pollution controls. The damages so averted constitute the basic benefit that society achieves from its investment in pollution abatement activities (see Table 6–3).

The environmental impact statements are required by the Council on Environmental Quality to assist federal agencies and to require them to build into their decision-making process "an appropriate and careful consideration of the environmental aspects of proposed action in order that adverse environmental effects may be avoided or minimized and environmental quality previously lost may be restored." However, these statements have been criticized as unnecessarily complex and consequently costly to prepare. Many business executives contend that these statements delay the development of productive facilities and demand substantial time to prepare, and therefore increase costs to consumers. The Council on Environmental Quality described the impact statements in its 1974 Annual Report:

Table 6–3

ESTIMATED NATIONAL AIR POLLUTION DAMAGE COSTS
WITH NO POLLUTION CONTROL, 1968 AND 1977
(In billions of dollars)

Damage Class	1968*	1977**
Health	$ 6.1	$ 9.3
Residential Property	5.2	8.0
Materials and Vegetation	4.9	7.6
Total	$16.2	$24.9

*In 1968 dollars
**In 1970 dollars
Source: Environmental Quality, fourth annual report of the Council on Environmental Quality, September 1973.

Many impact statements now resemble encyclopedias. They discuss the project's setting in overly elaborate detail and contain lengthy descriptions of all species of plant and animal life in the affected area. Frequently, this reflects a lack of understanding of what is important and what is not.

Some of the most severe criticism of the environmental legislation has come from the Congress itself, which apparently did not fully anticipate all the potential effects at the time the programs were enacted. An April 1975 report of the Subcommittee on Investigations and Review of the House of Representatives Committee on Public Works stated, "The complexity of PL 92–500 (the Federal Water Pollution Control Act) has not been fully comprehended. In some respects, the law sought to redesign the world to meet water quality objectives." The Congressional report went on to note "inherent contradictions" in the ecological law in that it sets target dates and deadlines that are "impossible to achieve," has timetables that underestimate the capital investment and construction need, and imposes severe penalties for noncompliance.

The capacity for environmental gains to be linked to a decline in economic progress was indicated by Robert Semple, chairman of the board of the BASF Wyandotte Corporation. His warning related specifically to advocates of "zero discharge" of pollutants by industry. Besides possibly being technically unfeasible in some instances, zero discharge requirements may not make good economic or practical sense. For example, in parts of Louisiana, industrial plants are required to return Mississippi River water cleaner than it was when it entered the plant.[6]

Decisions on expenditures for environmental quality must consider benefits as well as costs. As the Council on Environmental Quality (CEQ) phrases the problem:

> When the expected gains are large relative to the costs, it is clearly in our interest to move forward in cleaning up the environment. And such improvement should, of course, continue as long as the perceived added gains of attaining each higher level of environmental quality exceed the expected costs.
>
> Decisions on levels of environmental quality are collective judgments increasingly made more explicit through the establishment of standards. Setting these standards implies evaluation or accounting of the added benefits and costs of higher levels of quality, with account taken of inherent uncertainties and risks.[7]

The CEQ supported this line of reasoning with the example of improving the water quality of the Delaware estuary. The pertinent benefit/cost study esti-

---

[6]"Environment and Economic Growth," *Environmental Science and Technology,* July 1974, p. 609.

[7]U.S. Council on Environmental Quality, *Environmental Quality,* (Washington, D.C.: U.S. Government Printing Office. 1971), pp. 118–20.

mated recreational benefits from a certain level of improvement in water quality at $120 million to $280 million, far in excess of the cost of $65 million to $140 million. By increasing expenditures to a range of $85 million to $155 million, the resulting benefits rose to a range of $130 million to $310 million—still a favorable payout ratio. But with even higher water quality expenditures of $215 million to $315 million, benefits increased only marginally to $140 million to $320 million. Clearly, the calculations were useful in showing the economic limits to increases in pollution abatement outlays.

Plant Closings—Do The Benefits Exceed The Costs?

By court order, United States Steel Corporation is shutting down its open hearth furnaces in Gary, Indiana, because of failure to comply with EPA pollution regulations. One cost of the plant closing will be the loss of 2,500 jobs directly and another 1,500 indirectly. The EPA, whose suit brought about the situation and who subsequently refused an extension, has urged the company to continue operating the plant while paying a fine of $2,300 a day.

The foundry industry has probably experienced some of the most serious impacts of environmental regulations. Between 1968 and 1974, 427 foundries were closed. Although a variety of factors was cited for the terminations, including the added expense of meeting job safety requirements, the cost of compliance with environmental regulations was frequently cited as a factor in a sizable number of foundry failures; the greatest fatality rate occurred among the small foundries. In addition to contributing to closings, environmental standards have hampered the industry's growth and its ability to meet both military and civilian demands for its products. A 1975 report on the foundry industry prepared by the U.S. Department of Commerce noted that EPA air pollution requirements involving "possibly unproven technology," uncertainty over impending water quality standards, and the interactions between them all contributed to the industry's problems.[8]

In the period 1960–70, the number of foundries decreased by about 25 percent, while the tonnage demand increased approximately 23 percent. It is estimated, for the period 1958–81, that the number of foundries will be reduced from 6,250 to 4,500. In this same period, tonnage demand is projected to increase from 13 million to 26 million tons.[9] It would thus appear that one unintended side effect of these government regulations has been to achieve a more concentrated industry structure, in which a relatively few large firms tend to dominate the market.

[8]Robert E. Curran, *The Foundry Industry* (Washington, D.C.: U.S. Department of Commerce, Bureau of Domestic Commerce, March 24, 1975), p. 20.

[9]Charles E. Fausel, "The Foundry Industry, Too Much From Too Few?," *Modern Casting Market Insight*, p. 20.

The loss of many of the small foundries has hurt the industry, not only in loss of capacity but also in loss of specialized production expertise and capability. The loss of expertise in small-run jobs can force manufacturers to turn to more costly alternatives to casting. Foundry closings have precipitated material shortages, as suppliers of ferroalloys have been reduced from five to two and the number of coke producers cut in half.[10]

A report by the U.S. Department of Commerce recommends that both EPA and OSHA establish an independent appeal mechanism for foundries threatened with shutdown. Consideration would be given to "national needs" (defense, energy, industry requirements), local conditions (economic and environmental), and the financial condition of the involved firms.[11]

OUTLOOK

Strong environmental legislation is here to stay. Even antirecessionary pressures to divert spending to other uses and rising interest in an adequate energy supply appear able to slow down the rising trend only slightly. Two of those concessions may relate to indirect source standards and restricted automobile use in metropolitan areas. In the first case, EPA has stopped its attempts to regulate auto pollution produced at large shopping centers, apartment and office buildings, and parking garages. In addition, EPA has indicated that it may ease requirements curbing automobile use in cities where such action would result in severe social and economic disruption.

The force of the Clean Air Act is likely to continue, however, in regard to utility emissions, auto emissions, and protection from deterioration of areas now meeting clean air standards. Concerning the nondeterioration effort, Congress may require that states divide their air into three categories. In zone 1, no significant increase in pollution would be permitted. The effect of this restriction would be the exclusion of steel and power plants and other major polluters, who even with the best of controls emit some pollution. In zone 2, limited degradation of the air would be allowed, thus authorizing some development. In zone 3, pollution levels would be allowed to increase to the level of the most stringent national standards. In these areas, most forms of development would be permitted.

Not only is the current force of environmental legislation remaining primarily intact but several new environmental bills are awaiting congressional action. The reduction and regulation of solid waste is receiving considerable attention. One approach to this problem is to prevent waste at its source.

---

[10]Raymond E. Walk, "Foundries, An Industry in Crisis?," *Modern Casting Market Insight,* pp. 2–3.

[11]Curran, *Foundry Industry,* p. 4.

Labeled "source reduction," this system would include regulations on product design and packaging, durability standards and bans on throwaway containers.

Another bill concerning the control of toxic substances would impose pre-market testing and reporting requirements on the chemical industry. EPA would also be given the power to limit or ban the production of chemicals judged hazardous to health. A Dow Chemical Company official estimates the annual cost to the chemical industry of this bill at $844 million and contends that it would delay the introduction of new products. EPA Administrator Russell Train places the costs to industry at $140 million, reasoning that EPA would require only the most extensive testing for selected chemicals.[12]

With the passage of the Federal Energy Administration Act, a new federal agency was created, aimed at the conservation and efficient use of energy, the development of alternate energy sources, and the ultimate achievement of energy independence. It is evident that in the near term at least each of these national priorities, energy and environment, will have to be compromised in the numerous areas where they are at odds. For example, improved gasoline mileage for automobiles versus stricter emissions controls; utilities being encouraged to convert their power plants to a more abundant fuel, coal, which then results in considerably greater air pollution problems.

In the words of Professor Mitchell R. Zavon of the University of Cincinnati, "The rush to spare our environment is highly desirable, but more thought as to methodology is essential if we are not to multiply the indirect damaging effects of our well-intentioned actions."[13] Zavon goes on to point out such problems as the desulfurization of coal—to meet air pollution standards—which in turn requires the disposal of quantities of calcium sulfate. Meeting the air pollution control requirements thereby results in creating a waste disposal problem, with consequences for water pollution.

In the future, we may see Congress turning to greater reliance on scientific and technical data in the establishment of regulations and away from policies such as "zero discharge." A study has been commissioned by Congress whose very purpose is to answer the question "How does the Environmental Protection Agency acquire and utilize scientific and technical information for regulatory decision-making?"[14] The results of the study will not be fully available until 1977, but hopefully they will contribute to lessened costs, as well as to a more benefit-conscious regulatory process.

An understanding of how the environment came to be polluted may be helpful in seeing how to develop proper public policy. In the past, polluting and

---

[12] John H. Sheriden, "Pending Environmental Bills Would Add to Regulatory Maze," *Industry Week,* June 2, 1975, pp. 14–16.

[13] Mitchell R. Zavon, "The Contradictory Impacts of Health and Environmental Regulation on Industry," *Mutation Research,* 26 (1974), p. 351.

[14] "Much Ado About Decision Making," *Environmental Science and Technology,* May 1975, p. 404.

the wasteful use of energy have been cheaper and/or easier than not polluting or conserving energy. To quote ecologist Barry Commoner:

> Soap companies significantly increased their profits per pound of cleaner sold when they switched from soap to detergents; truck lines are more profitable than railroads; synthetic plastics and fabrics are more profitable than leather, cotton, wool, or wood; nitrogen fertilizer is the farmer's most profit-yielding input, and as Henry Ford has said, "Minicars make mini-profits."[15]

But contrary to Commoner's general approach, it is not necessary to fault the free enterprise system for this phenomenon. Industrialized countries with other political systems, notably the Soviet Union, have experienced comparable pollution problems to those of the United States. Simply, the social cost of resource waste and pollution has not been borne by the polluter but by society as a whole. If the act of polluting were made more expensive to the polluter, perhaps through the mechanism of taxation or other price increases, then the profit incentive would force changes in patterns of use. More fundamentally, making more expensive the products whose production and consumption involve relatively large amounts of pollution will provide a fundamental incentive to both business and consumers to shift to less pollution-intensive goods and services. Similarly, increasing the price of energy will encourage producers and consumers to shift to less energy-intensive activities. Thus, the market can respond to those changing price signals automatically and with a minimum of government intervention.

APPENDIX: CLEANING UP THE WILLAMETTE*

In one important respect the Willamette River in Oregon is now more like the river that Lewis and Clark saw in the early nineteenth century than it was 10, 30, or even 50 years ago. What used to be one of the nation's most polluted waterways has been transformed once again into a clean river. Fifty years ago men refused to work at riverside construction because of the water's stench. Now thousands regularly swim, fish, water ski, and boat on summer weekends.

The Setting

The Willamette Valley is approximately 150 miles long and 25 miles wide. It is bordered by mountains on both sides. At lower elevations the mountains are

---

[15]Barry Commoner, "As The West Sinks Slowly Into The Sun," *New York Times,* November 20, 1974, p. 34.

*The details of this section are drawn from U.S. Council on Environmental Quality, Environmental Quality (Washington, D.C.: U.S. Government Printing Office, 1973), pp. 43–70.

heavily forested. Lakes, rock outcroppings, and meadows appear at the higher elevations in the Cascades. Most of the Willamette's water originates in the mountains and flows down into the river by way of its major tributaries. The valley itself is relatively flat. The main river begins at the confluence of several tributaries at the southern part of the valley and meanders northward for 185 miles. At Oregon City, the river plunges dramatically over the 41-foot Willamette Falls. From there to the Columbia, the Willamette is subject to ocean tides.

Near the mouth of the Willamette and stretching along both banks as far as the falls is the metropolitan area of Portland, with a population of 900,000. It is a major port and a center of industry and finance. Portland's suburbs stretch southward along both banks of the river as far as Willamette Falls. Salem, the state capital with a population of 75,000, lies 47 miles south of Portland. Above the falls, agriculture begins. The land on both sides of the river is cultivated. Lumbering and food processing are primary economic activities.

The residents of the basin make up 70 percent of Oregon's population. The river has always played a major role in the history of the valley. By the turn of the century, Willamette Falls was harnessed to generate electric power. Sawmills used the river to transport logs and finished products. With the advent of pulp and paper mills, the river also was used to dispose of wastes.

The hydrology of the Willamette is important. Variability in flow is extreme. There is heavy precipitation in the winter months and very little in the summer. This pattern led to extremely high water in the winter and early spring and extremely low water from July through October. Before the construction of storage reservoirs, the natural flow of the river ranged from an estimated maximum of 500,000 cubic feet a second during the flood of December 1861, to summer minimums of less than 2,500 cubic feet a second. These variations in flow were important to pollution control.

Water Quality Restored

Pollution—the early days. Pollution of the Willamette was a concern as early as the 1920s. In 1926, the Oregon State Board of Health organized an "Antipollution League," and in 1927 the Portland City Club was studying the pollution of the Willamette. Several water quality surveys were undertaken. The studies concentrated on measuring the amount of dissolved oxygen (DO) in the water. Concentrations of dissolved oxygen are needed to support not only fish and plant life but also the natural biological processes by which organic wastes are converted to stable inorganic materials by bacteria and other organisms. As a general rule, DO concentrations of five parts per million are required if a river is to stay healthy.

The first comprehensive water quality survey was undertaken by the Oregon Agricultural College in 1929. The dissolved oxygen level was measured during the low summer flow from the headwaters to the Portland Harbor. DO was above eight parts per million for the first 130 miles. At Salem, DO dropped to seven parts per million and remained at that level as far as Newberg, 35 miles farther downstream. DO fell below five parts per million 15 miles above Willamette Falls and reached four parts per million at the upper end of Portland Harbor. Considering the volume of wastes entering the river at Portland, the study concluded that DO was less than 0.5 parts per million where the waters of the Willamette reached the Columbia River.

The water was polluted because all municipalities dumped their wastes into the river without treatment. Although the Willamette was able to absorb and stabilize the discharges of smaller communities, it could not handle the municipal loads from the larger communities such as Eugene and Salem. Of even greater consequence were the five pulp and paper mills in operation by the late 1920s. These plants produced pulp using the sulfite process, which means cooking wood chips under pressure and then separating the larger cellulous fibers to produce paper. The residue, primarily wood sugars and smaller wood fibers, was discharged into the river. In decomposing, the wood sugars exerted an immediate and severe demand on dissolved oxygen. The wood fibers exerted their demand over a more extended period. Often they formed sludge deposits on the bottom. During the low-flow summer months, the deposits frequently surfaced as unsightly, foul-smelling floating rafts. As much as 80 percent of the total demand on the dissolved oxygen in the river stemmed from the pulp and paper mills.

When these waste flows reached Portland Harbor, the water quality situation became serious. The municipal wastes of the city, which by 1930 had 300,000 inhabitants, flowed untreated into the harbor through 65 separate discharge sewers. Tidal action and backflows from the Columbia generally kept the wastes in the deep harbor for an extended period during the low-flow summer months. The result during the summer was often a total absence of dissolved oxygen along stretches of the harbor.

Public concern over the river's condition increased in the 1930s. In 1933, the governor of Oregon called the mayors of the cities on the Willamette together for a conference "responsive to a statewide demand for abatement of stream pollution." The first technical study of the pollution generated by the pulp and paper industry followed that meeting. In 1935, the Oregon State Planning Board made a study of the water pollution laws. After identifying 35 separate state laws, the Committee determined that the existing statutes fostered administrative duplication and ineffectiveness, made it impossible to undertake ameliatory regulation, and provided for unacceptably severe, and therefore unenforceable, penalties. The Committee concluded that "promiscuous adoption of unrelated and uncoordinated nuisance and penal statutes . . . cannot form the basis of a concerted and direct effort to prohibit pollution of streams."

First Plan

During 1937, the energies of those concerned about water pollution were directed at the state legislature. A bill passed that year was vetoed by the governor on the grounds that it would cause financial hardship to the cities and towns. In November 1938, through the efforts of the Izaak Walton League and other citizen groups, an initiative measure proposing the "Water Purification and Prevention of Pollution Bill" was placed on the ballot. No arguments against the bill appeared in the official state "Voters Pamphlet." The measure passed by a margin of 3 to 1. The act made it public policy to restore and maintain the natural purity of all public waters. It authorized establishment of water quality standards and created a six-member State Sanitary Authority to develop a statewide control program and to enforce the new requirements.

The Sanitary Authority, organized in February 1939, decided as a first priority that the cities should be required to clean up their wastes. The Authority determined that primary treatment and effluent chlorination would be sufficient to restore acceptable water quality. An important consideration in choosing this strategy, rather than one requiring higher levels of treatment, was the fact that several large multipurpose storage reservoirs were to be constructed by the Corps of Engineers on tributaries of the Willamette. These projects—authorized for flood control, hydroelectric power, irrigation, and navigation—would provide increased stream flows during the critical summer and fall months. Instead of natural low flows of 2,500 to 3,000 cubic feet a second at Salem, it was expected that a minimum flow of 6,000 cubic feet a second would be possible. The higher flows would provide a greater capacity to absorb wastes. The Authority, therefore, directed the municipalities to construct primary treatment facilities.

World War II delayed the construction program. However, in 1944, Portland approved a $12-million bond issue to finance construction of necessary interceptor sewers and a new primary treatment plant. The plan provided for interceptor sewers to collect and carry the wastes to a new primary treatment plant. After treatment, the effluent was to be discharged into the Columbia River because its low summer flow was generally 40 times greater than the Willamette's. The first two municipal plants were completed in 1949. Portland's was placed in operation in 1951 and Salem's in 1952. By 1957, all cities on the Willamette had at least primary treatment. All construction costs were borne by the municipalities themselves.

In 1950, the Sanitary Authority faced a difficult problem. On the one hand, significant improvement in water quality depended on abatement by the mills. On the other hand, there appeared to be no available technology by which the mills could reasonably reduce the oxygen demand of their wastes.

The Sanitary Authority adopted what it saw as a stopgap solution. It formally ordered the five mills to halt, by July 1952, all discharges of concentrated sulfite waste effluents during the summer months of June through October. All the mills complied with the order. Three constructed storage lagoons in which their wastes were impounded during the summer months and released into the river during high water periods. One mill at Willamette Falls was unable to find a site for an impoundment. It was granted permission to barge its wastes to the Columbia and release them into the larger river. The fifth mill changed to an ammonia-base sulfite process, which allowed the wastes to be concentrated by evaporation and spray drying for recovery of the solids as a saleable by-product.

In 1953 and 1954, the two largest of the Corps of Engineers dams began operating. The dams permitted a flow of between 5,000 and 6,000 cubic feet a second in the mid-1950s compared to the low flow of between 3,000 and 4,000 cubic feet a second in the 1940s.

The plan reexamined. In 1957, the Sanitary Authority assessed its original plan. Water quality was still poor. DO in Portland Harbor that summer was one part per million. Because of a tremendous increase in the sources of pollution since 1939—particularly a 73 percent increase in the population served by public sewer systems and a 93 percent increase in industrial waste loads—water quality in the Willamette had not improved. It was clear that higher degrees of treatment were necessary. In early 1958, the Sanitary Authority initiated a new set of requirements.

The cities of Eugene, Salem, and Newberg were directed to install secondary treatment facilities. The growth in their populations was not the only reason. A major fruit and vegetable processing industry had developed, whose waste discharges coincided with the low-flow summer months. For the most part, this industry depended on municipal facilities for waste treatment services, thereby significantly increasing facility requirements.

The city of Portland was also lagging in its program to intercept discharges from its 65 outfalls. In 1959, the Sanitary Authority filed a lawsuit against the city council—one of the few times that the Authority went to court during the entire course of the cleanup campaign. In 1960, the voters of the city approved an increase in the monthly sewer charge sufficient to finance the completion of the interceptor project over a five-year period. In addition, the pulp and paper mills were directed to reduce their pollution discharges sufficiently to eliminate slime growths and sludge deposits and to maintain a minimum dissolved oxygen concentration of five parts per million. Finally, all municipalities downriver from Salem were directed to adopt secondary treatment.

Further actions. On the basis of an updated water quality evaluation, the Sanitary Authority issued even more stringent policies in 1964. All pulp and paper mills were ordered to adopt year-round primary treatment to remove settleable solids. The sulfite mills were directed to apply secondary treatment during the low-flow summer months, providing an 85 percent reduction in oxygen demand. In 1967, the secondary treatment requirement was extended to cover the entire year. Secondary treatment for all other industries was also required, and the possibility was reserved of demanding still higher degrees of treatment in some cases.

This policy is still in effect. Secondary treatment is now universal in the Willamette Basin. The total oxygen demand of wastes has been reduced to one-fourth the 1957 level. Dissolved oxygen in Portland Harbor has remained above the standard of five parts per million every summer since 1969.

A living sign of the new health of the Willamette is the success of the Chinook salmon entering the river in the fall. Salmon had been successfully migrating upstream in the spring even during the 1940s and 1950s, because the pollution was not a hindrance given the high water common at that time of the year. No fall Chinook salmon run had existed on the Willamette due to low summer flows at Willamette Falls. Attempts to start fall runs failed because of the extremely low DO levels in the lower river. But the situation has changed: pollution has been abated, flows are higher, and a new fish ladder has been built at the falls. In 1965, 79 Chinooks were counted; in 1968, 4,040; in 1970, 7,460; and in 1972, 11,614. The outlook is for even larger numbers.

Evaluation

A series of factors was responsible for the success of the pollution control efforts in the Willamette Valley. First, the limited but steady progress made between 1939 and the 1960s set the stage for more comprehensive efforts. That the Sanitary Authority (now the Department of Environmental Quality) succeeded with limited resort to the courts is noteworthy. Without doubt the single major factor behind the cleanup of the Willamette was the strong concern of the people of Oregon. Citizen organizations worked hard for a cleaner river at all stages. The people of Oregon wanted "their river" cleaned up.

With broad public support, new state legislation was enacted in 1967 to strengthen the antipollution effort. The new law created a mandatory waste discharge permit program. This permit authority allowed the state to set legally enforceable limitations on the amount and concentration of wastes and to establish compliance schedules for each step in the clean-up process. The 1967 legislation also provided for state aid to local governments for sewage works construction and established a system of tax credits for industrial expenditures on pollution control.

The assumption by the federal government in 1965 of a stronger role in controlling water pollution was also important. Legislation enacted that year required each state to establish approved water quality standards for its interstate waters and to place industry and municipalities on schedules for building treatment facilities. The Willamette as far upstream as the falls was held to be interstate. In meeting the federal requirement, Oregon in 1967 reviewed and updated its water quality standards not only for the lower Willamette but for its other waters as well, and it was one of the first states to receive federal approval of its standards. The stronger role of the federal government was a spur, particularly for industry, which came to recognize that pollution control was inevitable and that the state of Oregon could deal firmly with industry without fear that jobs would be lost to another state. The federal government also gave financial assistance to municipalities for their waste treatment plants.

A final factor in the improvement of water quality was the achievement of a higher minimum flow through releases from the upstream reservoirs during the low-flow months.

Chapter 7

Regulation of Personnel Practices

In a great variety of ways, federal legislation influences the hiring, pay, promotion, firing, and other aspects of the personnel practices of private industry. Federally required fringe benefits are the most obvious examples of the added costs that result, and affirmative action programs are the most conspicuous and often controversial influences on company work force policies. The personnel area is a key example of the public's unwillingness to accept the impacts on society that result from the unregulated workings of the free market.

ADMINISTERING EQUAL EMPLOYMENT OPPORTUNITY

Government responsibility for ending job discrimination rests primarily with three federal agencies—the Equal Employment Opportunity Commission, the Labor Department's Employment Standards Administration, and the Office of Federal Contract Compliance (see Table 7–1).

The most familiar of these agencies, the Equal Employment Opportunity Commission (EEOC), was created by the Equal Employment Opportunity Act of 1972 to enforce the prohibition of discrimination because of race, color, religion, sex, or national origin in all employment practices, including hiring, firing, layoffs, promotion, wages, training, disciplinary action, and other terms,

Table 7-1

U.S. LAWS AGAINST JOB DISCRIMINATION

Executive Order 11246 as amended by 11375	Title 7 of the Civil Rights Act of 1964 as amended by Equal Employment Opportunity Act of 1972	Equal Pay Act of 1963 as amended by the Education Amendments of 1972 (Higher Education Act)
Which employers are covered?		
All employers with federal contracts over $10,000.	All employers with 15 or more employees.	Most employers.
What is prohibited?		
Discrimination in hiring, upgrading, salaries, fringe benefits, training, and other conditions of employment, on the basis of race, sex, color, religion, or national origin.		Discrimination in salaries (including most fringe benefits).
Who enforces the provisions?		
Office of Federal Contract Compliance (OFCC) of the Labor Dept. oversees anti-discrimination programs of 18 other agencies.	Equal Employment Opportunity Commission (EEOC).	Wage & Hour Div. of the Employment Standards Administration, Labor Department.
How is a complaint made?		
By letter to OFCC.	By a sworn complaint form, obtainable from EEOC.	By letter, phone call, or in person to nearest Wage & Hour office.
Who can make a complaint?		
Individuals or organizations on own behalf or on behalf of aggrieved individual(s). In the case of the EEOC, members of the Commission may also file charges.		
Can investigations be made without complaints?		
Yes.	No.	Yes.
Can the entire establishment be reviewed?		
Yes.	Yes.	Yes. Usually Wage & Hour reviews entire establishment.
Recordkeeping requirements and government access		
Employer must keep and preserve specified records relevant to the determination of whether violations have occurred. Government is empowered to review all relevant records.		
Enforcement power and sanctions		
Government may delay new contracts, revoke current contracts, and debar employers from eligibility for future contracts.	If attempts at conciliation fail, EEOC or the U.S. Attorney General may file suit. Aggrieved individuals may also sue. Court may enjoin respondent from engaging in unlawful behavior, order appropriate affirmative action, or order reinstatement of employees and award back pay.	If voluntary compliance fails, the Secretary of Labor may file suit. Aggrieved individuals may sue. Court may enjoin respondent from engaging in unlawful behavior, order salary raises and back pay, and assess interest.

Table 7–1 (continued)

Executive Order 11246 as amended by 11375	Title 7 of the Civil Rights Act of 1964 as amended by Equal Employment Opportunity Act of 1972	Equal Pay Act of 1963 as amended by the Education Amendments of 1972 (Higher Education Act)

Is harassment prohibited?

Employers are prohibited from discharging or discriminating against any person because he/she has made a complaint, assisted with an investigation, or instituted proceedings.

Notification of complaints

Notification of complaints has been erratic in the past.	EEOC notifies employers of complaints within 10 days.	Complaint procedure is very informal. Employer under review may or may not know that a violation has been reported.

Confidentiality of names

Individual complainant's name is usually given to the employer. Investigation findings are kept confidential by the government, but can be revealed by the employer. Policy on government disclosure of investigations and complaints has not yet been issued. Aggrieved party and respondent are not bound by the confidentiality requirement.	Individual complainant's name is divulged when an investigation is made. Charges are not made public by EEOC, nor can any of its efforts during the conciliation process be made public by EEOC or its employees. If court action becomes necessary, the identity of the parties involved becomes a matter of public record. The aggrieved party and respondent are not bound by the confidentiality requirement.	The identity of the complainant, as well as the employer (and union, if involved), is kept in strict confidence. If court action becomes necessary, the identity of the participants involved becomes a matter of public record. Aggrieved party and respondent are not bound by confidentiality requirement.

Source: Project on the Status and Education of Women, Association of American Colleges.

privileges, conditions, or benefits of employment.[1] Those covered by the act include all firms and labor unions of 15 or more persons, employment agencies, educational institutions, and state and local governments.

EEOC enforces this law through the following procedure. A person who believes that he or she has been discriminated against files a charge of discrimination (see Figure 7–1). After receipt of the charge, EEOC investigates it to determine if sufficient evidence of discrimination exists. If so, EEOC tries to persuade the employer to remedy the situation voluntarily. If the conciliation attempts fail, the EEOC files suit in federal court. In the words of the Commission, "Court ordered compliance with Title VII often results in large expenses to

[1]*EEOC At A Glance* (Washington, D.C.: US. Equal Employment Opportunity Commission, September 1974), p. 1.

(PLEASE PRINT OR TYPE)

CHARGE OF DISCRIMINATION	EEOC CHARGE NO.	FORM APPROVED OMB NO. 124-R0001

INSTRUCTIONS

If you have a complaint, fill in this form and mail it to the Equal Employment Opportunity Commission's District Office in your area. In most cases, a charge must be filed with the EEOC within a specified time after the discriminatory act took place. IT IS THEREFORE IMPORTANT TO FILE YOUR CHARGE AS SOON AS POSSIBLE. *(Attach extra sheets of paper if necessary.)*

CAUSE OF DISCRIMINATION

☐ RACE OR COLOR   ☐ SEX

☐ RELIGIOUS CREED

☐ NATIONAL ORIGIN

NAME *(Indicate Mr. or Ms.)*   DATE OF BIRTH

STREET ADDRESS   COUNTY   SOCIAL SECURITY NO.

CITY, STATE, AND ZIP CODE   TELEPHONE NO. *(Include area code)*

THE FOLLOWING PERSON ALWAYS KNOWS WHERE TO CONTACT ME

NAME *(Indicate Mr. or Ms.)*   TELEPHONE NO. *(Include area code)*

STREET ADDRESS   CITY, STATE, AND ZIP CODE

LIST THE EMPLOYER, LABOR ORGANIZATION, EMPLOYMENT AGENCY, APPRENTICESHIP COMMITTEE, STATE OR LOCAL GOVERNMENT WHO DISCRIMINATED AGAINST YOU *(If more than one, list all)*

NAME   TELEPHONE NO. *(Include area code)*

STREET ADDRESS   CITY, STATE, AND ZIP CODE

OTHERS WHO DISCRIMINATED AGAINST YOU *(If any)*

CHARGE FILED WITH STATE/LOCAL GOV'T. AGENCY ☐ YES ☐ NO	DATE FILED	AGENCY CHARGE FILED WITH *(Name and address)*

APPROXIMATE NO. OF EMPLOYEES/MEMBERS OF COMPANY OR UNION THIS CHARGE IS FILED AGAINST	DATE MOST RECENT OR CONTINUING DISCRIMINATION TOOK PLACE *(Month, day, and year)*

Explain what unfair thing was done to you and how other persons were treated differently. Understanding that this statement is for the use of the United States Equal Employment Opportunity Commission, I hereby certify:

I swear or affirm that I have read the above charge and that it is true to the best of my knowledge, information and belief.

DATE	CHARGING PARTY *(Signature)*

Subscribed and sworn to before this EEOC representative.

DATE	SIGNATURE AND TITLE

NOTARY PUBLIC

SUBSCRIBED AND SWORN TO BEFORE ME THIS DATE *(Day, month, and year)*

SIGNATURE *(If it is difficult for you to get a Notary Public to sign this, sign your own name and mail to the District Office. The Commission will notarize the charge for you at a later date.)*

EEOC FORM JUN 72 5   Previous editions of this form may be used.

U.S. GOVERNMENT PRINTING OFFICE : 1973-728-451/1250
GPO 871-168

Figure 7-1

the employer, usually exceeding the cost of effective voluntary affirmative action. Widespread voluntary compliance is by far the most desirable method for eliminating job discrimination."[2] Expensive settlements are at least partly a result of the retroactive liability of the employer. Companies are held liable for back pay for two years prior to the filing of the charge, and if two additional years were required to settle the case, the employer would be liable for four years' back pay.

The power of the EEOC as exemplified by its manpower and budget has increased substantially since its inception. The fiscal year 1976 budget allocates the EEOC $63.4 million, a 44 percent increase over the fiscal 1974 level. EEOC employs 2,400 people in 7 regional and 32 district offices.

The Office of Federal Contract Compliance examines the antidiscrimination programs of companies with federal government contracts of $50,000 or more and 50 or more employees. These companies must have affirmative action plans listing the specific goals and timetables for the hiring of women and minorities. Even if only one division of a company has a government contract of $50,000 or more, the entire firm must participate in the required affirmative action program.

The OFCC indirectly provides incentives as well as punishments to government contractors. Robert L. Malcolm, vice-president of Rockwell International Corporation, contends that Rockwell's success in meeting affirmative action goals was "a definite factor" in winning the $2.6-billion space shuttle contract.[3]

The Employment Standards Administration administers the Equal Pay Act, which prohibits discrimination in salaries or benefits because of sex. Through these laws, more than 133,000 employees, mostly women, have been awarded more than $71 million as compensation for discriminatory actions by their employers.[4] Also administered by ESA is the Age Discrimination Act of 1967.

Secretary of Labor John T. Dunlop testified before one congressional committee concerning the "plethora" of agencies enforcing the equal employment regulations: "One might question whether there is not a redundancy of authority, administration, and forums creating confusion among both those seeking to comply with the law and those attempting to seek enforcement."[5]

THE FEDERAL GOVERNMENT AND PERSONNEL PRACTICES

The importance given equal employment opportunity considerations, perhaps at the expense of employee productivity, is often evident in the statements

[2]Ibid., p. 1.

[3]"Acting Affirmatively To End Job Bias," *Business Week,* January 27, 1975, p. 94.

[4]Vivian Pospisil, "Winding Through The Equal Opportunity Maze," *Industry Week,* October 7, 1974, p. 61.

[5]Ernest Holsendolph, "Dunlop Criticizes Equal Job Rules," *New York Times,* June 25, 1975, p. 34.

of federal officials involved in the regulation of personnel practices. For example, the deputy director of the Equal Opportunity Program of the U.S. Treasury Department listed the following item in a 10-point "overall strategy for identifying and correcting EEO problems" as presented to a group of commercial bankers:

> 10. Refuse promotions or substantial wage increases to those who do not produce satisfactory EEO results, no matter what other performance results they achieve.[6]

In contrast, the ninth point in the "overall strategy" conveys a sense of balance among a variety of important objectives: "Make each line manager and personnel manager accountable for, and rewarded in terms of, equal employment opportunity results in his or her unit as well as other performance measures."

The Equal Employment Opportunity Commission has stated that it is concentrating on the nation's largest and most visible corporations. In the words of then Commission Chairman John H. Powell, Jr., "Once we get the big boys, the others will soon fall in line."[7]

The irony is that the large, national corporations often have the best civil rights records in industry. At the time it was sued by the EEOC, the General Motors Corporation had a work force that was 17 percent black and 15 percent female. According to Commission member Colston A. Lewis, "Sears has the best damn affirmative action program of any company in the country... The Commission is harassing Sears and GM, because this is the way the chairman can get headlines."[8]

Sears' view of affirmative action, in fact, does not stop with an effort in the area of jobs and promotions, but is extended to minority economic development. Ray Graham, the head of Sears' affirmative program, states, "We sell more than anyone else in the world, but we manufacture nothing. Obviously we have to buy a lot, and our buying creates a lot of business opportunities." Sears is trying to pass some of these opportunities along to minority businesses.[9]

Many large companies seem to have decided that the most practical course is to agree to the Commission's demands. Adverse publicity may be considered too high a price to pay for possible ultimate vindication in the courts. The resultant agreements often involve the companies consent to hire a stipulated quota, such as the nine major steel companies who agreed to fill one-half of the openings in trade and craft jobs with minority and women employees.

---

[6]Inez S. Lee, *Current EEO Regulations.* Speech to the Pennsylvania Bankers Association, Philadelphia, February 20–21, 1974, p. 12.

[7]Gerald R. Rosen, "Industry's New Watchdog in Washington," *Dun's,* June 1974, p. 83.

[8]Ibid.

[9]William Raspberry, "Action on Affirmative Action," *Washington Post,* July 30, 1975, p. A15.

Former Chairman Powell apparently was not convinced by the arguments over reverse discrimination. He was quoted as saying, "Such terms as 'quotas' and 'reverse discrimination' are merely shibboleths designed to confuse the issue." Colston Lewis disagrees with this position. A southern black, opposing the notion of forcing companies to hire less qualified people to fill quotas for minorities, he says, "It is wrong to force companies to hire unqualified applicants just because they are minority people. In the end, such practices will only serve to hurt the minorities."[10]

According to Professor George C. Lodge of Harvard University, the old idea of equality of opportunity has been replaced by equality of result or equality of representation:

> . . . You've got to have so many men telephone operators, so many women vice-presidents. You've got to have minority groups spread up and down the corporate hierarchy, roughly in proportion to their numbers in the community. That's a very new idea radically different from the old way.[11]

Yet the difficulties inherent in a reliance on a quota system to increase the proportion of certain groups in the labor force are described by Professor Richard Posner of the University of Chicago Law School:

> The problem of remedy becomes acute if the law is interpreted to require that the employer have some minimum number or percentage of black employees regardless of whether he or his white employees have been guilty of discrimination. To comply, the employer must lay off workers or, what amounts to the same thing, favor black over white job applicants for as long a period of time as is necessary to attain the quota. In either case white employees untainted by discrimination are made to bear a high cost in order to improve the condition of black workers. The result is a capricious and regressive tax on the white working class.[12]

Even more sweeping changes in employment policy have been proposed by U.S. District Judge Albert V. Bryant, Jr. To remedy job discrimination at a Richmond, Virginia, tobacco plant, he ordered:[13]

> "A flat ban on hiring anyone but blacks and women as foremen, assistant foremen, or their white-collar counterparts" until the percentage of women and blacks in these occupations equals their percentage of the population

[10]Rosen, "Industry's New Watchdog," p. 84.

[11]"Recovery and Beyond," *Saturday Review,* July 12, 1975, p. 25.

[12]Richard A. Posner, *Economic Analysis of Law* (Boston: Little, Brown, & Co., 1973), p. 306.

[13]"A Sweeping Remedy For Job Discrimination," *Business Week,* February 3, 1975, p. 21.

in the surrounding area. A white male can be hired only if no other qualified person can be found.

A "bumping" system where any black or woman can replace any pro-
duction-line employee with less seniority. No skill requirements may be
imposed by the company, but the new worker may be removed if he or
she cannot perform the job competently in a reasonable time. (See appendix at the end of this chapter for a federal law case upholding affirmative
action in the construction industry.)

According to the EEOC's long-range goals, the only way a company can
satisfy the Commission completely is if its work force reflects the minority
group situation in the area in which it is located. Commissioner Ethel Walsh
states, "Each plant should reflect the percentages of minority people that make
up the labor force in its locality."[14] A plant in Alaska, for example, should
employ a high percentage of Eskimos; a plant in Oklahoma should have a high
proportion of Indians.

The possibility, of course, arises that the strategy could backfire. A company could avoid the entire problem by locating its new plants in largely white
communities, making it more difficult for minority group applicants to obtain
jobs. In such an event, the EEOC's actions would hurt the very people it is trying
to help. There is some evidence to support this concern.

The St. Louis office of the EEOC is reported to follow standards that,
whatever their intention, serve to discourage prospective employers from locating in the central city, where most of the area's black population resides. This
situation results from the EEOC setting up a county (not metropolitan area)
standard whereby it will infer discrimination has taken place if a firm's work
force contains a smaller percentage of blacks than the county as a whole. Thus,
if a company locates in the city limits of St. Louis (about 42 percent black), it
has to work under a far more severe personnel restraint than if it locates in
suburban St. Louis County (16 percent black). Not too surprisingly, the opposition to the EEOC position has not arisen in the suburbs, but is led by two St.
Louis city aldermen who contend that the policy contributes to the exodus of
business to the suburbs.[15]

Laws forbidding job discrimination against handicapped workers are in
effect in many states as well as in the federal government. There are important
benefits, both public and private, to be achieved from the productive utilization
of the skills of handicapped workers. Savings in unemployment or welfare payments accrue to the society, as well as the increased output of the goods and
services that they produce. Moreover, handicapped individuals benefit from increased income as well as having the satisfaction of holding productive jobs. Yet,

[14]Ibid., p. 85.

[15]Marsha Canfield, "U.S. minority hiring guides here called unfair," *St. Louis Globe-
Democrat,* December 1, 1973, p. 3A.

the cost to the employer of compliance with these regulations can be substantial. A number of the laws require employers to make architectural adjustments around the requirements of workers or applicants with physical handicaps. Under federal law, an employer could also be required to restructure work schedules to meet the needs of the handicapped.[16] The significance of this regulation should not be understated. The government has, for the first time, made an affirmative action program a direct cost to employers—the employer must pay to make it possible for an employee to do the job for which he or she was hired.[17]

One of the basic problems encountered in the administration of any national regulatory program is the inevitable shortcomings that result from a bureaucratic, do-it-by-the-numbers approach. In the case of the equal employment opportunity program, this would appear to be a problem in terms of the substantive issues as well as the detailed administration.

The overhead costs, and notably the paperwork burden, associated with the equal employment opportunity program appear to be rising. In July 1974, the Department of Labor gave final approval to its Revised Order No. 14, with reference to the procedures that federal agencies must use in evaluating affirmative action programs by government contractors.[18]

As mentioned earlier, all prime contractors or subcontractors who have 50 or more employees and a contract of $50,000 or more are required to develop written affirmative action programs for each of their establishments. They must now list each job title as it appears in their union agreements or payroll records. Listing only by job group, as was formerly required, is no longer acceptable. The job titles must be listed from the lowest paid to the highest paid within each department or other similar organizational unit.

If there are separate work units or lines of progression within a department, separate lists must be provided for each such unit, or line, including unit supervisors. For lines of progression, the order of jobs in the line through which an employee can move to the job must be indicated. If there are no formal progression lines or usual promotional sequences, job titles must be listed by departments, job families, or disciplines, in order of wage rates or salary ranges. For each job title, two breakdowns are required—the total number of male and female incumbents, and the total number of male and female incumbents in each of the following groups: blacks, Spanish-surnamed Americans, American Indians, and Orientals.

The wage rate or salary range for each job group at the facility, with an explanation if minorities or women are currently being underutilized in any

[16]Jane E. Brody, "Equal Opportunity Job Laws for Disabled Have Little Effect," *New York Times*, May 3, 1975, p. 14C.

[17]Michael Markowitz, "Affirmative Action—Good Idea Gone Too Far," *NAM Reports*, January 13, 1975, p. 6.

[18]"Revised Order No. 14 Clarifies Rules," *NAM News*, July 29, 1974, p. 5.

group, also is required. Underutilization means "having fewer minorities or women in a particular job group than would reasonably be expected by their availability." Separate utilization analyses must be prepared for minorities and women. Clearly, these requirements will necessitate a significant increase in the amount and costs of recordkeeping and reporting required of federal contractors. Matters are made more difficult for federal contractors because compliance is administered by 15 separate agencies, each with its own approach. Todd Jagerson, president of EEO Services, a New York based consulting firm, provides a vivid description of actual practice:

> I've got a client who deals with six compliance officers for a single, 25,000-employee plant. No two of them will accept the same affirmative action program, so the company has six, with the required 170 items for each program. And that's small potatoes. Some big corporations with plants all over the U.S. may have 100 programs.[19]

A positive effect of OFCC affirmative action pressures has been the reexamination of requirements for certain positions. For example, the availability of black and women engineers traditionally has been small. For this reason, Westinghouse reanalyzed its entry-level professional and managerial positions to identify those jobs where a liberal arts degree would do as well as the engineering degree required previously.[20] The very real and serious lingering effects of past discriminatory practices, whether intentional or not, surely provide the continued impetus for substantial efforts to promote equal employment opportunity. Concern over specific enforcement practices need not deflect attention from the underlying social inequities whose correction are the object of public policy.

Equal Opportunity vs Seniority

Periods of economic recession have forced many employers either to erase gains in the employment of women and minorities or to turn their backs on the seniority system. When job layoffs are prevalent, blacks and women, often the last hired, are frequently slated as the first to be let go. If this occurs, affirmative action gains may be drastically reduced or negated completely. The position of employers resembles being in the middle of a triangle, threatened from three sides at once, with the forces including women's rights organizations, organized labor, and the civil rights enforcement agencies.[21]

EEOC asserts that minority and women workers warrant special considera-

---

[19]"Acting Affirmatively To End Job Bias," *Business Week,* p. 102.

[20]Ibid., p. 98.

[21]Ernest Holsendolph, "Layoff and the Civil Rights of Minorities," *New York Times,* January 29, 1975, p. 17.

tion and protection from layoffs as compensation for past discrimination. EEOC Chairman John Powell described the position of the EEOC during the recession of 1974–75, "Contrary to letting up, we're going to tighten up. We intend to use the full panoply of enforcement powers through the courts."[22] Many employers, especially those bound by union agreements, have used seniority as the basic determinant of who gets the pink slip. One survey of companies that experienced layoffs failed to find a single employer who openly flouted seniority to retain minority or women workers.[23]

Numerous layoff decisions have been tested in the courts, with differing and conflicting opinions from judges. In a case involving the Harvey, Louisiana, plant of Continental Can, using seniority as the guideline meant that 48 of 50 black employees were laid off. One federal district judge stated, in a ruling prohibiting the use of the seniority approach:

> The company's history of racial discrimination in hiring makes it impossible now for blacks (other than the original two) to have sufficient seniority to withstand layoff.
>
> In this situation, the selection of employees for layoffs on the basis of seniority unlawfully perpetuates the effects of past discrimination.[24]

An opposing view in a Court of Appeals decision stated that using the last hired, first fired principle "does not of itself perpetuate past discrimination." And in yet another ruling, a federal district judge held that after a layoff the company must have the same percentage of blacks and women employed as it did on a specified date prior to the layoff.[25] It seems that the law in this area is undergoing a period of testing and development.

Future Trends

An indication of the shape of things to come can be obtained from an examination of a draft of proposed Uniform Guidelines on Employee Selection Procedures, which has been developed by the Equal Employment Opportunity Coordinating Council. The guidelines were drafted to assure that selection procedures, in both the public and private sectors, do not discriminate against any group on the basis of race, color, religion, sex, or national origin.[26]

[22]Marilyn Bender, "Job Discrimination, 10 Years Later," *New York Times,* November 10, 1974, p. F5.

[23]"Seniority Squeezes Out Minorities In Layoffs," *Business Week,* May 5, 1975, p. 66.

[24]Holsendolph, "Layoff and the Civil Rights of Minorities," p. 17.

[25]Ibid.

[26]U.S. Equal Employment Opportunity Coordinating Council, *Uniform Guidelines on Employee Selection Procedures,* June 24, 1974, p. 1.

Although the objective may be commendable, the method of carrying it out has been strongly questioned. Division 14 of the American Psychological Association, representing about 1,300 psychologists specializing in research and its application in business and industry, has stated:

> ... as presently constituted, the guidelines would discourage selection research because on many points the standards are unclear, unworkable, unnecessarily negative, and, in places, technically unsound. Adoption of the current draft could, therefore, result in more unfair discrimination, rather than less, and result in less effective use of the nation's human resources.[27]

The statement of the practicing psychologists would seem to be unusually strong. However, an inspection of a draft of the federal regulations reveals the basis for their concern. The section on validity of personnel tests states in part:

> Under no circumstances will the general reputation of a selection procedure, its author or its publisher, or casual reports of its validity or practical usefulness be accepted in lieu of evidence of validity. Specifically ruled out are ... data bearing on the frequency of a procedure's usage; testimonial statements and credentials of sellers, users, or consultants, and other nonempirical or anecdotal accounts of selection practices or selection outcomes.[28]

In the words of the industrial psychologists, "The pervasive problem in this draft is the attempt to specify a universally applicable set of ideal procedures ... To create an impossible standard is to invite evasion and disrespect for the law."

From an inspection of the draft regulations, it appears that smaller employers would have great difficulty in even understanding the regulations, much less meeting their requirements, without paying for extremely expensive outside help. A sampling of the draft regulations follows. The excerpt relates to the requirement that each company demonstrate that the tests it uses are valid for the specific prospective employees to be tested:

> Evidence of validation studies conducted by other employers or in other organizations ... will be considered acceptable when ... there are no major differences in pertinent contextual variables which are likely to affect validity significantly, and with respect to criterion-related studies, no major differences in sample composition which are likely to affect validity significantly (Section 6 (a)).

[27]Cited in Ad Hoc Industry Group, *Uniform Guidelines on Employee Selection.* Washington, D.C., 1974, p. 1.

[28]Equal Opportunity Coordinating Council, *Uniform Guidelines*, pp. 6–7.

The following seems to be an attempt to ease the burden on the employer, providing that he or she understands it:

> If a criterion-related or construct validation study is technically feasible in all other respects, but it is not technically feasible to conduct a differential prediction study when required by subparagraph 14a(5) below and the test user has conducted a validation study for the job in question which otherwise meets the requirements of paragraph 14a below, the test user may continue to use the procedure operationally until such time as a differential prediction study is feasible and has been conducted within a reasonable time after it has become feasible (Section 8(b)).
>
> A selection procedure has criterion-related validity, for the purpose of these guidelines, when the relationship between performance on the procedure and performance on at least one relevant criterion measure is statistically significant at the .05 level of significance . . . If the relationship between a selection procedure and a criterion measure is significant but nonlinear, the score distribution should be studied to determine if there are sections of the regression curve with zero or near zero slope where scores do not reliably predict different levels of job performance. (Section 14(a) (5) (6)).

The quotations above are not isolated instances. They are indicative of the general tone of the proposed regulations. No mention of cost or minimum size of firm or the limits of practical application is contained in the proposal.

An ad hoc industry group, consisting of representatives of leading business and professional associations ranging from the Business Roundtable to the American Society for Personnel Administration, has warned that the proposed guidelines, if implemented, would eliminate objective test selection of employees. This could well cause a reversion to less job-related and potentially more bias-laden procedures, such as the uncontrolled oral interview.

There are strong indications that numerous companies have dropped or reduced the role of testing as a tool in hiring. A Supreme Court ruling involving the Albermarle Paper Company indicates that companies may be required to validate a test for every individual job in which it is used as a screening device. One firm, Duke Power Company, estimates the cost of validation studies at $15,000 to $20,000 each.[29]

It may be difficult to contemplate, but the notion of a company town could reemerge as a result of the efforts of the Civil Rights Commission. The Commission has recommended that the Office of Federal Contract Compliance require contractors and subcontractors, as a condition of eligibility for federal contracts, to demonstrate the adequacy of nondiscriminatory low and moderate

---

[29]Hal Lancaster, "Job Tests Are Dropped By Many Companies Due to Antibias Drive," *Wall Street Journal,* September 3, 1975, pp. 1, 12.

income housing in any community in which they are located or propose to locate.

The Commission states, "In the event the supply of such housing is not adequate, contractors should be required to submit affirmative action plans, including firm commitments from local government officials, housing industry representatives, and civic leaders that will assure an adequate supply of such housing within a reasonable time following execution of the contract. Failure to carry out the assurance should be made grounds for cancellation of the contract and ineligibility for future government contracts."[30]

FEDERALLY MANDATED FRINGE BENEFITS

A major example of legislation leading to higher product costs is legally required fringe benefits. The story is simple—legally required fringe benefits have grown enormously since World War II. In 1950, they totaled a little more than $4 billion. In 1973, they cost employers over $43 billion, an almost tenfold increase in 23 years.

By far the largest portion of these fringe benefits is social security (technically, old age, survivors, and disability insurance). Congress has continued to enlarge this program, adding on an 11 percent increase in benefits in 1974 (see Table 7–2). Unemployment insurance and workmen's compensation, at a cost of about $5 billion each to employers, are important but much smaller categories (see Table 7–3). The point being made here is not that these are undesirable social programs, but rather that they have a significant hidden economic impact. In a very real sense, these federally mandated benefits add to the cost of labor the employer must pay, which is then reflected in the selling price of the goods or service the firm provides or shifted backward in the form of lower direct wage payments than would otherwise be the case. These costs have grown at a faster rate than direct wages and salaries, rapidly increasing private firms' costs associated with labor. In 1950, the employers' share of legally required fringe benefits was over three percent of wages and salaries. Fifteen years later, in 1965, these costs had risen to a level of five percent of wages. In the following eight years, the required payments rose to an all-time high of over eight percent.

Under some circumstances, the cost of these government-mandated fringe benefits may not be fully passed on to the customer but are borne by labor in the form of lower wage rates than would otherwise be paid. To that extent, the higher incomes for social security recipients are financed by lower real incomes for current workers. As in the case of the other federally mandated costs on the private sector, an accommodating monetary policy is required and is generally forthcoming to "validate" the cost increases.

---

[30]Taylor Pennsoneau, "New U.S. Agencies To Curb Housing Bias In Suburbs Here Urged By Rights Panel," *St. Louis Post-Dispatch,* August 12, 1974, p. 1.

Table 7–2

SOCIAL SECURITY TAX INCREASES
Past, Present, and Future

Year	Tax Rate*	Tax Base	Maximum Tax*
1937	2.0%	$ 3,000	$ 60.00
1950	3.0	3,000	90.00
1960	6.0	4,800	288.00
1965	7.25	4,800	348.00
1966	8.4	6,600	544.40
1970	9.6	7,800	748.80
1971	10.4	7,800	811.20
1972	10.4	9,000	936.00
1973	11.7	10,800	1,263.60
1974	11.7	13,200	1,544.40
1975	11.7	14,100**	1,649.70
1976	11.7	15,300	1,790.10
1977	11.7	16,500	1,930.50
1978	12.1	18,000	2,178.00

*Combined employee-employer tax for Social Security cash benefits and Medicare (HI) programs.

**The 1972 Social Security amendments provided for automatic future increases in benefits whenever the Consumer Price Index (CPI) rises 3% or more a year. Financing of the benefit escalator is provided by automatic increases in the taxable earnings base starting in 1975. Estimated increases in the tax base prepared by Social Security Administration.

The figures in Table 7–3 reflect only the part of government-mandated fringe benefits paid directly by the employer. They do not include the money deducted from employees' paychecks as their contributions to social security, and so on.

Legally required personal contributions to social insurance by private firms were $33.9 billion in 1973, an increase of 40 percent from 1969.[31] Some part of these personal deductions may in some circumstances be compensated for by higher salaries to employees, and therefore passed on to the consumer.

These required payments by both employers and employees are in addition to private pension and welfare funds. The private funds are also a substantial cost to employers, totaling $39.2 billion in 1973.[32]

The hidden effects of the legally required fringe benefits are actually twofold. As discussed above, they increase the prices of goods and services to consumers because of higher labor costs to employers. In addition, the inflated costs of hiring labor due to the increasingly more expensive mandatory benefits may encourage firms to hire fewer workers and substitute machinery or other capital for them when possible, in all decreasing the demand for labor.

[31] *Survey of Current Business*, July 1973, p. 33; July 1974, p. 28.
[32] *Survey of Current Business*, July 1974, p. 16.

Table 7-3

COST BORNE BY PRIVATE EMPLOYERS OF LEGALLY REQUIRED
FRINGE BENEFITS
(millions of dollars)

Category	1950	1955	1960	1965	1970	1973
Old age, survivors, and disability insurance[a]	1,590	3,133	5,947	8,717	16,954	26,160
Hospital insurance	—	—	—	—	2,276	5,301
Unemployment compensation[b]	1,473	1,550	2,823	3,729	3,482	6,733
Workman's compensation	746	1,051	1,590	2,027	4,267	5,370
Cash sickness compensation	7	5	8	9	27	46
Total	3,816	5,739	10,368	14,482	27,006	43,610
Private wages and salaries	124,300	175,100	277,100	289,600	426,875	545,060
Legally required fringe benefits as a percent of wages and salaries	3.1%	3.3%	3.7%	5.0%	6.3%	8.0%

[a]Includes railroad retirement.

[b]Includes railroad unemployment insurance.

Source: U.S. Department of Commerce and Chamber of Commerce of the U.S.A.

The upward trend of these federally mandated personnel costs is likely to continue. Most of the proposed national health insurance plans, Democratic as well as Republican, would require the largest part of the cost (as much as three-fourths) to be borne by employers in the form of required payments to health insurance carriers.

The Department of Health, Education, and Welfare is attempting to require that companies offer their workers membership in health maintenance organizations (HMO's). Under the Health Maintenance Organization Act of 1973, this option must be offered to employees even if the union bargaining for them rejects it. On this point, the Labor Department and the unions object to the ruling. In the opinion of Peter G. Nash, general counsel of the National Labor Relations Board, the regulation is in conflict with national labor law.[33]

Court decisions have also increased the coverage of existing federally mandated fringe benefits. For example, in July 1974, a federal court ruled that women workers on forced maternity leave are entitled to unemployment compensation benefits.[34]

[33]"The HMO Movement Stalls Once More," *Business Week,* April 21, 1975, p. 31; "HEW Chief Proposes Firms Be Required To Offer HMO Plans," *Wall Street Journal,* February 14, 1975, p. 15.

[34]"Courts Rule on Pay for Maternity Leave," *Industry Week,* August 5, 1974, p. 13.

In a comprehensive analysis of employee benefit programs, the Conference Board concluded that the basic role of government in this area has changed from regulator to social planner. The study offered the following forecast:

> Regardless of which trends are followed by unions and corporate benefit staffs in the next ten years, the government is now almost certain to become a major, if not the dominant, force in the design of employee benefit packages during that time.[35]

By taxing various forms of compensation unequally, the government can encourage the development of certain types of employee benefits at the expense of money wages. A tax code that subsidizes compensation paid in the form of insurance premiums (which are not taxable to the employee while he or she is working) leads to the widespread adoption of such plans by employers. In the words of the Federal Reserve Bank of Kansas City, "It is clear that government intervention in compensation practices is largely responsible for the rapid growth of employee benefits."[36]

REGULATION OF PRIVATE PENSIONS

The 1974 pension reform law is likely to add substantially to the cost of private pension plans. The Employee Retirement Income Security Act of 1974 is widely considered to be one of the most complicated laws ever enacted. It is estimated that 90 percent of all private pension plans will have to be rewritten to comply with this law.[37] Basically, the pension law establishes seven areas of requirements to be met. Compliance is required for a company's pension plan to be acceptable to IRS, thus allowing the contributions and earnings on the plan to be tax-exempt.

Eligibility. An employee must be eligible to participate in the retirement plan when he or she is 25 and has worked for one year.

Vesting. Explicit regulations are established on the time it takes for an employee to earn the right to a pension. Once vested, the employee has a right to a pension at retirement even if he or she is not working at the company at the time.

Surviving-spouse Benefit. In the event of the retired employee's death, the surviving spouse must receive at least 50 percent of the pension benefit.

---

[35]Mitchell Meyer and Harland Fox, *Profile of Employee Benefits* (New York: Conference Board, 1974), p. 5.

[36]Dan M. Bechter, "The Elementary Microeconomics of Private Employee Benefits," *Monthly Review of the Federal Reserve Bank of Kansas City,* May 1975, p. 9.

[37]Vivian C. Pospisil, "The New Law And Your Pension," *Industry Week,* March 3, 1975, p. 24.

Funding. Employers must fully fund the annual cost of the retirement program. They must also contribute an additional amount to amortize existing liabilities over a designated period of time.

Fiduciaries. Fiduciaries, those who manage or administer a pension plan or those who give investment advice for a fee, are more widely defined and are placed under strict rules of conduct. Under the law, they must act as a "prudent man" would in similar circumstances. Fiduciaries are personally liable for violations of this responsibility.

Plan Termination Insurance. The U.S. Pension Benefit Guaranty Corporation was chartered to guarantee the payment of pension benefits should a plan be terminated with insufficient assets to pay pension liabilities. Initially, annual premiums for employers are $1 for each participant for single employer plans and 50¢ for each participant in multiemployer plans. Firms are liable for up to 30 percent of their assets if they terminate a pension plan that is not fully funded.

Reporting and Disclosure Requirements. Extensive reports on benefits are required of all employers, including a detailed plan description, a summary plan description understandable to the laymen, and an annual report.

The Labor-Management Services Administration, a division of the Labor Department, is responsible for enforcing the law with regard to disclosure and fiduciary standards. Civil penalties may be invoked and criminal penalties may apply to disclosure violations. The Internal Revenue Service enforces the provisions regarding vesting, funding, and participation.[38]

The paper work requirements of the new pension law may prove to be quite costly. It will hit small businesses hardest says John D. Stewart, chairman of the Bureau of National Affairs, "For the one that is too small to afford a computer, and yet has a substantial number of employees, the recordkeeping and added cost of administration will be a burden." "The act requires that plans be communicated in layman language, and then proceeds to make such requirements on what the plan summary should include that they've got to be very difficult to understand," says Peter Biggins, corporate benefits manager of Xerox Corporation.[39] Xerox solved the problem through a dual communications system. One publication explains the program in layman's language and another in technical, legal language that will satisfy the law.

Standard Oil of California has at least 102 pension plans covering 30,000 employees and 9,000 annuitants. Fifty of the plans were a result of merger and are no longer operative except to pay out old benefits. If Standard Oil has to meet all the reporting and disclosure rules for each plan, Robert Maggy, benefits manager, estimates the costs could reach $2.5 million to initiate the statistical system with ongoing costs of operation rising an additional $750,000 a year.[40]

[38]"The New Pension Law—What It Means To You," *Nation's Business*, November 1974, p. 62.

[39]Pospisil, "The New Law," pp. 27–28.

[40]"Pension Reform's Expensive," *Business Week*, March 24, 1975, p. 149.

The total effect of all the provisions of the 1974 pension reform law is to raise annual pension costs 10 to 15 percent for the average employer, according to Robert D. Paul, president of actuarial consultants Martin E. Segal Company. The result has been the termination of pension plans at three times the normal rate in the first half of 1975, representing primarily small companies, with the average cancelled plan having only 30 employees.[41]

APPENDIX: EQUAL EMPLOYMENT OPPORTUNITY IN CONSTRUCTION*

United States Court of Appeals, Ninth Circuit, May 17, 1971, No. 26048
United States of America, Plaintiff-Appellee v. Ironworkers Local 86 et al., Defendants-Appellants

Action wherein government charged unions and joint apprenticeship and training committees with having denied equal employment opportunities to blacks in violation of Civil Rights Act. The United States District Court for the Western District of Washington entered judgment in favor of government, and all but one defendant appealed. The Court of Appeals held that finding that building construction unions and joint apprenticeship and training committees associated with them had engaged in a pattern or practice of discriminatory conduct with respect to equal employment opportunities for blacks was not clearly erroneous when well documented with statistical evidence showing a distinct absence of black membership in unions and committees, failure of union hiring halls to grant black referrals, many overt acts of discrimination on part of unions and committees, and many facially neutral employment practices, which had a differential effect on blacks.

On October 31, 1969, the attorney general of the United States brought an action in the United States District Court for the Western District of Washington against five building construction unions, located in Seattle, Washington, and three joint apprenticeship and training committees associated with them. The complaint alleged that the named unions and joint apprenticeship and training committees had denied employment opportunities to blacks on account of their race and that certain policies, practices, and conduct, described therein, constituted a "pattern or practice" of resistance to full employment of blacks in violation of Title VII of the Civil Rights Act of 1964. The district court found that all the named unions and joint apprenticeship and training committees had pursued a pattern or practice of conduct that denied blacks, on account of their

[41]"Impact of Pension Plan Regulation," *U.S. News and World Report,* June 9, 1975, p. 12.

*This section contains excerpts from the law case upholding the federal government's affirmative action efforts in the construction industry, the so-called Philadelphia Plan.

race, equal employment opportunities in the construction industry; two judgments and decrees followed. All but one of the defendants have joined in the instant appeal.

Many of the basic facts were largely undisputed and were stipulated by the parties. Appellant building trades unions are labor organizations that represent a large number of workmen employed in the construction industry in and about Seattle, Washington. Through the union hiring halls, appellant unions effectively control a large percentage of the employment opportunities in the construction industry in that area. Under the bargaining agreements entered into between the contractor–employers and the unions, the unions must be given first opportunity to fill positions. Contractors may not employ nonunion workers unless the positions are not filled by the unions within a period of time stipulated under the bargaining agreement.

The joint apprenticeship and training committees who join in this appeal are entities legally separate and distinct from the specific unions with which they are associated. The committees consist of members representing both the unions and the employers, and are formed to oversee and run the apprenticeship programs whose purpose is to train apprentices to become journeymen in the respective trades. Once an applicant is accepted into the program, he becomes indentured to the joint apprenticeship and training committee for a period of years and participates in a program consisting of both on-the-job training and classroom instruction. It is through this program that participants gain admission to the union as journeymen, thereby obviating the necessity of taking the avenue of direct admission, which demands that an applicant meet certain requirements such as a specified number of years of experience, being within a given age range, having letters of recommendation, and passing a journeyman's examination.

The court found appellant unions and joint apprenticeship and training committees to have engaged in a pattern or practice of discrimination that denied blacks employment opportunities in the construction industry. It based its conclusions on specific findings of discrimination, which included (1) the employment of tests and admission criteria that had little or no relation to on-the-job skills and that had a differential impact upon blacks, operating to exclude them from entrance into the unions or referrals to available jobs; (2) the active recruitment of whites, at the same time giving little or no publicity to information concerning procedures for gaining union membership, work referral opportunities, and the operation of the apprenticeship training programs in the black community; (3) the granting of preferential treatment to friends and relatives of existing members of the unions; and (4) the differential application of admission requirements, often bypassing such requirements in cases of white applicants. In addition, several instances were shown where black workers who sought referrals were turned away without reason or after being given a spurious reason in support of the action; and in some cases, unions refused to place blacks on the referral lists, thus assuring their inability to secure work.

The relief granted by the court took the form of two judgments and decrees: the first related to the unions and the second related to the joint apprenticeship and training committees. In the first, the court enjoined the unions from engaging in future discrimination with respect to referrals for employment and the acquisition or retention of union membership. It ordered that the unions keep detailed records of their operations and actively disseminate information in the black community describing the operation of the referral systems, membership requirements, and available job opportunities. Specific relief was granted by the court to certain individuals or groups of persons ordering the unions to offer them immediate construction referrals in response to the next contractor requests for workers and to open their membership application lists to these persons. The court retained jurisdiction for such further relief as it deems necessary or appropriate to effectuate further equal employment opportunities.

The committees were enjoined from all future discrimination against applicants for apprenticeship on account of race. It further ordered the committees to disseminate information concerning the requirements and procedures for admission to the apprenticeship programs so as to apprise blacks within the geographical area of available opportunities. The respective committees were ordered to consider all applicants who met the standards set out by the court in the decree. In addition, an affirmative action program was included in the decree in the hope of eradicating the vestiges of past discrimination. Among the provisions under this program were the creation of special apprenticeship programs designed to meet the special needs of average blacks with no previous experience or special skills in the trade, or black applicants who have some previous experience or special skills in the trade but do not meet journeymen standards. The court also retained jurisdiction over the committees in order to grant such further relief as it deems necessary.

Findings of Fact

We are confronted initially with the appellants' contention that the "clearly erroneous" rule should not govern our review of the findings of fact made by the district court. They reason that the rationale underlying the rule is that an appellate court should defer to the judgment of the trial court because the trial judge has access to demeanor evidence and could readily assess the credibility of the witnesses. Hence, where, as they allege, "large reliance" is placed upon written instruments and depositions, they claim the rule does not apply as demeanor evidence played a small part in the trial judge's decision.

Appellants' characterization of the proceeding below as one in which the trial judge placed "large reliance" on documentary evidence and depositions ignores the fact that over 55 witnesses testified, many of whom were deponents prior to trial. Even if "large reliance" was placed on written evidence, the clearly erroneous rule would still apply. We examined this problem in *Lundgren* v. *Freeman,* 307 F.2d 104, and found the better rule to be that the clearly erroneous rule does apply, even where the factual issues are decided on written evidence alone. Appellants would have us review the evidence de novo and freely substitute our judgment for that of the trial judge. We decline to do so. The well-established rule is that we "may not substitute our judgment if conflicting inferences may be drawn from established facts by reasonable men, and the inferences drawn by the trial court are those which could have been drawn by reasonable men."

Appellants further contend that the district court's findings were based on evidence which it had previously excluded. Prior to trial, the attorney general examined the application forms found in the files of the joint apprenticeship and training committees. At trial, appellants objected to the introduction of charts which were made from information found in the application forms on the ground that they did not qualify for admission under the business records exception to the hearsay rule. The court, sustaining, in part, appellants' objection, held this evidence was inadmissible to prove the truth of the matters contained therein, but was admissible as evidence of the type of information sought by the committees and relied upon by them in reaching their evaluative decisions.

The contention of appellants is unsupportable, given the limited purpose for which the information contained in the applications was used, as we noted in *Phillips* v. *United States,* 356 F.2d 297, 307, where a similar argument was raised.

The purpose of that section (Business Records Act, 28 U.S.C. 1732 as amended, 28 U.S.C. 1732) is to provide, in the case of business records, an exception to the hearsay rule, and to provide an acceptable substitute for specific authentication of each business record. We are not here concerned with the hearsay rule because the letters and requests contained in exhibits 968 and 984 were not offered in proof of the statements contained therein. They were introduced only to show defendants had knowledge that such statements had been made. Nor are we concerned with authentication since the authenticity of the documents need not be established where the only purpose of the documents is to show notice. As in Phillips, supra, the information contained in the applications was not proffered to prove the statements therein, but to show what information was sought by the apprenticeship committees in the applications and relied upon by them in making their decisions. The application form information was properly admitted for this purpose.

The district judge's duty was to consider the evidence, reach all reasonable inferences therefrom, and make specific findings of fact and conclusions of law. This task was necessarily a difficult one and involved the review of extensive oral testimony, many depositions, and a great amount of accompanying documentary evidence. Its proportions are reflected in the size of the reporter's transcript, which alone numbers 20 volumes. In his carefully written and excellent opinion, covering some 50 pages, Judge Lindberg made separate findings of fact as to each party, carefully analyzing the supportive evidence found in the record. In these findings of fact Judge Lindberg has pointed out by page reference to the record, the testimony, stipulations, admitted facts, and exhibits upon which his findings were based. It would serve no purpose to repeat such references in this opinion. It is not our duty to relitigate the facts at this time. Having reviewed the findings below and the record before us, we are fully convinced that the findings are amply supported by the evidence.

Conclusions of Law

At the outset, appellants contest the use of racial statistics to prove a "pattern or practice" of discrimination as a matter of law. They categorize this mode of proof as a statistical "numbers game," incapable of proving a violation of Title VII. We believe this argument is without support as the use of statistics is well established in recent Title VII cases.

In the district court's opinion, a separate statement was made as to each appellant concerning the racial composition of its membership. As to appellate unions, it was stated: Ironworkers Local 86 had approximately 920 members in January 1970, only one of whom was black. Sheet Metal Workers Local 99 had approximately 900 members in its construction division, only one of whom was black; Plumbers and Pipe-fitters Local 32 had approximately 1,900 members in its construction classification, only one of whom was black. In addition, with respect to the appellant joint apprenticeship and training committees, the court noted: Sheet Metal Workers JATC had 100 apprentices indentured in its program and seven were black; Plumbers and Pipefitters JATC had 104 building trades apprentices and none were black.

The district court also made a specific finding applicable to all parties concerning the racial composition of the city of Seattle where the main offices, hiring halls, and training facilities of the appellants are found. Approximately 42,000 blacks reside in the city, constituting roughly seven percent of the population. This information came from an expert witness, a demographer, called to testify by the attorney general.

Since the passage of the Civil Rights Act of 1964, the courts have frequently relied upon statistical evidence to prove a violation. This judicial practice has most often taken the form of the use of such data as a basis for allocating the burden of proof. On the basis that a showing of an absence or a small black union membership in a demographic area containing a substantial number of black workers raises an inference that the racial imbalance is the result of discrimination, the burden of going forward and the burden of persuasion is shifted to the accused, for such a showing is enough to establish a prima facie case. In many cases the only available avenue of proof is the use of racial statistics to uncover clandestine and covert discrimination by the employer or union involved. One court, in *Parham* v. *Southwestern Bell Telephone Co.,*

433 F. 2d 421, 426 (8th Cir. 1970), held as a matter of law, without other supportive evidence, that the statistics introduced showing an extraordinarily small number of black employees, notwithstanding a small number who held menial jobs, established a violation of Title VII. Of course, as is the case with all statistics, their use is conditioned by the existence of proper supportive facts and the absence of variables, which would undermine the reasonableness of the inference of discrimination which is drawn. It is our belief that the often-cited aphorism, "statistics often tell much and courts listen," has particular application in Title VII cases.

Here, even if we were to accept appellant's assertion that statistics alone cannot show as a matter of law that there has been a violation, it would not command our overturning of the conclusions of law reached by the district court. We are not faced with a situation where a court has relied upon statistical data alone. On the contrary, in its findings the district court cited specific instances of discrimination on the part of the unions and apprenticeship committees. Thus the statistical evidence is complementary rather than exclusive. We see no merit in appellants' complaint regarding the use of statistics.

Appellants next argue that the conclusions reached by the court that appellants engaged separately in a "pattern or practice of resistance" are wholly unsupportable. They equate the phrase "pattern or practice" with "uniformly engaged in a course of conduct aimed at denying rights secured by the act." We feel that such an interpretation is overly restrictive and does violence to the meaning intended by Congress to be accorded the phrase. Moreover, it is our firm belief that the conclusions reached by the district court are not clearly erroneous and must be affirmed.

The phrase is not defined in Title VII, but some guidance is offered by an examination of the legislative history of this and other Civil Rights Acts employing the same words. Commenting on the meaning to be accorded the phrase in the debates on the Civil Rights Act of 1964, Senator Humphrey stated: "Such a pattern or practice would be present only where the denial of rights consists of something more than an isolated, sporadic incident, but is repeated, routine or of generalized nature."

In testimony before the House Judiciary Committee on the Civil Rights Act of 1960, Deputy Attorney General Walsh said: "Pattern or practice have their generic meanings. In other words, the court finds that the discrimination was not an isolated or accidental or peculiar event; that it was an event which happened in the regular procedures followed by the state officials concerned."

In *United States* v. *Mayton,* 335 F.2d 153, 158 (5th Cir. 1964), an action under the Civil Rights Act of 1960, in which the court found that racial discrimination in the voter registration process was pursuant to a "pattern or practice," the court addressed itself to defining the words and concluded that they "were not intended to be words of art." With respect to the phrase, Senator Keating commented that "[t]he 'pattern or practice' requirement means only that the proven discriminatory conduct of defendants was not merely an isolated instance of racial discrimination."

We are firmly convinced that it was the intent of Congress that a "pattern or practice" be found where the acts of discrimination are not "isolated, peculiar, or accidental" events. The words were not intended to be words of art. Applying this definition in the instant case, we are compelled to concur with the district court's findings that appellants engaged in a "pattern or practice" of discrimination. The findings are well documented with statistical evidence showing a distinct absence of black membership in the unions and the apprenticeship programs; the failure of the union hiring halls to grant black referrals; many overt acts of discrimination on the part of appellants; and many facially neutral employment practices, which had a differential effect upon blacks. We are not concerned with isolated or accidental acts by appellants but a "pattern or practice" or resistance by them, which has had an effect of denying black workers equal job opportunities in the Seattle area.

Therefore, we hold that the conclusions reached by the district court finding appellant unions and joint apprenticeship and training committees to have engaged in a pattern or practice of discriminatory conduct with respect to employment opportunities in the construction industry are not clearly erroneous.

Relief Granted

Appellants finally contend that the district court violated section 703(j) of the act in ordering appellant unions to offer immediate job referrals to previous discriminatees, and ordering appellant apprenticeship and training committee to select and indenture sufficient black applicants to overcome past discrimination, and to also meet judicially imposed ceiling requirements in apprenticeship program participation. This they condemn as "racial quotas" and "racial preferences." We cannot agree.

The act vests in the attorney general and the trial court power to eliminate both the vestiges of past discrimination and terminate present discriminatory practices. Under sections 706(g) and 707(a) unlawful employment practices may be enjoined by the court and such affirmative relief granted as the court may deem appropriate. The only statutory limitation on the availability of relief is the antipreferential treatment provision of section 703(j).

There can be little doubt that where a violation of Title VII is found, the court is vested with broad remedial power to remove the vestiges of past discrimination and eliminate present and assure the nonexistence of future barriers to the full enjoyment of equal job opportunities by qualified black workers. On the basis of this broad equitable power, the courts have allowed a wide range of remedial relief.

In Vogler, supra, 407 F.2d at 1053–1055, the district court ordered, in addition to an injunction against future discrimination and the immediate admission of four discriminatees, that the union develop objective criteria for membership and union size. As here, it was contended that the order established a "quota system to correct racial imbalance in violation of section 703(j)." Rejecting this argument, the court held the district court did "no more than ensure that the injunction against further racial discrimination would be fairly administered" Id. at 1054. The Vogler court succinctly stated that "where necessary to insure compliance with the act, the district court was fully empowered to eliminate the present effects of past discrimination." Similarly, in International Brotherhood of Electrical Workers, Local No. 38, supra, 428 F.2d at 149, the court felt that such an interpretation of section 703(j) "would allow a complete nullification of the purposes of the Civil Rights Act of 1964."

We therefore reject appellants' contention. The district court neither abused its discretion in ordering the affirmative relief, nor did it in any way establish a system of "racial quotas" or "preferences" in violation of section 703 (j).

The judgment of the district court is affirmed.

Chapter 8

Regulation via
Government Procurement

While many businessmen and scholars continue to debate the desirability of companies becoming more socially responsible, the debate may be largely over for an important sector of the American economy. For companies that do business with the federal government, the very act of signing the procurement contract forces them to agree to perform a wide variety of socially responsible actions. These requirements range from favoring disadvantaged groups to showing concern for the quality of life and the environment.

The magnitude of the government's procurement outlays, and particularly their importance to government-oriented firms, creates opportunities for implementing a host and variety of governmental economic and social aims through the contract mechanism.

THE NATURE OF THE GOVERNMENT MARKET

Because of the unique market basket of goods and services that government departments and agencies purchase, and the detailed laws and regulations that they must adhere to, a government market structure has developed that differs in many ways from normal commercial procurement.

A Monopsonistic Market in Large Part

In a procedural way, the government market (federal, state, and local) is a buyer's monopoly ("monopsonistic"), in that prospective contractors must do business the government's way, or they are violating the law or they do not get the government's business. In the case of many purchases related to national security (aircraft carriers, nuclear submarines, supersonic bombers, ICBMs, space exploration systems), the federal government is indeed the single customer. Because the market is so completely subject to the changing needs of this one customer, the relationship between buyer and seller differs fundamentally from the one existing in the commercial sector of the economy. Particularly in the military segment of the market, the government, by its selection of contractors, controls entry into and exit from the market, determines the growth patterns of the firms participating, and imposes its ways of doing business.

A contract is awarded as the result of negotiation with suppliers whom the buyer believes are in a position to undertake the magnitude of research, development, and production required. This single-customer market makes for an extremely keen but novel type of either-or competition. A company generally is not competing for a share of the market for a given product, but for all or none of the market. Boeing and General Dynamics both competed for the F-111 aircraft program. General Dynamics won and produced all of this type of aircraft. Similarly, McDonnell-Douglas builds all of the F-15 aircraft, as the result of a design competition it won against Rockwell International and Fairchild-Hiller.

It is not surprising that the military buyer, in the restless search for ever more sophisticated weaponry, assumes many of the risks that in more normal business activities are borne as a matter of course by the seller. Along with greater assumption of risk, the federal government also has been taking on increased operating responsibility for its suppliers' internal operations. (This is a point to which we will return.)

In the one-third of government purchases for defense and space programs, potential contractors' past records of technical achievement are often a dominant factor in awarding a contract. Whether a particular program will reach the production stage depends largely on the technical capability displayed during the research and development stage. In many cases, the military is not a buyer of products—frequently the products do not yet exist at the time of purchase—but of research and design capacity and the ability to convert research and development into fully developed weapon systems. For the other two-thirds of government procurement, mainly at the state and local level, bidding occurs generally among civilian-oriented firms that are merely offering standard commercial products.

For most civilian government agencies, price is all-important. Sealed bidding is the order of the day. No weight is given to conscientiousness of prior performance, as long as bidders are considered to be "responsible." For military and space systems, as pointed out, technical capability is given much greater weight. Since the significant competition for high technology systems frequently occurs before the final product is completely designed, estimates of total cost are tentative and of limited reliability or real usefulness. The seller's previous cost performance and demonstrated capabilities may be given much greater weight than the price estimate it offers.

Distribution and Marketing Channels

There may be little if any advertising done in the government markets. On military work the "allowable" costs, such as for advertising, are strictly regulated. Very limited marketing and distribution capabilities are needed. Often the manufacturer ships directly to the government purchaser, who may not necessarily be the actual user. Thus, it is the government rather than the private supplier that maintains the internal distribution system, be it General Services Administration warehouses or air force supply depots or a state purchasing department. The flow of material from the seller to central warehouses to the operating command and on to the final user is analogous in the commercial economy to the flow from manufacturer to wholesaler to retailer and on to the final customer. Given this distribution setup, many government contractors have developed only very limited marketing capabilities. At times, this has inhibited their ability during declines in military sales to shift their merchandising efforts to the civilian economy.

Government contractors generally do not need to devote as much attention as do civilian contractors to standard economic and industrial market forecast techniques. Concern focuses instead on sociopolitical trends and forces that influence the size and composition of public disbursements.

As shown in Table 8–1, government expenditures are only a starting point in analyzing the public sector market. Transfers, interest payments, and subsidies must be deducted. Account also must be taken of the fact that more than half of the category of "government purchases of goods and services" consists of wages, salaries, and fringe benefits paid to government employees; these items can be expected to rise steadily as a result of their statutory tie to expanding wage costs in the private economy. Less than one-third of total government expenditures are truly purchases from the private sector.

When the total of such purchases is broken down, it can be seen that the aggregate of federal procurement is less than the combined purchases of state and local governments, albeit a portion of the latter is financed by federal aid. Also of interest is the fact that durable goods and construction outlays account for almost half of total government purchases of goods. This is a basically

Table 8-1

COMPOSITION OF THE GOVERNMENT MARKET, 1973

Category	Billions of Dollars	Percent
Government expenditures*	449	100
Less: Transfers, interest payments, and subsidies	173	38
Equals: Government purchases of goods and services	276	62
Less: Compensation of government employees	148	33
Equals: Government purchases from the private sector	128	29

Breakdown by Customer			Breakdown by Type of Purchase		
Level	Billions of Dollars	Percent	Level	Billions of Dollars	Percent
Federal	54	42	Durable goods	25	19
State and local	74	58	Nondurable goods	24	19
			Construction	34	27
			Services	45	35
Total	128	100		128	100

Detail of Government Purchases

	Billions of Dollars			
	Construction	All Other	Total	Percent
Military	2	36	38	30
Other federal	3	13	16	12
Total, federal	5	49	54	42
Education	7	12	19	15
Other state and local	22	33	55	43
Total, state and local	29	45	74	58
Total	34	94	128	100

*National income accounts basis.
Source: U.S. Department of Commerce data.

different pattern from that in the consumer-oriented private sector, with its heavy emphasis on services and nondurables.

TYPES OF REGULATION

The federal government requires that firms doing business with it maintain "fair" employment practices, provide "safe" and "heathful" working conditions, pay "prevailing" wages, refrain from polluting the air and water, give preference to American products in their purchases, and promote the rehabilitation of prisoners and the severely handicapped. Table 8–2 contains a sample listing of such ancillary duties required of government contractors. From the viewpoint of this book, we are concerned about the important extent to which this required "social responsibility" reduces the discretion of private management and increases the costs of the goods and services that government agencies, as well as others, purchase from the private sector.

HISTORICAL DEVELOPMENT OF REQUIRED SOCIAL RESPONSIBILITY

One of the earliest attempts to bring about social change through the government procurement process was the enactment of the Eight-Hour Laws, a series of statutes setting standards for hours of work. In 1892, the eight-hour work day was first extended to workers employed by contractors and subcontractors engaged in federal projects.[1] President Theodore Roosevelt, by an executive order issued in 1905, prevented the use of convict labor on government contracts. This order was based on an 1887 statute prohibiting the hiring-out of convict labor.

The use of the government contract as a means for promoting social and economic objectives became widespread during the depression of the 1930s. In the face of high unemployment and depressed wages, Congress passed the Buy American Act, and most of the current labor standards legislation governing public contracts, including the Davis-Bacon Act and the Walsh-Healey Public Contracts Act.

The economic mobilization during World War II gave further impetus to this use of the government purchasing process. Executive orders requiring nondiscrimination in employment by government contractors were justified by the need to encourage maximum use of the nation's scarce manpower and other resources. A similar concern during the Korean War led to a provision encouraging the placement of government contracts and subcontracts in areas of substantial labor surplus.

Rarely have these social provisions been eliminated or scaled down, even when the original depression or wartime conditions that led to them were no longer present. Rather, the trend has been to extend their application. In 1964, for example, an amendment to the Davis-Bacon Act broadened the prevailing wage concept to include certain fringe benefits as well as actual wages.[2] The

---

[1] These statutes have been superseded by the Work Hours Act of 1962, 76 Stat. 357. See Murray L. Weidenbaum, "Social Responsibility Is Closer Than You Think," *Michigan Business Review,* July 1973, pp. 32–35.

[2] Public Law 88–349, 78 Stat. 238.

Table 8-2

SPECIAL SOCIAL AND ECONOMIC RESTRICTIONS
ON GOVERNMENT CONTRACTORS

Program	Purpose
Improve Working Conditions	
Walsh-Healey Act	Prescribes minimum wages, hours, age, and work conditions for supply contracts
Davis-Bacon Act	Prescribes minimum wages, benefits, and work conditions on construction contracts over $2,000
Service Contract Act of 1968	Extends the Walsh-Healey and Davis-Bacon Acts to service contracts
Convict Labor Act	Prohibits employment on government contracts of persons imprisoned at hard labor
Favor Disadvantaged Groups	
Equal Employment Opportunity (Executive Orders 11246 and 11375)	Prohibits discrimination in government contracting
Employment Openings for Veterans (Executive Order 11598)	Requires contractors to list suitable employment openings with state employment systems
Prison-made supplies (18 U.S. Code 4124)	Requires mandatory purchase of specific supplies from federal prison industries
Blind-made products (41 U.S. Code 46-48)	Requires mandatory purchase of products made by blind and other handicapped persons
Small Business Act	Requires "fair" portion of subcontracts to be placed with small businesses
Labor Surplus Area Concerns (32A Code of Federal Regulations 33)	Requires preference to subcontractors in areas of concentrated unemployment or underemployment
Favor American Companies	
Buy American Act	Provides preference for domestic materials over foreign materials
Preference to U.S. Vessels (10 U.S. Code 2631; 46 U.S. Code 1241)	Requires shipment of all military goods and at least half of other government goods in U.S. vessels.
Protect the Environment and Quality of Life	
Clean Air Act of 1970	Prohibits contracts to a company convicted of criminal violation of air pollution standards
Care of Laboratory Animals (ASPR 7-303.44)	Requires humane treatment by defense contractors in use of experimental or laboratory animals
Humane Slaughter Act (7 U.S. Code 1901-1906)	Limits government purchases of meat to suppliers who conform to humane slaughter standards

Table 8-2. (continued)

Promote Other Government/Objectives

Embargo on Ships Engaged in Cuban and North Vietnam Trade (ASPR 1-1410)	Prohibits defense contractors from shipping supplies on foreign flag vessels that have called on Cuban or North Vietnamese ports
Use of Government Facilities (ASPR 7-104.37)	Requires defense contractors to purchase jewel bearings from government facility
Use of Government Stockpile (ASPR 1-327)	Requires defense contractors to purchase aluminum from national stockpile

Source: Murray L. Weidenbaum, "Social Responsibility Is Closer Than You Think" *Michigan Business Review,* July 1973.

Service Contract Act of 1965 extended to service employees of contractors the wage and labor standards policies established by the Davis-Bacon Act and the Walsh-Healey Public Contracts Act. In 1969, the Contract Hours Standards Act was amended to give the Secretary of Labor authority to promulgate safety and health standards for workers on government construction contracts.

Federal contractors are being compelled to follow energy conservation measures that remain voluntary for all other companies. These restrictions include keeping heating levels in buildings and facilities down to 68 degrees and reducing indoor lighting standards.

The federal procurement process has been utilized as the cutting edge of the effort to reduce barriers to the employment of minority groups. In 1970, the hiring of apprentices and trainees was required on federal construction projects. In 1971, all government contractors and subcontractors were required to list job openings with state employment service offices.[3] This was especially intended to help Vietnam veterans reenter civilian labor markets. The Vocational Rehabilitation Act of 1973 extended the equal employment opportunity programs of government contractors to include handicapped personnel.

The advantages of using government contracts to promote basic social policies are quite clear. Important national objectives may be fostered without the need for additional, direct appropriations from the Treasury. Because restrictive procurement provisions seem to be costless, the government has been making increasing use of them.[4] Any disadvantages, being more indirect, receive less attention.

Although aimed at worthwhile social objectives, those special provisions are not without costs to the governmental procurement process. They increase overhead expenses of private contractors and federal procurement offices alike. Many of the provisions also exert an upward pressure on the direct costs incurred by the government. The basic concern of governmental buyers should be

---

[3]*Weekly Compilation of Presidential Documents,* 376 (1970), article III, section B4; Executive Order 11598, 3 CFR 161 (Supp. 1971).
[4]See *Report of the Commission on Government Procurement,* 1, 1972, pp. 110-24.

to meet public needs at lowest cost. Yet special provisions such as the Davis-Bacon Act have tended to increase the cost of public construction projects through government promulgation of wage rates higher than those that would have resulted if the market were allowed to operate without impediment.[5]

THE DAVIS-BACON ACT

Because it has been examined most intensively, some attention to the effects of the Davis-Bacon Act may be appropriate. Several studies have demonstrated that the act tends to increase the costs of the construction projects that the federal government finances or subsidizes. It directs the Department of Labor to set "minimum" rates for construction workers on these projects. Although the law stipulates that the minimums be set at the level prevailing in "the city, town, village, or other civil subdivision of the state in which the work is performed," in practice these rates are rarely the average of those paid all construction workers in the area.

In its study of the Davis-Bacon Act, the General Accounting Office interviewed several private contractors, who stated that they would not bid on federally financed construction projects because of the high wages they would have to pay, even though the added costs would be covered by the government contract. They believed that paying the higher wage rates, as required by the Department of Labor, would disrupt their operations because the workers on federally financed construction would receive higher wages than the workers on the company's other construction projects. The general contractor for the low rent public housing project in Lancaster, Pennsylvania, offered to reduce its price by $114,000 if the Davis-Bacon clause were omitted from its contract.[6]

"Minimum" wage rates set under the Davis-Bacon provision are almost always at least as high as the local union rates and, in some instances, higher. Contractors who want to bid on these projects must agree to pay at least these rates. Professor Yale Brozen of the University of Chicago reports that in many cases the Labor Department has set minimum rates above the union scale found in the area in which the work is performed. Higher union rates in some other area, 50 or 70 miles from where the work is to be done, are frequently used instead of local rates, despite the instruction in the law to the contrary. More than 50 percent of the time, the Labor Department has used union rates from a county other than that in which the work was done.[7]

[5]John P. Gould, *Davis-Bacon Act* (Washington, D.C.: American Enterprise Institute for Public Policy Research, 1971).

[6]Cited in Armand J. Thieblot, Jr., *The Davis-Bacon Act* (Philadelphia: University of Pennsylvania, The Wharton School, 1975), p. 104.

[7]Yale Brozen, "The Law That Boomeranged," *Nation's Business,* April 1974, pp. 71-72.

Davis-Bacon minimum wage rates in western Pennsylvania, for example, are based on the Pittsburgh construction union scale. The common labor rate for building construction in Pittsburgh is $6.75 an hour, plus 80 cents in fringe benefits; the prevailing wage for common labor in depressed Appalachia is $3 an hour. As a consequence, local contractors did not bid for water, sewage, and school projects. The "minimums" forced on them for these projects would have raised their wage scales so high that they would have been unable to compete for nongovernmental projects.

The temporary suspension of the Davis-Bacon Act in 1971 provided an opportunity for measuring the effect of this legislation. Several construction contracts were awarded during that period, which provide a direct comparison of the cost with and without the influence of this federal regulation. A contract to install government-supplied generators in a veterans hospital was to be awarded just before the suspension. The low bid, using the "prevailing" wage determination of Davis-Bacon, was $28,884. After the suspension, the contract was rebid. The new low bid, without Davis-Bacon, dropped to $22,769, submitted by the original low bidder. The work was completed at this price, a 21 percent saving.

A federally assisted hospital under construction in the northeast let a contract during the suspension for one phase of construction work. The result was a 23 percent saving over the cost of a similar phase that was subject to the Davis-Bacon Act.

In Florida, a contractor submitted two bids for the same work on a public housing project, the higher one under the Davis-Bacon procedure and the lower one without the restriction. The difference was $18,000, or a 6 percent saving. In the midwest, an electrical company was awarded two separate contracts for similar size phases of work on a college building being built with federal support. The phase that was not subject to Davis-Bacon cost 10 percent less than the phase that was.[8]

ADVERSE EFFECTS ON DEFENSE PRODUCTION

Many of these provisions that accompany government procurement contracts reflect the notions of an earlier age. The prohibition against convict labor was enacted because of the concern over "chain gang" workers, which was a live public issue several decades ago. Changing attitudes on rehabilitation since then have cast doubt on the validity of the negative approach. In fact, under another and more recent statute, federal prisoners may work for pay in local communities under work release programs.

---

[8]Chamber of Commerce of the United States, *Why Davis-Bacon Must Go* (undated), p. 1.

The greatest shortcoming of the use of government contracts to foster unrelated economic and social aims is the cumulative impact they have on the companies themselves. Forced to take on so many of the concerns and attitudes of government agencies, it should not be too surprising that the more government-oriented corporations have come to show many of the negative characteristics of government bureaus and arsenals. The advantages of innovation, risk-bearing, and efficiency may be lost to the public and private sectors alike. That may be a high price to pay for legislating social responsibility.

Some appreciation of the adverse consequences of government requiring companies to be "socially responsible" can be gained from examining the area of the industrial economy where government control over production is most intensive and of longest standing—the defense industry.

In its long-term dealings with those companies or divisions of companies that cater primarily to the military market, the Department of Defense gradually has taken over decision-making functions that are normally the prerogatives of business management. A new type of relationship has been created in which the military establishment, as the buyer, makes many of the management decisions about policy and detailed procedures within the companies or divisions of companies that sell primarily to the military, management decisions that in commercial business would be made by the companies themselves.[9]

The government's assumption of, and active participation in, private business decision-making takes three major forms: virtually determining the choice of products the defense firms produce; strongly influencing the source of capital funds that they use; and closely supervising much of their internal operations.

By awarding billions of dollars of contracts for research and development (R&D) each year, the Department of Defense strongly influences which new products its contractors will design and produce. The government customer thus directly finances the R&D efforts and assumes much of the risk of success or failure of new product development. In the commercial economy, in contrast, the R&D costs are not borne by the buyer, but by the seller, who only recovers the investment if it results in the sale of profitable products.

The Defense Department also uses its vast financial resources to supply much of the plant and equipment and working capital used by its major contractors for defense work. Military contractors hold over $8 billion of outstanding "progress" payments (government payments made prior to completion of the contract and while the work is still in progress).

The most pervasive way in which the military establishment assumes the management decision-making functions of its contractors is through the procurement legislation and regulations governing the awarding of these contracts. The military procurement regulations require private suppliers to accept, on a "take

---

[9] See Murray L. Weidenbaum, *Economics of Peacetime Defense*, chap. 6. (New York: Praeger Publishers, 1974).

it or leave it" basis, many standard clauses in their contracts that give the governmental contracting and surveillance officers numerous powers over the internal operations of these companies.

The authority assumed by the government as purchaser includes power to review and veto company decisions as to which activities to perform in-house and which to subcontract, which firms to use as subcontractors, which products to buy domestically rather than to import, what internal financial reporting systems to establish, what type of industrial engineering and planning system to utilize, what minimum as well as average wage rates to pay, how much overtime work to authorize, and so forth. Thus, when a business firm enters into a contract to produce weapon systems for the military, it tends to take on a quasi-public nature. This is given implicit recognition by requiring the firm to conduct itself in many ways as a government agency, to follow the same Buy American, equal employment, depressed area, prevailing wage, and similar statutes.

The following is just a sample of the authority over the private contractor that the Armed Services Procurement Regulation gives to the military contract administration office:[10]

Personnel
Review the contractor's compensation structure.
Monitor compliance with labor and industrial relations matters.
Remove material from strikebound contractor's plants.
Administer the defense industrial security program.

Production
Screen, redistribute, and dispose of contractor inventory.
Review the adequacy of the contractor's traffic operations.
Review and evaluate preservation, packaging, and packing.
Evaluate the contractor's request for facilities.
Evaluate and monitor reliability and maintainability programs.
Perform quality assurance.
Maintain surveillance of flight operations.
Assure compliance with safety requirements.

Research and Development
Provide surveillance of design, development, and production engineering efforts.
Review engineering studies, designs, and proposals.
Review test plans.

[10] Section 1–406 of the Armed Services Procurement Regulation; Seymour Melman, *Pentagon Capitalism* (New York: McGraw-Hill, 1970), pp. 38–42.

Evaluate the adequacy of engineering data.

Monitor value engineering programs.

Evaluate and perform surveillance of configuration management systems.

Evaluate the management, planning, scheduling, and allocation of engineering resources.

Purchasing

Review, approve or disapprove, and maintain surveillance of the contractor's procurement system.

Consent to the placement of subcontracts.

Assure compliance with small business and labor surplus area mandatory subcontracting.

Finance

Manage special bank accounts.

Review the contractor's insurance plans.

Monitor the contractor's financial condition.

Assure timely submission of required reports.

Determine the allowability of costs.

Negotiate overhead rates.

On occasion, the attempt to regulate in detail the operations of defense contractors can be self-defeating. For example, one section of the procurement regulations seeks to encourage prime contractors to subcontract as much of their work as possible to small business. Another section, however, attempts to prevent prime contractors from realizing large profits on the work that is subcontracted. In essence, the contractor is told that he will be given favorable treatment if he subcontracts to small business, but that his profits will be less than if he does the work himself—an odd combination of incentives.

Government policy-makers in the area of military contracting rarely consider the cumulative and long-term effects on company initiative and entrepreneurship. Viewed as a totality, these restrictions represent substantial government regulation of industry. This regulation is not accomplished through a traditional independent regulatory agency, such as the Interstate Commerce Commission, but rather through the unilateral exercise of the government's dominant market position.

Despite the talk from time to time about reducing the degree of government regulation of the defense firms, the trend and the stated policy go the other way. One senior Pentagon official described enthusiastically his visit to a large defense contractor: "I was impressed with the complete interrelationship of the service/contractor organizations. They are virtually colocated... The

Table 8-3

MAJOR MILITARY PROJECTS TERMINATED, 1957-70

Category	Number	Amount Spent $ millions
Missile projects	28	5,167
Aircraft projects	24	3,874
Space vehicle projects	2	1,897
Ordnance and other projects	27	838
Total	81	$11,776

Source: U.S. Congress, Senate, Committee on Armed Services, *Hearings on S. 939,* Part 4, 92nd Congress, 1st Session, 1971.

service is aware of and, in fact, participates in practically every major contractor decision. Both parties join in weekly management meetings."[11]

The same official recalled an earlier visit with the chief executive of a major public utility, during which the executive was asked about the governmental controls to which he was subject. The answer was a short pamphlet. In striking contrast, a comparatively minor support contractor for the military has over 450 major specifications, directives, and instructions to comply with, weighing in the aggregate several hundred pounds. The Pentagon official's conclusion may not be widely appreciated, but is amply borne out by the facts: "The reality is that there are infinitely more controls in the so-called free enterprise environment of the major weapons systems contractor than there are in the controlled environment of the public utility."[12]

It is hard to avoid concluding that the current environment for defense work attenuates the normal entrepreneurial characteristics associated with private enterprise. It is not surprising, therefore, that the design and production of weapon systems for the military establishment have been frequently characterized by cost overruns, technical shortcomings, and time delays.

A most comprehensive report on this subject was made by the General Accounting Office in May 1975. The report covered 50 major weapon systems with a total cost estimated in excess of $154 billion—hardly a small or unrepresentative sample. When the 50 projects first went into development, it was estimated that they would cost $105 billion. An increase of $49 billion occurred since then, or an average overrun of more than 46 percent.[13]

[11] Barry J. Shillito, "How to Implement Our Sound Weapons System Acquisition Policies," *Defense Management Journal,* Fall 1971, p. 26.
[12] Ibid.
[13] Comptroller General of the United States, *Status of Selected Major Weapon Systems,* Report PSAD-75-83, May 30, 1975, p. 3.

Between 1957 and 1970, the Department of Defense cancelled 81 major weapon projects on which it already had spent a total of $11.8 billion (see Table 8-3). Three of the projects had already cost the nation more than $1 billion each prior to cancellation—the air force's manned observation laboratory, the air force's B-70 bomber, and the navy's Regulus II missile. The Pentagon maintains that many of the cancelled programs contribute to the knowledge subsequently employed in weapon systems that do become operational. Yet, it is hard to avoid the conclusion that a great deal of the taxpayers money is wasted. It is not inevitable, of course, that the wave of government regulation of the private sector will lead to firms in other industries experiencing similar results. Yet, the ineffective nature of the detailed regulation of defense production provides a clear warning.

Chapter 9

Government as Financier

Over the years, many credit programs have been established by the federal government. Since most of these activities do not appear in the federal budget, they seem to be a painless way of achieving national objectives. In the main, the federal government is "merely" guaranteeing private borrowing or sponsoring ostensibly private institutions, albeit with federal aid. Existing examples include the federal land banks and the federal home loan banks. Serious proposals have been made in recent years to revive that credit instrument of the 1930s—the Reconstruction Finance Corporation.

Is this use of the federal government's credit power a variation of the proverbial "free lunch?" As will be demonstrated, upon closer inspection we find that this use of the governmental credit power does result in substantial costs to business as well as to taxpayers; it also generates obvious opportunities for the application of federal controls over private economic activity—credit serving as the sweetener for the recipient of the added regulation. Acknowledgement also needs to be made of the substantial benefits that may accrue from these programs in achieving various national priorities. The advantages of the use of government credit power arises from its effectiveness in channeling more credit—and ultimately additional real resources—to specific groups of the society. In each case, Congress has passed a law stating in effect that it believes that the national welfare requires that the designated groups receive larger shares of the available supply of credit than would result from the operation of market forces alone.

What may not be apparent is the costs and other side effects that result from the expanded use of government credit programs. In terms of their overall economic impact, they do little to increase the total pool of capital available to the economy. They result literally in a game of musical chairs. By preempting a major portion of the annual flow of savings, the government-sponsored credit agencies reduce the amount of credit that can be provided to unprotected borrowers, mainly consumers, state and local governments, and private business firms.

During periods of tight money, it is difficult for unassisted borrowers to attract the financing they require. They are forced to compete against the government-aided borrowers. Federal loan guarantees reduce the riskiness of lending money to the insured borrowers. The result of that uneven competition is still higher interest rates. More detailed analysis of the phenomenon of federal credit programs is warranted. Over the years substantial numbers of credit programs have made their way through the legislative process of the federal government. These programs emerged on an ad hoc basis, with each program directed toward providing assistance in overcoming a specific problem at hand. As a result of this gradual but very substantial accretion, federal credit program subsidies are now provided to a great many and variety of sectors of the American economy—housing, agriculture, transportation, health, education, state and local governments, small business—as well as to foreigners.[1] As shown in Table 9-1, there are three major uses of the federal government's credit power.

TYPES OF GOVERNMENT CREDIT PROGRAMS

Direct loans by federal departments and agencies. These, such as the two percent loans made by the Rural Electrification Administration, generally involve significant subsidies because of low lending rates. In many cases, the government also absorbs the administrative expenses and losses arising from loan defaults, thus further increasing the amount of the subsidy. Although not formally considered a federal credit program, the relatively generous progress payments made by the Department of Defense do represent interest-free provision of working capital to government contractors on a very large scale. Direct loans have become a less important form of federal credit aid, in part because they require the direct use of federal money.

Loans guaranteed and insured by federal departments and agencies. These account for the greatest share of the current expansion in federal credit subsidies, largely because the loans are made by private lenders and thus excluded from the federal budget. Also, there has been a substantial increase in the federal

---

[1] Detailed information on individual credit programs is presented in Special Analysis E, *Special Analyses, Budget of the United States, Fiscal Year 1976* (Washington, D.C.: U.S. Government Printing Office, 1975), pp. 82–100.

Table 9-1

MAJOR FEDERAL CREDIT PROGRAMS FISCAL YEAR 1974
(New commitments, dollars in millions)

Category and Agency	Direct Loans	Guaranteed Loans	Government-sponsored Enterprises	Total
Aid to Business				
Commerce	$ 19	$ 255	----	$ 274
Interior	19	35	----	54
Transportation	50	1,143	----	1,193
General Services Adm.	20	483	----	503
Emergency Loan Guarantee Board	----	60	----	60
Export-Import Bank	----	7,039	1,617	8,656
Small Business Adm.	249	2,703	----	2,952
Subtotal	357	11,718	1,617	13,692
Aid to Farmers				
Agriculture	3,901	2,870	----	6,771
Farm credit agencies	----	----	1,941	1,941
Subtotal	3,901	2,870	1,941	8,712
Aid to Local Governments				
District of Columbia	270	----	----	270
Washington Metropolitan Transit Authority	----	334	----	334
Environmental Financing Authority	----	----	300	300
Subtotal	270	334	300	904
Aid to Individuals				
Health, Education, and Welfare	132	1,671	----	1,803
Housing and Urban Development	15	15,269	----	15,284
Veterans Administration	412	8,643	----	9,055
Federal Home Loan Bank Board	10	----	4,995	5,005
Federal National Mortgage Association	----	----	3,354	3,354
Subtotal	569	25,583	8,349	34,501
Miscellaneous				
Funds appropriated to the President	1,125	664	----	1,789
Other agencies	70	308	----	378
Subtotal	1,195	972	----	2,167
Total	$6,292	$41,477	$12,207	$59,976

Source: Special Analyses, Budget of the United States Government for Fiscal Year 1974.

payments of part of the interest on insured loans for such programs as low income housing. Technically, all that the government does is to assume a contingent liability to pay the private lender if the private borrower defaults.

Loans by federally sponsored agencies, such as the Federal National Mortgage Association, the Federal Home Loan Banks, and the farm credit agencies. These involve relatively little direct subsidy. However, these ostensibly privately owned agencies have various tax advantages and are able to borrow funds in the market at low interest rates because of the implicit government backing of their debentures and other issues. Loans made by these sponsored agencies have increased sharply since the mid-1960s. They now comprise the dominant form of federal credit assistance to the private sector.

Impacts on Total Saving and Investment

The conclusions of the empirical literature on the impacts of federal credit programs on the total flow of saving and investment in the American economy are clear. These programs do little if anything to increase the total flow of saving or investment. They mainly change the share of investment funds going to a given industry or sector of the economy and, in the process of doing so, exert upward pressures on interest rates as investment funds are bid away from other sectors.

In commenting on existing programs of federally assisted credit to the private sector, Dr. Henry Kaufman, distinguished economist with the investment house of Salomon Brothers, has written: "Federal agency financing does not do anything directly to enlarge the supply of savings... In contrast, as agency financing bids for the limited supply of savings with other credit demanders, it helps to bid up the price of money."[2]

In referring to borrowing by the federal government and its agencies, Dr. Albert Wojnilower has made a similar observation:

> Because these governmental borrowers need have few if any worries about creditworthiness or meeting interest payments, they can preempt as much of the credit markets as they choose. As a result, the federal sector has become one of the most relentless sources of upward pressures on interest rates.[3]

In a comprehensive study of federal credit programs for the prestigious Commission on Money and Credit, Warren Law of Harvard University concluded

[2] Henry Kaufman, "Federal Debt Management: An Economist's View from the Marketplace," in Federal Reserve Bank of Boston, *Issues in Federal Debt Management,* 1973, p. 171.

[3] Albert M. Wojnilower, "Can Capital-Market Controls be Avoided in the 1970's?" in *Containing Inflation in the Environment of the 1970's,* ed. Michael E. Levy (New York: Conference Board, 1971), p. 42.

that they have created inflationary pressures in every year since World War II.[4] Professor Patricia Bowers has noted what she terms "costs" of federal credit programs. One cost arises from the fact that given the availability of funds, an increase in credit for housing means lesser amounts for other borrowers. The other two borrowing groups most adversely affected by tight credit are state and local governments and small businesses. A further cost is that the operations of the federal credit agencies tend to increase the level of interest rates above the level that would have prevailed if they had not entered the credit markets.[5]

This phenomenon occurs for a variety of reasons. The total supply of funds is broadly determined by household and business saving and the ability of banks to increase the money supply. This is the basic limit on the availability of funds referred to by Bowers. The normal response of financial markets to an increase in the demand for funds by a borrower, such as is represented by a federal credit program, is an increase in interest rates so as to balance out the demand for funds with the supply of saving. But the federal government's demand for funds is "interest-inelastic" (the Treasury will generally raise the money that it requires regardless of the interest rate), and the interest-elasticity of saving is relatively modest. Thus, weak and marginal borrowers will be "rationed" out of financial markets in the process, while the Treasury and other borrowers pay higher rates of interest.

Important insight into the effects of federal credit programs on capital markets has been provided by Bruce MacLaury, president of the Federal Reserve Bank of Minneapolis and a former deputy undersecretary of the Treasury:

> The more or less unfettered expansion of federal credit programs and the accompanying deluge of agency direct and guaranteed securities to be financed in the credit markets has undoubtedly permitted Congress and the administration to claim that wonder of wonders—something for nothing, or almost nothing. But as with all such sleight-of-hand feats, the truth is somewhat different.[6]

MacLaury goes on to point out that there are extra costs associated with introducing new government credit agencies to the capital markets, selling issues that are smaller than some minimum efficiently tradeable size, and selling securities that only in varying degree approximate the characteristics of direct government debt in terms of perfection of guarantee, flexibility of timing and

---

[4]Warren A. Law, "The Aggregate Impact of Federal Credit Programs on the Economy," in Commission on Money and Credit, *Federal Credit Programs* (Englewood Cliffs, N.J.: Prentice-Hall, 1963), p. 310.

[5]Patricia F. Bowers, *Private Choice and Public Welfare* (Hinsdale: Dryden Press, 1974), pp. 494–6. See also Alan Greenspan, "A General View of Inflation in the United States," in Conference Board, *Inflation in the United States* (New York: The Board, 1974), p. 4.

[6]Bruce K. MacLaury, "Federal Credit Programs—the Issues They Raise," in Federal Reserve Bank of Boston, *Issues in Federal Debt Management,* 1973, p. 214.

maturities, "cleanness" of instrument, and so on. He points out that, as a result of such considerations, the market normally charges a premium over the interest cost on direct government debt of comparable maturity. That premium ranges from one-quarter of one percent on the well-known federally sponsored agencies, such as Federal National Mortgage Association, to more than one-half percent on such exotics as New Community Bonds. In general, if cost of financing were the only consideration, it would be most efficient to have the Treasury itself provide the financing for direct loans by issuing government debt in the market.

Reduced efficiency occurs in the economy by providing a federal "umbrella" over many credit activities without distinguishing their relative credit risks. A basic function that credit markets are supposed to perform is that of distinguishing different credit risks and assigning appropriate risk premia. This is the essence of the ultimate resource-allocation function of credit markets. As an increasing proportion of issues coming to the credit markets bears the guarantee of the federal government, the scope for the market to differentiate credit risks inevitably diminishes. Theoretically, the federal agencies issuing or guaranteeing debt would perform this role, charging as costs of the programs differing rates of insurance premia. In practice, all of the pressures are against such differential pricing of risks.[7] This is a hidden cost of federal regulation via credit programs.

Impacts on Sectors of the Economy

The very nature of federal credit assistance is to create advantages for some groups of borrowers and disadvantages for others. The literature provides clear answers on who will tend to be rationed out in the process. It is unlikely to be the large well-known corporations or the United States government. It is more likely to be state and local governments, medium-sized business, private mortgage borrowers not under the federal umbrella, and consumers, thereby contributing to additional economic and financial concentration in the United States.

The competition for funds by the rapidly expanding federal credit programs also increases the cost to the taxpayer by raising the interest rate at which the Treasury borrows its own funds. As shown in Table 9–2 there has been a massive expansion in the size and relative importance of federal government credit demands over the past decade. In 1960, the federal share of funds raised in private capital markets, using the Federal Reserve System's flow-of-funds data, was 12.7 percent. By 1970, the government's share had risen to 23 percent, and has continued to grow.

Virtually every session of Congress in recent years has enacted additional federal credit programs. Since 1960, the Federal National Mortgage Association (Fannie Mae) has been joined by the General National Mortgage Association

[7]Ibid., p. 217.

Table 9-2

IMPACT ON CREDIT MARKETS OF FEDERAL AND FEDERALLY ASSISTED BORROWING

(Fiscal years, dollars in billions)

Category of Credit	1960	1965	1970	1973
A . Federal borrowing	$ 2.2	$ 4.0	$ 5.4	$ 19.3
B. Federally assisted borrowing (off-budget)[a]	3.3	6.8	15.1	27.6
C. Total federal and federally assisted borrowing (A + B)	5.5	10.8	20.5	46.9
D. Total funds advanced in credit markets	43.4	69.6	89.0	185.1
E. = (C) ÷ (D)	12.7%	15.5%	23.0%	25.3%

[a]Obligations issued by government-sponsored agencies or guaranteed by federal agencies.
Source: Federal Reserve System; U.S. Treasury Department.

(Ginnie Mae), Student Loan Marketing Association (Sally Mae), and, more recently, the U.S. Railway Association (Fannie Rae). The upward trend has not leveled off. In view of the financial problems faced in raising sufficient funds for the extremely capital intensive energy industry, proposals are now being seriously advanced for federal credit guarantees of private electric utility bonds and for the creation of an Energy Independence Authority to provide credit to private companies.

Relation to Government Controls

An examination of existing programs of federal guarantee of private credit reveals how the credit assistance is often accompanied by various forms of governmental controls or influence over the recipients of the credit. For example, federal credit guarantees for shipbuilders are part of a broader program whereby the federal government requires the builders to incorporate various "national defense" features into the vessels.

It is instructive to examine the largest federal program for guaranteeing private credit, that administered by the Federal Housing Administration (FHA), to observe the extent to which controls accompany the credit assistance. The FHA conducts an inspection of each residence to determine whether the builder has abided by all of the agency's rules and regulations governing the construction of the homes that it insures. There are four separate "veto" points facing a builder applying for FHA insurance of mortgages for a new project: (1) affirmative marketing to minority groups, (2) environmental impact, (3) architectural review, and (4) underwriting.

Because of the division of responsibilities among the various federal housing offices, considerable confusion and delay can arise. For example, after the underwriting has been approved, which gives an appraised value high enough to cover the builder's costs, additional requirements may be imposed by the environmental impact office or by the architectural review that substantially raise the cost of the project. If this occurs, the builder must return to the first office and attempt to obtain a revised underwriting.

Miles Colean, distinguished analyst of the housing industry, has commented on the deleterious effects on the housing industry of the increasing array of government controls that has been imposed via the FHA program: "The complications of FHA operations, by introducing numerous requirements irrelevant to the extension of mortgage credit, placed the market-oriented activity of FHA at a competitive disadvantage."[8]

In October 1972, the National Center for Housing Management contracted with the Department of Housing and Urban Development to study HUD's housing programs. The Center drew on a distinguished group of experts in the area of housing. In analyzing the requirements added in recent years to the FHA processing format—"such matters as affirmative marketing, environmental protection, and project selection"—the Center's report stated:

> ... the task force feels that HUD has not proceeded in the most logical fashion in dealing with these new requirements. It has tended to add them on to the process without even analyzing the effect that they would have on that process... The end result has been that the constant imposition of new socially useful requirements for FHA processing has produced a substantial loss of competitive status for FHA's single-family programs.[9]

Thus, the implicit credit subsidy to the FHA in effect is being absorbed to a large extent by the social objectives. The current cost of attempting to implement these social policies may be quite high compared to more direct alternatives. Once an industry has become dependent on the federal financial assistance, that situation can be used to impose additional controls, which may be unrelated to protecting the government's investment or contingent liability. An example is the 1974 report of the Congressional Joint Economic Committee, which deals with energy policy. Among its various proposals, it recommended that the Congress enact authority to require minimum standards for thermal efficiency in new buildings as a prerequisite for approval under any federal subsidy or mortgage insurance program.[10]

[8]Miles L. Colean, "Quarterly Economic Report," *Mortgage Banker,* March 1974, p. 63.

[9]*Report of the Task Force on Improving the Operation of Federally Insured or Financed Housing Programs* (Washington, D.C.: National Center for Housing Management, Inc., undated), pp. 69–70.

[10]U.S. Congress, Joint Economic Committee, *A Reappraisal of the U.S. Energy Policy,* 93rd Congress, 2nd Session, 1974, pp. 2–3.

The proposal for federal guarantees of electric utility bonds is a cogent example of the tendency for federal credit assistance to be accompanied by extensive and often expensive systems of federal controls. The draft bill to legislate the plan contains a variety of new federal controls over activities of electric utilities, which historically have been subject either only to state control or to the discretion of company management.[11]

Before a utility could apply for the federal guarantee, its state public utility commission would have to submit a "Statement of Need," which the Federal Power Commission deemed consistent with "national standards." Each public utility applying for a federal guarantee would have to demonstrate to the Commission that no other reasonable means of financing was available on "reasonable" credit terms. The net interest cost on each utility bond issue guaranteed by the FPC could not exceed what the chairman of the FPC deemed to be reasonable. The FPC would be required to determine that the management of the utility is "efficient."

SUMMARY

Boiled down to its basics, federal guarantees of bonds issued by business and other institutions really involve putting "the monkey" on someone else's back. They do not increase the amount of investment funds available to the economy. Rather, to the extent they succeed, they mainly take capital funds away from other sectors of the economy and lead to similar requests for aid by those sectors. These government guarantees also tend to raise the level of interest rates in the economy, both for private as well as government borrowers. They thus increase an important element of business costs.

Since an increasing proportion of private saving is being borrowed by governments, the inelasticity of demand of the money and capital markets has been rising. That is, governments elbow private borrowers out of the capital markets simply because the federal government and its agencies are willing to pay whatever interest rates are required to cover their financial needs. Private borrowers are restricted by competitive pressures and the limits of their own resources.

The pressure on interest rates forces the Federal Reserve System to increase the reserves of the banking system to supply financing to the private sector. This, in turn, contributes to the general inflationary condition of the economy. Federal credit programs therefore tend to raise the private cost of production in two ways: (1) by causing an increase in interest rates and (2) by resulting in a higher general rate of inflation.

[11] Proposed "Electric Utility Guarantee Act of 1974."

Several ways have been suggested to deal with the various problems that arise with the expansion of federal credit programs. One general approach is to require that all proposals to create new federal credit programs or to broaden existing ones be accompanied by an appraisal of the relation between the interest rate charged in the program, the rate which would be charged by competitive and efficient private lenders, and the rate necessary to cover the government's costs.

A more detailed method is to establish controls over the total volume of federally assisted credit. Even though no immediate impact on the federal budget may be visible in most cases, the influence on the allocation of resources—on the composition of income and employment—may be very considerable. At present, many of these federal credit programs tend to have virtually a blank check on the nation's credit resources. Under this second method, they would no longer be treated as a "free good."

One way of controlling federal credit programs is to impose a ceiling on the total borrowing of federal and federally sponsored credit agencies, both those "in" and those "out" of the budget. In addition, the Congress could enact a ceiling on the overall volume of debt created under federal loan guarantees. It would be important to establish procedures to permit review of commitments far enough in advance to permit evaluating their likely impact when the commitments become actual loans.

A third method of controlling federal credit programs more effectively is to require these programs to be reviewed and coordinated along with other federal programs in the preparation of the government's annual budget and economic plans. At the present time, numerous federal credit programs— guaranteed and insured loans, and loans by federally sponsored enterprises— escape regular budget and program review.

Perhaps the most fundamental proposal does not deal with federal credit programs at all, but with the underlying conditions of which they are symptoms. Hence, if we can create an economic climate more conducive to private saving and investment, that will reduce the need for private borrowers to seek federal credit assistance. The creation of that climate may require a tax system that tilts in favor of saving rather than consumption and a fiscal policy that avoids the large Treasury deficits whose financing competes with private borrowers. Until that fundamental change is achieved, continued expansion of federal credit programs seems likely.

Chapter 10

The Paper Work Burden

As of June 30, 1974, business and private individuals had to fill out 5,146 different federal forms (excluding tax and banking forms) in dealing with the government. This growing paper work burden is a direct cost resulting from governmental regulation and subsidy. That cost includes the expensive and time-consuming process of submitting reports, making applications, filling out questionnaires, replying to orders and directives, and appealing in the courts from other rulings and regulatory opinions. Individuals and business firms spent over 130 million man-hours a year filling out all of the necessary federal report forms.[1]

Federal departments and agencies require a substantial amount of information to carry out their statutory objectives. Standardized reports are often the most efficient way of obtaining this information. Thus, it is irrelevant to attack the general notion of business and other private individuals and organizations reporting to government agencies. Rather, the useful questions relate to minimizing the time and costs incurred by business, government, and the public in meeting the government's information needs.

The impact on a single business firm can be seen vividly in the case of the Standard Oil Company of Indiana, which is required to file approximately 1,000

---

[1]*Statement of Robert H. Marik, Associate Director for Management and Operations, Office of Management and Budget before the House Committee on Government Operations,* 93rd Congress, 2nd Session, September 12, 1974, p. 5.

reports annually to 35 federal agencies, including the Federal Power Commission, the Federal Energy Administration, the Bureau of Indian Affairs, and the Small Business Administration. In the first half of 1975, Standard added 16 major new reports to be submitted on a regular basis to its list of required paper work. Duplication inevitably occurs. Standard must report its oil and gas reserves, with each report taking slightly different form, to the FEA, the FPC, the FTC, and the U.S. Geological Survey.[2] It requires 636 miles of computer tape to store the data that the company must supply to the Federal Energy Administration. In total, Indiana Standard has 100 full-time employees whose work is centered around meeting federal regulations, at an annual cost of about $3 million.[3]

The extended process of decision-making by federal agencies inevitably produces a "regulatory lag," a delay that can run into years and can be an encumbrance to private managerial decision-making. For example, the Federal Trade Commission averages nearly five years to complete a restraint-of-trade case[4] (see Figure 10–1). Thirty percent of the electric utility rate cases decided in 1973 extended for more than one year, some of them taking more than two years to be settled.[5] It took the Federal Power Commission 11 years to determine how to regulate the price of natural gas all the way back to the wellhead.[6] Prior to the 1962 amendments to the food and drug law, the Food and Drug Administration processed an average new drug application in seven months. The more stringent regulation has resulted in increasing the regulatory lag to two and one-half years.[7]

Regulatory delay and government-required paper work can be particularly costly for small businesses. A firm employing not more than 50 people is required to fill out as many as 75 to 80 different types of forms in the course of one year.[8] The lack of understanding, which at times occurs between the regulators and those they regulate, is conveyed in the interchange reported by a small manufacturer who attended a meeting to discuss the paper work burden. When he was advised to have his staff complete the forms, he replied, "When I attend this meeting the staff is right here with me. It's me."[9]

[2] Honorable Richard R. Albrecht, Remarks before the Rotary Club of Seattle, *Department of the Treasury News,* June 4, 1975.

[3] James Carberry, "Red Tape Entangles Big Petroleum Firms In Complying with Federal Regulations," *Wall Street Journal,* September 3, 1975, p. 30.

[4] David Burnham, "Regulatory Agencies Scored on Delays," *New York Times,* June 15, 1974, p. 10.

[5] Murray L. Weidenbaum, *Financing The Electric Utility Industry,* chap. 5 (New York: Edison Electric Institute, 1974).

[6] Floyd G. Lawrence, "Can Industry Develop a Five-Year Strategy?," *Industry Week,* January 6, 1975, p. 43.

[7] Sam Peltzman, *Regulation of Pharmaceutical Innovation* (Washington, D.C.: American Enterprise Institute for Public Policy Research, 1974).

[8] U.S. Congress, Senate, Select Committee on Small Business, *The Federal Paperwork Burden,* 93rd Congress, 1st Session, 1973, p. 2.

[9] Ibid., pp. 3–4.

Processing Time Analysis of the Federal Trade Commission

Number of Years, Months and Days That Elapsed in Disposition of the Median Restraint-of-Trade Case

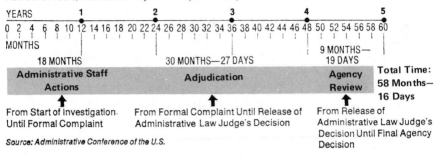

Source: *Administrative Conference of the U.S.*

Figure 10-1

Source: David Burnham, "Regulatory Agencies Scored on Delays," *New York Times,* June 15, 1974.

Two employees working half time to fill out government forms may not sound particularly burdensome to a small enterprise employing 75 people, until you consider that it might substantially reduce the plant's productivity increase for the year. In contrast, a plant employing 5,000 people can much more easily afford to employ a staff of 10 working full time to meet federal requirements. Figure 10-2 contains one of the shorter federal forms that accompany regulatory functions. It is the weekly one-page report on meat inspection that processing plants are required to submit to the Department of Agriculture.

Approximately 1,100 permits were required to build the Alaska pipeline. To obtain approval for a new drug, a 64-volume application, 10 feet tall, was submitted by one pharmaceutical company.[10] A small, 5,000-watt radio station in New Hampshire reported that it spent $26.23 to mail its application for license renewal to the Federal Communications Commission. An Oregon company, operating three small television stations, reported that its license renewal application weighed 45 pounds. These small stations apparently were required to fill out the same forms as the multimillion-dollar radio and television stations operating in major metropolitan areas.[11]

One small businessman, James Baker, president of Gar-Baker Laboratories in New York City, lamented the number of government forms his five-man firm must fill out:

[10]Lawrence, "Can Industry Develop a Five-Year Strategy?," p. 43.

[11]U.S. Congress, *The Federal Paperwork Burden,* p. 10.

- 205A -

FORM MI-404 (11-1-67)
U.S. DEPARTMENT OF AGRICULTURE
CONSUMER AND MARKETING SERVICE
MEAT INSPECTION

**PROCESSING OPERATIONS
AT OFFICIAL ESTABLISHMENTS**

WEEK CODE NO. | MONTH DAY MONTH DAY YEAR
From To
TO: OFFICER IN CHARGE | CIRCUIT
FORM APPROVED BUD. BUR. NO. 40-R2039
EST. NO.

PART 1 - MEAT AND MEAT FOOD PRODUCTS *(Express in pounds) This part is required under 9 CFR 320.3 and 21 U.S.C. 89.*

	CODE NO.	POUNDS		CODE NO.	POUNDS
CURED OR PLACED IN CURE			LOAF; HEAD CHEESE; CHILI; JELLIED PRODUCT	1410	
Beef Briskets	1012		STEAKS; CHOPS; ROASTS; BONELESS CUTS	1420	
Beef - Other	1019				
Pork	1020		SLICED PRODUCT		
Other Meats	1030		Bacon	1440	
SMOKED OR DRIED			Other (Sausage; loaves; ham; luncheon meat)	1450	
Hams - Regular	1122		HAMBURGER	1460	
Hams - Water added	1123				
Hams - Boneless	1124		GROUND BEEF	1465	
Picnics - Regular	1125		MISCELLANEOUS MEAT PRODUCT	1470	
Picnics - Water added	1126		FROZEN FOODS - Dinners; Entrees; Meat Pies; Specialties	1480	
Pork Butts	1127				
Bacon	1121		LARD - Rendered	1510	
Pork - Other	1129		LARD - Refined	1520	
Beef	1110		EDIBLE TALLOW	1540	
Other Smoked or Dried Meats	1130		PORK FAT - Rendered	1550	
COOKED MEAT			PORK FAT - Refined	1560	
Hams	1224		COMPOUND CONTAINING ANIMAL FAT	1570	
Pork - Other	1229				
Beef	1210		OLEOMARGARINE CONTAINING ANIMAL FAT	1580	
Other Cooked Meats	1230		CANNED PRODUCT - Commercial	1590	
SAUSAGE			CANNED PRODUCT - Government	1595	
Fresh finished	1310		BEEF - BONED (Manufacturing)	5350	
Dried or Semi-dried	1320		PORK CUT	5360	
Franks/Wieners	1330				
Bologna	1335		OTHER MEAT - BONED	5370	
Other Smoked and/or Cooked	1340		HORSE MEAT PRODUCT	6910	

PART 2 - BREAKDOWN OF CANNED PRODUCT TOTAL *(Express in pounds of finished product. Do not include product canned for governmental agency. The following section of this report will be used for statistical purposes. It is not required by law.)*

	LUNCHEON MEAT		CANNED HAMS			BEEF HASH		CHILI CON CARNE		VIENNAS	
	40 OZ. OR OVER	UNDER 40 OZ.	UNDER 3 LB.	3 to 6 LB.	OVER 6 LB.	40 OZ. or OVER	UNDER 40 OZ.	40 OZ. OR OVER	UNDER 40 OZ.	40 OZ. OR OVER	UNDER 40 OZ.
WEEKLY TOTAL											
CODE NO.	2611	2612	2621	2622	2623	2631	2632	2641	2642	2651	2652
	FRANKS, WIENERS IN BRINE AND SAUCE	DEVILED HAM	OTHER POTTED OR DEVILED MEAT FOOD PRODUCTS	TAMALES		SLICED DRIED BEEF	CHOPPED BEEF		MEAT STEW (All products)		
				40 OZ. OR OVER	UNDER 40 OZ.		40 OZ. OR OVER	UNDER 40 OZ.	40 OZ. OR OVER	UNDER 40 OZ.	
WEEKLY TOTAL											
CODE NO.	2660	2670	2680	2691	2692	2710	2721	2722	2731	2732	
	SPAGHETTI MEAT PRODUCTS (All types)		TONGUE (Other than Pickled)	VINEGAR PICKLED PRODUCTS		SAUSAGE	HAMBURGER; ROASTED or CORNED BEEF; MEAT AND GRAVY		SOUPS		
	40 OZ. OR OVER	UNDER 40 OZ.		40 OZ. OR OVER	UNDER 40 OZ.		40 OZ. OR OVER	UNDER 40 OZ.	40 OZ. OR OVER	UNDER 40 OZ.	
WEEKLY TOTAL											
CODE NO.	2741	2742	2750	2761	2762	2770	2781	2782	2791	2792	
	SAUSAGE IN OIL		TRIPE	BRAINS	CANNED LOINS AND PICNICS	ALL OTHER WITH MEAT AND/OR MEAT BY-PRODUCTS				HORSE MEAT (All kinds)	
						20% OR MORE		LESS THAN 20%			
	40 OZ. OR OVER	UNDER 40 OZ.				40 OZ. OR OVER	UNDER 40 OZ.	40 OZ. OR OVER	UNDER 40 OZ.		
WEEKLY TOTAL											
CODE NO.	2811	2812	2820	2830	2840	2851	2852	2861	2862	6940	

NAME OF FIRM | BY | TITLE | APPROVED BY INSPECTOR

Figure 10-2

1. 37 filings on 12 different federal forms, ranging from tax reports to data for the Census Bureau to registration with the Food and Drug Administration.
2. 26 sets of data for nine different New York State agencies, including employee and tax records, an alcohol permit, and information on disability-benefits insurance.

3. 25 forms for 12 different city departments, including a variety of tax records, a chemical permit from the fire department, two refrigerator permits, and one deep-freeze permit.[12]

A corporation with about 40,000 employees reports that it uses 125 file drawers of back-up material just to meet the federal reporting requirements in the personnel area. The equivalent of 14 full-time employees is required to staff the personnel reporting activity. The personnel manager estimates that one-third of his staff could be eliminated if there were no federal, state, or local reporting requirements.[13]

The Federal Trade Commission is attempting to obtain "line of business" (LB) data on the nation's 345 largest corporations. According to the FTC, the purpose of the report is to examine the extent and effectiveness of competition in the United States economy and to supply return on investment data as guides to investors.[14] The FTC, in arguing for the LB reports, claimed they would be useful to other federal agencies as well. But when the Office of Management and the Budget asked several agencies how they would use the information, they replied that no use was planned because they did not view the data as sufficiently reliable.[15] Despite the costs and questionable value of the information, the General Accounting Office issued the following statement as part of its evaluation of the LB program:

> The FTC and business respondents [should] get on with the task of developing reliable line-of-business information, recognizing that the initial information collected will be unreliable at best, and may be seriously misleading.[16]

The Commission's staff believes that the costs of the program will be "modest in relation to the substantial benefits" resulting from the additional information.[17] This conclusion is reached on the basis of their cost estimates from a sample of 25 major companies, which, on the average, figure the "setting-up costs" of providing the new information at $548,000 (see Table 10–1).

Assuming that the $548,000 figure is representative, this means that the total initial cost of this single report from the 345 companies will be about $190

[12]"Smothered In Paper Work—Businessmen are Fed Up," *U.S. News and World Report,* April 29, 1974, pp. 57–58.

[13]Correspondence with the author, July 17, 1974, St. Louis, Missouri.

[14]Robert K. Mautz and W. G. May, "The FTC Line of Business Reporting Program," *Financial Executive,* January 1975, pp. 15–16.

[15]Shirley Scheibla, "Illegal Search and Seizure," *Barron's,* February 17, 1975, p. 17.

[16]Ibid., p. 18.

[17]U.S. Congress, Senate, Subcommittee on Budgeting, Management, and Expenditures of the Committee on Government Operations, *Hearings on Corporate Disclosure,* 93rd Congress, 2nd Session (1974), p. 924.

Table 10-1

ESTIMATED START-UP COSTS FOR FTC LINE OF BUSINESS REPORTS

Company	Estimated Mean Start-Up Costs (thousands)
American Metal Climax	$ 75
Anaconda	1,000
Combustion Engineering	100
Crown Zellerbach	100
Deere	1,000
Dow Chemical	400
DuPont	500
Ex-cell-o	350
Exxon	1,000
General Instrument	100
Inland Steel	100
Lear Siegler	400
McGraw-Hill	45
Mobil	500
Nabisco	100
Northrop	300
Outboard Marine	100
R.J. Reynolds	1,000
Singer	500
Standard Oil, California	800
Union Carbide	1,100
U.S. Steel	2,000
Varian Associates	63
Westinghouse	2,000
Westvaco	75
Total	$13,708
Mean	548

Source: U.S. Congress, Senate, Subcommittee on Budgeting, Management, and Expenditures of the Committee on Government Operations, *Hearings on Corporate Disclosure,* 93rd Congress, 2nd Session, 1974.

million. This sum would appear to be a substantial overhead cost, which ultimately will be passed on, in good measure, to the customer.

Without disputing the merits of the suit itself, we can note the substantial paper work costs involved in a Justice Department antitrust suit against one of the nation's corporate giants. American Telephone and Telegraph Company estimates the government demands for documents in relation to its antitrust suit could cost $300 million and 20,000 man-years of effort, including a search of seven billion pages of material.[18] One Justice Department request from AT&T included every piece of paper "prepared, sent, or received since January 1, 1930, which relate or refer in whole or in part to, or which constitute instructions,

[18]"Data Would Cost $300,000,000, AT&T Says," *St. Louis Post-Dispatch,* February 20, 1975, p. 12A.

directives, or suggestions regarding the purchase by AT&T or any Bell Company of telecommunication equipment from Western Electric."[19]

In contrast, some of the reporting requirements of the newer federal regulatory agencies may result in a relatively heavier burden on small business. In its first several years of operation, the Occupational Safety and Health Administration, which was established under a law passed in 1970, required virtually all employers to keep three separate records: a log of occupational injuries and illnesses, a supplementary record of each occupational injury or illness, and a summary sheet of injuries and illnesses (OSHA Forms Number 100, 101, and 102, respectively). A supplemental quarterly survey was also required (OSHA Forms 102F and 102FF). These had to be kept up to date and accurate, even if an employer had only one employee.[20] Subsequently, Congress developed legislation that would have relieved all employers of 15 or fewer persons from the agency's recordkeeping and reporting requirements. As a result, OSHA determined that employers of seven or fewer persons could be exempted from its paper work requirements.

The OSHA reports and records are in addition to the traditional forms required by other federal agencies. To illustrate, the Graymills Corporation, which employed 120 workers in 1972, compiled a list of the 40 different government forms that it is required to fill out (see Table 10–2). Some of these forms must be filled out several times a year and others must be completed for each employee.

The ability to fill out these forms may require more educated, and hence more expensive, workers than are assigned to producing the company's products. Some of the frustration on the part of the small business executives, who are burdened with the growing array of federal forms, can be gleaned from the correspondence received by the Small Industry Committee of the Illinois Manufacturer's Association:

> The bureaucrats can't seem to comprehend that we out of the government have to work for a living and that these papers detract from our productive time. . .
>
> I have no argument with the policies of EEOC, OSHA, Corps of Engineers effluent controls, etc. But not enough thought has been put on minimizing unnecessary data and reports, in my opinion. In a small plant of 75 people, we have two men working half time on programs with attendant detailed plans and reports which were not necessary 2–3 years ago. . .
>
> Our greatest concern is the changing of forms each time they become due. Especially in small businesses where it is necessary for one person to take

[19]" 'Great Paper War' Begins in Lawsuit of U.S. and AT&T," *Wall Street Journal,* January 20, 1975, p. 14.

[20]U.S. Department of Labor, *What Every Employer Needs to Know About OSHA Record Keeping,* B.L.S. Report No. 412 (revised), 1973, p. 3.

Table 10-2

GOVERNMENT FORMS REQUIRED OF GRAYMILLS CORPORATION

Agency	Form or Subdivision	Form Number
Federal		
Department of Commerce	Census of Manufactures	MC-35M
Office of Equal Employment Opportunity	Employer Information Report EEO-1	265-41
Federal Trade Commission	Division of Financial Statistics	MG-1
Department of Labor	Log of Occupational Injuries and Illnesses	100
Department of Labor	Supplementary Record of Occupational Injuries and Illnesses	101
Department of Labor	Summary-Occupational Injuries and Illnesses	102
Department of Labor	Wage Developments in Manufacturing	BLS 2675b
Department of Labor	Employee Welfare or Pension Benefit Plan Description	D-1
Department of Labor	Employee Welfare or Pension Benefit Plan Description Amendment	D-1A
Department of Labor	Employee Welfare or Pension Benefit Plan Annual Report	D-2
Department of Labor	Information on Employee Welfare or Pension Benefit Plan Covering Fewer than 100 Participants	D-3
Department of Treasury	Federal Tax Deposits-Withheld Income and F.I.C.A. Taxes	501
Department of Treasury	Unemployment Taxes	508
Department of Treasury	Employers Annual Federal Unemployment Tax Return	940
Department of Treasury	Employee's Withholding Exemption Certificate	W-4
Department of Treasury	Reconciliation of Income Tax Withheld from Wages	W-3
Department of Treasury	Report of Wages Payable Under the Federal Insurance Contributions Act	941a
Department of Treasury	Return of Employee's Trust Exempt from Tax	990-P
Department of Treasury	U.S. Information Return for the Calendar Year 1971	1099
State of Illinois		
Industrial Commission	Application for Adjustment of Claim-Notice of Disputed Claims and Memorandum of Names and Addresses	None
Industrial Commission	Employer's Report of Compensable Injury	None
Industrial Commission	Memorandum of Names and Addresses for Service of Notices	None
Industrial Commission	Notice of Filing Claim	77
Employment Service	DOL-BES Form	None
Division of Unemployment Compensation	Notice of Possible Ineligibility	UC (I11.) Ben-22

Table 10-2 (continued)

Division of Unemployment Compensation	Employer's Contribution Report	UC-3D
Department of Revenue	Retailers' Occupation Tax, Use Tax, County, Municipal Service Occupation, and Service Use Tax Return	RR-1A
Department of Revenue	Employee's Illinois Withholding Exemption Certificate	I1-W-4
Department of Revenue	Monthly State Income Tax Payment Form	I1-501
Department of Revenue	Application for Renewal of Resale Certificate Number	RR-4904
State of Illinois	Report of Accident	C174
State of California		
Department of Business Taxes	State, Local, and District Sales and Use Tax Return	BT 401C
State of New Jersey		
Division of Taxation	Resale Certificate	SF-3
Division of Taxation	Blanket Exemption Certificate	1786 AC
City of Chicago		
Commission on Human Relations	Contractor Employment Practices Report	None
Metropolitan Sanitary District	Industrial Waste Surcharge Certified Statement	FI-235
Metropolitan Sanitary District	Report of Exemption Claim or Estimate of Liability for Surcharge	FI-236
Metropolitan Sanitary District	Computation of Initial Estimate of Liability for Surcharge	FI-236A
City of Los Angeles		
Department of Building and Safety	Application and Agreement for Testing Electrical Equipment	B&S E-147
Department of Building and Safety	Application for Approval Labels	B&S R9

Source: U.S. Senate, Subcommittee on Government Regualtion of the Select Committee on Small Business, *Hearings on the Federal Paperwork Burden,* Part I (Washington: Government Printing Office, 1972).

care of several phases of the work, we find we are having to spend many hours keeping informed of changes made on the forms, and studying all the fine print. . .[21]

Even large corporations with highly specialized staffs at times have difficulty in understanding federal regulations. Standard Oil of Indiana reports that phone calls to Washington for interpretation and clarification of new federal regulations have risen to approximately 27,000 a year, from 1,300 annually five

[21]U.S. Congress, Senate, Select Committee on Small Business, *Hearings on the Federal Paper Work Burden,* Part 1, 93rd Congress, 1st Session, 1973, pp. 122–3.

years ago. In addition, Standard employees take over 600 trips a year to Washington.[22]

The Office of Management and Budget estimates that the reporting burden imposed on American business by the federal government increased by 50 percent between December 1967 and June 1974.[23] Major new programs were the principal source of the increase—occupational safety and health activities, medicare and medicaid, environmental protection regulations, and equal employment opportunity compliance (see Table 10–3). Just keeping track of new reporting requirements can be difficult. Many firms rely on trade association publications and external consultants and lawyers to keep them advised of changes or new legislation or regulation pertaining to their business.

One of the problems seems to be that the various levels of government view proposed forms solely from the viewpoint of government, rather than from the vantage point of the private respondent. The Office of Management and Budget, which has the responsibility for minimizing the paper work burden at the federal level, was unable to tell a congressional committee exactly the number of forms or which forms a typical small business might be required to fill out each year.

The paper work imposed by government regulatory agencies on private industry is likely to expand because of more congressional action. As a result of a rider attached to the Alaska pipeline bill (Public Law 93–153), the authority to review proposed questionnaires of federal regulatory commissions has been shifted from the Office of Management and Budget to the General Accounting Office (GAO). In the process, the power to disapprove unnecessary reports has been converted merely to issuing advisory opinions to the agencies, who now have the final power to decide whether the report burdens that they impose on the private sector are necessary. Unlike OMB, GAO cannot now rule on "the necessity of the information." In the past, the value of the data requested was compared to the trouble and cost required to gather it before the questionnaires were approved.

The Securities and Exchange Commission, to which all publicly held corporations submit reports, is playing an ever increasing role in requiring new types of information from businesses. Pressure is mounting for the SEC to require some measurement of a corporation's social impact. One district court ordered the SEC to hold hearings and determine its response to a suit charging it with failure "to adopt regulations requiring broader disclosure in the environmental and equal opportunity areas."[24]

The SEC was not anxious to enter this new arena of reporting requirements, and there has been some question as to whether the Commission has the legal authority to request nonfinancial disclosures. It is generally unwilling to

[22] James Carberry, "Red Tape Entangles Big Petroleum Firms."

[23] *Statement of Marik,* pp. 8–9.

[24] "Disclosing Social Data," *Business Week,* April 14, 1975, p. 76.

Table 10-3

SOURCES OF MAJOR INCREASES IN THE REPORTING
BURDEN ON AMERICAN BUSINESS

December 1967–June 1974, in millions of man-hours

Category	Amount of Increase
Occupational safety and health	+ 4.6
Social security (mainly medicare and medicaid)	2.7
Manpower programs	1.3
Equal employment opportunity	1.1
Aircraft and airport regulations	1.0
Housing production and mortgage guarantee programs	0.9
Foreign trade documentation	0.7
Environmental protection	0.6
Employment statistics	0.6
Total	+13.5

Source: U.S. Office of Management and Budget.

yield to public interest groups who want a myriad of social data from corporations without any serious intention to invest. The SEC will require only disclosure of information sought by the "realistic investor."

Other pressures are evident for more detailed financial disclosure by business. The Interagency Steering Committee on Uniform Corporate Reporting recommended that federal agencies, including the SEC, require such information as:[25]

> A listing of the affiliations with other business or financial organizations for all company officers and directors of any company filing a report with a federal agency.
>
> A list of each contract or agreement of $1 million or more between the company and any organization with which an officer or director is affiliated.
>
> A list of each contract or agreement exceeding $600 during a calendar year between the company and an officer or director, other than salaries or director's fees.
>
> An extensive description of long-term debt, including the names of individuals or organizations holding over five percent of each debt issue.

In still another SEC proposal, businesses would have to report to the Commission any profits or earnings forecasts made to the press or to financial analysts. Reports also would have to be filed if a previous projection was no

[25]Stephen M. Aug, "Agencies Seek More Data," *Washington Star-News*, January 27, 1975.

longer valid or if a company decides to quit making projections. The reasons for these actions would have to be provided.[26] The effect of this new regulation likely may be to discourage companies from communicating with investors rather than facing the additional paper work and possible penalties. It is evident that the acceleration of the paper work burden on business is continuing with little attention to the costs involved for both business and government. As an economist would state the matter, "Information is not a free good."

Some federal regulations enacted to protect the customer, and as a result provide substantive benefits, also involve additional paper work costs. The Real Estate Settlement Procedures Act of 1974 is designed to provide greater disclosure of home mortgage closing costs and possibly help consumers save money on settlement charges. The new law requires lenders to disclose all closing costs to buyers at least 12 days before settlement. In practice, this has meant lengthening the time that it takes to complete a purchase of a home.

One bank estimates that the cost of the added paper work required by the 1974 law comes to about $50 a loan.[27] Although lenders are not permitted to charge directly for the extra documents required under the law, it is likely that they ultimately will be compensated for the additional expense, notably in the form of higher loan fees.

An effort also appears under way to shift many government questionnaires from a voluntary to a compulsory basis. At present, almost all quarterly and monthly surveys by nonregulatory agencies are voluntary. The Bureau of Labor Statistics has urged the Congress to make mandatory as many as 10 of its surveys on prices, wages, and employment.[28]

To deal with the paper work burden, in December 1974, Congress authorized a National Commission on Federal Paper Work. For a variety of reasons, no doubt including existing federal paper work requirements, the Commission did not hold its first meeting until late in July 1975. Adhering to the statutory schedule would put the new federal agency's issue of a "policy statement" and recommendations to the Congress and various federal agencies in late 1976.

---

[26]"SEC Disclosure Plan Challenged," *St. Louis Post-Dispatch,* May 23, 1975, p. 7B.

[27]"Business Bulletin," *Wall Street Journal,* July 3, 1975, p. 1.

[28]"Wringing Data Out of Business," *Business Week,* March 9, 1974, p. 49.

Chapter 11

Conflict and Duplication
in Government Regulation

With the growth in the number of government regulatory agencies and with the main concern of the newer agencies being a single function or department of all businesses, it is inevitable that authority will overlap and regulations will conflict. At present no mechanism exists to resolve these conflicts readily. The creation of state and local regulatory agencies concerned with the same worthy objectives—environment, product safety, job safety and health, and so on—has compounded the problem of consistency in regulatory practice.

AREAS OF CONFLICT

Ecology Versus Product Safety

The simple task of washing children's pajamas in New York State exemplifies how two sets of laws can pit one worthy public objective against another, in this case ecology versus safety. Because of a ban on phosphates in detergents, the mother who launders her child's sleepwear in an ecologically sound way may risk washing away its required flame-retardant properties.

In 1973, New York State banned the sale of detergents containing phosphates, in an effort to halt water pollution. Less than two months later, a federal regulation mandating that all children's sleepwear in sizes 0 to 6X be flame-retardant took effect across the country. New York housewives face a dilemma, because phosphates are the strongest protector of fire-retardancy. Phosphates hold soil and minerals in solution, preventing the formation of a mask on the fabric that inactivates flame-resistancy. Soap, and to a lesser degree many non-phosphate detergents, redeposit those harmful items during the wash cycle. Although flame-resistant phosphate substitutes are being tested, none has received general acceptance.

Ecology Versus Equal Employment Opportunity

An incident in Florida underscores the difficulties that arise when public policy is confronted with several aspects of compulsory "social responsibility." In the fall of 1973, Offshore Power Systems announced plans to construct a facility in the Jacksonville area to produce floating barges on which seawater-cooled nuclear reactors would later be installed. The company had worked out an affirmative action agreement with local community groups under which it was committed to ensure that 23 percent of the 11,000 to 14,000 jobs expected to be created by the new facility would be made available to minority group applicants. The agreement had been hailed in Jacksonville as a substantial step toward reducing the city's chronically high unemployment rate among blacks.

But the Florida Audubon Society objected to the project because it contended that the Corps of Engineers had not addressed "the concept and feasibility" of floating nuclear plants in its environmental impact statement and had failed to analyze adequately the possibility of alternate sites. Although the community groups argued that the economic advantages would outweigh any adverse environmental effects, the district court issued a temporary restraining order blocking the project.[1]

Energy Versus Transportation Regulation

The national goal of energy conservation and the fight against inflation both seem to be at odds with certain policies of the Interstate Commerce Commission. A small trucker in Long Island makes his living by hauling produce to New York City. He would like to haul something on his trip back to Long Island, but ICC regulations will not permit it. A trucking company in Omaha wanting to route a truck from Los Angeles to Little Rock, Arkansas, must have the truck stop in Lincoln, Nebraska, hundreds of miles out of the way, even if it has no pick up or delivery there. Thomas G. Moore of Stanford University's Hoover Institution has estimated that ICC regulations add between $3.8 million and $8.8 million a year to trucking costs.[2]

[1]"Audubon Society Tangles With Job-Opportunity Issue," *Public Interest Alert,* November 1, 1973, pp. 2–3.

[2]Peter T. Kilborn, "Empty Trucks and Inflation," *New York Times,* October 6, 1974, p. F3.

Job Safety Versus Equal Employment Opportunity

The controversy over rest rooms provides a cogent example of carrying a worthwhile principle too far, as well as of the conflicts among different federal agencies. The Labor Department, acting under the Occupational Safety and Health Act, has given industry instructions concerning the size, shape, dimension, and number of toilet seats. For well-known biological reasons, OSHA, as well as many state laws, requires some kind of lounge area to be adjacent to women's rest rooms.

However, the Equal Employment Opportunity Commission has entered this area of government-business relations by requiring that male toilet and lounge facilities, although separate, should be equal to those provided for women. Hence, either equivalent lounges must be built adjacent to the men's toilets or the women's lounges must be dismantled, OSHA and state laws to the contrary notwithstanding.[3]

Clean Air Versus Clean Water

Even within the jurisdiction of a single agency, objectives can be counterproductive. For example, before the issuance of the Air Pollution Control Regulations, the foundry industry as a whole had little if any waste water problems. The air cleaning mechanisms installed to comply with air pollution regulations necessitated tremendous water usage, which in turn required installation of water treatment systems at a cost equal to the original air cleaning system.[4]

Variations on the Theme

The financing of economic activity may be frustrated by new disclosure requirements for banks proposed by the Securities and Exchange Commission. The Federal Reserve System has warned that the SEC's efforts to force bank holding companies to divulge potential loan losses could make it extremely difficult for banks to raise necessary capital. Federal Reserve Chairman Arthur Burns explained, "If unreasonable or misleading disclosure requirements are imposed, banks and bank holding companies will simply tend to avoid the issuance of new securities" at a time when many holding companies must increase their capital.[5]

---

[3]J. Kenneth Kriegsmann, "Pity the Poor Personnel Man," *Dun's,* February 1973, p. 89.

[4]American Foundrymen's Society, *Foundry Industry Statement,* August 1974, p. 2.

[5]"Fed Says SEC Effort On Bank Disclosures May Hinder Financing," *Wall Street Journal,* May 8, 1975, p. 18.

Another area of conflict among government objectives occurs in the interaction between older statutes, such as antitrust, and newer ones, such as those governing safety and the environment. For example, the utility companies once sought to ensure the safety of gas burners used for heating by supplying gas only to users who had burners that passed their tests and received a safety seal. The manufacturer of one brand of burner that failed to get such a seal sued, claiming an antitrust violation. The court ruled that the complaint was sufficient to state a claim on which relief could be granted.[6] The same point was illustrated in another court decision, which held that "violations of antitrust laws could not be defended on the grounds that a particular accused combination would not injure but would actually help manufacturers, laborers, retailers, consumers, or the public in general."[7]

In the 1960s, the automobile industry assigned engineers to find the best and most efficient way to control automobile emissions in the smog-filled Los Angeles area. There was prompt antitrust objection to such an industrywide approach. As a result, the exchange of confidential technical data among company engineers was prohibited.[8] The result was costly duplication of effort, and perhaps lost time.

The goal of national security has not been without its bouts with other national objectives. When numerous United States foundries closed due to their inability to meet EPA and OSHA requirements, the Defense Department found the industry either unwilling or unable to take on military production. The key item in this case is the M–60 tank, which has been in short supply since the transfer of 1,000 tanks to Israel in 1973–74. Only Knox foundry in East Chicago makes castings for the M–60. But the domestic production shortage has been so great that the army has considered using foundries in Great Britain and West Germany.[9]

The Jones Act—requiring shipments of cargo from port to port in the United States to be made by American vessels—is another illustration of the conflict between two or more objectives. Ostensibly, the legislation was enacted to aid the high-cost American shipping industry. In practice, it tends to aid lower-cost foreign shipping industries and to reduce the availability of, or increase the cost of, goods to the American consumer.

The staff of the Senate Finance Committee estimates that the Jones Act adds 8 to 10 cents per million cubic feet to the cost of transporting liquified natural gas (LNG) between Alaska and the West Coast by American flag vessels

---

[6] *Radiant Burners, Inc. v. Peoples Gas Light and Coke Co.,* 364 U.S. 656 (1961).

[7] *Giboney v. Empire Storage and Ice Co.,* 376 U.S. 490, 496 (1949).

[8] Consent decree in *United States v. Automobile Manufacturers Association, Inc.,* 1969, quoted in Robert L. Werner, *Antitrust, social responsibility, and changing times.* Address to the Conference Board's Thirteenth Conference on Antitrust Issues, New York City, March 7, 1974, p. 11.

[9] John W. Finney, "Pentagon Asserts Tank Output Lags," *New York Times,* September 30, 1974, p. C13.

as compared to foreign flag vessels. Attempts to avoid this 8 to 10 cent "tax" result in the roundabout and more expensive process whereby Alaska exports LNG to other countries, and the rest of the mainland United States imports LNG from the South Pacific and Russia.

Another law aimed at boosting the American shipping industry has caused what may be an irreversible depression for ports on the Great Lakes. The Merchant Marine Act of 1970 requires shippers to transport in American vessels half of all goods shipped to the Soviet Union and goods used in foreign aid programs. However, no United States ship is both efficient enough for transocean trade and small enough to pass through the locks of the St. Lawrence Seaway.[10] The net result of the law is that many American shippers are unable to use the Great Lakes.

Another conflict between government objectives has been in the health and housing area. In Philadelphia, a controversy over lead-based paint has substantially reduced mortgage assistance for low income families. The problem arose as the result of a court ruling that prohibited the Department of Housing and Urban Development (HUD) from selling the stock of housing it had acquired before cleansing it of lead-based paint, which can cause lead poisoning in children if they swallow enough of it.

The federal government maintained that the cost of eliminating the lead-based paint was prohibitive. Hence, the government-owned houses sat vacant, and many were vandalized beyond repair. To compound the problem HUD instructed the regional office of the Federal Housing Administration not to guarantee any mortgages on homes unless they were certified to be free of lead-based paint. That further paralyzed the low income housing market in Philadelphia by removing virtually all of the rest of the moderately priced, inner-city dwellings from the reach of FHA's assistance programs.

The regional director of HUD was quoted as saying:

> It is a hell of a mess. Frankly, I'm not sure what's going to happen, and I don't think anyone else is either. . . I said, it is a horrible, heart-breaking, hell of a mess.[11]

Health and housing are also the theme in another predicament resulting from conflicting governmental objectives. In New York City, as a consequence of air pollution regulations, many apartment houses have switched from incinerators to garbage compactors. Complaints by tenants of rodent and vermin infestation have risen sharply. The situation has meant increased business for exterminators, who report that buildings requiring exterminating services once a

---

[10]"The Great Lakes Slump," *Time,* September 30, 1974, p. 90.

[11]James T. Wooten, "Lead Paint Ban Tying Up Mortgage Help for the Poor," *New York Times,* May 9, 1974, p. 1. *et. ff.*

month prior to installing compactors are now getting service three times a month.[12]

The Agriculture Department is giving up its program to exterminate fire ants because of restrictions on pesticides imposed by the Environmental Protection Agency. Fire ants, who aggressively attack intruders with a painful sting that can even cause death, invaded the United States from South America in 1918. Since 1957, the Department of Agriculture has waged war on fire ants through aerial sprayings of the chemical pesticide Mirex. Due to studies linking the pesticide to the death of fish and to cancer in mice and rats, the EPA has limited the number and scope of spraying to the point where the Agriculture Department deems the program unworkable.[13] Without the control program, Agriculture asserts that the ants can be expected to spread over a third of the country.[14]

The problem of noise control can place a business in a position of having to choose which regulation to obey. In the case of a meat plant, for example, surfaces must be easily cleaned to meet sanitary requirements of OSHA. The type of surface that fulfills this requirement is likely to be tile or stainless steel, which is also highly reflective of noise. Under these conditions, the required noise control is almost impossible.[15]

The educational system may be the victim of a tug-of-war between the Department of Health, Education, and Welfare and the Internal Revenue Service regarding the privacy of student records. IRS demands that its auditors be allowed to inspect student records at colleges, universities, and private schools for proof that discrimination is not occurring. IRS must be satisfied that there is no discrimination for a school to maintain its tax-exempt status. HEW contends that to allow IRS to see a student's file without his or her permission is a violation of the Buckley Amendment, and HEW subsequently would withdraw all federal funding. The result of this dilemma can be a situation such as described by John Kemeny, president of Dartmouth College:

> Last fall, auditors from HEW and from IRS were on our campus at the same time. The HEW people told us we were not going far enough [in attracting minority group students]. But the IRS people told us that we'd done so much that we might be guilty of reverse discrimination.

---

[12]Carter B. Horsley, "Rise of Vermin in Apartments Is Tied to Garbage Compaction," *New York Times,* March 27, 1975, p. 35.

[13]Jane E. Brody, "Agriculture Department to Abandon Campaign Against the Fire Ant," *New York Times,* April 20, 1975, p. 46.

[14]"Butz Says EPA Forces End to Fire Ant Program," *New York Times,* April 6, 1975, p. 63.

[15]Mitchell R. Zavon, "The Contradictory Impacts of Health and Environmental Regulation on Industry," *Mutation Research,* 1974, p. 350.

We tried very hard to get them to sit down and talk to each other [about the conflict] , but they weren't interested.[16]

WHO WILL REGULATE THE REGULATORS?

A rapid expansion has occurred not only in the types of business regulation, but also in the different levels of regulation. An example is the request of Consolidated Edison to convert two New York City power plants back to coal. This move was advocated by the federal energy office, then denied by the New York City environmental agency, and subsequently approved by the New York State agency. However, new appointees in the latter two agencies have indicated that they will reverse their predecessors, thus maintaining the contradiction.

As part of the effort to conserve on oil and natural gas, the Federal Energy Administration has ordered 79 power plants to convert to coal use. (Some of these plants converted from coal several years ago due to pressure to reduce air pollution.) "We're putting these changes into effect without knowing the cost to consumers," said John Hill, deputy chief of the FEA.[17] Another striking example is the division of pollution control of the Hudson River between state authorities in New York and New Jersey; each has jurisdiction from its own shore to the middle of the river.[18]

Representatives of the electric utility industry frequently complain about the multiplicity of approvals that are required before a new electric generating plant can be put into operation. The average person may discount this concern until he or she actually sees the extensive and repetitive nature of these controls. The schedule of authorizations required for the construction and operation of a single generating plant, shown in Table 11–1, was prepared by the U.S. Atomic Energy Commission. In the case of its proposed facility at Fulton, the Philadelphia Electric Company had to obtain 24 different kinds of approvals from five federal agencies, five state agencies, two townships, and a regional commission. The required permits and licenses range from approval of its towers by federal and state aviation agencies to the state environmental agency authorization of a trestle across Peters Creek.

A survey by the Atomic Industrial Forum of 95 nuclear power plant projects of 37 different utilities reported that 70 out of the 95 have experienced delays ranging from 2 to 66 months. An average delay of 24.3 months was reported for plants under construction, and 25.9 months for those awaiting

[16]Loye Millers, Jr., "School Official Stuck in IRS-HEW Tug-of-War," *St. Louis Globe-Democrat,* April 26–27, 1975, p. 4A.

[17]Karen J. Elliott, "FEA Moving to Shift Utilities to Coal Use Without Clear Idea of Consumer Impact," *Wall Street Journal,* May 12, 1975, p. 7.

[18]Alfred C. Neal, *The Business-Government Relationship.* Paper presented at UCLA, January 24, 1974, p. 5.

Table 11-1

MULTIPLICITY OF GOVERNMENTAL AUTHORIZATIONS REQUIRED FOR THE CONSTRUCTION AND OPERATION OF A NUCLEAR GENERATING PLANT

Proposed Fulton Generating Station of the Philadelphia Electric Company

Agency	Nature of Authorization
Federal	
Atomic Energy Commission	Construction permit
Atomic Energy Commission	Operating license
Atomic Energy Commission	By-product material license
Atomic Energy Commission	Special nuclear materials license
Corps of Engineers	Dredging in navigable streams and tributaries permit
Corps of Engineers	Construction of structures in navigable streams and tributaries
Environmental Protection Agency	National pollution discharge elimination system permit
Federal Aviation Administration	Construction of meterological towers
Federal Aviation Administration	Construction of cooling towers
Federal Aviation Administration	Construction of transmission towers
Department of Transportation	Authorization to transport fuel in approved containers
State	
Department of Environmental Resources	Air pollution permit for auxiliary boilers and radioactive off-gas facilities
Department of Environmental Resources	Industrial waste permit for thermal, chemical, and radioactive liquid discharges
Department of Environmental Resources	Water obstruction permit for trestle across Peters Creek
Department of Environmental Resources	Steam-encroachment permits for construction extending into the Susquehanna River
Department of Environmental Resources	Sewage permit
Department of Environmental Resources	Certification of water quality for plant water
Department of Labor and Industry	Use and occupancy permit for buildings
Department of Transportation	Notice of construction (same as Federal Aviation Administration)
State Police-Fire Marshal	Flammable liquids permit to store and use potentially hazardous materials
Public Utility Commission	Certificate of necessity to exempt plant buildings from local zoning ordinances
Local	
Drumore Township	Building permit
Fulton Township	Building permit
Susquehanna River Basin Commission	Surface water withdrawal

Source:　U.S. Atomic Energy Commission, *Draft Environmental Statement Related to the Proposed Fulton Generating Station Units 1 and 2, Philadelphia Electric Company,* May 1974.

permits. By far, the most frequently cited reason for the lagging schedule was governmental licensing and regulatory requirements.[19] The Federal Energy Administration (FEA) has urged the Congress to reduce the prolonged hearings and repetitious licensing procedures, which interfere with the objective of increasing the nation's energy supplies.

The FEA also urged alteration of the dual hearings procedure, which has prevailed under the concept of treating each nuclear reactor on a "one of a kind basis." Presently, section 189a of the Atomic Energy Act requires a public hearing before issuance of both the construction permit and the operating license. The FEA recommended eliminating the mandatory hearing at the construction permit stage "where no valid contested issues are raised and no real purpose is served by a public hearing." If a hearing is held at the construction permit stage, FEA urged that it be comprehensive and thus render further hearings unnecessary, unless there are changes that could significantly affect public health and safety.[20]

One major utility estimates that delaying a power station may involve continuing costs of up to $1 million a week.[21] The multiplicity of regulatory reviews for new utility facilities, and the resultant delays, are, of course, one factor among several in the spate of utility rate increases.

An interesting case of government regulators hamstringing private industry by failing to follow federal requirements involves the Kennecott Copper Corporation and the Environmental Protection Agency (EPA). The source of the complaint is the lack of an EPA-approved plan for the state of Nevada to meet federal clean air standards, which is preventing the company from going ahead with an emissions control plan.

A tentative plan was submitted in January 1972, but more than two years later the federal agency had neither approved it nor offered an alternative, as required by the Clean Air Act. The law provides for EPA to act within six months. Kennecott is going ahead with a $24 million project to clean up emissions from its Nevada smelter, hoping that ultimately it will receive the agency's approval. "It's ironic that the longer the delay in approval, the dirtier the air gets," a Kennecott spokesman said.[22] Kennecott has notified EPA that it plans to sue the agency for failure to obey the Clean Air Act of 1970. Such notification is required before the suit can be instituted.

---

[19]"Government is Main Atom Plant Roadblock," *Industry Week,* May 27, 1974, p. 24.

[20]*Statement by Robert H. Shatz, Assistant Administrator of the Federal Energy Office, before the Joint Committee on Atomic Energy at the Hearings on Nuclear Power Plant Siting and Licensing,* March 21, 1974, p. 5.

[21]Gordon R. Corey, *Central Station Nuclear Electric Power in Meeting the Energy Crisis.* Lecture at the City College of New York, May 14, 1973, p. 3.

[22]"EPA Faces Charges That It Disobeyed The Clean Air Act," *Wall Street Journal,* May 9, 1974, p. 19.

STATE AND LOCAL GOVERNMENT REGULATION

The maze of government regulations is intensified when one considers the laws administered by state and local governments. In addition to regulating many of the same areas as the federal government, such as pollution control and job safety, state and local governments introduce numerous other types of regulations. Some can be anticompetitive in their impact.

The requirement for licensing of certain professions is a popular means of limiting the number of those engaged in a particular trade. Every state has at least 10 licensing boards, and some have as many as 40. Occupations requiring licenses range from television repairmen to midwives. New Hampshire licenses lightning rod salespeople and Hawaii licenses its tattoo artists. A majority of states have laws forbidding the advertising of the prices of prescription drugs, eyeglasses, or hearing aids. As a result, in Texas, where price advertising is allowed, single-vision eyeglasses sell for $20; in California, where a price blackout exists, the same glasses can cost $60.

Thirty-six states have fair trade laws, which require retailers to charge the price set by the manufacturer. These laws prevent price competition and ensure dealers an attractive markup on the merchandise.[23]

An example of a sector experiencing duplication of regulation by federal, state, and local agencies is the milk industry. Sixty-one federal milk orders and 18 state laws fix the prices that processors must pay dairy farmers. Some states go a step further and fix resale prices in addition to producer prices. These regulatory programs set prices that producers must pay for approximately 90 percent of the fluid milk and milk products consumed in the United States.[24]

Milk plants also experience an extraordinary variety of inspections. More than 20,000 state, county, local, and municipal milk jurisdictions exist in the United States. A USDA study reveals that milk plants are inspected about 24 times annually, even though the Public Health Service recommends only two inspections a year. In one state, each milk plant averaged 95 inspections during a year. One milk plant, licensed by 250 local governments, 3 states, and 20 other agencies, reported that it was inspected 47 times in one month in 1964.[25]

[23]Jack Anderson, "How State Laws Rip You Off," *Parade,* April 6, 1975, pp. 7–8; Lee Benham and Alexandra Benham, "Regulating Through The Professions: A Perspective On Information Control," *Journal of Law and Economics,* October 1975.

[24]*Milk Facts 1974*, Milk Industry Foundation, Washington, D.C., 1974, p. 7.

[25]*A Study of State and Local Food and Drug Programs,* U.S. Department of Health, Education, and Welfare, Food and Drug Administration, May 1965.

CONCLUSION

If there is any lesson that economics has to offer, it is the need to make difficult choices. As a nation, we cannot carry an endless array of governmental responsibilities whether they are financed via the public purse or through higher prices. The government cannot be expected to assume all sorts of new burdens without removing some of the present load. A Vietnam television clip comes to mind—the one that shows so many soldiers attempting to climb aboard a helicopter that the vehicle never gets airborne at all.

II

THE ADAPTATION
BY BUSINESS

Chapter 12

Impacts on Top Management

OVERVIEW OF BUSINESS REACTIONS

Three basic patterns of reaction to government controls over business are likely to be followed by companies. In practice, a company will utilize a blend of these three approaches to federal regulation, varying its responses with external conditions, the capabilities of its management, and the nature of the firm.

Passive. Some corporate managements simply react to each new or expanded federal control. They may criticize the developent or they may attempt to postpone its effects through litigation and administrative appeals. But, sooner or later, they gear their firm's operations to meet the new government requirements.

Anticipatory. Other corporate managements rely on their planning capability to estimate in advance likely changes in federal controls over business. Thus, for example, prior to congressional passage of restrictions on the use of private land, they will reorient their construction projects to minimize the likelihood of subsequently running afoul of new federal regulations. They also voluntarily may take socially responsible actions to make the initiation of more government controls less likely. Some food retailing chains have put nutritional information on private brand products and have instituted unit pricing systems, even when not required by law to do so. One major financial institution has appointed an executive vice-president to take charge of the company's action programs in such areas of social policy as consumer problems, minority affairs, and environmental protection.

As corporate managers become more sensitive to evolving social demands, they will consider response to at least some of the public's expectations as being a normal aspect of conducting business. To the extent that this development occurs voluntarily, businesses themselves will be providing an important constraint on the degree of political pressure that social action interests can effectively exert against them.

Active. Still other business executives attempt to head off or shape the character of federal intervention by playing a more active role in the development and enactment of such legislation. Thus, some companies are strengthening the divisions of their Washington offices that deal with pending legislation, or are setting up such operations if they do not exist. Trade associations that are active on Capitol Hill are being supported more strongly. Despite the growing restrictions on political contributions and practices, many businessmen and businesswomen—as individuals—attempt to exercise leverage on government decision-making by participating more actively in the political process.

Business is seeking means of participation in the political process in addition to the conventional route of campaign contributions. Some business executives take leaves of absence to run for office or to work actively in election campaigns. Many more will join and take greater interest in the political party of their choice at the precinct and county levels, from which come most of the political figures that ultimately reach national prominence.

Business firms are making more extensive use of in-house publications, communications to shareholders, and other media to raise the public awareness of political issues that affect the future of the business community. Businessmen and businesswomen increasingly serve on government committees and participate more actively in public hearings.

An improved knowledge of the public policy process enables business and its representatives to affect, in entirely legal and legitimate fashion, the formulation of new and revised federal controls. Often the most effective form of influence is making available to government decision-makers prompt, knowledgeable, and detailed analyses of the various impacts of proposed legislation, in contrast to the traditional methods of "political" pressure.

IMPACTS ON TOP MANAGEMENT

Internal Monitoring

The growing array and increasingly serious effects of federal controls are changing the role of top management, in some ways expanding and in other ways restricting it. The result will be important changes in the entire corporate structure.

Operating management is increasingly more directed toward the internal corporate functions, because so much more attention needs to be devoted to such matters as hiring and promoting practices, personnel safety, product evaluation, and developing and reporting new types of information. With these pressures on his or her time, the chief operating officer (usually the president or the most senior executive vice-president) has less time for such matters as public and industry meetings and the external reactions to the company's activities. Such functions increasingly are becoming the primary responsibility of the corporation's chief executive officer (either the board chairman or the president) and his or her immediate associates. Thus top management will need to monitor these externally oriented functions much more closely.[1]

As an example of this trend, the chairman of the Consumer Product Safety Commission hopes to get company boards and top managements personally involved in safety standards, which have hitherto generally been the responsibility of engineering and other line or operating departments. Government relations, in all of its many manifestations, increasingly will become a major concern of a company's board of directors.

Liabilities and Restrictions

Senior corporate officials are devoting more attention to government controls because the newer regulatory agencies increasingly are placing responsibility with top management in an effort to obtain more rapid corporate responses. The CPSC requires that the chief executive officer of the company sign and certify the information sent to the Commission. If the authority is delegated to a subordinate, the chief executive must so notify the Commission in writing. The chairman of the Commission has stated that, in the case of a criminal proceeding, he is inclined to cite the board chairman or the corporate president, in addition to operating officials.[2]

The chief executive, in the words of the Occupational Safety and Health Administration, "must be willing to accept the responsibility for occupational safety and health as an integral part of his job."[3] He or she is charged with setting the company's safety policies and stimulating an awareness of safety in others. At the present time, approximately one-half of all corporate safety officers report to the director of personnel or industrial relations. About one out of five report to the president or a general manager.

The official responsible for the equal employment opportunity program in

---

[1]"The Top Man Becomes Mr. Outside," *Business Week*, May 4, 1974, pp. 38–42.

[2]"Product Liability: A Sleeping Giant," *Industry Week*, September 3, 1973, pp. 13–14.

[3]U.S. Occupational Safety and Health Administration, *Guidelines for Setting Up Job Safety and Health Programs* (Washington, D.C.: U.S. Government Printing Office, 1972), p. 1.

one utility, an officer of the company, states flatly, "No Affirmative Action program will ever work without active and strong support from a company's top management. . . the whole process is tied together. If the support for EEO didn't exist at the top, every other person involved in an EEO effort would be hard put to make any real progress."[4]

In another pronouncement with similar overtones, one federal court decision levying an unusually high antitrust fine cited as the reason for the severity of the penalty the failure of the company's top executives to exert sufficient pressure on subordinates to obey an earlier antitrust order.

The Supreme Court ruled in 1975 that chief executives are personally responsible for making certain that their firms are in compliance with pure food and drug standards. In that case, Acme Super Markets pleaded guilty to charges that its food shipments had been exposed to rodent contamination in a warehouse, and the company president, John R. Park, was convicted for the offense (his fine was $250).

Park contended that he had consulted company officials responsible for sanitation and that he was informed that corrective action was being taken; thus he did whatever he could have "constructively" done. The court disagreed, stating that persons in supervisory positions are not only required by the Food, Drug and Cosmetic Act to seek out and remedy violations, but also "to implement measures that assure that violation will not occur . . . The requirements of foresight and vigilance imposed on responsible corporate agents are beyond question demanding and perhaps onerous." But the court stated that the public had a right to expect that from executives of companies distributing products affecting health.

Thus, proof of wrong action was not needed in the Park case. According to the Supreme Court, the act dispenses with the conventional requirement for criminal conduct—the awareness of some wrongdoing by the person found guilty.[5]

To reduce the possibility of conflicts of interest on the part of officers and directors of the companies that they regulate, several government agencies have required such officials to file statements of outside business interests. For example, the comptroller of the currency requires the members of the boards of directors and the principal officers of the approximately 4,600 national banks to provide such information in the case of business enterprises in which they have an ownership of 10 percent or more or where they have the power to direct management or set policies. A debt owed by the business enterprise to an officer or director of a nationally chartered bank must be reported if it amounts to $100,000 or five percent of the enterprise's outstanding debt. Although these statements must be kept on file at each bank, so that the federal officials can

[4]"The Meaning Behind the Words," *Continental System Communicator,* June 1975, p. 10.

[5]*U.S. v. Park,* 43 LW 4687–4695.

review them, the company is not required to make them available to share-holders or the public.

The Investor Responsibility Research Center has urged companies to take specific steps to prevent unethical or illegal behavior on the part of its officials. These include the following:

1. Adopting a statement of practices to be avoided. The statement should make clear that severe disciplinary measures will be invoked against any employee who engages in such practices.
2. Putting into effect controls to monitor the behavior of employees. A useful model might be the systems that many companies use to monitor the activities of purchasing officers. Such systems often require an annual written affirmation by personnel with purchasing authority that they have paid no more than fair market value for goods and services and have not accepted any bribes or kickbacks.
3. Monitoring the conduct of senior corporate officers through a group of outside directors (who are not themselves officers of the company).
4. Making public the information that would assure those interested that the company had done nothing improper. To be most helpful the public disclosures should include a brief description of the company's policies and monitoring practices and a statement describing any improper transactions that had been detected or noting that there had not been any such transactions.

The adoption of these measures may not eliminate the possibility of illegal or unethical corporate behavior. However, the Center believes that voluntary good faith implementation of systems of this sort would prove far more effective than the whole range of existing government enforcement efforts in deterring corporate officials from engaging in those kinds of transactions.[6]

Internal and External Communication

More information is pouring into the corporation and is being transmitted up and down each division, and between divisions and positions, creating new relationships among the functions. Some positions are upgraded in the process. For example, managers of quality control are becoming vice-presidents and are included in more executive group meetings so that they can receive inputs from legal counsels and other senior officials; directors of personnel are being upgraded to vice-presidents, where such action has not already taken place.

As chief executive officers become more personally liable to the government for the actions of their subordinates, and as they find their managerial prerogatives curtailed, there will be a growing incentive to become involved in

---

[6]Elliott J. Weiss, *The Corporate Watergate,* (New York: Investor Reponsibility Research Center, 1975).

the government and political arenas, where the requirements that limit management are initially established. Mobil Oil Corporation has assumed this role in its campaign to educate the public and politicians to its view of the energy crisis. It has placed full-page advertisements in leading magazines and newspapers, but has thus far been blocked in attempting to relay its message via television. The television networks have the right to refuse controversial commercials, and they have exercised this option in Mobil's case despite the corporation's offer to buy time for critics to reply.[7] Mobil is lobbying for congressional action to amend the law, thus giving them the right to editorial commercials.

Government relations are becoming a major concern of company boards of directors and, in particular, of full-time chairmen or chairwomen. More members of top management, particularly from well-known companies, frequently are speaking out on public affairs as part of their basic function. Important new positions are developing in the planning, legal, and government relations divisions in response to the added duties imposed by government regulatory activities.

There is a growing realization that senior corporate executives increasingly are placed in situations where their images and speaking abilities are crucial to public, and therefore consumer, reaction to their companies and products. As Carl Gerstacker, board chairman of Dow Chemical Company, stated: "We are quickly approaching the point when it must be asked of candidates for executive posts in major corporations, 'How does he come across on television?'" Gerstacker went on to explain this relatively new function of top management:

> Too often, we who represent business are competing today in a situation where the opposition are pros and we are amateurs. The public, therefore, sees us in a bad light, doesn't understand and doesn't buy our point of view. Yet it is safe to assume that at some point in his career, the senior corporate executive might well have to cope with an audiovisual situation involving George Meany, Evelyn Davis, Ralph Nader, Clergy and Laymen Concerned, Philip Hart, or the Symbionese Liberation Army.[8]

A new breed of consultants has originated to cater to this concern among business executives. These consultants instruct corporation officers on such specifics as the type of clothing to wear and the tone to take in public announcements. Such outside assistance has been utilized particularly by companies suffering the greatest criticism from consumer groups, environmentalists, and political figures. As Harry Bridges, president of Shell Oil Company and an alumnus of a Dialog Telecommunications Development Course, stated the matter: "I enrolled because I am not a natural to appear on the television set or

---

[7]"Notable and Quotable," *Wall Street Journal,* December 24, 1974, p. 4.

[8]"Grooming the Executive for the Spotlight," *Business Week,* October 5, 1974, p. 57.

to be publicly interviewed. This business of communicating has become as important as finding more oil."[9]

But, as pointed out by Elisha Gray II, former chairman of the Whirlpool Corporation and now chairman of the Council of Better Business Bureaus, "We have got to establish the public's confidence in the marketplace before we can establish our credibility." Thus, more fundamental than speaking out to overcome misconceptions about their activities, businesses must correct mistakes and shortcomings. According to Kenneth Schwartz, vice-president of Opinion Research Corporation, "Performance is more important than rhetoric."

C. Jackson Grayson, Jr., who served as chairman of the Price Commission during the 1971–73 period of federal wage and price controls, concluded that many business executives, consciously or unconsciously, are adding to the probability of more government control over the economy by seeking ways to reduce competition. To illustrate this point, he quoted letters sent to him by various businessmen:

> We need government protection because we can't compete against the big companies.
>
> We must have minimum milk prices if we are to have an orderly market.
>
> If we allow liquor prices to fluctuate freely, competition will be ruinous and the Mafia might move in.[10]

IMPACTS ON CORPORATE PLANNING

Corporate planning departments are devoting more attention to analyzing factors that may result in changes in government regulatory policies and practices. On the whole, planning is becoming a more difficult function because of the conflicts among different government policies—for example, the desire to reduce the use of energy while avoiding the pollution of the environment, to produce safer products under healthier working conditions and avoid large price increases.

In addition to covering traditional economic and market trends, planning staffs need to focus in detail on federal regulations that can limit or greatly influence company managements in selecting new products, production processes, and/or marketing methods. They also now need to give more weight to government controls in forecasting future markets and product sales. Their approach needs to be multifaceted since federal regulations can either create new derivative markets or reduce the demand for existing products. For example:

[9]U.S. Consumer Product Safety Commission, National Electronic Injury Surveillance System, *NEISS News,* July 1973, pp. 1–10.

[10]C. Jackson Grayson, Jr., "Let's Get Back to the Competitive Market System," *Harvard Business Review,* November/December 1973, p. 104.

More stringent environmental controls are leading to the curtailment of the use of coal, and simultaneously are creating increased demands for devices to reduce pollution.

Job safety and health regulations impinge on production processes declared unacceptable, but they also open new opportunities for companies to supply safety equipment and alternative methods of production.

IMPACTS ON RESEARCH AND DEVELOPMENT

Increasingly, business is operating in an environment in which the application of the fruits of science and engineering to products and services is coming under public scrutiny in advance of their widespread use. Federal controls are having their impact at every major stage of the product cycle. Tightening federal standards for product safety are resulting in increased attention to original product design, because this is the phase where safety can be improved with minimum changes in existing production equipment. Thus, design staffs need to improve their understanding of a product's intended operating environment—especially because legal liability may depend in part on whether or not the manufacturer could have foreseen the product's safety hazard. In addition, the OSHA rules need to be considered when R&D develops new manufacturing processes.

To the extent that existing products and processes do not meet new, more stringent government standards, R&D departments are facing different, but not necessarily reduced, demands for their function. For example, in the automobile industry some innovative engineering efforts have shifted from such traditional areas as style to bumper designs, emission improvements, and devices to prevent drunken drivers from being able to start their cars. The intense efforts of one automobile company to meet, and perhaps anticipate or forestall, federal emissions standards is demonstrated by the substantial increase in personnel employed in its emissions control research and development function (see Table 12–1). A more than fourfold increase occurred during a five-year period.

Within the next several years, federal safety standards are scheduled to be adopted for such consumer products as television sets, swimming pools, playground equipment, firecrackers, and architectural glass. In addition to measurable product-related injury rates, more subjective criteria—such as necessity of use and reliability—will receive greater consideration in the regulatory process.

Some indication of the specific areas that may receive special federal attention can be obtained by examining the CPSC's tabulations reporting product-related injuries, which the Commission distributes widely (see sample in Table 12–2). Such data need to be interpreted with great care. The statistics indicate only that a product was "associated with" an injury. Richard O. Simpson, chairman of the Consumer Product Safety Commission, frankly acknowledges the shortcomings of the data:

Table 12-1

EMISSION CONTROL RESEARCH AND DEVELOPMENT PERSONNEL
IN ONE AUTOMOBILE COMPANY

Year	Number of Persons
1967	1,041
1968	1,196
1969	1,523
1970	1,892
1971	2,972
1972	4,745

Source: Harold W. Henry, "Pollution Control: Corporate Responses," *AMA Management Briefing*, 1974.

Note that I said injuries *associated* with consumer products and not necessarily injuries *caused* by products. Just how many injuries are caused by the products is anybody's guess. . . .[11]

Nor does the list show the ratio of product-related injuries to the total number of products in use or whether the individual voluntarily and knowingly used a product that is inherently risky. Nevertheless, such data can be useful to R&D management by indicating which products are receiving the attention of federal safety authorities. Thus, changes may be designed to either forestall or meet possible future government regulatory requirements. In the words of Commission Chairman Simpson, "Industry has a choice—either question the validity of our data or take actions that will result in the product in question moving further down the hazard index. This is the preferred approach."[12]

Particularly with the expanding activity of the recently established Office of Technology Assessment, federal requirements for technology assessment likely will increase.[13] One result will be more overhead expenses for corporate R&D departments. Another will be personnel or organizational shifts. If some form of technology impact statement should become common practice, corporate laboratories will require personnel with such nontraditional capabilities as evaluating social and economic effects of proposed new products. Alternatively, this function may be handled elsewhere in the corporation; because inputs will come from R&D and other departments, this type of assessment will be a difficult interdisciplinary task.

[11]"Producing Safe Products: An Interview With Richard O. Simpson," *ASTM Standardization News*, April 1975, pp. 8–9.

[12]Ibid., p. 10.

[13]Herbert Fore, "The State of the Art of Technology Assessment," *Astronautics and Aeronautics*, November 1974, pp. 40–47.

Table 12–2

PRODUCT INJURY TABULATION
July 1, 1972 — June 30, 1973

Products	Number of Cases	Products	Number of Cases
General Household Appliances		*Home Furnishings & Fixtures*	
Dryers—Electric	34	Bath & Shower Structures	2,020
Dryers—Gas	11	Beds & Bedding	5,496
Fans—Electric	565	Carpeting & Rugs	592
Vacuum Sweepers—Electric	274	Chairs, Couches & Slip Covers	4,890
Washers with Wringers	433	Ladders	2,614
Washers without Wringers–Other	266	Power Cords	185
Water Heaters	219	Tables	6,905
Total	1,802	Total	22,702
Kitchen Appliances		*Home Alarm, Escape &*	
Electric Stoves & Ovens	170	*Protection Devices*	180
Gas Stoves & Ovens	428	Total	180
Irons	451		
Microwave Cooking Devices	0	*Home Workshop Apparatus*	
Portable Cooking Devices	246	*& Tools*	
Portable Kitchen Appliances	534	Auto Tools, Batteries/Chargers	810
Refrigerators	506	Manual Tools & Accessories	2,681
Total	2,335	Paint Sprayers	12
		Power Jointers	1,427
Space Heating, Cooling &		Power Saws	1,435
Ventilating Appliances		Torches, Soldering & Welding	
Furnaces—Floor	86	Equipment	232
Furnaces—Other & Equipment	1,180	Total	6,597
Space Heaters	271		
Vaporizers	35	*Home & Family Maintenance*	
Total	1,572	*Products*	
		Adhesives & Related Compounds	157
Housewares		Antifreeze	55
Cutlery, Cutting & Chopping		Bleaches & Dyes	586
Devices	8,597	Cleaners—Caustic, Solvent, etc.	1,085
Drinking Glasses	2,501	Gasoline, Kerosene, Paint	
Fondue & Table Stoves	47	Removers, etc.	1,039
Pressure Cookers	156	Lubricants	103
Total	11,301	Paint, Varnish, Shellac, etc.	264
		Polishes & Waxes	202
Home Communications,		Total	3,491
Entertainment & Hobby			
Equipment		*Farm Equipment*	612
Record/Tape Players, HiFi &		Total	612
Stereo	384		
TV Sets	653	*Household Packagings &*	
Total	1,037	*Containers*	
		Containers—Metal & Self-	
		openers	3,044

Table 12-2 (continued)

Products	Number of Cases	Products	Number of Cases
Household Packagings & Containers (cont.)		*Personal Use Items*	
		Clothing	181
Glass Bottles & Jars	4,879	Footwear	422
Plastic Bags & Wrapping,		Hair Curling & Drying Devices	39
except for cooking	30	Lighters & Lighter Fluids	168
Pressure & Vacuum Containers	232	Pens & Pencils	1,793
Total	8,185	Personal Protection, Incl.	
		Tear Gas Pens/Guns	31
Sports & Recreational Equipment		Razors & Shavers	2,095
		Saunas	10
Bicycles & Bicycle Equipment	16,367	Sun & Heat Lamps	488
Cooking & Heating Equipment	272	Total	5,227
Lighting	26		
Mini-Bikes	929	*Other Products*	
Playground Equipment	5,195	Equipment for Sick or Aged	718
Snow Skiing	1,878	Matches	480
Snowmobiles	480	Seasonal Decoration & Equipment	159
Swimming Pools &		Total	1,357
Associated Equipment	1,717		
Team Sports	35,902	*Home Structures & Construction Materials, etc.*	
Unlicensed Motor Scooters &			
Go-Karts	229	Doors & Assoc. Hardware, Excluding	
Water Sport Equipment	506	Structural Glass	7,511
Total	63,501	Fences—Non Electric	2,781
		Floors, Porches & Balconies	3,503
Toys		Stairs & Railings	21,396
Chemistry Sets & Other		Windows & Glass Walls/Panels	
Science Toys	25	& Doors	7,864
Fireworks	270	Wires—Non Electric	1,067
Fuel & Fuel Powered Toys	39	Total	44,122
Skates & Skate Boards	2,346		
Sleeping Bags & Play Tents	8	*Products Covered By Existing Federal Regulations*	
Toy Balls, Inflatables & Marbles	289		
Toy Guns, Cap & Sling Weapons	254	Cosmetics	594
Total	3,231	Drugs	5,444
		Pesticides	499
Yard & Garden Equipment		Total	6,537
Sprayers & Insect Control Devices	22		
Hand Mowers & Edgers	168		
Manual Yard & Garden Tools	1,780		
Power Mowers, Edgers &			
Trimmers	2,304		
Power Yard & Garden Tools	451		
Total	4,725		
Child Nursery Equipment & Supplies			
Baby Exercisers, Swings & Walkers	258		
Cribs, Bedding, etc.	445		
Playpens	91		
Strollers/Carriages, Infant &			
Car Seats	424		
Total	1,218		

Source: Consumer Product Safety Commission.

The cost pressures resulting from more stringent federal regulation of product safety, energy use, and ecological effects will result either in limitation of product variety or in higher prices. More uniform, standardized, and conservatively and expensively designed products are likely to result. For example, power tools that are less likely to burn out from extended use are usually the more expensive items in a producer's product line. In the pharmaceutical area, a slowdown in the pace of innovation is apparently linked to the more stringent regulations in the United States governing the introduction of new drugs. According to Professor William Wardell of the University of Rochester Medical School, the United States was the 30th country to approve the antiasthma drug metaproterenol, the 32nd country to approve the anticancer drug adriamycin, the 51st country to approve the antituberculous drug rifampin, the 64th country to approve the antiallergenic drug cromolyn, and the 106th country to approve the antibacterial drug co-trimoxazole.

In some cases, the company's responses to new governmental concerns may result in an altogether positive approach. This is most visible in the energy conservation area, where the national priority of fostering domestic energy independence is bolstered by the relatively new desire of company management to minimize the rising cost of one of its traditional inputs. As described in the appendix to this chapter, successful energy conservation programs often entail the participation of all levels of management.

APPENDIX: RESPONDING TO A NEW NATIONAL PRIORITY, ENERGY CONSERVATION*

The establishment of national energy independence as a long-range goal for the United States, coupled with the impact of rising costs, has led many companies to respond with efforts to reduce their use of energy. This section describes the activities of four firms, which range from a small family-owned business to one of the nation's largest manufacturing corporations.

Behrenberg Glass Company

Company description. Behrenberg Glass Company, a family-owned business, is located in Delmont, Pennsylvania, 30 miles east of Pittsburgh. Founded by the grandfather of the present owners, John and Jim Behrenberg, the company has been in the "glass bending" business for 50 years in the Pittsburgh area.

*The material in these cases is taken from U.S. Federal Energy Administration, *Energy Management Case Studies* (Washington, D.C.: U.S. Government Printing Office, 1975), pp.1–15.

Behrenberg was one of the early suppliers of the glass logos used in globes that identified gasoline pumps prior to World War II. Since then, the company has supplied decorative glass to about 50 assemblers, who produce a substantial share of the lighting fixtures used in the country. The firm's sales run about $1 million, and it has fewer than 50 employees. The small industry has only 10 benders. Most of the firm's customers serve the housing industry.

John Behrenberg, 44, a graduate glass technologist, became president of the company when his father retired in 1972. He always has been involved in the family business, working the lunch-hour breaks on the furnaces while he was in high school and operating every machine in the plant at some point in his career. After college at Alfred University School of Ceramics, a year with Sylvania Electric, and an army stint, he came home to stay at Behrenberg. He runs the production operations, while his brother Jim, company vice-president, heads the design activities of the firm. John Behrenberg is proud of the fact that, since business regularly comes through the door without a marketing or advertising effort, he need only concern himself with delivering quality products. The company's success is shown by the retention of most of the same customers over the past 20 years.

Although always in the Pittsburgh area, the company moved to Delmont 11 years ago. The Delmont facility, expanded four years ago by adding a warehousing section to the basic plant, has changed little of the internally designed equipment over the years.

The company has always designed its own furnaces. John Behrenberg describes the business: "We're in an oddball industry where standard equipment doesn't usually work. We've always had to design for our own purposes. As product demands change, we adjust our speeds and mixture of product accordingly." The company produces no stock item. Rather, they are all made to customer specifications—as few as 100 at a time.

Behrenberg's process. Behrenberg produces decorative glass for lighting fixtures from a wide variety of flat glass. Input raw material consists of 90 percent clear window glass and 10 percent colored rolled glass, which may have a wide variety of surface patterns.

The operations at Behrenberg can be characterized as of three types—glass preparation, decoration, and firing.

Behrenberg energy supplier. During the winter of 1969–70, the local gas distributor, the People's Natural Gas Company, was informed by its parent company and supplier that natural gas might have to be curtailed. People's, through Consolidated Gas Supply Corporation, receives 80 percent of its supplies from the southwest, where natural gas reserves are declining. At that time, People's began an active gas conservation program among its customers to avoid any interruption or serious curtailment of service.

Initially, the company's efforts were directed at obvious waste—getting people to turn off equipment that was not in use. More recently, People's industrial customer representatives have been directly involved with 220 industrial customers, helping them identify ways to cut gas consumption. Operating from regional field offices, the industrial representatives provide pertinent technical information on conservation to their customers. If a customer requests guidance or assistance in analyzing his or her operations for ways to improve energy utilization, People's provides assistance, especially in cases where the allocation of natural gas has hindered the expansion of a customer's business.

The results of conservation efforts by the People's Natural Gas Company are impressive. Most customers are producing more than in 1969, but with the same quantity or less of natural gas. Behrenberg and People's Gas have worked closely many times, although Behrenberg is not the gas company's major customer. Eight years ago, People's suggested a makeup air system for the plant. Behrenberg used its engineering talents to adapt the suggested system to its site, and the result was cleaner inner-plant air. The plant used to be filled with "blue air," but as soon as the makeup air system went into operation, the air cleared completely. Although OSHA was not in effect at the time, the gas company's suggestion probably prevented violations when the law did become effective.

Behrenberg adds: "People's has been very helpful in other ways. For the past several years I haven't been able to add gas connections. It was suggested I add a propane tank for emergencies. I did, and set it up so that connections to propane can occur in only a minute if needed. A conversion to propane is expensive, so while I'm more secure, they've given me more incentive to conserve energy."

Bending furnace energy savings. The bending furnace is the key to the process at Behrenberg. By the time the glass reaches the furnace, all other processing operations have occurred. Therefore, the furnace operation must be carefully managed to assure a quality product with minimal waste. Improper annealing or heating, which results in breakage or obvious mold marks, reduces productivity and increases operating and raw materials costs.

At the furnaces, flat pieces are placed in or on top of a stainless steel mold, which rests on a continuous, flexible chain grating. In the furnaces, the glass is heated by natural gas burners to "fire in" the color and bend the glass to conform to the mold.

The bending operation in the furnace occurs in three successive temperature stages. As the grating moves into the furnace, the glass enters a radiant heating zone in which the temperature is maintained at about $900°F$ to remove organic color vehicles in the glass prior to softening. Next, the glass passes through a section in which it is heated to about $1,250°F$, where it bends under its own weight to conform to the shape of the mold. Finally, the glass passes through the annealing section at $900°F$, and subsequently cools to room temperature.

The side walls and suspended crown of the furnaces, or bending lehrs, had been constructed of refractory and red brick to withstand the continuous high temperatures. Although the walls were quite thick, substantial heat losses occurred, which Behrenberg believed to be wasteful. After discussions with the insulation supplier, Behrenberg replaced the heavy brick crown of the furnace with one of sheet metal and high temperature insulation material. Insulation was added to the walls as well. The total cost of modifying two lehrs, 45 feet long by 6 feet wide by 5 feet in height, was about $3,500.

The gas savings were immediate and substantial. Because of the change from massive refractory to light insulation, the daily time required to heat up the one furnace that cycled was reduced from 2½ hours to about 30 minutes. This alone saves over 3,000 cubic feet of natural gas per day. Over the course of a normal 16-hour day, the savings are 4,300 cubic feet per furnace. Annual reduction in total gas consumption is estimated at 1.9 million cubic feet, for a saving at present cost of about $2,000 a year and a payback of 1¾ years, if these were the only savings.

Once the changes were complete, intangible economic benefits of the energy saving were more apparent. The comfort of the personnel operating the furnaces improved with the reduction of radiant losses, lowering the ambient temperature near the furnace by 20°F. In terms of operation, temperature uniformity in the furnace improved as well, providing a slight increase in flexibility in the combinations of pieces that could be bent simultaneously. During bending runs of one formerly difficult product, the breakage rate was reduced from 70 percent to 20 percent due to improved heat distribution.

Because of the long heat-up time, one furnace ran on a 24-hour basis and the other only one or two shifts. Thus, the plant had to be open, manned, and illuminated for all shifts. Now both furnaces run on two shifts, saving one full shift of manpower and energy to light the plant.

Reduction in maintenance of the furnaces also was a benefit. Currently, when the baffles that control heat distribution must be repositioned or replaced, only a few hundred pounds must be moved instead of the former several thousand pounds. Should the furnace have to be shut down for repairs, the new construction cools faster, shortening the downtime.

Although these items cannot be quantified, Behrenberg believes that his savings will keep the company's earnings about even although business has slackened.

Chesebrough-Pond's, Inc.

Company description. Chesebrough-Pond's, Inc., is a diversified consumer marketing and manufacturing company, making such well-known products as Vaseline Petroleum Jelly, Pond's creams, Wind Song perfume, Q-Tips Cotton Swabs, Ragu spaghetti sauces, Adolph's meat tenderizer, and Healthtex children's apparel.

The company had sales for the year 1973 of $463 million, ranking 313 among Fortune's top 500 U.S. companies, and earned over $37 million, or 8.1 percent of sales that year. Sales continued to increase in 1974, and during the first 6 months, showed a 16.5 percent increase over the similar period for 1973.

Of Chesebrough-Pond's 22 producing plants in the United States, one of the largest is located in Clinton, Connecticut, a town of 10,000 people located 25 miles east of New Haven. This plant is a key local employer with 800 to 1,000 employees. The Clinton plant dates back to 1873 and was the original Pond's Company, which made witch hazel from the area's native hazel root. Following the merger with the Chesebrough Company in 1955, the Chesebrough and Prince Matchabelli lines were added to Clinton, so that today the plant produces beauty creams, lotions, powders, and fragrances under many well-known brand names. Annual sales of approximately $100 million result from the manufacturing operations at Clinton.

Role of energy in the company. The company's internal growth tends to keep the corporate manufacturing and engineering staffs busy designing and building new facilities. During 1974, operations began at new textile manufacturing facilities in Centreville, Alabama; Cumberland, Rhode Island; and Cabo Rojo, Puerto Rico; and a new Q-Tips Cotton Swabs plant in Las Piedras, Puerto Rico. In addition, construction is under way for a textile facility at Gadsden, Alabama, and a tomato paste plant at Merced, California, has just been enlarged.

Chesebrough-Pond's businesses are neither energy nor labor intensive. Energy costs make up roughly $2 million of the domestic corporate expenses.

Process layout in the Clinton plant. Clinton plant management has attempted to create a working environment in which communication between management and employees is viewed as vital. The Clinton plant manager regularly (once every few weeks) holds a meeting with the personnel manager and one employee from each department. In addition, each month the heads of all departments hold meetings with the department employees. These hour-long meetings are aimed at transferring information and providing a forum for employee complaints. The meetings have existed for some time and are an accepted means of employee communication.

The Clinton plant produces the Prince Matchabelli and Pond's lines of products. Production at the plant has doubled over the past five years, primarily due to the introduction in 1972 of Vaseline Intensive Care products, all of which are manufactured at Clinton. This increase has created cramped production facilities, and the result is a production flow not considered adequate by plant officials. New facilities are planned for Huntsville, Alabama, to produce the Prince Matchabelli line, which will relieve some of the pressure at Clinton.

The Clinton plant consists of three floors containing 240,000 square feet, of which 100,000 square feet is manufacturing space and the rest warehousing. At the plant, bulk liquid and powder feedstocks are received, compounded, and proportioned; the products are then prepared and packaged. Since the product mix is varied, the plant is laid out by function; that is, all compounding of powder is performed in one location, liquid bottling in another.

Utilities provided to the plant's manufacturing areas are low pressure steam, compressed air, and electricity. In many respects, this plant is typical of numerous light manufacturing operations in a wide range of diverse industries.

Development of a conservation policy. Over the years, energy consumption was never a major concern at Chesebrough-Pond's. Prior to 1973, the Clinton plant energy bill did not exceed $225,000 a year. But 1973 was different. Ralph Ward, Chesebrough's president since 1968, moved quickly to counteract rising fuel costs. On November 13, 1973, he wrote to all employees: "In recent months, we have all become aware of the developing energy crisis in this country, particularly as it relates to petroleum products. This crisis is real, and strong energy conservation steps are required not only by industry, but by each of us individually in our daily lives."

Ward appointed Perry Lindholm, vice-president of manufacturing and a 14-year veteran of Chesebrough-Pond's, to head the corporate energy conservation program. Lindholm directed the establishment of energy conservation committees at each company location to develop and carry out local conservation programs.

At Clinton, for example, George Lahn, plant engineer, was named to set up and implement the energy-saving program. As a first step, Lahn organized an energy conservation committee and established a weekly reporting system through the chain of command, to follow up on the steps taken to conserve energy.

Lahn believed that any energy-savings program would require complete cooperation from the employees, and that employees must be kept informed of the energy conservation efforts. By reporting to the employees the effects of their energy-saving ideas, management succeeded in engendering an energy consciousness among the employees. The plant's employee bulletins also played a role, publishing energy saving ideas and accomplishments regularly.

In the beginning, employees were told that some attempts at energy saving could have unforeseen effects and that in no way was it desirable to make working at Chesebrough-Pond's uncomfortable, hazardous, or generally less pleasant. With the preparatory work done, attention was directed toward reducing the plant's energy requirements.

Process changes and energy savings. The major sources of electrical consumption were plant lighting and compressed air used in the processes. Lighting was studied first. Through a series of gradual changes, light was reduced in the production areas to a point where electric usage was one-third less, with no evidence of employee dissatisfaction. In addition, this reduction was extended to halls, cafeterias, conference rooms, and storage areas.

The night lighting was of special concern since plant security had to be maintained. To solve this problem, switch locks were installed on all lights that were to be left on. All other lights were to be turned off by the employees or the guards. The result was an easily controlled light reduction program with sufficient light still available for the plant guards.

The control of compressed air was more difficult since it was essential for the production of the plant's products. This air is used for a variety of operations, including driving mixer motors in the bulk compounding process, conveying small containers in the packaging process, and the actual bottling of products. The solution to the compressed air usage problem was embarrassingly simple—install shutoff valves on the production line machinery so that air could be shut off during work breaks and when otherwise not required. Each production supervisor examined carefully every time the air could be turned off without any adverse effect on production.

In the manufacturing and office areas, building thermostats and control valves were adjusted to keep temperatures at 68°F. In the warehouse, even more substantial temperature control steps were taken when half of the steam coil unit heaters were deactivated. It was determined that steam pressure could be reduced from 125 pounds per square inch gage (psig) to 100 psig in various plant activities with no measurable effect on the processes. Further, no reason was found why hot water temperatures had to be 180°F., so they were reduced to 140°F. As Lahn explained: "These pressures and temperatures were set years ago and no one ever considered the reasons for them until energy became important." Finally, maintenance efforts were stepped up. Faulty steam traps were repaired, new insulation was applied, and faulty automatic door seals and approximately 50 broken windows were replaced.

Employee cooperation, not only in willingness to accept changes, but also in initiative by offering energy-saving ideas, played a major role in the Clinton plant's energy management success. One employee's idea, which led to substantial heating savings during the winter, illustrates this cooperation.

The warehouse on the first floor is adjacent to the automatic packaging area. The packaging area uses automatic equipment, which generates considerable heat during its operation. During the summer, that area becomes very hot, and the company installed a fan to draw cool air from the outside through the warehouse into the packaging area.

During the process of looking for energy-saving ideas, a woman employee in the packaging area, after noting that the area exceeded 68°F. and that heaters were needed in the warehouse, suggested that the fan between the two areas be reversed in the winter and warm air from the packaging area be drawn into the warehouse. The net result was that the warehouse required substantially less heat and the employees participated in the save-energy efforts.

To assure that savings were obtained, several monitoring procedures were established. Each weekend the plant was inspected to ensure that utility usage was at the lowest possible rate. Lighting, compressed air, and temperature levels were checked. Additionally, a weekly report was prepared for top management detailing progress in energy saving during the previous week.

In terms of results, the Clinton plant achieved a total of 40 percent reduction in fuel usage and 20 percent reduction in electrical consumption during the first six months of 1974. The company finds it difficult to relate these figures on a unit-of-production-basis, but believes direct-labor man-hours accurately provide a comparison of the 1973 and 1974 energy needs. The direct man-hours for the first five months of 1973 and 1974 are almost identical, making direct comparison possible. Despite the price of fuel and electricity nearly doubling, Clinton's energy budget for 1974 is only $284,000, or 26 percent over the actual use in 1973, indicating energy use declined more than 30 percent for comparable levels of production.

Chemetron

Company description. The chairman of Chemetron (1973 annual sales of $353 million) describes the company as one with a strong flavor toward "industrial consumables." In his words: "Rarely has more than 25 percent of our sales volume been in capital goods. . . Rather, the great proportion of our sales was of products that were immediately consumed and then reordered."

The company is divided into three groups: chemicals; gases and related products; and metal products and process equipment. The metal products and process equipment group includes the Tube Turns Division.

The Tube Turns Division was formed in 1927 to produce welded pipelines and fittings by a process developed in Germany. These fittings were specified for the first major buildings to be constructed using modern welded piping—the Union Carbide Building in Chicago and the Empire State Building and the Waldorf Astoria Hotel in New York City. Tube Turns products are produced at three locations, Philadelphia, Louisville, and Houston.

Management's philosophy is to have decisions affecting profitability made as far down in the organization as possible. The Chicago headquarters houses the four corporate vice-presidents, but the staff activities there are limited. Chemetron has traditionally allowed local managers great authority over local operations.

C. C. Candee, who had been with the company for 18 years, headed the energy effort. He assumed the responsibility in February 1974, continuing until his retirement that October. Candee had the kind of reputation within the company to make novel programs work. When the first of Chemetron's three operating groups was formed in 1968 (the chemicals group), Candee was chosen to be the corporate vice-president in charge. The designation of a senior executive in Chicago in charge of overall energy matters was contrary to the normal corporate philosophy and seemed to reflect his availability rather than a typical strategy-related decision.

Energy Conservation in the Tube Turns Division.   Although other areas of the company have conservation programs, the most intensive one is in the Tube Turns Division. The Tube Turns mill in Louisville produces steel elbow and tee forgings, gas transmission line elbows, and steam distribution system fittings. In addition, nuclear power plant penetration seals, forgings for automotive gears, large connecting rods, and other products constitute a line of select products produced on special order. Energy costs at the Louisville plant are 3.1 percent of the manufacturing costs.

The Tube Turns Division has for several years had a major cost-cutting effort under its Profit Improvement Program (PIP). The division management responded to the energy crisis by establishing an energy task force under the PIP program. The purpose was to improve housekeeping and daily practices and to examine all processes using energy forms; to review and justify all possible cheaper or alternate fuels and processes; then to develop programs, see that they are implemented, and audit the results.

Considerable use is made of a computer system in the overall task force functions. The computer is a key factor in managing the energy audit that is made of all the energy utilized for company operations. All equipment and devices that use energy are accounted for and catalogued as to type and amount of energy used. The objective of the audit is to gather enough data from each product process to compare the energy expended to the product production volume and cost.

An energy audit form has been created to identify each piece of equipment that utilizes energy and the amount it uses. Upon completion of the audit forms, they are catalogued in accordance with equipment type and function. The data provides a categorized baseline of all the major equipment energy users. The sum of the incremental energy functions provides the basis for an energy model of Tube Turns.

"The overall continuing function of the Energy Task Force depends on the exchange of ideas. The composition of the membership lends itself to this purpose," explains Task Force Chairman Bob Benson. "However," he points out, "further involvement of all employees is believed to be a necessity, and plans are being made to implement an education program to provide free flow of information and keep energy conservation a prime thought in everyone's mind."

Energy conservation projects are suggested by members of the task force. Each is analyzed as to its payback, and then its priority is established. Each project selected for implementation is followed closely during the construction phase. In turn, each project undergoes postauditing on an annual basis to evaluate the original analysis.

The group reviews two types of programs for energy conservation. In the first category are the housekeeping measures—reducing building temperatures, hot water service temperature, and lighting levels when appropriate. In the second category are the process-related energy-savings opportunities. The basic approach is to identify and alter extraneous processes and thus conserve energy and labor effort. This case focuses on one painting process for small fittings at Louisville.

It was believed after analysis that the speed of the conveyor system, the temperature of the rinse water, and the distance between rinsing and painting stations made the oven no longer necessary for drying the product. On a trial basis, gas to the oven was shut off and the effect on product quality was evaluated. It was found that the parts were completely dry before reaching the paint station and the drying oven could be removed from the process. Natural gas savings by the removal of this step amount to 4,600,000 cubic feet a year for an annual saving of $3,000.

Some projects in the energy conservation program also have solved other problems, such as meeting OSHA standards or controlling air pollution. In the large diameter elbow shop, two car-bottom assembling furnaces have been completely rebuilt. The refractory was stripped away back to the steel frame, and modern insulating firebrick was installed. In addition, burners with greater efficiency than those used previously were provided. Before modification it was found that, for some batches requiring a low furnace temperature, an air pollution problem developed due to the formation of aldehydes. Since the furnace was modified, 10,000,000 cubic feet of natural gas is saved a year with an attendant cost savings of $6,500 annually. In addition, the air pollution problem has been solved at considerable cost avoidance.

Other changes have improved manufacturing operations as well as saved energy. For example, a simple burner change on one of the small batchtype, car-bottom, heat-treat furnaces in the Louisville plant led to a reduction in natural gas consumption of more than 4,000,000 cubic feet a year, while obtaining an improved temperature uniformity inside the furnace chamber. Previous uniformity had been ±25 degrees. The new system provided ±5 degrees, with a decreased time to bring the furnace to the required operating temperature. The company realized $2,600 a year direct decreased operating cost of natural gas and has decreased the percentage of heat-treat failures with the improved furnace uniformity.

In another area of the plant, an air curtain was installed to kill the cold air draft caused by building negative pressure and winter air. The principle of this air curtain operation was to warm all incoming air, thereby eliminating cold drafts. This installation would result in $2,000 a year decreased operating costs. This one unit would eliminate several steam heaters presently used to spot heat areas that would have been affected by the cold air drafts. Additionally, decreases in operating costs were expected to result from decreased door repairs in that the door now would stay open at all times. Four more air curtains were scheduled to be installed in other buildings.

One of the more dramatic savings occurred in the engineering department where low light levels had been a morale problem for some time. Recently it became obvious that the air conditioning requirements for the department exceeded capacity and that a new air-conditioning system might be needed. Instead, the engineers designed a new lighting system, which both increased light levels and decreased the heat produced by the lights. The new system raised the lighting level from 25 to 60 footcandles to the 85 to 100 footcandles required by OSHA.

The old system consisted of a suspension ceiling of egg-crate diffusers with bare fluorescent bulbs on two-foot centers located above the ceiling. Some of the egg-crate sections were replaced with fluorescent panels, which were far more efficient in delivering light to the work area. Since the existing wiring was utilized, added costs have been only $6,000. Direct electrical savings of $860 a year, combined with the cost avoidance of $6,000 for air-conditioning work, made this energy-saving project financially attractive.

A water recirculation system was also installed in the Louisville facility that would save both water and energy. Existing equipment used water in large quantities and dumped it directly to the sewer after only one use. A study revealed that the facility processed 172,000,000 gallons of water annually. With the proposed recirculation system, sewer charges could be reduced by $41,000 and water costs by $64,000 annually. The total system would cost approximately $120,000. Operating costs were expected to be $10,000 a year. The system would have payback of 2.06 years.

A second water recirculation system has been designed. Components will be purchased at a later date. This system for the rotary hearth furnace would consume 82,000,000 gallons of water a year. Savings would be on the order of $8,200. The internal rate of return has been estimated at 162 percent, with a payback of 1.6 years.

Another major accomplishment resulted from the operation of one boiler in lieu of two. This was explained by a company spokesman: "Previously it was felt that two 60,000-pound-per-hour boilers had to be operated to provide the necessary steam for our hammer shop. By study and observation, we found that it is actually only necessary to operate one boiler to supply the necessary steam. The boiler is operating at a more efficient level and the cost of fuel, chemicals, and support equipment as a by-product have decreased."

As a result of these and other energy-saving activities, the corporation produced considerably more goods in 1974 and for the same amount of energy used in 1973.

Raytheon

Company description. Raytheon Company, a diversified electronics manufacturing firm, has annual sales exceeding $1.5 billion. It ranks 103 in Fortune's list of the 500 largest United States manufacturing companies. The firm is the largest employer headquartered in Massachusetts, with half of its

54,000 employees working in the state. The company has 45 major plants and laboratories nationwide.

Raytheon's traditional product line—military and commercial electronics—made up over 60 percent of its 1973 sales, although significant contributions to overall sales came from the engineering and construction division, major appliances, heavy construction equipment, and publishing subsidiaries. Nearly half of the company's business (48 percent) comes from government-related work and 20 percent from international operations.

Role of energy in company. Raytheon has an inherent interest in the energy business. Three subsidiary companies are benefiting from the mounting demand for new energy sources. As described in the 1973 annual report, the energy-related businesses include: "Design and construction of petroleum refineries and petrochemical plants—the Badger Company, geophysical exploration for oil and natural gas—the Seismograph Service Corporation, and the engineering and building of nuclear and conventional power plants—United Engineers and Constructors."

The opportunities for cost savings through energy conservation created additional interest within the company and prompted an early look at ways to improve in-house energy management. A companywide program to conserve energy was established and a full-time manager of environmental and energy conservation was appointed in 1973.

Development of a conservation policy. Raytheon is described by one company vice-president as "a big company made up of a lot of little companies." Thus each "little company" has its own problems, including energy availability and cost impact, which vary substantially from plant to plant. For example, the Andover, Massachusetts, plant chose to use only electric power rather than fuel oil or natural gas due to local air pollution concerns, while most of the company's other northeastern facilities are heavy fuel oil users.

It was not corporate citizenship alone that motivated Raytheon to action in the energy area, but savings possible from the high energy costs of the company. Corporate energy costs exceeded $15 million annually.

In October 1973, impetus for conservation was provided when D. Brainerd Holmes, executive vice-president of Raytheon, made energy conservation a matter of corporate policy. Accordingly, the corporate Office of Manufacturing was assigned overall responsibility for energy-related activities. James K. Rogers, then manager of environmental quality, was assigned the additional job of coordinating energy conservation in the corporation's facilities.

One individual in each division was made responsible for that division's energy conservation, and was instructed to submit each month to corporate headquarters detailed statements of energy consumption by source (fuel oil, natural gas, and electricity). Significant savings in energy consumption resulted from the program. During May 1974, Raytheon's savings were 46 percent in fuel oil, 11 percent in electricity, and 26 percent in natural gas compared to the previous year. For the period November 1973 through July 1974, reductions were 30 percent in fuel oil, 15 percent in electricity, and 17 percent in natural gas.

Actions taken early were largely the common ones—reducing building temperatures, sealing air leaks, improving heating/cooling systems maintenance, and reducing lighting where possible. It was realized, however, that although these techniques are important, a different sort of plan was required if truly innovative measures were to be taken to combat the pressing problem of expensive fuel supplies.

Accordingly, a search was begun in the corporation for a person with strong technical expertise in energy-use management. The man selected was Thola Theilhaber, an engineer who had worked on boiler design for the Raytheon Mini Furnace, a gas-fired heat transfer module for home and commercial heating. Previous experience with high temperature, hot water heating systems, boiler design, and combustion systems development provided Theilhaber with a strong background applicable to the corporate energy-saving program. Reporting to energy conservation coordinator Jim Rogers, Theilhaber's job was to act as an energy consultant to the plant engineers and to identify and help implement energy-saving measures at all of Raytheon's plants.

The conservation office was to be, in Rogers' words, a "catalyst." And, explains Raytheon's vice-president for manufacturing: "We decided not to solve their own problems. I'll help move people around who have the specialities to help implement, but that's all." This policy forced each plant to appoint a person to coordinate the individual energy programs.

At the same time, Raytheon's in-house Plant Engineers Council stepped up its energy conservation programs. The group, comprised of plant engineers from 17 Raytheon locations, scheduled meetings and seminars aimed at upgrading skills and disseminating information on energy conservation methods and practices.

Rogers discussed the program further, explaining that a checklist of more than 130 items was prepared and sent around: "The checklist wouldn't have worked, however, unless local plant people cared. Anyone can read checklists, but you need the talent to do things at the plant."

With Theilhaber as a consultant and using individual plant talent, a number of successful energy-savings projects have been undertaken at various Raytheon plant locations.

Process changes and energy savings.   An early assignment began at a plant in California, which has several electrically fired processing furnaces. The facility was told by its local power company (Pacific Gas and Electric) that a plan should be developed for a 15 percent reduction in electrical availability in the 1973–74 heating season. It looked for a while as if production would have to be reduced, with dramatic effects on the whole plant operation. Theilhaber found, however, that by ducting away hot exhaust gases from the furnaces, providing enclosures at air leakage points, and redesigning the front end of the furnace to reduce radiant energy losses, the air-conditioning load on the area could be reduced by 50 kilowatts.

Another project being studied involves a plant that has a large quantity of dry refuse, which is currently removed by commercial waste hauler. The plant also has a large plating department requiring heated water for rinse tanks and steam for heating and air conditioning (absorption type). Under consideration is a plan to incinerate the refuse and heat the rinse water using a waste-heat boiler on the incinerator effluent. In this case, the installation of incinerator and boiler would have a three- to four-year payback.

Another service performed by the conservation group at Raytheon is the review of capital spending for energy-saving plants. At one plant a project was planned to reduce steam distribution losses by closing down the plant's steam boiler in the summer months and using electrical steam generators to service the summer steam demand at a remote part of the plant. Theilhaber found that the project, although conceived in the spirit of energy conservation, would actually save very little, if any, energy and would never pay for itself.

A final example of energy conservation practices at Raytheon may be applicable to a wide variety of industrial plants. One Raytheon facility is cooled and heated by 131-ton rooftop units (24 of them) incorporating freon cooling systems and electric resistance heaters. After consulting with the equipment manufacturer, Theilhaber found that it is possible to modify the air-conditioning units to operate as heat pumps in the winter at considerable energy savings. In a heat pump, the energy delivered to the air for heating purposes is greater than the input electrical power. In this case, a coefficient of performance of approximately two will be realized—meaning that for each electrical British thermal unit (Btu) delivered to the compressor motor, two Btu's will be delivered to the air steam being heated. Calculations show that electrical heating will not be necessary until the outside temperature drops to approximately 10°F. At this point the resistance heaters will cut in to augment the heat pump. Costs associated with the conversion are $9,000 for engineering the change in circuit and new controls and $16,000 a unit for modifications required. A total cost for all units is $393,000. Annual savings anticipated at current electrical rates are $208,000 for a simple payback period of under two years. Because the units are not originally designed to operate as heat pumps, only one unit was modified for the 1974–75 heating season. During that period, extensive tests on performance and energy usage were to be conducted prior to modifying the remaining units.

Raytheon's approach to energy management—having an energy manager with an in-house consultant on energy matters reporting to him—is well suited to a large corporation with a number of facilities involved in a wide range of manufacturing functions.

Chapter 13

Impacts on Company Operations

Government regulations affect the production and distribution of goods and services in many ways. These requirements can change the methods by which some products are made and they can increase the cost of others. The range of company operations affected by government can include work procedures, manufacturing processes, marketing methods, and markets served.

MANUFACTURING FUNCTIONS

Changing Production Processes

A major impact of federal regulation on manufacturing is in the form of increased production expenses. As long as the Congress does not directly assess to industry the costs stemming from legislated controls, but concentrates primarily on the intended social benefits of the regulations, this situation can be expected to continue.

Although government regulations generally result in cost increases, some companies are finding that, in the long run, their adaptations to certain requirements can result in cost savings. Better process operation and control may be a consequence, in addition to improved "housekeeping," such as fewer leaks, more reprocessing of wastes, recycling of water and raw materials, energy conservation, and so forth. Although existing facilities often will require the addition of expensive pollution controls, new structures at times can be designed with less expensive pollution devices at the outset.

One example of cost reduction resulted from government efforts to standardize packaging, fostered by the Fair Packaging and Labeling Act of 1966, which led to less variety in package sizes. Between 1966 and 1974, the number of different types of toothpaste packages decreased from 57 to 5.

Various other impacts occur as a result of government regulation of production processes. To meet increasingly specific consumer product safety standards, many industries have been changing their materials mix.[1] Some manufacturers of sleepwear for children, for example, are using a higher proportion of cotton for thermal underwear to increase fire-retardant properties. Certain positive benefits result for companies that have successfully produced lines of flame-resistant clothing. This relatively new capability can be used to diversify into other areas of textile production, and the fire-retardant characteristic is also a promotional asset.

Capital/labor ratios are likely to rise as a result of increasing use of safety features, such as photoelectric presence-sensing systems, brake monitoring devices, barrier guards, and other devices that tend to reduce the need for manpower. Companies in industries with historically high accident rates are especially feeling the impact of increased federal control of production processes. OSHA has identified several "target" industries or occupations that are to be inspected with particular frequency: wood and wood products, roofing and sheet metal, meat packing, longshore, and construction.[2]

One result of the pressures for production processes to meet government environmental and safety requirements is that a rising share of company investment is being devoted to these required social responsibilities rather than to increasing output. This situation could lead to a significant decline in the longterm growth of productivity, at least as it is conventionally measured.

Employer Responsibility for Safety

Many manufacturing departments have been revising their procedures to conform to the expanding occupational safety and health regulations pertaining to air, noise, and heat. Asbestos producers are now required to meet strict minimum operating requirements, and numerous other areas of manufacturing are being studied by the National Institute of Occupational Safety and Health to determine if additional standards should be promulgated. The often substantial cost to the manufacturer of complying with the new array of health and safety

---

[1] U.S. Consumer Product Safety Commission, *CPSC Issues Final Standard for Children's Sleepwear, Sizes 7 to 14,* April 26, 1974, pp. 1–3.

[2] U.S. Occupational Safety and Health Administration, *The Target Health Hazards* (Washington, D.C.: U.S. Government Printing Office, 1972).

standards is shown in Table 13–1. Although the cost of compliance rises, on the average, with size of the company, it is apparent that the increases are not proportional. Hence, the smaller firms tend to bear a disproportionately large share of the expenses that arise from employee safety and health regulation.

Organizational changes are also a consequence of the stepped-up pace of federal regulation. An interdepartmental work safety committee is becoming a common mechanism for responding to rising government and public concern with job safety and health (see Table 13–2). Depending on the size of the company and the geographic dispersion of its activities, such safety committees may be set up at the plant, division, or corporate levels. Their role may vary from coordination to staff assistance to actual line authority over the safety aspects of production activities.

Despite the dollars and the manpower devoted to OSHA compliance, there is some question as to whether these resources are aimed in the right direction by emphasizing adherence to governmentally determined standards. Professor Walter Oi of the University of Rochester in New York has noted studies showing that violation of safety standards account for small proportions of industrial accidents. In one New York study, it was found that violations of state standards were contributory factors in only 23 percent of the 3,123 cases investigated. Under the Wisconsin workmen's compensation program—where a worker is entitled to additional benefits if he or she can show that the injury was caused by a violation of state safety standards—less than two percent of the cases examined qualified for the added payments.[3]

Also, OSHA inspection rates tend to be lower in high risk industries and higher in low risk industries.[4] The probability that a typical worker in a small firm (100 or fewer employees) will see an OSHA compliance officer is about four times greater than in the case of a worker in a large manufacturing establishment. The benefits of inspections in the smaller firms in relation to costs are low because of the small absolute number of workers exposed to risks that a given inspector can review. This is true even though reported accident "rates" are higher in the smaller companies. In contrast, allocating inspectors to larger firms tends to have a higher payoff because one inspector can cover a working environment that affects many more workers.[5]

The OSHA approach to safety regulation is based on the notion that employers can best prevent accidents and disease. As stated by the U.S. Occupational Safety and Health Review Commission, "the (OSHA) law exhorts employees to comply with job safety and health standards, but its enforcement procedures are directed solely at employers." In a series of cases before the Commission testing this question, the employers were given the onus for unsafe acts of their employees. The Commission ruled that the employers should have

[3]Walter Y. Oi, *On Evaluating the Effectiveness of the OSHA Inspection Program,* May 15, 1975 (processed), pp. IX–X.
[4]Ibid., p. 35.
[5]Ibid., pp. 37–38.

Table 13-1

ESTIMATED AVERAGE COST OF OSHA COMPLIANCE

Company Size (Number of Employees)	Estimated Expense (Weighted Average)		
	Safety	Health	Total
0 - 100	$ 24,000	$ 11,000	$ 35,000
101 - 500	50,500	23,000	73,500
501 - 1000	141,140	209,627	350,767
1001 - 2000	272,000	58,630	330,630
2001 - 5000	552,000	278,000	830,000
over 5000	2,226,500	2,455,000	4,681,500

Source: Occupational Safety and Health Management Research Survey, National Association of Manufacturers, 1974.

Table 13-2

FUNCTIONS OF A COMPANY HEALTH AND SAFETY COMMITTEE

1. Establishing procedures for handling suggestions and recommendations of the committee.
2. Inspecting a selected area of the establishment each month for the purpose of detecting hazards.
3. Conducting regularly scheduled meetings to discuss accident and illness prevention methods, safety and health promotion, hazards noted on inspections, injury and illness records, and other pertinent subjects.
4. Investigating accidents as a basis for recommending means to prevent recurrence.
5. Providing information on safe and healthful working practices to the foremen.
6. Recommending changes or additions to improve protective clothing and equipment.
7. Developing or revising rules to comply with current safety and health standards.
8. Promoting safety and first aid training for committee members and other employees.
9. Promoting safety and health programs for all employees.
10. Keeping records of minutes of meetings

Source: U.S. Occupational Safety and Health Administration

done more than merely make protective equipment available. It was held that employers must establish an effective policy to ensure that the equipment is used, and must continually monitor the program to make certain that their employees are complying with it.[6]

[6]*The President's Report on Occupational Safety and Health* (Washington, D.C.: U.S. Government Printing Office, 1973), pp. 92-93.

There are limits, however, to the company's responsibility for lack of safety consciousness by its employees. In one case (*Secretary of Labor* v. *Standard Glass, Inc.*) where the evidence demonstrated that the employer had done all that could reasonably be required to assure that employees used their protective equipment, the Commission ruled that their isolated failures to use it was not a violation by the employer. The Commission held that the employer could not be expected to guarantee that all employees would observe good safety practices at all times.

Some studies indicate that substantial percentages of accidents are wholly or partially caused by factors best controlled by employees. The Occupational Safety and Health Act, however, does not provide sanctions for employees who violate safety practices through reckless or risk-creating actions. An analysis by the Wisconsin Department of Labor revealed that approximately 45 percent of the accidents surveyed were due to behavioral problems of workers, such as the reluctance to wear face masks because of discomfort. An additional 30 percent were attributable to momentary physical hazards not susceptible to correction by inspection.[7]

In contrast to the bureaucratic approach fostered by OSHA—if the company follows the agency's standards it will not get into trouble—some business firms have been taking a more positive, results-oriented attitude to occupational safety and health. DuPont, for example, sets formal safety goals for all supervisors in terms of lost-time injuries per million hours worked; line supervisors are held responsible for the safety of all work in their areas. Safety professionals are only used in an advisory capacity.

Once a DuPont manufacturing department, in cooperation with the company's Laboratory of Toxicology and Industrial Medicine, determines that a substance it is handling may be toxic, a number of crucial steps are taken. The first is initiating a program to safeguard the health of employees, which may include revision of work practices, requirements for additional protective equipment, changes in production processes, or other improved engineering controls.

Next, a program for monitoring and measuring exposure levels is instituted, along with an examination of employee medical histories to determine any possible adverse effects on health. Medical surveillance procedures, as well as the recording of employee exposures, are also undertaken.

Depending on the circumstances, a variety of groups may be notified of the actions taken; these may include employees, customers, government agencies, other producers, and the media. If safe production cannot be assured, it is company policy to shut down production and halt sales of the items involved until adequate safeguards can be developed.

To deal with the possibility of accidents occurring while a product is in shipment, DuPont has developed a Transportation Emergency Reporting Pro-

---

[7]James R. Chelius, *Expectations for OSHA's Performance: The Lessons of Theory and Empirical Evidence*, March 1975 (processed), pp. 22-23.

cedure (TERP); this activity keeps track of company materials in transit. In the event of an accident, TERP can provide the carrier and local police and fire personnel with immediate advice, and often it follows with technical people to assist. TERP ties in with the Chemical Transportation Emergency Center (CHEMTREC), which the company helped to set up. CHEMTREC provides round-the-clock assistance throughout the United States in any transportation emergency involving chemicals.[8]

DuPont reports that its injury rate has dropped from 3 per million worker-hours in 1935 to 0.16 in 1972. The company estimates an annual saving of about $27 million compared with the average all-industry injury experience. In fact, the company receives a modest amount of income from the fees that it receives from other companies for the evaluation and review done for them by the DuPont occupational safety and health group.

Unions are becoming increasingly vocal in pressing for new and more stringent health and safety standards. The Occupational Health and Safety Act has given labor the leverage to bargain on health and safety items with less fear of sacrificing money or fringe benefit issues for safety considerations. Organized labor's demands also may make compliance more expensive for the employer. Labor stresses improvements in the condition of the workplace itself and considers wearing extra equipment often only a stopgap measure. As Leonard Woodcock, president of the United Auto Workers, commented concerning workplace noise:

> Earplugs, earmuffs, or other ear protection do not provide an answer. We will accept them only for that time needed to develop engineering methods and controls that will bring the workplace noise levels down to acceptable safe levels.[9]

QUALITY CONTROL FUNCTIONS

As a result of the stepped-up activities of the various federal regulatory agencies, many companies are finding it necessary to expand their quality control departments. In the process, some companies have been separating quality control operations from production, so that the two departments report to different vice-presidents. The establishment of such independent quality control units is further upgrading the function, in some cases resulting in the promotion of the chief quality control official to vice-presidential rank.

The quality control function is finding it especially necessary to focus on

[8]Edwin A. Gee, "Report on Safety," *DuPont Context,* 1, 1975, p. 7; Paul F. Jankowski, "Report on Safety: DuPont's Long Record," *DuPont Context,* 1, 1975, p. 14.

[9]Richard F. Gibson, "Labor Pushing Harder for Safer Workplaces," *Industry Week,* December 16, 1974, pp. 43–44.

prevention of increasingly expensive, time-consuming, and publicly embarrassing product recalls. Many companies require a safety analysis of each of their products and of the ingredients that go into them. The resultant "safety profiles" enable the company to correct potential problems before their products reach the marketplace.

In the Whirlpool Corporation, the product safety audit is a formal product review. It is usually led by the engineering laboratory group charged with the responsibility for the total product evaluation program. It never is conducted by the engineers who did the product design work in the first place. Attendees at a product safety audit include the director of engineering of the operating division responsible for the product; the director of engineering for the product under review; the engineering director of a totally unrelated product; personnel from design, testing, manufacturing, and quality control; a representative of the reliability group; and people from the customer assurance and service departments.

The Whirlpool product audit covers the following subjects:

Shipping containers and shipping performance.
Provisions for handling the packed product.
Unpacking procedures and instructions.
Product identification on the carton.
Product installation.
Instructions, cautions, and labels.
All performance characteristics.
Electrical, chemical, and construction standards.
Reliability of the product.
Serviceability, including access to parts.
Disposal of the product.[10]

Some firms are retaining outside experts to perform "product audits" with the purpose of having an independent authority review the firm's quality control procedures to verify both compliance with government regulations and the authenticity of company advertising claims. The product auditor also can act as an expert witness before federal regulatory bodies or in court cases. Although use of such independent experts is not new, it has become more important as a result of government programs of product safety, increased enforcement of truth-in-advertising, and the trend toward placing the burden of proof for safety on the manufacturer.

As a result of federal requirements, quality control departments, as well as company health groups, are receiving added responsibilities for testing the physical environment in which production takes place. As the pressures from govern-

[10]Howard E. Brehm, "How to Establish a Product Safety Program," *Quality Progress*, February 1975, pp. 28–29.

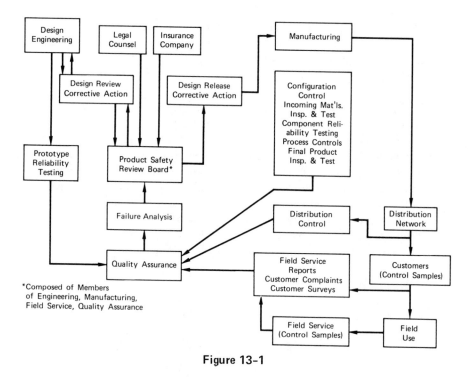

Figure 13-1

A SUGGESTED COMPANY SYSTEM FOR PRODUCT SAFETY

Source: James P. Kuhn, "How to manage product safety," *Industry Week,* April 22, 1974.

ment safety agencies increase, many companies are setting up product safety review boards responsible for monitoring and taking corrective action on all phases of the product development cycle (see Figure 13–1). Such interdivisional organizations are composed of representatives of quality control, engineering, manufacturing, marketing, and legal departments—and may be assisted by the company insurer. These boards can directly or indirectly influence a large share of company expenditures and potential liabilities—ranging from product liability costs to liability insurance premiums and legal fees to expanded outlays for risk prevention through product testing, certification, quality assurance, and product service.

MARKETING FUNCTIONS

The possibility of intermittent but direct federal intervention in company pricing decisions is one of the more significant areas of government regulation affecting marketing. Overall, long-term market planning may need to take account of the likelihood of some form of federal influence over private industry pricing for one or more periods in the years ahead.

"Caveat emptor" (buyer beware) is a concept being relegated to the business history books. Stepped-up enforcement by the old-line regulatory agencies, such as the Federal Trade Commission, and the establishment of newer activities (notably in the product safety area) mean that the seller must be aware of the dangers of inadequacy of his or her product. As the marketing departments are feeling the brunt of this aspect of government control, they are gradually undergoing a broadening of their outlook and a curtailment of their discretion as staff offices, notably the corporate legal and insurance staffs, are more heavily involved. More of the marketing department's efforts are now geared to reviewing and criticizing the internal product development efforts of the company prior to the products reaching the marketing stage, where the company may find itself in conflict with unofficial or formal consumer advocate agencies.

Product Recalls

As a result of expanding government regulation and enforcement of existing controls, marketing departments are increasingly responsible for provisions for "reverse distribution"–product recalls. In addition to the highly publicized cases of motor vehicles, growing numbers of nonautomotive products are recalled, including adhesives, bicycles, computers, deodorants, drain cleaners, electric shavers, epsom salts, gas ovens, heart monitors, lawn mowers, power drills, safety helmets, soup bowls, television sets, and toys.

Many companies, especially those catering to consumer markets, are introducing numerous modifications in their operating procedures to reduce the expense and anxiety associated with recall situations. For example, a coded identification number for each product or batch of products can expedite product recalls. Computers keep track of the numbers throughout the distribution chain. The minimum identification includes the labeling of each shipping package and container with a code indicating item, batch or period, day, month, year, and plant. In the example of grocery manufacturers, the following records and actions have been recommended by their trade association to facilitate locating a product subject to recall:[11]

> A record of the cases, by identification code, packed in a batch so that a reconciliation with total shipments can be quickly accomplished if needed.
> Shipping specific batches of goods to defined distribution regions, rather than scattering them across the country.
> Retain documents at each shipping point to show the codes and number of cases for each item shipped.

[11] *Guidelines for Product Recall* (Washington, D.C.: Grocery Manufacturers of America, 1974), pp. 57–58.

Keeping these documents until it is certain that the product has gone through the grocery marketing system, but not less than two years. Record retention for perishable products, however, may be limited to six months.

Where practical, shipping only one batch of each item for each order.

Where practical, reconditioned merchandise should not be packed with more than one batch to a case. Cases containing mixed codes should be clearly marked.

Instructing each public warehouse to follow predetermined product recall procedures.

In those cases where the stock is taken beyond the distributor warehouse, encouraging subsequent warehouses to follow similar identification procedures.

In most cases the normal distribution system can be reversed for return and pick up of the recalled products. In addition, of course, inventory and accounting systems must make adjustments for product recalls and wholesalers must be reimbursed.

Postage paid, detailed warranty cards are a method of providing the manufacturer with the names and addresses of purchasers of certain types of products. Some companies have conducted "dry runs" of recall procedures. The Hartford Insurance Company now offers a "Hazardous Product Reporting Kit" to its policyholders. The kit is designed to aid companies in complying with the reporting regulations of the Consumer Product Safety Commission, including a sample press release to alert the public to a hazardous product.[12] Often, a single executive is assigned recall responsibilities, with the authority to halt production and to begin notification of dealers and customers. An example of a possible action plan, resulting from a situation that may require a product recall, is shown in Figure 13–2.

The stepped-up emphasis within the marketing function on the recall problem is resulting in a number of visible changes. For example, a major expansion is under way in recordkeeping so that the holders of the recalled products—final purchasers as well as wholesale and retail distributors—can be promptly notified and so that the required information can be furnished to the appropriate government agency. Figure 13–3 contains a proposed format for notifying the Food and Drug Administration of product recalls. The necessity often arises of establishing a network of service firms to replace substandard parts or substitute new products.

The federal government eventually may require that manufacturers keep records of all complaints concerning products, which will be turned over to a government agency on request. At least that notion has been reported under consideration by the Consumer Product Safety Commission. Such information could form the basis for future product recalls. Corporations are devoting more attention to correspondence from consumers than has been the case in the past.

---

[12]"Marketing Observer," *Business Week,* October 5, 1974, p. 100.

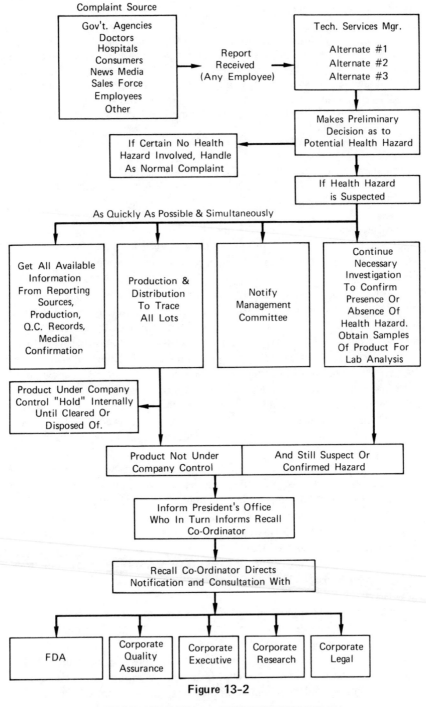

Figure 13-2

A PRODUCT RECALL CONTINGENCY PLAN

Source: Guidelines for Product Recall, Grocery Manufacturers of America, Inc., 1974, pp. 28-29.

If After Consultation and Analysis, the Complaint Is A Confirmed Hazard The Recall Co-Ordinator Shall Direct As Follows.

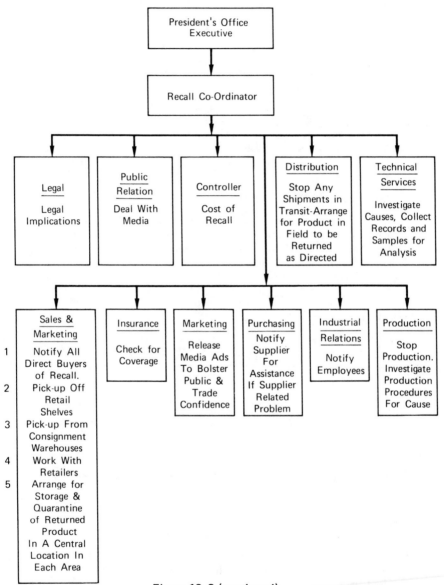

Figure 13-2 (continued)

This outline is intended to assist the affected Division in supplying the information necessary for company designee, such as Recall Coordinator of Corporate Affairs, to notify FDA.

I. PRODUCT INVOLVED

    Give product, product code, labeling, packaging and description

    _____

    _____

II. PRODUCTION CODE DATES

    List all production code dates in full (include plant designation).

    _____

    _____

III. ESTIMATED AMOUNT ON MARKET

    Total amount produced _____
    Indicate best estimate of product as yet unconsumed
    Area of country affected _____

IV. REASON FOR RECALL
    Describe precisely the reason for recall _____

    _____

V. INJURIES, DEATHS

    Furnish a statement, even if negative

    _____

VI. RECALL COMMUNICATIONS

    Furnish a copy of the recall telegram sent to the trade.

Figure 13-3

AN FDA NOTIFICATION FORMAT FOR A PRODUCT RECALL

Source: Guidelines for Product Recall, Grocery Manufacturers of America, Inc., 1974,
         p. 43.

Such response also can be used as evidence of the company acting in good
faith should a product subsequently be declared hazardous.

The cost of a recall varies with the number of products sold; the amount
of time and effort required to track down purchasers; the percentage of products
that require repair, replacement, or refund; and the cost per unit to remedy the
problem. It cost one motor vehicle manufacturer $3.5 million for postage alone
to notify by certified mail, as required by law, the 6.5 million owners of cars
with questionable motor mounts. The cost of the recall may far exceed the price
of the product itself. One company estimated that it cost on the average $5 to

recall each defective 19-cent item. The costs included notifying each user by return receipt letter or personal call; locating, taking inventory, removing and disposing of suspect items at various locations; redesigning the item; overtime manufacturing of new items, printing labels and instructions, packing, shipping, installing and testing new items; recording and reporting the actions taken; and the cost of medical and legal fees in connection with consumer complaints—all in addition to lost sales.[13]

Overall, as design, manufacturing, and quality control procedures are increasingly geared to federal requirements, the incidence of product recalls may peak and then decline. However, in the short term, the number of product recalls is likely to rise with the stepped-up pace of enforcement by government agencies, as well as the increased attention to product safety by company managements.

Warranties

The Magnuson-Moss Warranty and Federal Trade Commission Improvement Act, which took effect July 5, 1975, for the first time sets standards for what must be incorporated in a product warranty and how the warranty must be worded. The law is expected to bring sweeping changes in product warranties. Some companies may simply decide to drop the entire warranty procedure to avoid the federal controls. Other companies, which will continue issuing warranties as part of the competitive "package" offered to customers, will make theirs more comprehensive and specific. The major provisions of the act include the following:

> Warranties shall "fully and conspicuously disclose in simple and readily understood language the terms and conditions of such warranty." The complex legal language previously used in many warranties is no longer permissible.
>
> Warranty information shall be made accessible to consumers to aid in their decision to buy. The burden of education seems to be on the manufacturer, who should encourage, or demand if possible, that retailers pass the information on to buyers.
>
> Companies must label the warranty either "full" or "limited." If a warranty is labeled full it must meet minimum standards, including the company's pledge to repair any defects within a reasonable time and without charge. After a reasonable number of attempts at repair (the Federal Trade Commission defines "reasonable"), if the product still does not work it must be replaced or the full purchase price refunded; this is the so-called lemon provision. If the warranty does not meet these prerequisites, it must be conspicuously promoted as a "limited" warranty.[14]

[13]Richard M. Jacobs and August B. Mundel, "Quality Tasks in Product Recall," *Quality Progress*, June 1975, pp. 16–17.

[14]E. Patrick McGuire, "Taking the Lemons Out of the Warranty," *New York Times,*

The "repair, replace, or refund" trend in customer restitution may spread to other federal regulators. OSHA is considering penalties for products failing to meet industrial safety standards, while CPSC requires refunds to customers for recalled products. The Federal Trade Commission has asked the Supreme Court for permission to seek refunds to customers victimized by deceptive marketing practices.[15]

Labeling

Some of the emphasis in consumer product packaging is shifting from merely decorative coverings to informational labeling. Increased government response to consumer concerns is leading to expanding amounts of information on labels. The product contents and usage of components are more and more frequently being described. For example, the Federal Trade Commission is requiring detergent producers to list all ingredients so that buyers can avoid allergy-causing chemicals.[16]

The Food and Drug Administration requires companies that enrich foods or make nutritional claims about them to include nutritional information on the package.[17] The FDA has urged Congress to require that the labels of nonprescription drugs show the quantity of all active ingredients, and it is considering regulations requiring ingredient labeling of cosmetics. The Consumer Product Safety Commission has the authority to set standards for packages containing hazardous substances. (see Figure 13–4 for an example). The CPSC also regulates packaging so that products containing harmful substances cannot be opened easily by children under age five.

The Department of Commerce has requested manufacturers voluntarily to label household appliances regarding their cooling capacity, power requirements, and energy efficiency ratio (EER) as part of the national effort to conserve energy. The higher the EER, the more cooling capacity is obtained from a watt-hour of usage. The labels for high EER products may become a positive marketing device—that is, they may help overcome consumer resistance to buying a more expensive model, provided that it is more economical in terms of energy usage (see Figure 13–5 for a sample).

Additional government labeling specifications are being developed for re-

---

July 6, 1975, p. 10F; "The Guesswork on Warranties," *Business Week*, July 14, 1975, p. 51.

[15] James D. Snyder, "Washington's New Watchwords: 'Repair, Replace, or Refund'," *Sales Management*, February 17, 1975.

[16] U.S. Federal Trade Commission, *Care Labels*, Buyers Guide No. 10, Washington, D.C., July 1972.

[17] U.S. Food and Drug Administration, *The New Look in Food Labels*, DHEW Publication No. FDA 74-2036, Washington, D.C., 1974.

Front panel   Front panel

POISON

CAUSES SEVERE BURNS—VAPOR HARMFUL
Read carefully cautions on back panel

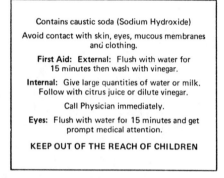

Back panel   Back panel

Contains Hydrochloric Acid

Keep away from skin and eyes

Do not mix with chlorine type bleaches
or other household chemicals

First Aid: **External:** Flush with water for 15 minutes.

Internal: Drink large quantities of water or milk.
Follow with milk of magnesia, beaten eggs
or vegetable oil.

Call Physician immediately.

Eyes: Wash with water for 15 minutes and get
prompt medical attention.

KEEP OUT OF THE REACH OF CHILDREN

Contains caustic soda (Sodium Hydroxide)

Avoid contact with skin, eyes, mucous membranes
and clothing.

First Aid: External: Flush with water for
15 minutes then wash with vinegar.

Internal: Give large quantities of water or milk.
Follow with citrus juice or dilute vinegar.

Call Physician immediately.

Eyes: Flush with water for 15 minutes and get
prompt medical attention.

KEEP OUT OF THE REACH OF CHILDREN

Figure 13–4

EXAMPLES OF LABELS MEETING REQUIREMENTS FOR PRODUCTS CONTAINING HAZARDOUS SUBSTANCES

Source: Lawrence E. Hicks, "Product Labeling and the Law," *AMA Management Briefing,* 1974, p. 21.

frigerators, freezers, water heaters, washers, and dryers; many likely will be adopted by industry. The federal government has prepared legislation making such labeling mandatory (the proposed National Appliance and Motor Vehicle Labeling Act). In any event, specification labeling is becoming more common. For example, clothing labels grow increasingly complex; many feature long lists of "dos" and "don'ts" for the user.

Advertising

Writers of copy are frequently being instructed about the product's liabilities—as well as its attributes—relative to those of other brands in the product category.

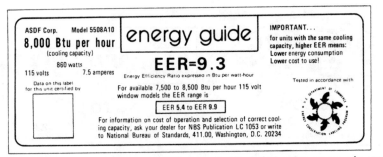

The U.S. Department of Commerce Energy Guide Label rates room air conditioners according to their "energy efficiency ratio," or EER.

Figure 13-5

Advertisers and advertising agencies, spurred by federal action, are displaying a greater awareness of consumer safety in product advertising. Advertising copy prepared with an awareness of safety can provide such tangible benefits as enhancing product acceptability and reducing the possibility of unfavorable publicity and safety related lawsuits.[18]

Some companies that are heavy advertisers in consumer markets, or their agencies, are setting up formal panels to review the approach to safety in their advertising. These panels include advertiser and agency personnel who are in some way particularly familiar with actual consumer experiences with the products involved—for example, parents of young children. The National Advertising Review Board, an industry self-regulatory organization, has developed the following checklist for reviewing company advertising to minimize the likelihood of violating federal product safety requirements:

> Is anything shown, described, or claimed in the advertisement that raises questions of consumer safety?
> Is everything known that should be known about the product's performance under both normal and misuse circumstances?
> Is there anything in the advertisement that might prove harmful to children who cannot comprehend the most familiar hazards in consumer products and tend to imitate what they see?
> Is allowance made in advertising situations for the susceptibility to suggestion of the elderly or the consumer predisposed toward risk-taking?[19]

As companies become more active in public affairs, they pay increasing attention to the distinction between political and ordinary business advertising.

[18]U.S. National Business Council for Consumer Affairs, *Safety in the Marketplace* (Washington, D.C.: U.S. Government Printing Office, 1973), pp. 1–11.
[19]National Advertising Review Board, *Product Advertising and Consumer Safety*, New York, 1974, p. 5.

The Internal Revenue Service generally prohibits tax deductions for political advertising, which it defines as that intended to "promote or defeat legislation or to influence the public with respect to the desirability or undesirability of proposed legislation." At times, disagreements occur as to where to draw the line between political advertising and merely public expression of the company's view on issues, particularly those that may strongly affect the company's markets and costs. In such cases, advice from the legal staff is needed.

INTERNATIONAL OPERATIONS

The major impacts of federal regulation on corporate international operations are mainly indirect. Through certain controls presented under the guise of tax reform, new investments in overseas business activities are likely to become less profitable. For example, public pressures are rising for taxing profits of some United States businesses abroad before the parent American company receives them. Public and congressional concern over the so-called export of jobs isssue may result in further government controls on the direct overseas investment of American businesses. Considerable controversy exists as to whether overseas operations do damage by exporting jobs or simply represent an effective way of surmounting foreign trade barriers.

The federal government is relying in good measure on provisions that encourage direct exports. Balance of payments considerations have led the federal government to enact legislation to encourage companies to favor exports over domestic sales or direct overseas investment. Since 1971, the Internal Revenue Code specifically authorizes companies to set up so-called Domestic International Sales Corporations (DISC) to handle their export sales from the United States. So long as the income remains in the DISC subsidiary, only one-half of export profits is subject to the federal corporate income tax.

Some existing tax advantages are likely to be limited in the future, especially for international petroleum producers. The stated aim would be to make direct exports of domestically produced goods relatively more attractive and imports from United States overseas subsidiaries less attractive. In addition, however, the domestic political environment in the United States appears increasingly to favor the adoption of some type of controls over multinational corporations, especially large companies that produce and sell their products in a variety of countries. Much of the pressures arise from the belief, often mistaken, that these corporations have eclipsed many individual governments in the scope of their authority and activity.

Specific federal controls may benefit domestic companies at the expense of overseas business, including the foreign subsidiaries of American corporations. The most conspicuous example of such controls is the Buy American policy of federal procurement agencies. Passed in 1933 as an antirecessionary measure, the

Buy American Act requires federal agencies purchasing commodities for use within the United States to pay up to a six percent differential for domestically produced goods. Pursuant to a presidential executive order issued in 1962, as much as a 50 percent differential is paid for military goods produced at home. The desire to reduce the defense burden on the United States balance-of-payments is the general justification for the special treatment to domestic producers.

As pointed out in an earlier chapter, American flag vessels must be used to transport at least 50 percent of the gross tonnage of all commodities financed with United States foreign aid funds. Most of the goods financed by the program are procured in the United States.[20] As shown in Table 13–3, many state governments have comparable practices. The preferences granted to domestic suppliers range from the North Carolina practice of favoring domestic bids when the terms of foreign and domestic proposals are essentially the same to Idaho's policy of purchasing only domestic materials. Some of these restrictions have been challenged in the courts, and others are so vague as not to be generally enforceable. Indirectly, American exporters may suffer from these policies, at least to the extent that they encourage other nations to adopt similar restrictions.

There also are laws that prohibit or limit foreign investments in certain sectors of the American economy for reasons of national security or to protect what are considered "essential" national interests. These sectors include atomic energy, domestic airlines, shipping, federally owned land, communications and media, and fishing. There are many laws that provide the government with authority to control foreign economic activities in specific areas such as defense.

The Department of Defense may deny security clearances required to do classified (secret) work for the government to any firm under "foreign ownership, control, or influence." Foreign ownership of producers of defense materials is not expressly prohibited, but it is effectively deterred by the prospect that such acquisition would likely cause the firm to lose its classified government business. Exports of arms are closely controlled.

The federal government has advised that it will expect any foreign government contemplating a major direct investment in the United States to seek advance consultations with our government on the prospective investment.[21]

A more direct impact on the international operations of American business firms is occurring in the wake of disclosures of widespread practices concerning legal and illegal payments involving government personnel of foreign nations (often called "mordita" or "baksheesh"). The payments have ranged from minor bribes to customs agents (at the equivalent of $5 to $10) to millions of dollars, via middlemen to senior officials of other governments. The practice of funnel-

---

[20]Norman S. Fieleke, "The Buy-American Policy of the United States Government," *New England Economic Review*, July/August 1969, pp. 2–6.

[21]*Statement by Gerald L. Parsky, Assistant Secretary of the Treasury Before the Senate Committee on Banking, Housing and Urban Affairs*, Washington, D.C., July 22, 1975, pp. 13–16.

Table 13-3

STATE BUY AMERICAN PRACTICES

State	Practice
Alabama	Requires use of U.S. materials "if available at reasonable prices" in cases of public works financed entirely by state funds
California	Requires use of materials of U.S. origin (subject to court challenges).
Georgia	Requires state agencies to buy American products if price and quality are equal.
Hawaii	Establishes a scale of preferences for domestic products.
Idaho	Requires state bids to carry a clause restricting use of foreign materials.
Indiana	Restricts use of foreign steel and aluminum.
Kentucky	Discourages state agencies from requesting foreign-made products.
Maine	Reserves the right to reject bids involving foreign products when in direct competition with American products.
Massachusetts	Grants preference "other considerations being equal" to instate products first and then to other American products.
New Jersey	Requires U.S. domestic materials to be used unless their cost is "unreasonable."
New York	Restricts use of foreign products through general specifications for bids.
North Carolina	Follows a policy of purchasing domestic products "wherever we deem we are not penalizing ourselves as to competition, availability, service and ultimate cost."
North Dakota	Requires certain bids to carry the phrase "bid domestically produced material only."
Oklahoma	Requires purchases of domestic goods and equipment unless a foreign product is of "equal quality" and also "substantially cheaper" or is of "substantially superior quality" and is sold at a "comparable price" to domestic products.
Pennsylvania	Prevents use in state projects of foreign steel and aluminum products made in countries that "discriminate" against American products.
South Dakota	Writes state specifications for American-made products; if foreign made is bid, award is made on condition of acceptance by the state agency.
Wyoming	Generally discourages use of foreign goods.

Source: Norman S. Fieleke, "The Buy-American Policy of the United States Government," *New England Economic Review,* July/August 1969.

ing cash into the hands of government officials or their representatives is long-standing and is defended by many business executives as the only way they can compete effectively abroad.[22]

One businessman in Africa said in an interview, "You have to pay small bribes, called 'dash,' to get anything done. It's part of the price of visas, getting customs clearance on materials—even getting your suitcase . . ."

An executive of a United States-controlled multinational electronics group in Western Europe stated:

> To do business in . . . European countries, you have to render all sorts of favors, including outright bribery.
>
> It's up to your ingenuity to disguise such practices in reports to your board and in financial statements . . . Don't expect company headquarters to give you any instructions on how to handle such situations. You are completely on your own—just keep the sales performance going up.[23]

Nevertheless, such practices violate the mores and established modes of conduct in the United States, even though it is not a violation of American law to bribe an official of a foreign government. Also, the payments of the bribes may run afoul of federal laws and regulations requiring American corporations to keep adequate records and to make adequate disclosure to their shareholders and the public. A following chapter deals with the new and expanded enforcement of federal financial regulations that have resulted in good measure from the extremely adverse public reaction to the reports of business bribery overseas.

The federal government also may be participating with other national governments in developing a code of international business behavior. American-based and other multinational corporations thus may find their operations increasingly subject to the rules set by such international bodies as the United Nations and the European Economic Community (EEC). The EEC has been reviewing guidelines for a comprehensive communitywide policy toward multinationals. The following aspects are being considered for inclusion in such a policy:

> Protection of employees in mergers.
> Creation of rules on stock exchange operations and investment funds.
> Cooperation between and amalgamation of national stock exchange authority.
> International cooperation and assistance regarding information, monitoring, and taxes.
> Drawing up a joint schedule of license fees and intracompany pricing.
> Establishment of a body of law on groups of companies.

[22] Michael C. Jensen. "U.S. Company Payoffs Way of Life Overseas," *New York Times,* May 5, 1975, p. 1.
[23] Ibid., p. 52.

Improvement of information-gathering on the international activities of multinationals.[24]

Individual foreign nations also may adopt approaches developed by such voluntary agencies as the Organization for Economic Cooperation and Development, of which the United States is a member. Unlike the United States, several Western European governments are requiring that companies located in their countries appoint one or more labor union representatives to their boards of directors. In West Germany, employees are equally represented, at least in theory, with shareholders on the supervisory boards of the approximately 650 companies with more than 2,000 employees. The supervisory boards in turn choose the management boards that actually oversee company operations.

The restrictions to be imposed on multinational firms may vary from limiting the transfer of funds to equalizing tax burdens or to controlling the international transfer of technology. In the latter case, guidelines may be set as to the minimum amount of research and development work that must be performed in a developing country, together with requirements for training indigenous personnel for technical and managerial positions.

The increasing cost to American-based companies of regulations that are and will be imposed will make their competitive position more difficult, especially in relation to foreign firms that can produce without these government restrictions. Stronger efforts will be made, via international organizations, to get other nations to adopt the high environmental and safety standards that prevail in the United States. Although such efforts may have some limited success, they are not likely to offset entirely the adverse international competitive effects of the United States government's regulation of industry.

APPENDIX: THE MARLIN TOY CASE*

In 1972, the U.S. Food and Drug Administration banned two toys produced by the Marlin Toy Company of Horicon, Wisconsin, as hazardous substances and included them in published banned products lists. This led to the company changing the products so as to eliminate the unsafe features and thus to qualify for removal from the ban list. After taking over administration of the Federal Hazardous Substances Act, the U.S. Consumer Product Safety Commission continued FDA's practice of periodically publishing such lists. In a list published on October 1, 1973, the Commission inaccurately listed the toys as still hazardous. Marlin claimed to have lost many thousands of dollars in sales

---

[24]"Whither Multinationals?," *European Community*, February 1974, pp. 19–22.

*The material in this case is taken from Comptroller General of the United States, *Banning of Two Toys and Certain Aerosol Spray Adhesives*, MWD–75–65, (Washington, D.C.: U.S. General Accounting Office, 1975) pp. 4–12.

because of the Commission's action. The Commission acknowledged its mistake to Marlin in October 1973, and stated that it would include a retraction on its next published list. But it did not publish another banned products list containing a retraction until June 1, 1974, eight months after the error.

Banning of Marlin Toys

As part of a toy safety survey in October 1972, FDA representatives in St. Louis identified Marlin's "flutter ball" toy as a possible mechanical hazard under the Hazardous Substances Act and acquired a sample for testing. Flutter ball was a transparent plastic ball with toy butterflies mounted on a rod and small plastic pellets. Both the rod and the pellets moved freely inside the ball.

FDA's Bureau of Product Safety tested the flutter ball on October 30, 1972, and found that the toy presented an unreasonable risk of injury or illness to children because it could be easily broken or shattered, creating the danger of inhaling, swallowing, or choking on the pellets. On November 1, 1972, FDA banned the toy as a mechanical hazardous substance.

The Hazardous Substances Act states that an article may be determined to present a mechanical hazard

> . . . if, in normal use or when subjected to reasonably foreseeable damage or abuses, its design or manufacture presents an unreasonable risk of personal injury or illness (1) from fracture, fragmentation, or disassembly of the article, (2) from propulsion of the article (or any part or accessory thereof), (3) from points or other protrusions, surfaces, edges, openings, or closures, . . . (7) because the article (or any part or accessory thereof) may be aspirated or ingested, (8) because of instability, or (9) because of any other aspect of the article's design or manufacture.

The act prohibits banned hazardous substances from being delivered in interstate commerce and authorizes several methods, including seizure, fines, and imprisonment, for removing them from the marketplace. Through formal rulemaking procedures (including such due process provisions as public hearings and public notice), FDA issued regulations for manufacturers, distributors, and retailers to follow in complying with the act (21 C.F.R. 191). Because such regulations had been issued, the toys were banned immediately after FDA determined that they did not conform to those regulations. Such immediate actions are authorized under the act.

On November 1, 1972, FDA notified Marlin that its flutter ball and any similar toys with like hazards were banned from interstate commerce and that any banned toys remaining in the market were subject to regulatory action, including seizure. In a subsequent meeting at Marlin's plant, FDA representatives learned that a similar Marlin toy—"birdie ball"—could also be hazardous. Birdie ball was basically the same as flutter ball, except it contained plastic birds instead of butterflies.

Late in November 1972, FDA obtained three samples of each ball to test before possibly seizing the balls as banned toys. Both types failed FDA's tests. On December 5, 1972, FDA notified Marlin that birdie ball had failed the test and that both balls were banned under the Federal Hazardous Substances Act.

After expressing displeasure and resistance to FDA's decision, Marlin agreed to modify the balls in stock and production, but hesitated to recall those already distributed. Marlin stated that it would be an extreme financial hardship to recall those balls already distributed because it reportedly manufactured an estimated five million flutter and birdie balls during the previous 12 years. After Marlin's continued resistance to recalling the toys, FDA initiated seizure action and seized 88 balls from the marketplace.

Early in January 1973, shortly after the seizure, Marlin informed FDA that the two toys had failed the FDA tests because a supplier substituted an inferior grade of transparent plastic than Marlin had used to make the balls. Marlin subsequently informed FDA that it was recalling defective balls it had distributed and was excluding plastic pellets from future balls produced. Marlin said that flutter and birdie balls made with the higher grade transparent plastic and without pellets would pass FDA tests.

Since Marlin planned to continue marketing balls similar to, but not the same as, the ones banned, Marlin and FDA agreed that the banned toys would be listed as those *with* plastic pellets to distinguish them from those that were not banned (those *without* plastic pellets). The record does not show whether FDA tested the balls with the higher grade transparent plastic.

Inaccurate Listing of Marlin Toys

To inform manufacturers, distributors, retailers, and consumers of banned products, FDA periodically published lists of products that it had banned. These lists include the products' names, the manufacturers' names and addresses, the reasons for banning, and the dates banned. FDA intended to publish monthly lists of all products banned the previous month and semiannual lists of all products banned during the preceding six months. Although this plan was not followed precisely, FDA published six banned products lists before the transfer of its functions under the Hazardous Substances Act to the Consumer Product Safety Commission in May 1973.

The Marlin balls appeared on FDA monthly lists issued in November 1972 (flutter ball) and January 1973 (birdie ball)—those issued after the banning of each ball. These lists properly labeled the toys as flutter ball and birdie ball, without any reference to plastic pellets. Both lists were issued before Marlin and FDA had agreed that future lists would specify that the ban pertained only to those balls with plastic pellets.

FDA added a note to the banned products list of February 1, 1973, stating that the only versions of flutter and birdie balls classified as banned hazardous substances were "those containing pellets." Future lists including flutter and birdie ball entries were to list the two banned balls as those with plastic pellets.

On October 1, 1973, the Consumer Product Safety Commission published a cumulative list of products banned since FDA began its toy safety program in December 1970, including Marlin's flutter and birdie balls. Both balls were inaccurately described. Flutter ball was listed without any notation concerning plastic pellets, and birdie ball was listed as " 'Birdie Ball' (without plastic pellets)," the opposite of what was intended.

On October 17, 1973, Marlin representatives informed the Commission of the errors in the October 1 list. It was Marlin's understanding that after six months a banned toy would no longer appear on the list. Further, Marlin claimed to have lost many thousands of dollars in business because of the Commission's actions, and believed it was entitled to some form of compensation.

The Commission acknowledged its inaccurate listing of birdie ball, agreeing that the toy should have been described as those with plastic pellets. It did not specifically acknowledge the inaccurate listing of flutter ball until the retraction was published. The Commission said it would include a retraction in the next list. However, it did not have an anticipated publication date. The next list, published on June 1, 1974, included a retraction stating that the only versions of birdie and flutter balls that had been banned were those with plastic pellets.

The Commission informed Marlin that the inaccurate listing was "an editorial error." The Commission staff explained that the inaccurate listing resulted from several factors. The manually prepared note in FDA's banned products list (February 1, 1973) was not picked up in the Commission's computer-prepared list on October 1, 1973. There was a major change in personnel responsible for preparing the list. Moreover, Commission staff did not discover the error when proofreading the October list before printing.

The Commission told Marlin that the cumulative banned products list (October 1, 1973) was issued because some previously banned toys were still on the market. The Commission pointed out that, although banned products are removed from production, they still might be in retail stores. Also, the originally designed version of a banned product is banned permanently, but a redesigned product would not be banned unless found to be hazardous through further testing.

The Commission informed Marlin that confusion might have arisen about a product appearing on the list for only six months. To help clarify the matter, the Commission told Marlin that FDA had planned to publish banned products lists each month and a cumulative list semiannually. Thereafter, items would remain banned but would not appear on new published lists. Marlin representatives may have interpreted this as meaning that the banned products would be listed for only six months.

The Commission gave Marlin no explanation for its delay in publishing a banned products list containing a retraction or for not publishing a separate retraction. Subsequently Commission staff told investigators of the General Accounting Office that the major reason for the delay was that, knowing of other errors, the Commission wanted to scrutinize and purify the list to improve its accuracy and usefulness. Banned products were to be more clearly identified, and reasons for their banning more fully explained.

The Commission wrote Marlin two letters—one in November 1973 and another in March 1974—acknowledging its error and explaining its intention to publish a retraction in the next banned products list. Publishing a separate retraction was not considered economical because of the wide distribution of the banned products list of October 1, 1973—about 240,000 copies—and the Commission's belief that a retraction in the next issue would be sufficient. Commission representatives also told the government investigators that Marlin could have used the Commission's letters to Marlin to inform its customers of the Commission's error and intention to publish a retraction. Although it did not tell that to Marlin, the Commission believed that Marlin was responsible for informing its customers of the error and the planned retraction. The Commission rejected Marlin's request for reimbursement because it did not have the authority to make such compensation payments. Marlin's recourse was to file a claim in the United States Court of Claims.

In a letter to the Commission dated May 6, 1974, Marlin said that it was forced out of the toy business because the two balls were inaccurately listed. According to Marlin, 40 percent of its business was from sales of flutter and birdie balls, and the Commission's November 1973 letter acknowledging the error and planning a retraction was "too little and too late." Marlin requested that the Commission permit it to sue and let the courts determine whether and to what extent the Commission was liable.

Lack of Procedures For Retracting Inaccurate Information

Since that episode, the Commission's Bureau of Compliance has installed procedures to upgrade the banned products list through controls and other verification practices. Commission officials believe these prepublication controls should eliminate inaccurate lists. The Commission, however, has not established any policy, regulations, or procedures for insuring prompt retractions.

Recognizing that the Commission may err in attempting promptly to advise the public of its activities to protect consumers from hazardous products, section 6(b) of the Consumer Product Safety Act requires it to retract erroneously published data. Section 6(b) states:

If the Commission finds that, in the administration of this Act, it has made public disclosure of inaccurate or misleading information which reflects adversely upon the safety of any consumer product, or the practices of any manufacturer, private labeler, distributor, or retailer of consumer products, it shall, in a manner similar to that in which such disclosure was made, publish a retraction of such inaccurate or misleading information.

The Hazardous Substances Act does not contain a similar provision. Therefore, although the banned products list of June 1, 1974 included a retraction, the Commission was not legally bound to issue retractions of information published in this case because the two balls were banned under the older law. However, in practice the Commission does attempt to follow the spirit and intent of section 6(b) in retracting any inaccurate or misleading information published under any of the acts that it administers.

Commission officials say that publishing separate retractions in most cases would not be economically justified, and that publishing a retraction in the next issue of the list would be sufficient. Unsatisfied manufacturers could go to the courts for relief.

The Consumer Product Safety Commission, subsequent to this case, has indicated that it would be willing to send any manufacturer or other concerned party a retraction letter explaining an inaccurate listing and expressing the Commission's intent to publish a retraction in the next list. The manufacturer could use such a letter to inform its customers of the error and planned retraction. Commission representatives believe it would be the manufacturer's, and not the Commission's, responsibility to disseminate the letter to the customers—and presumably to request such a letter in the first place.

Although a letter written to a manufacturer would be beneficial, this retraction method is, of course, weaker than section 6(b) of the Consumer Product Safety Act. That law provides that the retraction be issued in "the same manner" as the original inaccurate statement.

Pending Litigation

In June 1974, two bills (S. 3666 and H.R. 15403) were introduced in the 93d Congress that would provide for the payment of an unstated amount to Marlin in settlement of its claim for the erroneous description of its toys in the banned products list. Senate and House resolutions (S. Res. 344 and H. Res. 1181) referred the two bills to the chief commissioner of the United States Court of Claims to determine the facts in this matter. Marlin filed a petition for its claim in the Court of Claims on October 11, 1974.

The Consumer Product Safety Commission was given an opportunity to comment on the bills and resolutions. On July 19, 1974, in letters to the House and Senate Committees on the Judiciary, it said that the two balls were inaccurately listed in the October 1, 1973 list. The Commission urged that Marlin be given an opportunity to prove its reported financial losses in the Court of Claims.

The Commission's recommendation, however, included a three-part quali-fication: The Commission's general support of the bills was not to be interpreted to mean that it generally favored relief for any company claiming to have been damaged by a Commission action. By supporting the bills, it did not admit its liability but felt that Marlin should have the opportunity to prove such liability in the Court of Claims because of the particular circumstances of this case. The Commission also suggested that the wording of the bills be revised to explain more correctly the nature of Marlin's claim—that the two balls were inaccurately described, not that they were erroneously included, on the list.

Conclusions

It would appear that the Federal Hazardous Substances Act was appropriately applied in banning Marlin's flutter and birdie balls as hazardous substances be-cause FDA's interpretation of its test results showed that the two Marlin balls met the requirements for banning unsafe products. Due process was served with the publication and application of formal regulations before the banning.

The Consumer Product Safety Commission's subsequent description of the two balls in the October 1, 1973 list was an error that took eight months to retract. The Commission acknowledged to Marlin its mistake and expressed its intentions to publish a retraction in the next list. However, it did not publish a retraction until June 1, 1974. Alternative retraction methods were discounted as being uneconomical even though Marlin informed the Commission that the in-accurate listing resulted in substantial financial loss.

The Commission's subsequent actions to strengthen its controls over the publication of banned products lists should better ensure the accuracy of future lists and thus reduce the potential for inflicting undue financial hardship on manufacturers. No case similar to the Marlin incident was reported in the follow-ing two years. However, the Commission had not established a formal policy to guide it in making timely and appropriate retractions of inaccurate or misleading information. Such procedures could reduce the hardships on manufacturers, the government's possible financial liability, and court actions that might arise from publicly disclosing erroneous or misleading information. In practice, it would seem that the substantial adverse public and Congressional reaction to the Marlin case did have a positive impact on the operating procedures of a relatively new regulatory agency.

In its report to the Congress, the General Accounting Office urged that the Consumer Product Safety Commission establish a formal policy, regulations, and procedures for timely retracting of inaccurate or misleading information that is publicly disclosed under any of the acts it administers.

Chapter 14

Impacts on Company Staffs

Company staffs bear much of the responsibility for company response to government regulation. This added function is especially evident in such areas as personnel, finance, and facilities. Effects of regulation can range from who a firm can hire or fire to what a company must tell its stockholders, including how often and in what form the information must be communicated. Increasing controls over land use and requirements for comprehensive, complex environmental impact statements limit the physical alternatives for expansion and add new environmental parameters to the decision to relocate or enlarge existing facilities.

PERSONNEL FUNCTIONS

Federal regulatory agencies increasingly are affecting most of the important aspects of company personnel policies and practices: hiring, promoting, and training activities; employee testing; compensation, including fringe benefits; the composition and funding of pension plans; the physical working environment; and basic work relationships, such as discipline, job termination, union negotiation, and communicating with employees.

In some cases, a government agency has authority to approve or disapprove company actions (for example, qualification of company pension contributions as a tax deduction). In numerous other situations involving requirements that range from equal employment opportunity to the health and safety aspects of the job, federal agencies can file legal charges against companies and seem disposed to do so with growing frequency (see Table 14–1).

To some extent, the importance of these government policies is reflected in the internal evaluation of company personnel. For example, some corporations now rate supervisors for their performance in meeting federal equal employment policies.

The General Electric Company, through a reporting system begun in 1968 which accompanies the annual review of a manager's performance and through a penalty-reward policy linked to executive compensation, has increased minority employment at all levels by 57 percent.[1] GE thus requires its managers to give priority to a thoughtful examination of the numbers of women and minorities supervised, whether that number is representative of local population or labor supply, plans for training these individuals for promotions, and the like. The results of GE's efforts can be seen in Table 14–2. In 1974, GE stated its policy evidencing the importance it accords equal employment considerations:

> Goals should be definitely established and a measurement and audit process for the achievement of these goals be put in place with an appropriate reward and penalty system for each foreman, supervisor, or manager who has the responsibility for hiring and terminating employees.[2]

Training and Recruitment

The widening array of government regulatory legislation is requiring corporate personnel departments to expand their existing orientation programs and to establish new programs. Training to meet new occupational safety and health requirements is particularly important.[3] Foremen need to be highly trained in many aspects of safety and health. Skills that must be taught vary from the ability to administer first aid to the leadership capability necessary to convince employees to use personal protective equipment continually (as we have discussed, the company often is liable if its employees do not use required safety devices).

Companies often need to use outside resources to meet the new training requirements. For example, at seminars held at seven universities in the summer

---

[1] Theodore V. Purcell, "How GE Measures Managers in Fair Employment," *Harvard Business Review,* November–December 1974, p. 99.

[2] Ibid., p. 104.

[3] U.S. Occupational Safety and Health Administration, *Training Requirements of the Occupational Safety and Health Standards* (Washington, D.C.: U.S. Government Printing Office, 1973); Timothy Larkin, "The Audiometric Assistant: New Recruit in the War Against Noise," *Job Safety and Health,* June 1974, pp. 20–24.

Table 14-1

FEDERAL INFLUENCE ON COMPANY PERSONNEL ACTIVITIES

Federal Agency	Employment	Training and Promotion	Compensation and Fringe Benefits	Working Relationships	Physical Environment
National Labor Relations Board	□	□	□	□	□
Equal Employment Opportunity Commission	□○	□○	□○	□	□
Federal Contract Compliance Office	□	□	□○	□	□
Wage and Hour Division			□○		
Internal Revenue Service			■○		
Occupational Safety and Health Administration		□		□	□○

□ = Federal agency can file charges

■ = Federal agency can approve or disapprove

○ = Federal agency receives reports

Table 14-2

EMPLOYMENT OF WOMEN AND MINORITIES, GENERAL ELECTRIC COMPANY, 1968 AND 1973

Job categories	All employees			Women			Minorities		
	December 1968	December 1973	Percent increase	December 1968	December 1973	Percent increase	December 1968	December 1973	Percent increase
Officials & managers	23,024	26,486	15.0	119	473	297.5	195	678	247.7
Professionals	53,624	44,905	-16.3	1,289	2,020	56.7	1,068	1,902	78.1
Technicians	19,846	15,377	-22.5	1,742	1,473	-15.5	726	964	32.8
Sales workers	4,599	7,622	65.7	336	595	77.1	79	362	358.2
Office & clerical	40,807	36,301	-11.1	28,898	27,068	- 6.3	1,844	3,558	93.0
Craftsmen	53,802	57,215	6.3	801	1,367	70.7	2,340	3,791	62.0
Operatives	88,910	101,099	13.7	41,869	46,856	11.9	11,182	18,703	67.3
Laborers	23,745	19,193	-19.2	8,663	8,869	2.4	3,489	3,385	-3.0
Service workers	3,689	3,011	-18.4	424	657	55.0	660	572	-13.3
Total	312,046	311,209	- 0.3	84,141	89,378	6.2	21,583	33,915	57.1

Source: Theodore V. Purcell, "How GE Measures Managers in Fair Employment," Harvard Business Review, November–December 1974.

of 1974 on the new consumer product safety laws, safety, legal, insurance, and product liability experts briefed corporate executives.

Greater numbers of specialized personnel are being hired—safety directors and engineers, industrial hygienists, in-house medical staffs, and material buyers with special knowledge of protective clothing and nonhazardous equipment. Moreover, because required reports and applications, such as environmental impact statements, necessitate inputs from many disciplines, companies are finding that they must either increase the array of experts on their own staffs or receive more expert opinions via consulting arrangements. These specialists are involved in such fields as ecology, economics, sociology, geology, climate, engineering, mining, forestry, and aquatic life, as well as in public communications. Businesses also use specialized consulting services, both to provide advice on meeting CPSC and OSHA standards, and to provide more health services to employees (for example, periodic examinations and return-to-work checkups).[4]

One issue of the *New York Times* (August 31, 1975) contained a variety of "help wanted" advertisements for positions that seem either to have been established or expanded as a result of requirements imposed by governmental regulatory agencies. A sampling follows:

> *Chief Toxicologist* . . . Responsibilities will include . . . a knowledge of state and federal laws, FDA regulations. . . .
>
> *Manager, Government Relations.* Assist on projects related to activities of federal agencies and congressional committees.
>
> *Manager, Toxicology/EPA Liaison* . . . this newly created position will be responsible for all dealings with the EPA and other governmental regulatory agencies regarding the registration of products; liaison between top management, research management, and the regulatory agencies. . . .
>
> *Tax Accountant* . . . experience in the preparation of corporate federal, state, and local tax returns. Responsibilities also include . . . various FTC and census reports.
>
> *Speech Writer* . . . to work with the chairman of the board . . . experience could have been gained through government, corporate or in free-lance practice.
>
> *Licensing Engineer.* Position involves coordination of various technical activities leading to the timely attainment of all licenses and permits needed from federal, state, and local regulatory agencies . . . will be directly involved in meetings with federal, state and local regulatory agency personnel. Will participate in public hearings.
>
> *Noise Control Engineer* . . . Environmental Impact Assessment. . . .

The personnel requirements associated with the equal employment opportunity program have led to the establishment of companies specializing in helping other companies attain their affirmative action goals. The *Affirmative Action*

---

[4]See Research Media, Inc., *Introduction to OSHA: A Complete Training Program,* Hicksville, N.Y., 1974.

Register, for example, provides—for a fee—a service whereby vacancies are brought to the attention of minority and female job candidates.

Equal Opportunity

Personnel departments, as well as supervision at all levels, are placing more emphasis on meeting federal equal employment opportunity and affirmative action requirements (see Figure 14–1). The importance of equal employment opportunity considerations, and their at times turbulent effects, is vividly displayed by statements of the general counsel of one very large organization after watching the bored reactions of a group of middle managers to a discussion of nondiscrimination laws.[5]

> Gentlemen, including back pay awards, this company has already spent hundreds of thousands of dollars on preparing, defending, and *losing* nondiscrimination cases in the federal courts. We do not intend to continue to do so.
>
> This meeting was called to tell you what the laws require. The attorneys on the other side are likely to be very able. And we now know that the courts intend to enforce these laws fully.
>
> If *you* do not expect to comply with all the nondiscrimination laws, consider this to be fair warning. You will be fired.

A "catch-up phase" is resulting in the need to train minority group candidates to enhance their opportunities for promotion to higher job levels. Equal employment regulations are being expanded to cover women, handicapped workers, and veterans. In a series of decisions, the courts levied substantial fines on companies that were held to discriminate against women and older workers in hiring, training, promotion, and firing practices. Meeting charges of discrimination against older workers during a general layoff can prove difficult, especially where supervisors have been preparing uniformly favorable or innocuous annual evaluations of their employees.

Companies holding federal contracts valued at $500,000 or more are now required to report on their treatment of handicapped applicants. The courts have clearly defined the only acceptable reason for discrimination as "business necessity." But this is a narrowly and rigidly defined "out." As stated in a United States Court of Appeals decision:

> Thus, the business purpose must be sufficiently compelling to override any racial impact; the challenged practice must effectively carry out the business purpose it is alleged to serve; and there must be available no accept-

[5]Ruth G. Shaeffer, *Nondiscrimination in Employment: Changing Perspectives, 1963–1972* (New York: The Conference Board, 1973), p. 3.

Could you be practicing illegal job discrimination— and not even know it?

Answer: True. Due to outdated policies or failure to understand the law, many employers do discriminate in the way they hire, fire, promote or pay.

Take this 30-second test and see where you stand.

An employer...	True	False
1. can refuse to hire women who have small children at home.	____	____
2. can generally obtain and use an applicant's arrest record as the basis for non-employment.	____	____
3. can prohibit employees from conversing in their native language on the job.	____	____
4. whose employees are mostly white or male, can rely solely upon word-of-mouth to recruit new employees.	____	____
5. can refuse to hire women to work at night, because it wishes to protect them.	____	____
6. may require all pregnant employees to take leave of absence at a specified time before delivery date.	____	____
7. may establish different benefits - pension, retirement, insurance and health plans for male employees than for female employees.	____	____
8. may hire only males for a job if state law forbids employment of women for that capacity.	____	____
9. need not attempt to adjust work schedules to permit an employee time off for a religious observance.	____	____
10. only disobeys the Equal Employment Opportunity laws when it is acting intentionally or with ill motive.	____	____

<u>Answers:</u> The answers to 1 to 10 above are false. The Equal Employment Opportunity Act makes it against the law for an employer to discriminate on the basis of race, religion, color, sex or national origin. It's a tough law, with teeth, but most Americans think it is a very fair law. Yet unfair practices continue — in big business and in small. So, if you are in private industry, state or local government, or educational institutions, it is your business to know your rights and obligations. Contact your local EEOC office, listed in the phone book under U.S. Government or write to us in Washington, D.C.

**Equal Employment Opportunity.
It's the law.
It's right.
And your key to a better employee.**

The Equal Employment Opportunity Commission Washington, D.C. 20506

Figure 14-1

TYPICAL PERSONNEL POSTER PREPARED FOR INDUSTRY
BY GOVERNMENT

able alternative policies or practices which would better accomplish the business purpose advanced, or accomplish it equally well with a lesser differential racial impact.[6]

Hiring and promotion decision-making processes are increasingly scrutinized by government agencies. In New York State, for example, preemployment physical examinations must abide by the requirements of the Human Rights Law. It must be demonstrated that any minimum physical standards adopted by a company are reasonably necessary for the work to be performed. The standards also must be uniformly applied to all applicants for the particular job category. General questions, such as "Do you have a disability?," are considered unlawful. Questions must be limited to those specific disabilities that relate to a particular job to be performed.[7]

Commenting on the personnel requirements that EEO has imposed on the Bell System, the affirmative action officer of another telephone system stated that Bell no longer has EEO goals. "They have quotas that have been mandated by the government. If they don't meet specific quotas—numbers of women and minority members hired and promoted—within a specific time period, the pressure and the fines will be laid on even more heavily." The officer went on to describe the adverse effects that can result:

Any time a company gets itself in that kind of situation—one of dealing with numbers instead of people—bad things begin to happen. Suddenly, the time that's necessary to develop and train a minority group person for higher level positions isn't available any more. That's when the old cliché about EEO being a program that puts people into jobs they're not qualified for becomes true.[8]

Many of the people concerned with affirmative action programs may need to be reminded of the ultimate goal of such efforts, as so ably stated by Rafer Johnson, a black officer of the Continental Telephone Company, whose responsibilities include the equal employment opportunity program:

We—and I'm talking about the country as well as the company—must get to the point where both the person being considered for a job and the person doing the considering are making decisions based strictly on the skills and potential that person can bring to his employer. EEO will be a

---

[6]*Robinson v. Lorillard Corporation,* U.S. Court of Appeals, Fourth Circuit (Richmond), 444 F.2d 791 (1971).

[7]"Discrimination for Disability," *Industrial Relations,* New York State Chamber of Commerce and Industry Bulletin, July 9, 1975, p. 1.

[8]"The Meaning Behind the Words," *Continental System Communicator,* June 1975, p. 10.

complete success only when the color or race or creed or sex of a potential employee becomes no more than an afterthought.[9]

The Rehabilitation Act of 1973 does strongly imply that the employer must make "reasonable" accommodations to the mental and physical limitations of the handicapped. The law does not seem to require a company to utilize a significantly less effective job design so that a disabled worker can be hired. But, according to Professor Richard Deane of Georgia Tech, in some cases an employer may be expected to restructure jobs slightly to accommodate a handicapped worker. This shows a good faith effort to use the skills of the handicapped. The failure to offer any accommodations at all for the handicapped worker may subject the company to charges of discrimination.[10]

Innovative job designs may include using special fixtures to aid the arm movements of paralysis victims, replacement of foot controls with hand controls (or vice versa), and use of alternate sensory devices for blind workers.

Medical Care

Recent and prospective federal health insurance legislation will further complicate the job of personnel departments in administering fringe benefits. In addition, company personnel costs have increased substantially. Most of the proposed national health insurance plans before Congress would require employers to pay the largest part of the increased costs in the form of required payments to health insurance carriers.

The Health Maintenance Organization (HMO) Act, approved in December 1973, requires all companies employing 25 people or more to offer their employees membership in an HMO, if a qualified one is available as an alternative to the company's conventional medical insurance plan. HMOs provide almost total health care for a fixed monthly fee.

Companies that cover all of their employee health costs have an especially large stake in evaluating the quality and effectiveness of HMOs—particularly HMO claims concerning long-run cost savings. Even though the existing law states that no employer need contribute more for the HMO than he or she does for the existing health package, some unions are likely to press for higher employer payments to make up all or part of the difference. On the other hand, the HMO emphasis on preventive medicine ultimately may result in savings to employers because of reduced downtime and workmen's compensation costs.[11]

Since the employer must offer both the HMO and conventional hospital

[9]Ibid., p. 11.

[10]Richard H. Deane, "The IE's role in Accommodating the Handicapped," *Industrial Engineering,* July 1975, p. 17.

[11]"HMO: A Health Care Option Your Firm Will Have to Offer," *Industry Week,* February 4, 1974, pp. 20–22.

insurance options if both are available, personnel officers must learn two approaches to health financing. Moreover, they need to instruct employees concerning the different plans. Some corporations may follow the example of the Kaiser Plan and start their own HMOs, either for their employees alone or as profit-making ventures. Others may provide start-up money for nonprofit HMOs sponsored by unions, employer groups, hospitals, or doctors. (These health organizations may provide a special market for the firm's products, such as computers and office supplies.)

Pension Plans

The federal income tax system continues to be a means through which the federal government requires company pension plans to meet ever more stringent national standards. Moreover, the 1974 pension reform law requires that up to 30 percent of a company's net assets be available to meet its pension program liabilities. The percentage is likely to be raised rather than lowered by subsequent amendments. In addition, the pension law inundates employers with additional reporting requirements (see Table 14–3). One impact of these increased costs and liabilities will be that some employers, especially those in smaller and/or new companies, will be discouraged from setting up retirement programs.[12]

Unfunded pension liabilities (the difference between the amount the corporation has set aside for pension benefits and the amount of its obligation if the pension plan were liquidated today) pose still another problem for many corporations. A study of 1,200 corporations showed their total unfunded pension liabilities exceeding $38 billion. General Motors had the largest such liability, $6.1 billion, with other automobile and steel manufacturers also having unfunded pension liabilities in the billions of dollars.[13] The new pension law requires employers to fund fully the yearly cost of their retirement program, and additional amounts must be contributed to amortize existing liabilities over a specified time period.

The new pension reform law is also altering the investment philosophy being followed. In many cases there is now more emphasis on a strategy that will minimize the legal liability on the manager of the portfolio. This is in contrast to the traditional approach of attempting to maximize the return on the pension contributions. The fear of legal consequences has also increased the documentation costs that the pension fund manager has to bear. The purchase of personal liability insurance has become more widespread for those in charge.[14]

[12]Cornell University, "Private Pensions and the Public Interest," *Industrial and Labor Relations Report,* Fall 1974, pp. 12–25.

[13]"Unfunded Pension Liability in Billions for Some Firms," *Money Manager,* July 14, 1975, p. 17.

[14]Shoya Zichy, "How Small Funds Are Coping With the New Pension Law," *Institutional Investor,* September 1975, pp. 19–20.

Table 14-3

REPORTING REQUIREMENTS OF THE EMPLOYEE RETIREMENT INCOME SECURITY ACT OF 1974

Reports to be filed with U.S. Department of Labor:

- Plan description, 120 days after the plan is subject to the reporting and disclosure provisions
- Summary plan description, 120 days after the plan is subject to the reporting and disclosure provisions
- Any change in plan description or material modification to plan, 60 days after its adoption
- Updated plan description at such times as the Secretary of Labor may require but no more frequently than once every 5 years
- Annual report, 210 days after the end of the plan year
- Certain terminal reports for plans winding up their affairs
- Plan documents and other information, if requested by the Secretary of Labor

Reports to be filed with the Pension Benefit Guaranty Corporation:

- Annual report, within 6 months after the end of plan year
- Intent to terminate, no later than 10 days before termination date
- Certain events that indicate financial adversity ahead, within 30 days after plan administrator knows or had reason to know of their occurrence
- Notification as soon as possible if any insufficiency develops after plan administrator has begun termination
- Such other reports as the corporation may require from a plan administrator who has initiated termination proceedings
- Notice of withdrawal of a substantial employer from a multiemployer plan, within 60 days

Reports to be filed with the Internal Revenue Service:

- Annual Registration Statement, listing employees separated from service of plan, for plans subject to vesting standards due as prescribed by regulation
- Notification of change of status, for plans subject to vesting standards, due as prescribed by regulation
- Annual return for certain pension and deferred compensation plans
- Actuarial statement of valuation for certain pension and deferred compensation plans, not less than 30 days before merger, consolidation, or transfer of assets or liabilities
- Actuarial report for defined benefit plans for the first year that new funding requirements apply and every third year thereafter, or within time prescribed by regulation

Source: Labor Management Service Administration, U.S. Department of Labor.

Wage Controls

Another aspect of federal regulation involving personnel departments is so-called incomes policy—intermittent and varying forms of federal restraint on wage increases. These actions generally occur in conjunction with federal price actions, discussed previously in the section "Marketing." As in the case of prices, federal involvement in wage decisions likely will be greater during the coming decade than it has been during the past ten years.

Recordkeeping

As a result of the federal controls described above, there are increasing requirements for recordkeeping and reporting on various aspects of employee characteristics and actions—including prehiring procedures and results of periodic physicals. Figure 14-2 shows an extract from the log of injuries and illnesses that OSHA requires employers to maintain. Many companies, particularly those with large work forces, find it useful to automate their personnel records. Personnel department staffs are expanding to meet the added federal requirements.[15]

The paper work burden imposed by the equal employment program on government contractors is becoming particularly heavy. All prime contractors or subcontractors having 50 or more employees and a contract of $50,000 are required to provide reports analyzing each job category to determine whether women and minority groups are being "underutilized." If this is found to be the case, the contractors must provide cogent explanations. The analyses are to cover such factors as pay, lines of job progression, and usual promotional sequences.

In addition to the new recordkeeping requirements for personnel departments, other corporate divisions are bearing added paper work burdens. Already noted are those connected with product recalls and health and pension plans. The requirements for more extensive information can be especially onerous for corporate finance departments. More staff, solely for recordkeeping, is often needed in divisions such as R&D or legal. Furthermore, some products or services may be discontinued and new lines not undertaken because the stringent recordkeeping requirements will make them too costly or simply unfeasible.

FINANCE FUNCTIONS

A fundamental impact of the federal government on company financial practices is that a rising share of the economy's investment funds are being funneled to business firms and other borrowers through government credit agencies. Thus, United States corporations are more frequently competing for money in credit markets dominated by federal financial institutions. During periods of extreme credit stringency, the federal government may resort to more direct

---

[15]U.S. Occupational Safety and Health Administration, *Recordkeeping Requirements* (Washington, D.C.: U.S. Government Printing Office, 1973); U.S. Department of Labor, *What Every Employer Needs to Know About OSHA Recordkeeping* (Washington, D.C.: U.S. Government Printing Office, 1973).

OSHA NO. 100

LOG OF OCCUPATIONAL INJURIES AND ILLNESSES

Form Approved
OMB NUMBER 44R 1453

Case or File no.	Date of injury or initial diagnosis of illness. If diagnosis of illness was made after first day of absence enter first day of absence (mo./day/yr.)	Employee's Name (First name, middle initial, last name)	Occupation of injured employee at time of injury or illness	Department to which employee was assigned at time of injury or illness	DESCRIPTION OF INJURY OR ILLNESS		EXTENT OF AND OUTCOME OF INJURY OR ILLNESS					
					Nature of injury or illness and part(s) of body affected (Typical entries for this column might be: Amputation of 1st joint right forefinger Strain of lower back Contact dermatitis on both hands Electrocution-body)	Injury or illness code See codes at bottom of page.	Fatalities	Lost Workday Cases		Nonfatal Cases Without Lost Workdays		
							Enter date of death (mo./day/yr.)	Enter workdays lost due to injury or illness (see instructions on back.)	If, after lost work-days, the employee was permanently transferred to another job or was terminated, enter a check in the column below	If no entry was made in columns 8 or 9, but the injury or illness did result in: Transfer to another job or termination, or; medical treatment, other than first aid, or; diagnosis of occupational illness, or loss of consciousness, or; restriction of work or motion; Enter a check in the column below	If a check in column 11 represented a transfer or termination, enter another check in column 12
1	2	3	4	5	6		7	8	9	10	11	12

Company Name _____

Establishment Name _____

Establishment Location _____

Art 14

Injury Code
10 All occupational injuries

Illness Codes
21 Occupational skin diseases or disorders
22 Dust diseases of the lungs (pneumoconioses)
23 Respiratory conditions due to toxic agents
24 Poisoning (Systemic effects of toxic materials)
25 Disorders due to physical agents (other than toxic materials)
26 Disorders due to repeated trauma
29 All other occupational illnesses

Figure 14-2

LOG OF OCCUPATIONAL INJURIES AND ILLNESSES

methods of rationing capital. It may establish a temporary "capital issues" committee to assure that available funds are channeled into uses that the government considers of highest priority. Another impact resulting from the government's increasing regulation of business financial activity and demands for more information on company operations is an increase in the size and budgets of financial departments.

Reporting

Government regulatory agencies are specifying in increasing detail the financial information that companies must provide to their shareholders and to the public.[16] Headquarters and divisional finance departments bear the brunt of demands for statistical information from federal regulatory agencies. Many such requests result from continued public distrust of private business. The greater amount of information, in turn, may make possible even more detailed regulation of business.

The FTC is attempting to obtain line-of-business sales and profits information from the nation's 345 largest businesses; 225 different lines of business categories have been established. The costs for a large corporation to set up the capability to fill out this one report are estimated at about $550,000.[17]

The FTC also is seeking data on outlays for advertising and sales promotion, and research and development. The probable resulting picture of industry competition is likely to enable the FTC and the Justice Department to pursue more effectively their antitrust cases against individual corporations. Conglomerates and other widely diversified corporations are likely to be particular targets of increased governmental litigation.

In addition to classifying sales and profits by product line, companies subject to SEC jurisdiction are required to show separately federal, state, local and foreign taxes. Partially in response to public concern over companies that report relatively low payments of United States corporate taxes, the SEC is ordering corporations that pay federal income taxes at a rate other than the standard 48 percent of profits to explain the difference. This requirement may be particularly burdensome to petroleum and other natural-resource-based companies granted depletion allowances and special tax incentives and to multinational corporations receiving credit for the income taxes they pay to other countries.

The SEC also requires companies to disclose more information about leasing, a measure especially affecting capital-intensive industries that lease such items as airplanes, railroad cars, nuclear fuel, and buildings. In the future, the

[16]Frank T. Weston, "Prepare for the Financial Accounting Revolution," *Harvard Business Review,* September–October 1974, pp. 6–8 *et. ff.*

[17]U.S. Senate, Committee on Government Operations, *Hearings on Corporate Disclosure* (Washington, D.C.: U.S. Government Printing Office, 1974), Part 2.

balance sheets for such companies will not look as attractive as they did without notation of such large contingent financial liabilities.

New Securities and Exchange Commission regulations have brought about substantial changes in the information provided in corporate annual reports. The SEC now requires that annual reports include:

> Certified financial statements for two fiscal years.
>
> A five-year summary of operations. The presentation must include sales, cost of goods sold, interest expense, taxes, earnings, dividends, and the effect of discontinued operations, extraordinary items, and accounting changes.[18]
>
> Management analysis, in plain English, of the financial information and the company's competitive position in its field.
>
> Operating information listed by line of business or classes of product.
>
> Identification of corporate officers and directors, including their outside business affiliations.
>
> Statement regarding the exchange or market where the stock is traded, market price ranges, and the dividends paid for at least the most recent two years.

In addition, the annual report must state that the 10-K report, the extensive financial statement required by the SEC, is available to any shareholder on request and without charge.

Quarterly reports seem to be the next target for SEC regulation. The agency is intent upon improving interim corporate reporting by requiring more auditor involvement in the preparation of the reports. One proposal under consideration would require that companies disclose more financial information, give explanations, and divulge sales information in their quarterly reports. Outside auditors also would be required to check the information. Several large brokerage firms have supported the SEC's effort to improve the quantity and quality of information in quarterly reports. Many corporations, however, have loudly objected to the increased auditing costs that would result. H. C. Knortz, executive vice-president and comptroller of International Telephone and Telegraph, estimates ITT's auditing costs could increase 25 percent. Other firms have estimated audit costs rising up to 50 percent.[19]

Companies are also being told to disclose the extent of "inventory profits"—the increase in apparent earnings that comes from the use of the FIFO (first-in, first-out) method of inventory accounting, whereby goods being currently sold are valued at historical cost rather than the higher replacement cost. Companies also may be required to provide a narrative statement on the "quality

---

[18]"An Open-Door Policy for Annual Reports," *Business Week*, May 12, 1975, p. 48.

[19]Kenneth H. Bacon, "Concerns Say New SEC Disclosure Rules Would Sharply Boost Auditing Expense," *Wall Street Journal*, March 18, 1975, p. 36.

of earnings," spelling out such factors as the effect of nonrecurring expense and revenue items on present and future earnings.

The discovery that several major American companies have engaged in payoffs to foreign governments and in illegal political contributions has prompted the SEC to push for disclosure on how corporations earn and spend their money. But the agency itself is faced with a dilemma over how far it should go in this effort. It faces the paradox that its actions to force disclosure of foreign payments in order to protect investors could have the opposite effect.[20] If the disclosure of a payoff leads to the nationalization of the foreign operations of a company, the stockholder is not likely to be overjoyed. In addition, many corporations deal with sensitive work of the Defense Department and the Central Intelligence Agency. Disclosures in these areas would be embarrassing, at the least, but could also raise questions of national security.

Specialized regulatory agencies are also enlarging their already substantial paper work requirements. The Federal Power Commission is expanding its reporting demands for electric utilities. Previously ordered to project their activities a month ahead, the companies are now required to forecast a year in advance and update these projections quarterly. The FPC is also considering requiring utilities to provide more information on ownership and indebtedness. Special changes include making each company list its top 30 stockholders and report them by institutional or individual name in addition to "street name" (brokerage house). There also may be a requirement that companies report holders of 5 percent or $500,000 or more of a utility's long-term debt issue.[21] Overall, such regulations will increase corporate overhead expenses and reduce the privacy of shareholders.

The Comptroller of the Currency requires that all national banks maintain, at headquarters, a current listing of the business affiliations of their directors and executive officers. Bank examiners will scrutinize the lists to determine instances of "self-dealing lending," thus reducing potentials for corporate conflicts of interest.

An effort is also under way to make compulsory many government questionnaires now answered on a voluntary basis. At present, almost all quarterly and monthly surveys by nonregulatory agencies such as the Census Bureau are voluntary. The Bureau of Labor Statistics has urged Congress to make as many as 10 of its surveys on prices, wages, and employment mandatory.

If companies must publish forecasts of their financial results, certain technical capabilities will have to be obtained or expanded. Executives will need to become more knowledgeable and informed about sophisticated forecasting techniques. Information systems will have to be developed so that publishable

[20]Kenneth H. Bacon, "Full-Disclosure Push by SEC on Companies Worries Some Critics," *Wall Street Journal,* May 15, 1975, p. 13.

[21]U.S. Federal Power Commission, *News Release 20207,* April 9, 1974, and *News Release 20238,* April 19, 1974.

forecasts can be prepared quickly and with minimum effort. Shareholders must be educated concerning proper interpretation of company forecasts and the accuracy and limitations of such information.[22]

Accounting

In the future, all divisions of a company selling goods and services to the federal government—not just those working on defense contracts—may be required to adhere to the expanding regulations of the Defense Cost Accounting Board. Some firms will economize on bookkeeping by adopting the board's concepts and procedures for all of their corporate accounting. Examination of the board's planned research efforts gives an indication of the future scope of this form of federal regulation of corporate accounting. These undertakings cover such fundamental accounting questions (not unique to government markets) as adjustments for price inflation, measurement of the cost of capital, records of deferred incentive compensation, and capitalizing leased equipment.

Credit Policies

Under new regulations relating to the Equal Credit Opportunity Act, retailers, banks, and others no longer will be able to discriminate on the basis of sex or marital status in the granting of credit. Still broader regulations barring discrimination in giving credit on the basis of race, color, religion, national origin, or age have been proposed.[23] Many of these considerations have been key factors in the point system used by numerous banks and retailers in determining who receives credit.

FACILITIES FUNCTIONS

Although the Congress has not yet enacted general land-use control legislation, some specific federal land-use statutes already are on the books. For example, section 208 of the Federal Water Pollution Control Act provides for the regulation of "the location, modification, and construction of any facilities that may have discharges. . . ." The Flood Disaster Protection Act of 1973 required that (by July 1975) all communities in areas officially designated as "flood-prone" enact new zoning and building codes.

---

[22]James D. Edwards and Carl S. Warren, "Management Forecasts: the SEC and Financial Executives," *MSU Business Topics,* Winter 1974, pp. 51–55.

[23]Eileen Shanahan, "Federal Rules Aim at Bias in Credit," *New York Times,* April 25, 1975, p. 1.

Federal legislation covering general land-use controls likely will be adopted within the next few years. Direct federal involvement probably will be limited to such critical aspects of facilities planning as intervention in power plant siting, deepwater port facilities, and surface mining. The states will play a large role in deciding such issues, which traditionally has been left to local decision-making. With the incentive of federal financial aid, statewide land-use laws are expected to focus on control of four types of development:

Shorelines, beaches, flood plains, historic sites, and other areas of environmental concern.

Airports, highway interchanges, frontage access streets, major recreational systems, and facilities for development, generation, and transmission of energy.

Regional public facilities or utilities.

Large scale developments, including land sales and land development projects.

More widespread federal land-use policies, often implemented at state and local levels, will restrict the discretion of corporate facilities departments in locating new factories, office buildings, warehouses, and distribution centers. To meet environmental regulations, the establishment of new facilities at times may have to be accompanied by some form of mass transportation, ranging from company-provided buses to publicly owned transit systems.

Future environmental impact analysis will involve more than preparing detailed analyses for governmental review (see Table 14–4). The process will also provide for greater community participation in determining whether the project should be built at a given location—particularly if considerable social and aesthetic consequences may result.[24]

In addition to examining the direct physical and economic impacts, environmental analyses increasingly deal with the indirect ("second order") effects, including the implications of the planned facility for regional development patterns; the effects on demand for housing and public utilities; and the possibility of further technological development that might have subsequent impacts. New emphasis also is being placed on how the benefits of the facility are to be distributed in the community, and especially how they will affect different economic, social, and ethnic groups. Thus, due to the comprehensive nature of these environmental impact statements, they have been both costly and time-consuming to prepare. Based on the experience of utility companies providing environmental impact statements for proposed facilities, the cost of the study for each facility would range from $300,000 to several million dollars.[25]

---

[24]Michael J. Walker, "The Impact of Environmental Impact Statements," *Management Review,* January 1974, pp. 25–29.

[25]Statement of Richard D. Godown on behalf of the National Association of Manufacturers before the Securities and Exchange Commission, 1975.

Table 14-4

RANGE OF REQUIRED ENVIRONMENTAL IMPACT ANALYSES FOR A TYPICAL RESIDENTIAL CONSTRUCTION PROJECT

Conditon to Be Examined	Existing Physical Environment—Natural and Man-Made	
	Required to Analyze	Example of an Analysis
Land and Climate	Soil (general characteristics, load bearing capacity, existing and potential erosion, permeability)	No special climatic, subsurface, or other unusual conditions.
	Topography (general characteristics, slope grade of site)	Soil—permeable, clayey.
	Subsurface conditions (geologic characteristics, geologic faults)	Topography—average, 3% slope.
	Special conditions: flood plain or other unique landscape features; potential for mudslide, subsidence, or earthquake; aerial or underground transmission lines and right-of-way	
	Unusual climatic conditions: subject to very high rainfall, flashfloods, hurricanes or tornadoes, strong winds, extremes of temperature, and so forth	
Vegetation, Wildlife, and Natural Areas	Extent and type of vegetation and wildlife; existence of on-site or proximity to unique natural systems (stream systems, wildlife breeding area, parks)	Site 50% covered with beech, oak, sassafras, and dogwood trees.
		Adjacent to 20-acre urban park.
Surrounding Land Uses and Physical Character of Area	Type of development (family or high-rise residential, industrial, commercial, open space, mixed); land use configuration; densities; building height and design; lot sizes	Mixed: single family, high-rise, and open space area.
		Density—about 60 dwelling units per acre in immediate site area.
Infrastructure	Water supply, sanitary sewage and solid waste disposal, storm sewers and drainage, energy, and transportation facilities (roads, public transit, parking) servicing site	Site controlled by city water system and sanitary and sewer system. There is ample capacity.
		Site on bus line and arterial street.
		Parking garage on same block.
		All electric project.

Table 14-4 (continued)

Condition To Be Examined	Required to Analyze	Example of an Analysis
	Existing Physical Environment—Natural and Man-Made	
Air Pollution Levels	Extent of pollution (smog, dust, odors, smoke, hazardous emissions) in relation to local/state standards, and standards of health and safety (frequency of inversions, air pollution alert, or emergency) and in relation to the rest of the metropolitan area (conditions peculiar to the site and immediate area)	No obvious dust, odors, or smoke in site area. Community does have smog alerts periodically throughout summer months.
Noise Levels	Source (nearby airport, railway, highway); noise levels in relation to HUD standards; vibrations	Project is not located in vicinity of airport or railroad. Project is on major arterial road, but noise exposure is minimal.
Water Pollution Levels	Ground and surface water relevant to site and area (drainage basin, source of water supply, water bodies with implications for health and recreation uses, and so forth)	No streams are on project site; there are no bodies of water nearby.
Community Facilities and Services	Description: general description; location; responsible organizations; relation of capacity to existing demand of schools, parks, recreational and cultural facilities; police and fire and health facilities servicing the site and area	Complete community facilities within walking distances of site, i.e., 200-bed hospital, library, museum, police, and fire station.
Employment Centers and Commercial Facilities	Employment centers and commercial facilities servicing site	Shopping center ¼ mile from site. Site is located 1-½ miles from downtown central business district.
Character of Community	Socioeconomic and racial characteristics	Immediate community is mainly white, 30% black, 4% Spanish-speaking, and 10% elderly. Community employees are about 50% professional (lawyers, bankers, and so forth) and 50% blue collar and clerical.
Existing Aesthetic Community	General aesthetic characteristics; special features (natural or man-made); existence on site or proximity to significant historic, archaeological, or architectural sites or property, including those listed on, or being considered for nomination to, the National Register of Historic Places; scenic areas and view	The Historic Society is across the street from the site.

Source: U.S. Department of Housing and Urban Development.

239

LEGAL AND CONSULTING STAFFS

The proliferation of regulatory agencies is enlarging the role of many corporate legal staffs and their outside law firms. Although many companies continue to rely heavily on private law firms, the role of house counsel is expanding as a result of the growing body of government laws and regulations affecting day-to-day business operations. The internal counsel can be particularly valuable in advising the various operating departments on how to conduct their affairs in accordance with ever-changing federal legal requirements. For example, increasing consumer product regulation is expanding the number of legal actions necessary to minimize company liability for products ruled to be unsafe or defective. Product liability insurance is being more widely used as the size and frequency of product safety suits rise.

For companies that are large users of the mail, particularly for advertising and direct marketing purposes, lengthy proceedings before the Postal Rate Commission are necessary at times. When Congress had responsibility for setting postal rates, mail rate proposals were handled by lobbyists. However, companies and their associations, such as the Direct Mail Marketing Association, now devote considerable legal resources to proceedings before the Commission, which may take a year or more to rule on a proposed rate increase.

The expansion in government control of business is also creating a growing market for consulting firms that can advise businesses on how to operate in the new regulatory environment, notably in pollution control and job safety. In response to suggestions by the Consumer Product Safety Commission, ad hoc associations are being established in industries where no trade organizations have existed so that industry standards may be developed that are acceptable to the Commission.

III

SHAPING THE BUSINESS-GOVERNMENT ENVIRONMENT

Chapter 15

Government Relations Functions

As government becomes more involved in day-to-day business activities, companies are expanding resources devoted to government relations. Virtually every company must develop the capability to know what present and future developments in the federal government relate to its activities. Firms of substantial size generally maintain Washington offices, while smaller companies rely primarily on their trade associations as well as on Washington-based attorneys and consultants. The full-time Washington representative is no longer limited to the major government contractors (for example, aerospace and electronics) or the closely regulated industries (such as transportation and drug manufacture).[1]

THE WASHINGTON REPRESENTATIVE

Most large corporations maintain one or more full-time representatives in the nation's capital. Their offices vary from one man plus a secretary to large operations with annual budgets of $250,000 or more. Large government contractors traditionally have maintained representation in Washington, and many commercially oriented firms, including medium-sized ones, are establishing a

[1]Paul Cherington and Ralph Gillen, *The Business Representative in Washington* (Washington, D.C.: Brookings Institution, 1962).

permanent presence in the capital. The expansion of government controls over business has led to "protective reaction" on the part of many companies that historically have had little knowledge of or direct relationship with the federal government.

Activities of Washington offices vary substantially according to the industry and markets served, the size of the firm, and tradition (see Table 15–1). One major company compares its Washington office to an embassy in that it follows and interprets actions of the federal government that have significant impact on it, helps to formulate positions on those actions, and serves as the principal channel for communicating the company's views to the government.[2] Five primary functions are often performed by Washington offices:

1. Supplying information to the home office.
2. Rendering services to visiting home office personnel.
3. Providing marketing assistance.
4. Providing legislative representation.
5. Supplying analyses of government programs and policies.

Supplying Information

Virtually all corporate offices established in the national capital provide a "listening post" for the home office. A constant flow of information is supplied to corporate officials on current government policies and on future plans and actions that might affect company operations. Although trade associations and industry publications are useful, at times a company's unique concerns best can be met by company personnel on the Washington scene. Some companies refer to this intelligence function as an "early warning" system.

Various communication channels are used. Representatives of some large companies prepare daily newsletters that are sent to senior executives in headquarters and operating divisions. Often information is passed along entirely by telephone, either because of urgency or because it is preferable not to maintain a written record on sensitive matters. The Washington office also may have day-to-day dealings with members of the government bureaucracy in order to follow up questions or complaints by company personnel on specific regulatory actions. A substantial amount of company information and views also may be provided to federal agencies. Such a "two-way street" relationship can help to provide a more cordial welcome to company personnel making inquiries at a federal agency; it can also enhance the weight given to the company's expressed concerns.

The more successful Washington representatives also have some effect on company policies and operations. In contrast to the traditional company attitude on public affairs ("if they only saw our side of the story, they would

---

[2]Private communication to the author, July 31, 1975.

Table 15-1

FACTORS AFFECTING SIZE OF D.C. OFFICES

Size of firm (e.g., automobile manufacturers)
- Most larger firms have some direct representation
- Economies of scale and variety of interests
- Greater public exposure

Importance of government markets (e.g., aerospace companies)
- Day-to-day contract administration function
- Market intelligence and forecasting
- Support base for sales efforts

Extent of regulation (e.g , ethical drug houses)
- Day-to-day dealings with regulatory agencies
- Desire to influence regulatory climate—through Congress and the media

Concern of management (e.g., petroleum corporations)
- Subjective factors, such as attitude toward social responsibility
- Level of civic awareness or concern with national policy

Degree of public exposure (e.g., conglomerates)
- Defensive—to counteract adverse media and congressional attention
- Offensive—to obtain greater public exposure for government marketing purposes and as institutional advertising

understand"), the Washington office may help to adapt corporate actions to changing national policies. In this regard, much depends on the status and effectiveness of the head of the Washington office. It is often desirable for the personnel stationed in Washington to make periodic visits to headquarters and other company locations to acquire and maintain a "feel" for the problems and outlook of company executives.

The need for such professional advice on communicating with government decision-makers is underscored by a survey of members of Congress by *Industry Week* magazine. The following—in large part, negative—congressional responses were received to the question, "Which of the following do you most often find true of industry communication with your office?":[3]

Reflex reactions to "government"	28%
Usually against and seldom favoring	24
Suggesting problems rather than solutions	24
Polished but impersonal	20
More constructive than most	20
Based more on concern than on facts	20
Narrowly self-serving	16

[3]"How Well Does Industry Communicate With Congress?" *Industry Week*, May 14, 1973, pp. 42–43.

Naive concerning economic realities	16
Timely and to the point	16
Representing management rather than employees	16
Often relates to "principles" and not issues	8

Several congressmen responding to the survey provided specific suggestions for business executives, as well as comments on business effectiveness in communicating its views:

> How could business be worse? Labor is so much more effective in Washington than business. Business is defensive, timid, and scared of the government. (Representative James M. Collins, Texas.)

> As a general principle, it seems to be always the same few companies who are well-informed on the issues and whose opinions are therefore most taken into account. Most companies provide too little, too late. (Senator Charles H. Percy, Illinois.)

> A personal letter from top management is more helpful than a form letter. Send to your member of Congress company magazines, newsletters, and reports on a continuing basis. It allows the congressman and his staff to become familiar with your company and its problems. (Representative G. William Whitehurst, Virginia.)

> We need factual information on how proposals affect you in specific terms. We get too many generalities reflecting association literature. (Representative Glenn R. Davis, Wisconsin.)

> I believe industry can improve the quality and timeliness of its communications with my office by doing a better job of studying legislation while it is pending rather than after it is passed. (Representative Harold R. Collier, Illinois.)

> Do not assume the legislator is familiar with your industry or its problems; explain as clearly as possible from a layman's point of view the problem or request. (Representative John H. Dent, Pennsylvania.)

> Thank those who support your position so they know they are supported. (Representative Philip M. Crane, Illinois.)

Service to the Home Office

To some extent, the Washington office serves as a "coffee and donuts brigade," assisting officials of the home office or operating divisions who are not fully familiar with government procedures. The assistance may vary from obtaining public documents and specialized studies to arranging appointments with federal officials and embassy personnel to meeting the board chairman's airplane. For senior officers, the aid may include getting theatre tickets and renting a limousine for dinner at the White House. The emphasis is shifting toward more important services, such as arranging and participating in high level contacts and meetings, and briefing corporate officials before congressional and agency hearings or other important public appearances.

The Marketing Function

For many Washington offices, marketing is the basic "bread-and-butter" justification of their existence and may account for the presence of the majority of the personnel assigned to the office. A variety of market research, selling, and contract administration activities may be involved. It is often considered the responsibility of the Washington office to keep the company abreast of emerging new government product requirements, so that engineering and advance design departments can be prepared for formal "requests for proposal."

On-the-scene representation may result in the company participating, officially or informally, in the development of government specifications for the products that it wants to sell to federal agencies. The basic objective usually is to assure that the products of the company meet government requirements. Representation and work on specifications being developed by government procurement agencies also provide advance information on future sales possibilities, as well as the opportunity to qualify company products. In the process, the company may learn of and bid on exploratory research and development contracts that the government will be awarding prior to the actual production phase of a major project.

Although much actual selling may be performed by company marketing and engineering personnel assigned to the home office, the Washington based staff may be in a better position to maintain day-to-day liaison with federal research and development and procurement offices, and to "open doors" for company specialists. In addition, by virtue of its location, the Washington office can expedite the often numerous and complicated steps involved in government contracting: obtaining the detailed bidding specifications; ensuring attention to company contract proposals; securing the necessary signatures; assuring company compliance with federal procedural requirements; and expediting payments for work performed. Some Washington offices also take advantage of their location in developing contacts with the embassies of foreign governments that may provide market potential.

Representation

The effective Washington office is the focal point of a company's relations with the federal government, serving especially as the principal channel for communicating the company's views on matters of major importance to legislators and executive branch officials. In good measure, the office is a coordinator, drawing on specialized talents in the corporate office, such as the legal, engineering, and public affairs staffs.

Although many company representatives try to avoid using the term, "lobbying" may be a primary part of their total function. One experienced Washington office director, who previously had served as legislative assistant to a leading senator, defines lobbying in very straightforward terms:

> Lobbying is a communication with public officials to influence their decisions in a manner harmonious with the interests of the individual or group communicating. . . . A lobbyist's purpose is selfish in the sense that he seeks to persuade others that his position is meritorious. . .[4]

The total lobbying activity includes direct relations with legislative and executive branch officials and, in addition, dealings with the media and the private policy analysis groups that abound in the nation's capital. Thus, the Washington office of a large national corporation may provide access to key reporters and influential columnists that cannot be obtained by senior management located in a more remote area.

Lobbying has changed dramatically from the flamboyant, power play oriented stereotypes. As the *New York Times* describes him (or her), "Today's lobbyist, whether working for a large corporation, a trade association or a labor union, tends to be a dun-colored organization man who fades easily into the background—and likes it that way."[5]

Increasing emphasis is being placed on subtle forms of lobbying. Because so many lobbyists crowd the stage, greater attention is given to innovative, offbeat techniques incorporating public relations, political action, and subtle influence. For example, Amoco Oil Company sponsors a weekly FM radio program in the Washington, D.C., area, featuring a guest conductor who selects the music for that particular program. Each week the guest conductor is a different member of Congress. Interspersed in the program are commercial messages by the sponsor on such subjects as why oil prices should not be regulated and why higher petroleum taxes will only lead to higher gasoline prices. Also in the program is a complimentary profile of the "guest conductor." One major retail chain sends each member of Congress a birthday cake, and a large trade association presents each lawmaker with a blank photograph album suitably engraved.[6]

The liaison with the legislative branch may serve both an "offensive" and a "defensive" function. The former is designed to get the company's views on

[4]Richard W. Murphy, "Lobbies as Information Sources for Congress", *Bulletin of the American Society for Information Science,* April 1975, p. 22.

[5]James Deakin, "Lobbying is Fine Art in Washington," *New York Times,* November 17, 1974, p. 1.

[6]Tom Littlewood, "Lobbyists Resort to Subtlety," *St. Louis Post-Dispatch,* April 21, 1975, p. B–1.

pending legislation of special interest across to senators, members of Congress, their aides, and committee staff members. Increasingly, these efforts are geared to opposing or at least amending the rising flow of federal legislation that results in greater government control over business decision-making. The "defensive" function—less widely known—is geared to avoiding embarrassing investigations of and attacks on the company. This may be accomplished by providing additional information, and the "other side of the story," at an early stage of a committee's operations. Moreover, continuing liaison, although perhaps involving nothing more than an occasional luncheon or cocktail party, may help to soften or even avoid unpleasant encounters by introducing into the situation the natural reluctance to confront one's friends.

When Congress is actively considering a piece of legislation deemed vital to the company, the Washington office may arrange for a corporate officer to be invited to testify, then draft the actual testimony, and prepare the officer for cross-examination and public interviews. Much influence on congressional deliberations, however, may come from informal telephone or face-to-face contact in a senator's or representative's office, rather than at a formal committee hearing. Formal "lobbying" activities are subject to statutory control.

Under the Regulation of Lobbying Act of 1946, lobbyists are defined as those individuals whose "principal" purpose is to influence legislation by direct contact with members of Congress. These legally defined lobbyists must register with Congress and give quarterly reports on their spending for lobbying activities.

Because enforcement of current legislation has been very limited and because of the many individuals active in governmental liaison work who have not judged their primary activity to be lobbying, new legislation in this area has been under active consideration in the Congress. Provisions of proposed legislation (S.815—94th Congress, the proposed Open Government Act of 1975), which seem likely to be incorporated into law, at least in some form, include the following:[7]

> An expansion of the definition of lobbying to encompass any communication with a member of Congress or the executive branch made in order to "influence the policy making process." Press communications and formal congressional testimony would be excluded.
>
> Criteria for qualifying as a lobbyist may consist of making eight or more oral contacts in a three-month period with members or officials of Congress or the executive branch; having lobbying as a "substantial purpose" of employment and receiving at least $250 a quarter or $500 a year for this work; spending at least $250 a quarter or $500 a year, excluding personal travel and lodging costs, for lobbying activity.

[7]Milton A. Smith and Stanley T. Kaleczyc, Jr., *Proposed New Federal Lobbying Laws* (Washington, D.C.: Chamber of Commerce of the United States, 1975), pp. 1–21; George D. Webster, "Proposed Lobbying Legislation Raises Constitutional Questions," *Association Management*, July 1975, pp. 14–17.

Persons thus qualifying as lobbyists would be required to register, listing details of their employment. Lengthy quarterly reports would have to be filed with the Federal Elections Commission, including such information as income; expenditures; gifts or loans; which phase of the policy making process he or she tries to influence; each committee, department, or agency with whom he or she communicates; and how the communication is expected to influence a specific action.

S.815 was introduced by Senator Robert Stafford (Republican of Vermont) and cosponsored by Senators William Brock (Republican of Tennessee), Dick Clark (Democrat of Iowa), Edward Kennedy (Democrat of Massachusetts), Charles Percy (Republican of Illinois), and Abraham Ribicoff (Democrat of Connecticut). A similar bill was introduced in the House of Representatives by Congressman Thomas Railsback (Republican of Illinois)—H.R.15, the proposed "Public Disclosure of Lobbying Act of 1975."

In contrast to the broad scope of coverage of S.815 and H.R.15, Representative Olin Teague (Democrat of Texas) has introduced a bill with more modest provisions—H.R.1112, the proposed "Lobbying Information Act of 1975." No expenditure reporting would be required and registration would be limited to persons retained specifically for the purpose of lobbying. Constitutional objections have been raised with reference to the proposed lobbying revisions that go beyond the Teague bill. As the late Justice Jackson stated in a noted dissenting opinion (*U.S.* v. *Harris,* 347 U.S. 612, 1954), ". . . to reach the real evils of lobbying without cutting into the constitutional right of petition is a difficult and delicate task. . . ."

Lobbying in the executive branch is not now regulated by statute. Elliot Richardson, when attorney general, required officials of the Department of Justice to log every outside call (except those from the press) on matters before them. In September 1974, the Federal Energy Administration adopted regulations that required its top officials to keep written records of all their contacts with lobbyists or other individuals or organizations seeking to influence policy decisions.

The FEA regulations require that names of persons meeting with top agency officials (from the administrator down to the level of office head) be published every two weeks and distributed to the media and the general public. These biweekly listings are to include not only the names of the visitors but the subjects they discussed. FEA employees in Grades GS–15 and above are required to keep written records of conversations with persons not directly involved in proceedings before the agency in those cases where the conversations concern applications, investigations, or enforcement proceedings.[8]

Washington office personnel also participate in various business organizations and trade associations. This activity may be part of the function of main-

[8]U.S. Federal Energy Administration, *FEA Requires Public Disclosure on Contacts With Lobbyists,* Washington, D.C., September 20, 1974.

taining the information flow, as well as a method of obtaining access to government decision-makers. Senior officers from headquarters are, however, more likely to serve on the policy boards of these associations. Another area of representation is with the press and other media that have increasingly built up their Washington staffs.

Analysis

A few companies, usually large government-oriented corporations, have developed in-house "think tanks" in conjunction with their Washington offices. These units often concentrate on forecasting and evaluating future markets in the public sector. Their staff members may interact with government and private planning groups and with the growing array of public policy analysis organizations that have been established in Washington, such as the American Enterprise Institute for Public Policy Research, the Brookings Institution, the Center for Strategic and International Studies, and the Committee for Economic Development.

As may be surmised, these four functions are closely interrelated. Much of the intelligence furnished by the Washington office leads to advice recommending company positions on major issues. As the focal point for communicating the company's views in Washington, the office can help to devise, for any given issue, a strategy of advocacy that takes into account the political and other realities of the Washington scene.

Staffing the Washington Office

Although many current Washington representatives or their key assistants have served previously in other capacities in the company, these positions are now frequently filled by men and women who have worked in and around the federal government for a number of years. The senior corporate representatives include former White House officials, cabinet and subcabinet officers, and members of Congress. Others are former congressional staff members or personnel from middle level positions in executive agencies and departments of the government.[9]

As the array of government controls over business expands, Washington offices are shifting more of their emphasis from marketing to representation before the Congress and the regulatory agencies in the executive branch. Thus, the personnel staffing these offices increasingly consists of lawyers, economists, and others versed in regulatory matters, in addition to the traditional complement of engineers and sales representatives.

[9] "Why the Corporate Lobbyist is Necessary," *Business Week,* March 18, 1972, pp. 62–65.

The head of a company's Washington office has usually reported to a vice-president in the marketing area or has been a relatively junior vice-president him- or herself. The current trend is to confer vice-presidential status on the firm's top official in the Washington office and have that individual communicate directly with the corporation's top management.

Washington representatives are being given greater authority to contact and direct personnel throughout the company. In addition, the discretion given to them in making statements in behalf of the company grows as the "reaction time" for government decision-making is reduced and as the issues become more complex and specialized. Their knowledge of the organization and its industry, as well as of the federal government, can be major determinants of their effectiveness.

There are obvious limits to the role of a company's Washington office. It is typically not the sole medium for communicating with the federal government. Lacking the array of expertise, it cannot substitute for the ongoing contacts by company engineers, lawyers, economists, and such, with their technical counterparts in the government. It can monitor and coordinate those relationships. At the most senior level, it cannot displace the visit by the chief executive officer or members of the senior management with key legislators and other high officials in the government on matters of concern to the company. The office, however, can identify the proper contacts, arrange appointments, and furnish the necessary background for these visits, as well as taking care of any follow-up activities.

SERVICE ON ADVISORY COMMITTEES

Companies are more frequently drawing upon trade associations to assist them in participating in the process of government decision-making. In addition, more companies find it advantageous to provide personnel to serve on federal advisory committees. Service on these groups permits company officials to obtain access to government decision-makers.

Representing the corporation to the executive branch of government may involve both attempts to influence future policy and efforts to learn of current developments and how the company might successfully adjust to them. Serving on government advisory committees can be a desirable form of unpaid public service, enabling the government to get a broad array of views prior to taking action. In addition, it may have the effect of marshalling public support for such action.

Virtually all federal agencies have set up one or more public advisory committees. These range from the Department of Defense's prestigious Industry Advisory Council (IAC) to the Business Research Advisory Council (BRAC) of the Bureau of Labor Statistics. The IAC, composed of senior management members of some of the major defense contractors, advises on Pentagon procurement policy, while the BRAC consists of economists, statisticians, and other company specialists who comment on price indices and such technical matters.

Table 15–2 illustrates the different patterns of representation on federal advisory committees for the utility, defense, automobile, and petroleum companies.[10] Highly regulated companies, such as AT&T, are far more active on federal advisory committees than are less regulated firms, such as Monsanto. Similarly, major defense contractors, for example, Lockheed, have more advisory memberships than do more commercially oriented corporations, such as Procter and Gamble. The variety of these business-government relations can be extensive; they range beyond the obvious agencies such as Commerce, Defense, and Transportation to include Agriculture, Health, Education, and Welfare, Interior, and State.

Advisory committees vary from those dealing with major matters of policy to bodies charged with providing advice on statistics and other technical matters. Some of these groups are designed to provide professional and technical expertise that the federal government may not possess. For example, the advisory panels of the National Science Foundation have one major and clearly defined task—to review and make recommendations on proposals for research grants that have been submitted to the Foundation in their area of expertise (economics, mathematics, physics, and so on). This essentially is a "peer group" review process, whereby academicians and other professionals evaluate research to be undertaken by their colleagues in their profession.

On the other hand, the advisory committees to the Bureau of the Census— there is one each appointed by the American Economic Association, the American Marketing Association, and the American Statistical Association—have a much broader scope. They review the various internal research and reporting programs of the entire bureau. The role of these advisory groups is substantially less precise and perhaps more difficult. To a very considerable extent, they listen to presentations on, and are asked to comment on, tasks that have been authorized and are already under way. The outside advisors may thus provide both technical expertise and an aura of scholarship to the government's own research undertakings.

Other advisory committees deal with aspects of governmental decision-making of a more operational character. For example, the Department of the Treasury meets four times a year with two committees who advise it on the quarterly financings of the public debt: the Government Borrowing Committee of the American Bankers Association and the Government Fiscal Policy Committee of the Securities Industry Association (formerly the Investment Bankers Association). This process has been subject to some criticism, because the advisors are also heavily involved in the subsequent purchases of government securities. Yet, the advisors provide an extremely knowledgeable input to the gov-

[10] M. L. Weidenbaum, "Private Advisors and Government Policy-making," *Policy Analysis*, January 1975, pp. 101–114.

Table 15–2

NUMBER OF REPRESENTATIVES OF SELECTED COMPANIES ON FEDERAL ADVISORY COMMITTEES, 1972

Department or Agency	AT&T	Exxon	General Motors	IT&T	Litton	Lockheed	Monsanto	Procter and Gamble	U.S. Steel
Agriculture	2	—	—	—	—	—	—	—	—
Commerce	9	4	9	3	3	1	11	5	3
Defense	18	1	3	5	6	9	—	—	2
Health, Education, and Welfare	7	1	1	—	2	—	—	—	1
Interior	3	12	—	—	—	—	1	—	—
Labor	8	2	4	—	—	2	1	—	11
State	37	2	2	19	4	2	—	—	—
Transportation	4	4	7	—	1	7	—	—	—
Treasury	—	—	—	—	1	—	—	—	—
Atomic Energy Commission	2	1	—	—	—	—	1	—	—
EPA	57	9	—	—	—	—	—	1	2
FCC	—	—	2	64	9	17	3	—	4
Federal Power Commission	—	12	—	—	—	—	—	—	—
Interstate Commerce Comm.	—	3	—	—	—	—	—	—	—
NASA	4	1	1	1	—	4	1	—	—
National Science Fnd.	9	—	2	—	—	—	1	—	—
Office of Economic Oppty.	—	—	—	—	1	—	—	—	—
Office of Mgt. & Budget	—	—	—	—	—	—	—	—	1
OTP	—	—	—	1	—	—	—	—	—
SEC	—	—	—	1	—	—	—	—	—
Other	4	1	2	—	—	—	—	—	—
Total	164	53	33	94	26	42	19	6	24

Source: U.S. Senate, Committee on Government Operations

ernment without the Treasury revealing any special information to them. The government's decisions on terms, size, and timing of the financings are made quite independently of the two committees. Moreover, the recommendations of the two groups frequently differ.

Another function of advisory committees is to provide a sounding board or at least a mechanism for the exchange of views by various private interest groups. An interesting variation is used by the Department of Labor. The Bureau of Labor Statistics has for many years organized two parallel but completely separate groups of advisors—the Business Research Advisory Council, consisting of economists, statisticians, and other executives of business firms, and a Labor Research Advisory Council, consisting of economists, statisticians, and other labor union officials.

The two groups always have been kept separate, never meeting jointly. Thus, the Labor Department would seem able to enjoy the role of the mediator or, at least, to occupy the high central ground in any dispute. In practice, both groups deal with technical questions related to the composition of price indices, the measurement of the labor force, and so forth.

Much may depend on the level of representation. In contrast to the staff officials who serve on the BLS committees, the Department of Defense has appointed senior management members of some of the major defense contractors and other large industrial corporations to its Industry Advisory Council. That council at times has provided a major vehicle for the defense industry to present its views to the key officials in the Pentagon, on such vital questions as changes in the regulations and procedures that the Department establishes in its dealings with the firms doing business with it.

Contrary to the general impression, professors from colleges and universities rather than business executives constitute the bulk of the memberships on governmental advisory committees (see Table 15–3). Business firms provide the second largest aggregation, accounting for 31 percent of the advisors. Participation varies substantially from industry to industry.

REVISED ORGANIZATIONAL STRUCTURES

To deal with increasing government control, many companies find it necessary to revamp their organizational structures. The growth of public interest groups (often with an antibusiness orientation) is another factor encouraging business firms to expand their government relations staffs. Initially, these changes may be modest, such as the previously discussed expansion of the Washington office or establishment of company interdepartmental committees on job safety, consumer affairs, or energy conservation.

In some cases, more substantial changes are made. For example, a major headquarters office on government relations may be established, with direct ties

Table 15-3

REPRESENTATION ON FEDERAL ADVISORY COMMITTEES BY MAJOR INTEREST GROUPS, 1972

Category	Number of Institutions	Number of Representatives	Percent of Representatives
Colleges and Universities (total)	56	3,157	58.2%
Public	33	1,774	32.7%
Private	23	1,383	25.5
Business Firms (total)	36	1,708	31.5
Aerospace and Defense	11	498	9.2
Oil	6	215	4.0
Airlines	4	140	2.6
Utilities	2	206	3.8
Other	13	649	11.9
Labor Organizations	3	341	6.3
Trade Associations	3	153	2.8
Research and Nonprofit	2	66	1.2
Total	100	5,425	100.0%

Source: U.S. Senate, Committee on Government Operations.

to each of the operating departments. Such offices may be given clearance authority on company actions ranging from introducing new products to price changes to personnel practices. On occasion, the head of such a government relations office may become a member of the corporation's top management and a primary advisor to the board of directors. Several large enterprises have designated a new vice-chairman of the board of directors to be concerned primarily with government and public relations in a very broad and comprehensive sense.

Chrysler has set up an office of public responsibility, directed by a vice-chairman of the board of directors. The office has been assigned the task of monitoring and coordinating the company's efforts in safety, environmental affairs, consumer relations, and improving job opportunities for minority groups. Mobil Oil has created a position of vice-chairman of the board responsible for explaining company policy and actions to congressional, consumer, and environmental critics. The Bank of America has designated an executive vice-president to be in charge of social policy. This post, which is viewed as a functional responsibility, oversees operations in the areas of consumerism, minority affairs, and environmental problems.

Other companies have assigned these tasks to a line division, and have made them more operational. Union Carbide's Chemical and Plastics Division has set up a Department of Safety, Health, and Affairs Related to the Environment (SHARE), headed by a vice-president. SHARE is charged with the corporate responsibility of communicating and protecting the environment and in-plant working conditions of the company's employees. In 1974, SHARE's operation cost $29 million.

One of the main responsibilities of the department, which was organized in March 1973, is to put into operation waste-water treatment facilities in company plants. It is charged with assuring that the water and air burdens from the manufacturing processes are reduced to permissible levels to meet applicable standards. The department works with research and development personnel to design systems to ensure permissible levels of operation.

SHARE meets regularly with the legal staff, toxicology experts, corporate environment staff, marketing personnel, and others. It also has authority to review and approve all new capital projects for environmental, safety, and health features.

Often, a major adverse experience with government regulators will trigger an organizational response by a company. Such was the case with the pharmaceutical producer, G. D. Searle and Company, which reacted in the fall of 1975 to a hostile congressional hearing on questions relating to its submission of test data to the Food and Drug Administration. Searle responded to the adverse public reaction by establishing a corporate committee of social scientists to study economic and political trends and determine how they are likely to affect the company. It also retained a Washington-based lobbying firm to gain more insight into congressional deliberations and to present its views more effectively.

The company also started to educate its employees on major public issues, ranging from drug pricing to the operations of the private enterprise system. It urged them to take more active roles in local civic affairs. It set up a council of management officials to review community relations and public attitudes toward business and to propose methods of dealing with those issues. The company also moved the regulatory compliance function from the divisional level to the corporate office.

PUBLIC RELATIONS EFFORTS

Although a relatively new phenomenon, business is increasingly turning to the public to exert pressure on government for reforms it believes desirable. For the first time in 14 years, General Motors in 1975 solicited the support of its stockholders to secure a five-year postponement of tougher emissions and safety standards. In a mailing to its 1.3 million stockholders, 13,000 dealers, and 19,000 suppliers, GM helped to communicate this sentiment to lawmakers by

Table 15-4

MAJOR BUSINESS ISSUES AT THE STATE LEVEL

Lobbying laws
Land-use planning
Environment
Consumer affairs
Taxation
Labor law
Product safety
Job safety and health
Legislature modernization

Source: Public Affairs Council.

enclosing names and addresses of the senators and representatives from the appropriate state.[11]

In the fall of 1975 Marathon Oil Corporation began mailing to its one million credit-card holders a series of leaflets designed to expand the ownership base of American business. The material was originally developed by the National Association of Investment Clubs as a part of its "Campaign 1976." Other companies tied in with "Campaign 1976" in other ways, such as Cutler Hammer, Inc., which adapted the material for its employee publication, "The Record."

Company managements are looking to their shareholders as an important but neglected constituency. William S. Mitchell, president of Safeway Stores, Inc., called for the development of a business activist movement. He suggested that the more than 60,000 Safeway shareholders be the nucleus for such a movement or at least active participants, "... 31 million communications from 31 million stockholders would cause a ground swell that could not be ignored."[12]

Due to what it believes has been the unanswered call for business to speak up in its own defense, the *Reader's Digest* in 1975 initiated a year-long series of articles entitled "Our Economics System: You Make It Work." Each monthly installment is labeled "Advertisement" and is sponsored by the Business Round-Table, an organization of top executives of 150 major United States corporations. The *Digest,* however, contributes editorial work and will pay to have the articles reprinted as advertisement in 50 college newspapers. The program appears to be a mass education effort, as the *Digest* itself calls it a "mini course in economics."[13]

[11]"GM's Political Pitch to Its Stockholders," *Business Week,* February 17, 1975, p. 27.

[12]William S. Mitchell, "Why Government Neglects the Stockholder," *Nation's Business,* August 1975, p. 51.

[13]Philip H. Dougherty, "New Series at Reader's Digest," *New York Times,* January 9, 1975, p. 57.

Business managers need to understand that not all public relations is necessarily negative. For example, in April 1973, the Minnesota Isaak Walton League presented an award to United States Steel for its conservation efforts in developing and operating its Minnesota ore operations. It should be noted that this was not a matter of public relations after the fact. United States Steel asked the group for its advice in planning the facility in view of the vast quantity of water used in processing taconite. Ninety-five percent of the water is reused via an extensive closed-circuit system of separators and tailings basins.[14]

INTERACTION WITH STATE GOVERNMENT

The introduction of federal revenue sharing indicates that a greater proportion of public sector responsibilities is being assumed by state and local governments. Thus, more business firms are setting up formal liaison activities with the state legislatures and agencies that affect their operations. In some cases, similar offices are being established to work with the larger county and municipal governments.[15]

The revitalization of state governments is often making a company representative in Sacramento or Albany almost as important as the one in Washington. State legislatures are moving in a variety of areas of concern to business (see Table 15-4). In addition to the traditional areas of taxes and labor, they are now deeply involved in job safety, environmental controls, land use, product packaging, and transportation systems. In 1972, at least 63 bills establishing or giving greater power to environmental agencies were introduced in 38 states. Many states also have land-use agencies, and, along with many municipalities, have created consumer protection offices. Zoning, once the exclusive province of local political subdivisions, is becoming a concern of the state. Whereas 20 years ago there were perhaps a few hundred rather weak state administrative agencies, today there are more than 1,500 with considerable power.

As a result, some companies are either expanding their state government relations efforts or establishing whole new programs. As in the case of the Washington representative, a state director of public affairs can be a "watchdog" maintaining an early warning system to alert the company on coming government action that may affect its plans or operations. Thus, he or she can identify at an early stage those bills that will have significant impact on the company, and corporate views can be presented before legislative positions become hardened. The state relations representative also may be a repository of knowledge about the mechanics of state government. Many company managers—particularly

[14]"Conservationists Salute Minntac," *U. S. Steel News,* July–August 1973, p. 10.

[15]John S. McClenahen, "Is Business Ready for New State Power?," *Industry Week,* November 12, 1973, pp. 56–60; Martin R. Haley and James M. Kiss, "Larger Stakes in Statehouse Lobbying," *Harvard Business Review,* January–February 1974, pp. 127–132.

technical specialists in engineering, manufacturing, or finance—lack sufficient understanding of committee structures and the mechanics of legislative processes.

Conferring on legislation at the state level often may be easier than in the Congress. Individual state legislators may be more approachable by business representatives. Typically, they possess less staff and official information sources, and may come to rely on business representatives for factual information on various issues. As one soft drink manufacturer recommended in a newsletter to the company's bottlers, "State legislators say that a visit from a soft drink bottler, where he explains the basis of his concern for support or change of a proposed measure, is much more persuasive than any requests for action received by mail. . . It is time again for 7UP developers to take positive action and carry proposals to their state government."[16]

The older forms of special access and personal relations are giving way in the new lobbying framework. Lunches, banquets, small favors, and year-round remembrances are still welcome as tokens of civility. But as techniques of influence they are being overtaken by specialized knowledge, integrative analysis, and planning. Sound research and professional expertise frequently can be critical ingredients in influencing governmental policy formulation. State legislators often lack well-staffed committees or good research services. For them the lobbyist can be a critical resource.

With 43 of the nation's governors possessing an item veto on appropriations bills, the executive branch should not be overlooked either. The well-prepared company representative, with established access to the executive offices, is able to offer advice on appointments to advisory commissions, to influence approval or veto of legislation, and to contribute to a more favorable political climate for business.

Although state laws on lobbying differ very substantially, there are several common threads that pervade many of them. As of August 1975, 46 states required lobbyists to register (although the precise definition of "lobbying" varied among the states). Seventeen states also required lobbyist employers to register.

In the case of several states—including California, Massachusetts, Texas, and Washington—lobbyists before executive branch agencies of state government must register for that purpose, in addition to registering for lobbying members of the legislature. Thirty-three states require the lobbyist and/or his or her employer to file financial reports.[17]

Washington State has set up a special regulatory agency to monitor the activities of lobbyists. Persons coming within the lobbying statute must register

---

[16]*Environmental Information,* The Seven-Up Company, January 31, 1975, p. 1.

[17]William Hoffer, "Associations Face Tough State Lobbying Laws," *Association Management,* August 1975, p. 46.

and file detailed financial reports weekly, monthly, and quarterly. The law also provides a "bounty hunter provision," whereby an individual citizen can sue a lobbyist and the employer for violating the act and receive as much as 50 percent of any resulting fine.

California has established a Fair Political Practices Commission, with an annual budget in excess of $1 million. One of the key duties of the Commission is to audit annually the books of every registered lobbyist. Lobbyists are prevented from spending more than $10 a month on any one item of legislation. Monthly reports are required and lobbying funds must be kept in a separate, designated bank account. California has adopted a bounty hunter provision similar to the state of Washington law.

Some enlightened business association executives have urged their members to take the lead in promoting and passing strict but reasonable lobbying laws, and to clean up any abuses that may exist in their organizations. In the words of one senior association official, "That's not the plaintive cry of a frazzle-haired liberal. That's the calm statement of a concerned association executive. Drag your members kicking and screaming into the 20th century."[18]

[18]Ibid., p. 47.

Chapter 16

Trade Associations and Government

Business firms have been utilizing trade associations ever since the Rhode Island candlemakers banded together in 1762. In more recent years, business corporations have been using their trade associations more frequently to assist them in dealings with the federal government. These associations traditionally have performed services in data collection, education, and other standard and relatively low profile areas. Now, they are taking a more positive role in public affairs, particularly in five areas of government regulation of business: health and safety, consumer affairs, the environment, wage and price controls, and energy (see Table 16–1).[1]

GOVERNMENT RELATIONS ACTIVITIES

Modern trade associations have been characterized as "organizations in the middle," standing between government and business.[2] Thus, they increasingly interpret government actions and attitudes toward business, and vice versa. Some of the ways in which this mission is accomplished is through testifying at con-

[1] "Associations Are Put to the Test," *Industry Week*, January 29, 1973, pp. 50–54.
[2] Reuel W. Elton, *How Trade Associations Help Small Business*, Management Aids No. 32 (Washington, D.C.: U.S. Small Business Administration, 1961), p. 1.

Table 16-1

KEY ACTIVITIES OF ASSOCIATIONS

Activity	Percent of Associations Performing Activity
Inform members of congressional developments	92
Help members express views to senators and congressmen	87
Inform members of federal administrative actions	87
Inform members of state and local legislative developments	81
Testify before Congress or state legislatures	76
Make recommendations on legislation	71
Provide data to state governments	66
Include speakers on legislation in convention programs	57
Draft legislation	55
Lobby and inform Congress of industry views	54
Provide data to federal government	49
Report federal court decisions	46
Train members to become active in politics	29
Collect and distribute political funds to candidates	27
Arrange plant tours to help government expose foreign visitors to U.S. industry	23
Sponsor courses on political participation	15
Assist members with customs, tariffs, and trade agreements	12
Represent industry in tariff negotiations	9
Assist government in foreign trade fair participation	8

Source: American Society of Association Executives.

gressional hearings on matters affecting the industry, appearing in proceedings before government agencies and regulatory bodies on issues of concern to the industry, and contributing to precedent-making cases before the courts.

Similarly, trade associations often interpret government to business by informing member companies of the attitudes and problems of various government bodies, and by making available information that the government is anxious to get into the hands of business executives. Trade association personnel often cooperate with government by serving voluntarily without pay on various advisory committees. As collectors of statistics for their industries, many trade groups may provide government agencies information that may not be otherwise available.

The use of the statistical information developed by trade associations often extends far beyond the members of the industry. Such regular annual publications as *Aerospace Facts and Figures* (Aerospace Industries Association), *Statistical Yearbook of the Electric Utility Industry* (Edison Electric Institute), *Annual Statistical Report* (American Iron and Steel Institute), and *National Fact Book* (National Association of Mutual Savings Banks) have become basic research sources used by government officials and private scholars. In addition, numerous specific statistical releases are issued by these organizations, such as the Edison Electric Institute's quarterly surveys of rate case decisions and its year-end summary of the electric power situation.

The critical relationship between the federal government and most trade associations has not been in the area of lobbying for or against new legislation. Rather, in most cases, it has been dealing with the rules and regulations that government agencies issue with increasing frequency.

Soon after the Arab oil embargo in October 1973, the Pharmaceutical Manufacturers Association (PMA) assembled an energy task force of 11 key executives from major drug companies to deal with the then new Federal Energy Administration. The task force first conducted a comprehensive survey of the member firms to determine the likely effects of a reduction in the energy supply. While the industry's needs for petrochemicals and fuels were found to be relatively small in comparison to other industries, the impact of a shortage of fuel or petrochemicals was considered likely to constitute a serious health hazard. On the basis of this analysis, the FEA granted the pharmaceutical industry priority in the allocation of certain distillates and residual fuel oils.

As federal agencies establish newer forms of controls over business, member companies more commonly look to their associations to explain the new rules to them, as well as to take public stands that they may not want to take individually. Federal agencies often foster this relationship by encouraging many companies in a given industry to present their views through a single association representing them rather than meeting with the companies individually. For example, the Secretary of the Treasury meets four times a year with two industry association committees that advise the Department on the quarterly financing of the public debt.

In contrast to this very high level, nationally focused activity, the Timber Operators Council (TOC) consists of hundreds of small plywood, lumber, and logging firms in the Pacific northwest that have banded together to develop a better understanding of the OSHA standards that apply to them. The TOC provides safety consultation services, hygiene counseling, and engineering advice on improved machine guarding and sound enclosures. It buys workmen's compensation as a group, thus obtaining more favorable rates for the member firms. TOC staff also perform "dummy" walk-through inspections complete with sound-level surveys.[3]

Because relatively few companies can afford professional safety and health experts, the establishment of OSHA has given a new or expanded role to many trade associations. The National Roofing Contractors Association has published *Roofing Contractors Guide,* listing the most serious hazards in the roofing industry. The National Association of Sheet Metal and Air-Conditioning Contractors set up a committee to develop safety standards.

The meat products industry created an industrial safety committee and has

---

[3]"Big Help for the Little Man," *Job Safety and Health,* February 1974, p. 19.

published an analysis of meat plant injuries; the lumber and wood products industry established a committee to develop guidelines for compliance with the OSHA act. A 10-hour course on occupational safety and health, offered by the New York City Building Trades Employers Association, has been completed by 1,000 construction supervisors and employees.[4]

The Grocery Manufacturers of America has prepared a 100-page study, *Guidelines for Product Recall,* to help members of that industry to cope with an increasingly frequent by-product of governmental regulation. The voluntary guidelines set forth in the report, which had been discussed previously with the Food and Drug Administration, cover organizational arrangements, distribution systems, and communications aspects.

The Milk Industry Foundation provides a recurrent publication, *Milk Order Roundup,* to keep its members informed on the great variety of regulations issued by federal and state agencies. Similarly, the Foundation's releases, *Information About Energy* and *Ecogram: Ecology and Environment,* are continuing efforts to keep milk processors abreast of two relatively new and rapidly changing areas of government regulation.

The American Petroleum Institute is an example of a large, well-financed trade association working for an industry that is strongly affected by government actions. Its 1974 budget of $15.7 million supported 330 employees, 11 of whom were formally registered as lobbyists. A major producer of statistics on the petroleum industry, the Institute has established a policy analysis division to examine proposed legislation and to provide information to the Congress. It is strengthening its ties to state and regional oil associations and providing more speakers to local radio and television talk shows, all in an effort to increase "grass roots" support for the industry's position.

Many associations with headquarters in cities closer to their constituents' industrial environment have opened subsidiary offices in Washington, but many more have moved their central offices to the nation's capital. As recently as 1974, New York City was still home for the largest single share of the nation's associations, especially because of the proximity of advertising, marketing, and publishing companies that provide important services to them. Nevertheless, a rising proportion of business associations has been locating in Washington. By early 1975, 26 percent (compared to New York's diminished share of 24 percent) were situated in the capital.[5] Industries that cater heavily to the government market—including the Aerospace Industries Association, the Electronics Industries Association, and the National Security Industrial Association—traditionally have located their trade associations in the capital. Others now located there are the American Advertising Federation, the American

---

[4]*The President's Report on Occupational Safety and Health* (Washington, D.C.: U.S. Government Printing Office, 1973), pp. 20–21; "High on Safety," *Occupational Safety and Health,* July 1974, p. 11.

[5]"Hard Times Strengthen Trade Groups," *Industry Week,* February 1, 1975, p. 10.

Bankers Association, the American Gas Association, the American Petroleum Institute, the American Newspaper Publishers Association, the Atomic Industrial Forum, the Bicycle Manufacturers Association, the Chemical Specialties Manufacturers Association, the Mortgage Bankers Association, the National Association of Furniture Manufacturers, the National Association of Manufacturers, and the National Shrimp Congress.

The continued expansion of federal control over private industry will further the tendency of trade associations to locate all or at least a major part of their operations in Washington, D.C. They also will be devoting a rising share of their resources to government relations. A recent survey by the American Society of Association Executives reported that 22 percent of member trade associations devoted one-fifth or more of their budgets to government relations activities.

THE RISE OF "UMBRELLA" ORGANIZATIONS

To counter the increasing impact of other interest groups, there is a new tendency for business associations to combine forces, at least for some overriding issues. Thus, the three major associations of defense contractors—the Aerospace Industries Association, the Electronics Industries Association, and the National Security Industrial Association—have founded a Council of Defense-Space Industry Associations (CODSIA). Although each of the three individual associations is continuing to perform its traditional functions, CODSIA provides a broader type of representation on issues affecting defense contractors across-the-board, notably changes in military procurement policy.

A more recent innovation is the joining of forces by the two largest general associations of business interests, the Chamber of Commerce of the United States and the National Association of Manufacturers (NAM). The move of the NAM to Washington has made such cooperation feasible; the Chamber of Commerce historically has been located in the capital.

In October 1973, the Chamber of Commerce and the NAM issued their first joint letter in 70 years—an appeal to the president to remove all wage and price controls. In December 1973, the two organizations sent the president another letter on the subject. (The wage and price control legislation was allowed to lapse in April 1974). The two associations have jointly testified before Congress on foreign trade legislation. They also have formed an Energy Users' Conference, designed to represent the nation's major industrial and commercial consumers of energy; the conference has become a major business link with the FEA. The heads of the two associations lunch together regularly and are frequently joined by the Secretary of Commerce.

The Chamber of Commerce also has been instrumental in organizing the Association Advisory Group on Product Safety, representing 30 different trade and professional associations who have joined forces for a common front. The group has dealt with the Consumer Product Safety Commission on industrywide problems, such as the publicity given the raw data obtained through the hospital network, known as the National Electronic Injury Surveillance System.[6]

The Chamber of Commerce and the NAM have joined with three other organizations to form the Committee on Business Overview. Working with the Business Roundtable, the Public Relations Society of America, and the Young Presidents Organization, the new group is designed to counter political assaults on the business community.

Of all of these broad-based organizations, the newest and least vocal but perhaps most influential is the Business Roundtable. Comprised of the chief executive officers of 158 of the largest and most prestigious companies, the Roundtable has its own staff and activities, although it does work with the older and larger groups. It is a specific vehicle for getting members of top management personally involved in presenting business views to the Congress and to senior officials in the departments and agencies. The staff of the Roundtable is kept at a minimum, with the organization relying mainly on the efforts of executives in the employ of its member companies. Committees are active in such areas as construction, labor-management, public information, and antitrust legislation.

The Roundtable operates with an annual budget of about $1.5 million. Much of its expenses are borne directly by the member companies whose executives serve on its committees or talk directly to members of Congress and executive branch policy officials. Annual dues range from $2,500 to $35,000, depending on the size of the company. The membership includes the three largest automobile manufacturers, the three largest banks, seven of the biggest oil companies, major retail organizations, several utilities, and a variety of other industrial firms.[7]

The trend toward the formation of more business "umbrella" organizations in Washington is likely to continue as federal regulations extend to nationwide activities, rather than being limited to a single regulated industry.[8]

ORGANIZATIONAL MATTERS

Most associations still conduct traditional activities, such as setting standards, gathering statistics, publishing information about the industry, main-

[6]"Chamber Dialogue Underway With CPSC," *Washington Report,* December 30, 1974, p. 2.

[7]Eileen Shanahan, "Antitrust Bill Stopped by a Business Lobby," *New York Times,* November 16, 1975, p. 1.

[8]"Harmonizing Business' Voices," *Industry Week,* June 24, 1974, pp. 50–52; Andrew J. Glass, "NAM's New Look Is Toward Goal of Business Unity," *National Journal Reports,* January 5, 1974, pp. 15–23.

taining public relations, and performing educational functions. However, government relations has become the dominant function for many of them. One result has been that association staffs have been growing in both quantity and quality. Relatively few associations still call their top staff people "executive secretary." The title "president" is more in vogue, with salaries often matching the added stature; on occasion, they may exceed $100,000 a year. Associations are attracting former government officials for top staff jobs.

The trade association field has taken on added professional stature as a result of an intensive educational program begun by the American Society of Association Executives, in which hundreds of association staff members have qualified for a certified association executive designation by passing a written examination. At least one educational institution, Florida Atlantic University, now offers a master's degree in association management. The ASAE sponsored 37 courses for association executives between October 1975 and June 1976, covering finance, management, publications, working with governments, and leadership. Table 16–2 indicates the contents of the first year course in association management sponsored by the U.S. Chamber of Commerce at six major universities.

A special three-day Communications Workshop prepares members for appearances on television, presentation of testimony, and press conferences. In the Workshop, television cameras, videotape recordings, and playback equipment are used for demonstrations and personalizing the educational experience.[9]

Educational activities of associations also extend to their member companies, especially smaller companies without their own management development staffs. The operational management sessions of the National Soft Drink Association, held in 1974, drew 1,800 participants on such subjects as security, energy conservation, and employee communications. The Edison Electric Institute conducts a four-week Graduate Management Course for upper level executives of the industry, covering management skills, oral communications, and current electric utility industry problems.

Some trade association executives are sensitive about being termed "lobbyist," preferring such terms as "government liaison" or "government representative." Many see themselves as conduits between business and government, acting mainly as message carriers. The effectiveness of the message being delivered may depend in good measure on the association's ability to get member companies to agree on strong common stands on controversial issues. For example, manufacturers of a product with a large foreign sales operation may well prefer a different stand on tariff issues than other companies in the same industry that are faced with severe import competition. For this reason, many large companies are active members of a variety of trade associations and also

[9]"New Opportunities for Executive Development," *Association Management,* July 1975, p. 75.

Table 16-2

PROGRAM OF A FIRST COURSE IN ASSOCIATION MANAGEMENT

Organization Structure, Policy, and Programming

Types of associations. Elements of the organization structure. Role of the manager, staff, and members. Techniques for developing a policy. Techniques for developing a program. Techniques for communicating the policies and program.

Finance and Budgeting

How to develop financial policies for an association. Setting up the financial structure. Fundamentals of cash and accrual accounting methods. The use of a budget as a planning and control tool. How to develop a budget. Procedures for assuring internal control.

Government Relations

The importance of government relations. Steps in developing a government relations program. Importance of policy in government relations. Developing membership support. Techniques for legislative representation. The "do's and don'ts" of political involvement.

Law

Basic knowledge of federal statutes that affect associations. Legal organization of an association. Activities that are clearly legal and clearly illegal. The executive's responsibility in association law. Techniques and procedures to help assure legality of activities.

Communication

Functions of communication. The communication process. The relationship between language and communication.

Power Relationships of People and Groups

Ways of looking at power relationships. Emergence of power relationships — formal and informal. Connection of power and organization.

Group Action

Components of group action (motivation). Concepts of group dynamics and the social structure of groups. The necessity for developing and implementing a philosophy of group action.

Task Force Management

Use of committees — their role in the organization. Types of committees. Selection of committee chairmen and members. Working with committees.

Developing External Manpower

How to determine volunteer leadership needs. Techniques for identifying potential volunteer leaders. Recruiting and developing volunteer leaders and potential leaders. How to evaluate performance. The role of the manager and staff in developing volunteer leadership.

Source: Chamber of Commerce of the United States.

maintain large offices in Washington. This dual form of representation provides flexibility, allowing a company to band together with other firms in the industry on some issues, while taking an independent stance on other matters.

The American Association of Association Executives is in the process of setting up a program for the voluntary accreditation of trade groups. The formal evaluation will be a three-stepped affair:

1. The applicant association will submit a self-evaluation report using the ASAE's Association Evaluation Guidelines.
2. A site visit will be made by an evaluation team of three persons made up of two ASAE member executives and a staff member.
3. The evaluation team will submit a written report to the ASAE's chief staff executive officers.[10]

THE FLOW OF INFORMATION

One of the problems facing business associations, and resulting in the upgrading of their personnel, is how to develop more sophisticated ways of dealing with the rapidly growing flow of information from government agencies and related research institutions. The traditional newsletter to the top management of member companies frequently is not considered sufficient. Conferences, television, a variety of printed publications, and other media are used to present and tailor information on government activities for the growing variety of users in member companies.

Several associations publish very professional looking magazines, which deal with issues of public policy and also inform the industry of the impact of current and prospective government activities. Examples include the Mortgage Bankers Association's monthly *Mortgage Banker* and the Edison Electric Institute's bimonthly *EEI Bulletin.*

The Milk Industry Foundation, in conjunction with the International Association of Ice Cream Manufacturers, regularly provides its membership with two series of reports on various aspects of government relations: *Thrust,* a relatively technical publication, describes and evaluates the effect of state and federal standards, labeling regulations, and enforcement activities. *Alert,* a more popularly written release, covers critical issues affecting the industry, such as proposals for requiring regulatory agencies to consider the costs that they impose on business.

The NAM recently has computerized many of its activities. Member firms have been categorized according to congressional districts as well as the standard

---

[10]"Accreditation Program Approved by ASAE Board At Annual Meeting," *Association Management,* October 1975, p. 99.

industrial classification (SIC) used by federal statistical agencies. A computerized profile of each member of Congress also has been prepared. As legislative issues arise, the NAM staff in Washington hopes to be better equipped to pinpoint the companies most directly affected by proposed legislative changes or executive action. The data will also help to determine where the association's government representation efforts should be focused.

In addition to assisting the information function of the individual corporate offices in Washington, trade associations also can be useful in obtaining "access" to government decision-makers in both the legislative and executive branches. While such officials may be reluctant to meet privately with the representatives of a single company, they frequently accept invitations to attend meetings sponsored by an association representing an entire industry. Employees of a company thus can make initial informal contacts with key government people at association luncheons, dinners, cocktail parties, conferences, and other meetings.

To be sure, not all of the activities of trade associations have generated uniformly favorable public reactions. Labor unions and other interest groups from time to time have attacked what they have considered to be improper or excessive influence that business associations have exerted on government policy makers. Many of the criticisms seem to boil down to the fact that members of certain industries, notably petroleum, are heavily represented on government advisory committees.[11] Some of the specific concerns, however, have a stronger base than that, as was the case of the U.S. Geological Survey.

Until April 1974, the Geological Survey consulted a committee of oil industry representatives before establishing regulations for offshore drilling on the continental shelf of the United States. The agency's practice was to circulate its proposed regulatory orders to the Offshore Operators Committee, composed entirely of industry representatives, before making the information public via publication in the *Federal Register.*

The change in procedure came about after Representatives Henry S. Reuss and Guy Vander Jagt, chairman and ranking minority member of the House of Representatives Subcommittee on Conservation and Natural Resources, complained to the Secretary of the Interior that the procedure deprived the public of knowing what the federal agency proposed initially. The revised practice is to make the proposed regulations public before soliciting the industry's comments.[12]

On occasion, companies in a given industry have cooperated in setting up organizations to develop new information and research findings, often in response to governmental regulatory activities. One example was the formation

[11] Norman Medvin, "How Big Oil Influences Government," *American Federationist,* December 1974, pp. 16–19.

[12] M. L. Weidenbaum, "Private Advisors and Government Policymaking," *Policy Analysis,* Winter 1975, pp. 110–111.

in 1975 of the Chemical Industry Institute of Technology, jointly funded by 11 large chemical companies. The Institute aims at generating, assessing and disseminating health and safety data on industrial chemicals. The testing and other factual outputs of the Institute are expected to help the chemical industry meet an increasing array of federal regulation, including EPA, FDA, CPSC, and OSHA.

Chapter 17

Business Participation in Politics

The rising impact of government regulatory activities on business decision-making is resulting in renewed interest by business executives in participating directly in the political process. Watergate and all its ramifications dampened the enthusiasm of some for political activities. But the substantial political role of other interest groups, such as labor and agriculture, and the antibusiness orientation of some political activists working under the banner of public interest groups, continue to encourage business people to enter the political arena more actively.

Although numerous industry leaders attempt to use the political process as a way of slowing federal intervention in the private sector, they will be increasingly restricted in their efforts. Some legislation has been enacted to deal with such abuses as those exposed to much public attention beginning in 1972 and kept in the limelight throughout the Watergate scandal. Hence, corporate executives need to become far more knowledgeable concerning the legal limits of their political activities. More rather than less restrictions on business participation in politics are likely in the future.

PERMISSIBLE POLITICAL ACTIVITIES

Corporations can participate legally in a wide variety of political activities. Federal law governs only political activities involving candidates for president, vice-president, and the congress. Involvement in state and local campaigns is governed by state statutes and local ordinances.[1]

[1]Lewis R. Freeman, Jr., "Permissible Political Activities," *NAM Reports,* September 9, 1974, p. 10.

A corporation may encourage its employees and stockholders to register and vote, but it may not recommend to employees *how* they should vote. Candidates may tour a company plant or office to meet employees or may stand at an entrance to greet them, but the company must grant *all* candidates that right. However, it need not specifically invite *every* candidate.

The management of a company has a right to state its position on public issues affecting the company's well-being, including legislative proposals before the Congress. It also may communicate to its employees and stockholders information on members of Congress and candidates for office, such as voting records. Company-sponsored programs explaining how to be effective in politics are another permissible form of political activity.

A corporation can provide political education programs for employees, and it can actively promote, on a nonpartisan basis, its employees' voluntary involvement in direct political action on their own time. An employee also may be granted a leave of absence without pay to work on a political campaign.

A survey in 1972 by the Conference Board of the 1,000 largest industrial firms revealed that 28 percent had formal policies covering employee participation in political activities; 17 percent had informal policies. Most of the remainder handle each request on an individual basis; 9 percent stated that the question of a leave for political reasons has never been raised in their companies.

Of the formal company policies on political participation, most encourage employees to be active in political work and offer leaves of absence without pay to employees elected or appointed to public office. Leaves are usually restricted to one term, after which an employee is considered to have chosen a career in politics.[2]

Under the 1974 election reform law, business partnerships may contribute to federal candidates, although corporations and labor unions may not. The Federal Election Commission has ruled that any candidate receiving a donation from a partnership must, to comply with the limitation on individual donations, divide the amount received among the individual partners "in relation to each partner's interest in the partnership's profits." The campaign organization must get that information within 30 days or return the contribution.[3]

METHODS OF SUPPORTING POLITICAL CANDIDATES

Direct financial contributions by individual business executives and corporate officials are likely to continue as a basic method of business participation in political activities. Although according to federal law such contributions must be

---

[2]Grace J. Finley, *Policies on Leaves for Political and Social Action* (New York: Conference Board, 1972), pp. 1–4.

[3]Walter Pincus, "Making Campaign Rules Complex," *Washington Post,* September 15, 1975, p. A22.

entirely personal, they tend to increase the importance of individual companies and of the entire business community in the eyes of present and future government officeholders.[4]

Special prestige groups are often established by political parties for large contributors. These may be in the form of a president's club or a congressional boosters club. Such clubs can provide a means for business people to gain initial entree to important public officials.

Corporate officials often pool their contributions, so that one company official presents all of the donations from company employees who support a given candidate. This approach is likely to increase the firm's political impact on the recipient. The LTV Corporation conducts an active citizenship program, which also includes education and get-out-the-vote efforts, as well as a special committee for donors of more than $100.

Such efforts may be industrywide and patterned after similar efforts by labor unions. The National Association of Manufacturers sponsors a Business-Industry Political Action Committee. Bankers have established a Banking Profession Political Action Committee (BANKPAC), and the American Bakers Association have a Bread Political Action Committee (BREADPAC). Doctors, with help from drug firms, have set up an American Medical Political Action Committee (AMPAC). Other industry groups that raise funds for political candidates include the Construction Equipment Political Action Committee (CEPAC), the Life Underwriters Education Fund and Political Action Committee, and the Milk Industry Foundation. These committees generally contribute to the campaigns of legislators who are favorable to business or to their specific industry.

Under the 1974 election law reform, funds receiving political contributions from more than 50 persons and receiving or spending more than $1,000 a year are considered to be "political committees." Such organizations must file regular reports to the Federal Election Commission and are limited to contributions of $5,000 per candidate in each election. The Federal Elections Commission has ruled that separate state committees fund raising will count toward the $5,000 overall ceiling on the parent (nationwide) committee.

Some bona fide sales of goods and services to campaign organizations at times turn out to be involuntary contributions if full payment is not made. Because of widespread abuses of this nature during 1968, especially by losing candidates, Congress passed some restrictive legislation. Pursuant to the Federal Election Campaign Act of 1971, the CAB, the FTC, and the ICC have issued regulations limiting the extension of unsecured credit for transportation and communication services to political candidates.

Businesses may legally make indirect contributions to political parties. Corporate officers and directors may take positions in political parties, often in

[4]Edwin M. Epstein, "Corporations and the Political Imperative," *Business and Society Review,* Summer 1972, pp. 54–67.

connection with fund raising. While these officials function in an individual capacity, their corporate affiliations usually are known, and their activities can result in political goodwill for the firm, at least in the case of winning candidates. Corporations are rarely monolithic in the political sympathies of their individual executives, and frequently some members of management will actively support one candidate while others back the opponent.

Corporations may advertise directly in convention and anniversary publications issued by political parties. Under current legislation, a company may deduct the cost of advertisements printed in national presidential convention programs if that cost is deemed reasonable in light of the business that the advertiser expects to gain. However, the Federal Election Commission in 1975 prohibited political parties from accepting services, such as free automobiles or buses, which business firms had customarily donated for use at national political conventions.

Members of Congress and state and local legislators, as well as candidates, may be invited to speak before trade associations, company management clubs, chamber of commerce groups, and similar business-oriented organizations. Their remuneration may range from merely having a convenient platform to present their views to generous honoraria. The 1974 election reform law set a limit of $1,000 (plus travel expense) for a speech, appearance, or article by a federal official, and an annual ceiling of $15,000 for each such individual. Once a government official becomes a candidate, the Federal Election Commission treats the honoraria as political contributions if the speech is made "before a substantial number of people within his (or her) electorate."

Any newspaper reader in recent years can readily recall numerous instances of flagrant abuse involving business and political campaigns—and attention to the less savory aspects of the subject is surely warranted. Nevertheless, it is useful to note the findings of Professor Edwin Epstein of the University of California that in the politically active year of 1968, only about one out of five officers and directors of the very largest industrial firms, including government contractors, contributed to political parties. Since large manufacturing firms, particularly those strongly influenced by governmental decisions, have generally had higher rates of political contributions by their officials than other businesses, the 20 percent figure is probably a generous indicator of the financial participation of business as a whole.[5]

Epstein views aggregate corporate political participation as a continuum along which individual companies can be placed with regard to both the scope and the magnitude of their operations. Businesses in practice vary in their political efforts from, at one pole, no conscious participation by company executives, to an occasional letter or phone call to a member of Congress or a $100 cam-

[5] Ibid., p. 61.

paign contribution to, finally, continuous and comprehensive governmental and electoral activity by political specialists on the company payroll.

Although most corporations engage in some form of participation in the political process, this activity varies substantially with a number of factors. These influences include the size of the firm, the degree of regulation of the enterprise by the government, and the extent to which company business and well-being depend upon governmental decisions. As would be expected, the larger the firm and the greater the importance of governmental decisions to its operations, the greater is likely to be the scope and magnitude of its involvement in political activity.[6]

The substantial contributions by other interest groups should not be ignored in any balanced treatment of the subject of political activity. In the fall of 1974, labor unions were reported to have contributed $333,300 to 141 members of the Congress who supported a bill to require that eventually 30 percent of all oil imports be shipped in American vessels, staffed by union crews. The largest donation, $20,000, went to the senator who served as floor manager of the bill. President Gerald Ford subsequently vetoed the bill on the grounds that it would result in higher fuel bills and larger government subsidies to shipping.[7]

Business executives need to understand, however, that, at least in the current environment, labor's political contributions do not receive the public attention that comparable business efforts do. A cogent contrast was provided by the case of Senator Harrison A. Williams of New Jersey, who was simultaneously chairman of the Committee on Labor and Public Welfare and chairman of the subcommittee of the Banking Committee that handles securities industry legislation. The $34,600 that members of the securities industry donated to the Senator's reelection campaign in 1975 became the source of considerable public controversy in view of his key role with reference to a major bill regulating the securities industry. These relationships between the industry's contributions and Senator Williams were the subject of a 28-inch article in *The New York Times*. It is interesting to note that buried in the same article was a short reference to the fact that the Senator's reelection campaign had also received $23,100 from labor groups. In the words of the reporter, "It is the securities industry donations, however, that have aroused controversy."[8]

These more typical relationships of businesses to politics have been obscured by the series of reports of highly improper and often blatantly illegal business activities in the political sphere, especially in connection with the 1972

---

[6]Ibid., p. 64.

[7]"Unions Back Shipping Bill With $333,000," *St. Louis Post-Dispatch*, September 16, 1974, p. 2A. For other examples, See Bryan E. Calame, "Unions and Politics," *Wall Street Journal*, January 29, 1974, p. 1 *et. ff.*

[8]Martin Tolchin, "Securities Industry Gave Senator Williams 25% of Election Fund," *New York Times*, June 22, 1975, p. 42.

presidential campaign. The Minnesota Mining and Manufacturing Company, for example, admitted in early 1975 that it maintained an illegal political fund totalling $634,000. Five of its officers agreed to pay $475,000 to the firm to settle a shareholder suit involving illegal donations to the 1972 campaign of former President Richard Nixon.[9]

In late 1974, the Northrop Corporation settled a class action suit that had been filed after the disclosure that it had made $150,000 of illegal corporate contributions to the Nixon campaign. The chief executive officer of the company was required to relinquish the post of president and to repay the company for $50,000 of the improper political gifts. This was in addition to a previous reimbursement of $122,000 to cover legal fees and other expenses to the company.[10]

Several other companies were fined for their illegal contributions to the 1972 presidential campaign, including American Airlines, Ashland Oil, Braniff, Goodyear, Greyhound, and Phillips Petroleum. The Gulf Oil Corporation has admitted that it had made secret political contributions of more than $10 million in the United States and abroad during the period 1966–73, some of the expenditures being demonstrably illegal. In many of the cases, senior management has left the company or resigned from the boards of directors of other corporations.

Business, quite properly, took it on the chin as these numerous revelations of so-called political slush funds were uncovered. It is altogether fitting that such lawbreaking be exposed and punished. As pointed out earlier, corporate contributions to federal election campaigns are clearly illegal. In addition, setting up the illegal funds often involved violating securities and income tax laws.

Yet there is another, usually ignored aspect of these illegal business contributions to political causes. When we turn to more traditional types of crime, we find that the progressive thinking is not limited to punishing crime, but it extends to uncovering the causes of crime. By identifying the conditions that breed crime, it is hoped that public policy can be modified so as to reduce or eliminate those conditions—a preventative approach to lawbreaking.

A rough parallel can be drawn to the Watergate-related cases of unlawful corporate political contributions and their attempted cover-up. What was the underlying motive for these illegal acts? On the basis of the evidence made public thus far, the dominant motive does not seem to have been to enrich the individual corporate executives who were involved, or even to enhance their positions in the company hierarchy. Neither was the typical motive the desire to

---

[9]"3M Firm Admits Keeping Slush Fund," *St. Louis Post-Dispatch*, January 2, 1975, p. 12D.

[10]"Northrop Tentatively Settles Class Action Over Illegal Gifts to '72 Nixon Campaign," *Wall Street Journal*, November 21, 1974, p. 14. Subsequently, investigation uncovered a pattern of Northrop contributions to foreign government officials in connection with the company's overseas sales.

get the federal government to grant a particular favor to the firm ("favors" in the form of government contracts were the object of many of the payments to citizens of other nations).

Rather, the illegal contributions were usually a response, sometimes reluctant, to the demands from the representatives of a powerful government administration in the position to do great harm to the company. Whether the government would abuse its vast power in the absence of an adequate payment was a risk that many managements decided not to take. But it is not surprising that so many of the executives who were implicated held positions in corporations that are dependent upon government in important ways—firms that hold large defense contracts, airlines that have government-approved route structures, and companies that otherwise are either recipients of special subsidies or subject to stringent federal regulation.

Those corporate executives—and indeed there were many—who turned down the outrageous demands of the Nixon campaign representatives were at the time (prior to the Watergate episode) exhibiting a special form of courage. In retrospect, of course, their reaction turned out to be the course of wisdom as well as honor.

It may not be too wide of the mark to consider at least some of those illegal corporate payments as a form of "protection" money given to prevent action harmful to the company. Viewed in this light, the underlying cause of this particular type of white collar crime does not arise in the company itself. Rather, the fundamental reason for the lawbreaking can be seen as the tremendous and often arbitrary power that the society has given the federal government over the private sector.

Thus, the eradication of this particular form of white collar crime would be seen to involve more than the necessary tighter auditing standards and improved laws on political financing. It would also require abstaining from the further expansion of governmental power over the private sector, and instead embarking on efforts to reduce the arbitrary decision-making authority that many federal agencies now possess in their dealings with business firms.

Some of the attacks on business participation in the financing of election campaigns, although fully justified, may be too narrow from the viewpoint of developing appropriate public policy. For example, the practice of voluntary political contributions by individual executives to a company or industry fund was based on an earlier innovation in the political campaign financing process introduced by labor unions. Their membership often agree to "voluntary" checkoffs of contributions to political funds controlled by union officers.

The basic point should not be misunderstood. Lawbreaking, whether by business executives or others, should not be condoned. It should be ferreted out and punished according to law. Simultaneously, it is naive—and it may be ineffective as well—to ignore the basic forces that give rise to the lawbreaking. In the area of business contributions to the political process, much of the basic thrust seems to come from the awesome power that—through the political process—government has been given over business, power that ranges from awarding contracts and subsidies to withholding approval of new products and facilities.

One way to reduce the potential for lawbreaking is to curtail the vast authority of government agencies to favor or harm specific groups of the society via the galaxy of federal regulatory, procurement, and subsidy programs. That might also help in shifting the resources of business, labor, agriculture, and other producer groups to more productive channels than financing the political process. Such action would simultaneously reduce the need to pay "protection" money against the threat of loss of subsidy or other federal largesse.

In response to the public concern over improper corporate political activities, some companies have been adopting a radically more open policy on the subject of campaign contributions. DuPont, the nation's largest chemical firm, adopted in July 1975 a policy of publicly disclosing all United States political contributions by its top executives. In addition, all solicitations for more than $1,000 and responses to those requests are made public for inspection by reporters, shareholders, and employees.

W. Michael Blumenthal, president and chief executive officer of the Bendix Corporation, has called for the establishment of a formal institute to promote ethical business practices. Such a group would deal with concrete questions of business ethics. It would not be an advocate of business interests per se, but would comprise representatives of other segments of the society as well. The institute would focus on devising new codes of ethical behavior to which all businesses could be expected to subscribe.[11]

NEW LIMITATIONS AND FEDERAL INVOLVEMENT

In reaction to revelations concerning the 1972 presidential election campaign, the Congress adopted wide-ranging legislation to limit the amount that an individual can contribute to a candidate, and also to provide for substantial federal financing of election campaigns. Government financing of political activity, in whole or in part, is likely to reduce the impact of business on government policy. The system of private campaign contributions plays a role in strengthening the voice of general business in political life, as well as representing the interests of individual industries.

A variety of proposals had been urged upon the Congress. The Nixon Administration itself recommended a $15,000 limit on individual donations to presidential campaigns and $3,000 on congressional races. More stringent limits

---

[11]W. Michael Blumenthal, "New Business Watchdog Needed," *New York Times*, May 25, 1975, p. F–14.

have been urged by others. Common Cause, a public interest group, advocates a $500 ceiling on individual contributions to presidential campaigns and $250 for congressional races.[12]

The Committee for Economic Development urged the prohibition of all political contributions, whether in cash or in kind, by corporations, trade associations, labor unions, business partnerships, or affiliated "political education" organizations. At present, 21 states allow corporate gifts to state and local election campaigns, and 45 states allow labor unions to do so. The CED also proposed government support of activities that reduce the cost of campaigns, such as subsidizing public television for citizen enlightenment on political affairs and using the Postal Service and the Government Printing Office to publish and distribute voter information on a nonpartisan basis. Another proposal for reducing campaign costs was to shorten campaign time by scheduling registration, primaries, conventions, and the election closer together.[13]

The response of the Congress was to enact the Federal Election Campaign Act of 1974, which went into effect on January 1, 1975. The new law limits the contributions that an individual can make to all candidates for federal office to $25,000 a year and $3,000 per candidate per campaign ($1,000 each in the primaries, a runoff, and the general election). Organizations are restricted to contributions of $5,000 in each of the three possible races for one candidate, up to a total of $15,000. Cash contributions in excess of $100 are prohibited. Loans and gifts of securities and other assets are also considered to be contributions.

From the point of view of presidential candidates, any Democrat or Republican (technically any party whose candidate drew at least 25 percent of the vote in the previous presidential election) who decides to enter the primaries can become eligible for taxpayer financing. To qualify, the candidate must raise $100,000, with $5,000 each from 20 states in contributions of $250 or less. The federal government matches that $100,000 plus additional contributions of $5,000 up to a total of $4.5 million. Primary candidates cannot spend more than $10 million for the nomination.

The winners of the Democratic and Republican presidential nominations can receive up to $20 million for the general election from the government or they can choose to depend entirely on private gifts. In either case, a presidential nominee is limited to spending $20 million. The government contribution would be financed by the voluntary $1 checkoff on the personal income tax. Beyond the $20 million spending ceiling, the state and national committees of a candidate's party can support his or her campaign at a rate of 2¢ a vote—for a total of about $3 million. The nominating conventions of both major parties are sup-

[12]Common Cause, "Integrity in Politics," *Report From Washington,* December 1973–January 1974, pp. 3–22.

[13]Committee for Economic Development, *Restoring Confidence in the Political Process* (New York: CED, 1974).

ported by the checkoff fund with $2 million each. This is roughly what the two parties spent in 1972. The Republican and Democratic nominees for the presidency will be limited to spending $20 million each in the 1976 general election, to be raised by the checkoff option on income tax returns. The new law has been challenged in the courts on constitutional grounds by groups including Republican Senator James L. Buckley and former Democratic Senator Eugene J. McCarthy.

Under attack are the law's ceilings on campaign contributions and expenditures, far-reaching public disclosure requirements, federal subsidies for presidential elections, and creation of the new and powerful Federal Election Commission to administer the law. In defending the 1974 reform act before the Supreme Court, Harvard Law Professor Archibald Cox, the first Watergate special prosecutor, described it as an attempt to halt "an arms race in political expenditures."

Professor Ralph K. Winter, Jr., of the Yale Law School, replied that the law not only curtails political speech but that it does so in a way that discriminates in favor of incumbents, including members of Congress who retain money-saving franking privileges and other advantages of holding office.[14]

The new federal campaign law also appears to have given organized labor some special leverage. Under the law, the value of a union's services in soliciting votes for a candidate among its members and in getting out the vote on election day are not legally counted as contributions to the candidate. These services were reported to have been particularly effective in behalf of the successful Democratic candidate in the September 1974 special Senate race in New Hampshire, the first time that the new law was operational. Corporations are given an identical exemption with respect to stockholders and their families, but no corporate campaigning was discernible in New Hampshire.[15]

THE OUTLOOK

Congress has been urged to ban all voluntary or involuntary political loans, which may be disguised donations, and to end so-called contributions in kind—donations of campaign workers, private aircraft, and other goods and services that may be paid from the funds of a corporation, a labor union, or other organization.

It is unlikely that Congress will eliminate all private contributions to political parties or to individual candidates for public office. The federal government,

[14]John P. MacKenzie, "Cox Defends Election Reform Law," *Washington Post,* November 11, 1975, p. A2.

[15]Warren Weaver, Jr., "Voting Law Gives Leverage to Labor," *New York Times,* September 24, 1975, p. 12.

Table 17-1

SEMINAR ON POLITICAL CAMPAIGN MANAGEMENT

Program Outline	Program Outline
Research and Surveys	Computers and Automated Devices
Planning Strategy	Profile of a Successful Campaign
Fund Raising, Advertising, and Publicity	Reaching Special Classifications:
Direct Mail	Absentee Ballots
Campaign Organization	Campus Votes
Volunteer Activities	Rural Votes
Graphics and Photography	Votes in High-Rise Apartments
Campaign Law	Print and Electronic Advertising

Source: Chamber of Commerce of the United States.

however, clearly is becoming a more important factor in election campaigns, and the Treasury is now a significant fund raiser for presidential candidates of the major parties.

Since 1972, each taxpayer has had the opportunity to check off on his or her individual income tax return a $1 contribution from the U.S. Treasury to the forthcoming presidential election campaign ($2 for married taxpayers filing jointly). Another effort to increase the role of small contributors to election campaigns—and thus to lessen the impact of major interest groups—is the tax treatment of private campaign contributions. Since 1972, each taxpayer has been permitted to deduct up to $50 of political contributions from his or her taxable income ($100 in the case of married taxpayers filing a joint return); or the taxpayer may credit half of such contributions against his or her tax liability, up to a maximum of $12.50 ($25 in the case of joint returns by married taxpayers). As these provisions become widely used and are augmented by direct appropriations from the U.S. Treasury, the dependence of political parties on large contributors will be reduced substantially.

Business executives, as well as the public, might well bear in mind Peter Drucker's thoughts on this subject:

> If I were to have a criticism of the American businessman, it is that he has made no attempt to understand the political process. He attempts to influence it without understanding it.[16]

Some business organizations are attempting to meet Drucker's challenge. The National Chamber of Commerce has been sponsoring a series of political campaign management seminars. Designed to be nonpartisan in nature, the seminars are aimed at business executives who may become involved in cam-

---

[16]"Inside Peter Drucker," *Nation's Business,* March 1974, p. 63.

paigns for public office at various levels—federal, state, and local. The sessions are aimed at potential candidates, campaign managers, finance chairmen, as well as rank-and-file volunteers. Staffed by professional campaign consultants, the seminars show the various steps in developing a campaign, including administrative and financial aspects.

Table 17–1 reproduces the program outline of a political campaign management seminar in the fall of 1975. The sponsors stress that the sessions are devoted to techniques of political campaigning and avoid advocating positions on specific issues or supporting any candidates or political parties.

Chapter 18

The Rising Government Presence in Business Decision-Making

The increased federal presence in business management is far more fundamental than the more obvious cost and efficiency effects that arise from the multitude of government regulations of business. These less visible effects are in terms of the changing locus of decision-making and responsibility for private sector activities.

The first "managerial revolution" was noted by Berle and Means more than four decades ago and given the title by James Burnham three decades ago. They were referring to the divorce of the formal ownership of the modern corporation from the actual management.[1] A second managerial revolution is now under way, a silent bureaucratic revolution, in the course of which much—but certainly not all—of the decision-making in the American corporation is shifting once again. This time the shift is from the professional management selected by the corporation itself to the vast cadre of government regulators who are influencing and often controlling the key managerial decisions of the typical business firm.

---

[1] "In the corporate system, the 'owner' of industrial wealth is left with a mere symbol of ownership, while the power, the responsibility, and the substance which have been an integral part of ownership in the past are being transferred to a separate group in whose hands lie control." A. A. Berle, Jr. and G. C. Means, *The Modern Corporation and Private Property* (New York: Macmillan, 1932), p. 68; see also James Burnham, *The Managerial Revolution* (Bloomington: Indiana University Press, 1941).

A SECOND MANAGERIAL REVOLUTION?

This revolution is neither deliberate nor violent. But a revolution it truly is—in forcing a fundamental change in the structure of our society. The traditional concerns and debates in business-government relations ("Are we moving toward socialism?" "Are we in the grips of a military-industrial complex?") should be recognized as dealing with an age that already has passed.

It is not who owns the means of production, but who makes the key decisions that is crucial in evaluating the relative distribution of public and private power. What lines of business to go into? Which investments to undertake? What products to make? Under what conditions to produce them? What prices to charge? As we have seen, government rules and officials loom increasingly large in the process through which these questions are answered.

There are few examples of outright nationalization of specific industries and firms in the United States. Rather, the current trend is, as has been noted in earlier chapters, for the government to take over or at least share many of the key aspects of decision-making of all firms. We must also recognize that this is a silent revolution in many ways. For one thing, it is not led by a host of noisy trumpeters. In fact, in the main it is not even intentional or noticeable to the day-to-day observer. But that does not alter its deep impact.

Finally, the change that our industrial economy is undergoing must be understood as a bureaucratic revolution, but not as a conspiracy. Rather, what is involved is the lawful efforts of government civil servants going about their routine and assigned tasks—tasks which in concept are hard to speak ill of. Who is opposed to cleaning up the environment? Or enhancing job safety? Or improving consumer products? Or eliminating discrimination in employment?

Yet, if we step back and assess the long-term impacts on the private enterprise system of the rapidly growing host of government inspections, regulations, reviews, and subsidies, we find that the entire business-government relationship is being changed in the process. To be sure, the process is far from complete—and it proceeds unevenly in its various phases—but the results to date are clear enough: the government increasingly is participating in and often controlling the internal decisions of business enterprise, which are at the heart of the capitalist system.

It is important to understand that this silent bureaucratic revolution is not intended to undermine the capitalistic system. The men and women involved are patriotic citizens who are attempting to carry out high priority national objectives, which are considered to be basic to the quality of life in America.

Yet, those who have assigned them these tasks—the Congress and the executive branch leadership—often have failed to appreciate the significance of what they have been doing. If specific laws had been proposed or regulations promulgated for the government formally to take over private risk-bearing and initiative, the problem would have been faced head on, and the proposals likely defeated. That, of course, is one of the most significant aspects. This silent revolution is unintentional; it is merely an unexpected by-product—but far more than a merely undesirable side effect—of the expanding role of government in our modern society. President Ford, who served in the House of Representatives for 24 years, has stated, "Most members of Congress don't realize the burdens that are placed upon business by the legislation they pass."[2]

Senator Hubert Humphrey of Minnesota has offered a similar criticism:

> The government goes around willy-nilly making decisions of consequence. There was no estimate of the economic impact of the Occupational Safety Act, for example. I happen to be for the occupational safety program, but what were its economic implications? Did anyone think that through? No.[3]

Professor Thomas Ehrlich, dean of the Stanford Law School, has used the term "legal pollution" to describe what he calls the growing feeling that it is almost impossible to move "without running into a law or a regulation or a legal problem."[4]

As has been shown, the new type—and the almost infinite variety—of governmental regulation of business is not limited to the traditional regulatory agencies, such as the FTC, SEC, FPC, ICC, FCC, and so on. Rather, the line operating departments and bureaus of government—the Departments of Agriculture, Commerce, HEW, Interior, Justice, Labor, Transportation, and Treasury—are now involved in actions that affect virtually every firm and most of the key departments of each firm. Governmental controls make an impact on manufacturing, research and development, finance, personnel, marketing, facilities, and planning. The organizational chart of a hypothetical industrial firm, in Figure 18–1, is an attempt to convey graphically the diverse nature of federal involvement in so many aspects of business. The precise nature of business-government relationships, of course, will vary by industry, size of firm, location, and types of products produced and markets served.

Certainly the majority of public policy changes affecting business-government relations have been in the direction of greater government involvement—environmental controls, job safety inspections, equal employment opportunity enforcement, consumer product safety regulations, energy restrictions, and

---

[2] Juan Cameron, "Suppose There's A President Ford In Your Future," *Fortune,* March 1974, p. 206.

[3] Hubert H. Humphrey, "Planning Economic Policy," *Challenge,* March–April 1975, p. 22.

[4] "Complaints About Lawyers," Interview with Thomas Ehrlich, Dean, School of Law, Stanford University, *U.S. News and World Report,* July 21, 1975, p. 46.

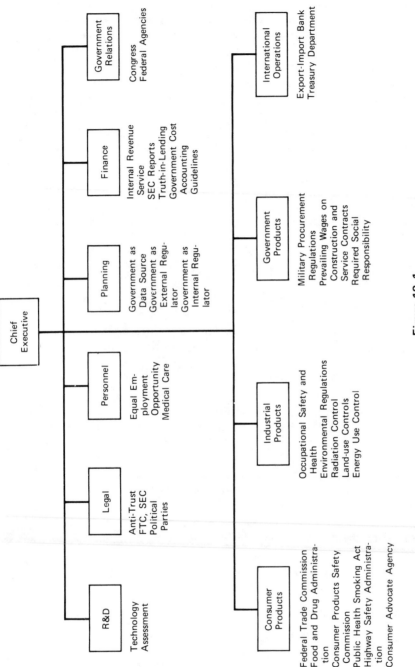

Figure 18-1

TYPICAL INDUSTRIAL CORPORATION AND FEDERAL GOVERNMENT RELATIONS

recording and reporting of items varying from domestic illnesses to foreign currency transactions. Indeed, when we attempt to look at the emerging business-government relationship from the business executive's viewpoint, a very considerable public presence is evident in what ostensibly, or at least historically, have been private affairs.

No business official today, neither the head of a large company nor the corner grocer, can operate without considering a multitude of governmental restrictions and regulations. His or her costs and profits can be affected as much by a bill passed in Washington as by a management decision in the front office or a customer's decision at the checkout counter.

PRESSURES FOR INCREASING THE GOVERNMENTAL PRESENCE

The rising government presence in internal business decision-making is a phenomenon that is still in the process of development, rather than one that has attained a "steady state." The basic factors causing the change are diverse, ranging from the concern by some with the quality of life to the desire by others to increase the social responsiveness of business enterprise. Yet, proposals for changes in public policy affecting business are virtually all variations on a single predictable theme: to increase the scope and degree of governmental involvement while shifting costs from the federal treasury to the products and services that consumers buy. Restrictions on the use of land owned by private individuals and companies is one obvious area that has received great congressional and public attention. Yet, more indicative of future policy changes may be the bill introduced by 23 members of the Congress in January 1975 (H.R. 76, the proposed National Employment Priorities Act of 1975). H.R. 76 would require that employees and affected communities be given two-year advance notifications of plant closings or relocations if the action would result in 15 percent or more of the employees (or 15 percent of the employees who are members of any labor union) losing their jobs. For "good cause," the Secretary of Labor may approve notification in a shorter period. The company's notification must include the following information:

1. The reasons for the proposed closing or transfer.
2. Alternatives to closing or transfer.
3. The unemployment loss that would result.
4. Plans to alleviate the effects of the job loss.
5. The "economic circumstances" of the plant, including profitability and future investment, employment, and production plans.
6. The "economic circumstances" of the overall company and the opportunity for transferring personnel elsewhere.

Should the Secretary of Labor rule that the proposed closing or transfer is not justified, the company would lose a variety of tax benefits for up to 10 years, including the investment credit, the accelerated depreciation range, the foreign tax credit, and deductions for ordinary and necessary expenses related to the transfer. Even if the plant closing or transfer is determined to be justified, these penalties can be invoked if the Secretary of Labor determines that the action could have been avoided had the company accepted the special federal assistance that would be established by the bill. The federal government would be given great discretion to provide grants, loans, and interest subsidies to companies qualifying for such aid. Hearings on a similar bill (H.R. 13541) were held in October 1974. The possibility thus looms that it literally may be difficult to go out of business, without at least some form of federal review.

A more basic expansion in government influence on private sector decision-making may result from the efforts that are under way to establish a formal system of national economic planning. In recent years, the Federal Budget and the Annual Economic Report of the President have been utilized as vehicles for presenting broad-gauged, long-term projections of future economic conditions and of national priorities, at least to the extent that the changing allocation of federal financial resources indicates revisions in the relative importance of the major program and policy areas. The initial suggestions for a more formalized planning system are in terms of planning information, especially forecasts of future needs, to guide decision-makers in the private sector.

In the words of the Initiative Committee for National Economic Planning, "The planning office would not set specific goals for General Motors, General Electric, General Foods, or any other individual firm." But the proposed new central planning office would indicate the number of cars, the number of generators, and the quantity of frozen foods that the American public is expected to require in, say, five years, and it would try "to induce" the relevant industries to act accordingly.

But suppose that General Motors or General Electric wishes to rely on its own market surveys rather than on the forecasts of the government planners? Strong hints of coercion are visible in the Initiative Committee's proposal. The inducements would be laws, as specific as necessary, on taxes, subsidies, and environmental problems. In the words of the Committee, "The heart of planning is to go from information to action."[5]

To be sure, long-range planning techniques are in widespread use in the private sector. But there are many differences between business and government planning. Boiled down to its fundamentals, it is the difference between forecasting and reacting to the future and trying to control it. Corporate planning of

[5]"For a National Economic Planning System," *Challenge,* March–April 1975, pp. 51–53.

necessity is based on the principle of trade—attempting to persuade the rest of society that they ought to purchase the goods and services produced by a given plan; the controls that may accompany the plan are internally oriented. If things go wrong, the onus falls on the officers, employees, and shareholders. In striking contrast, the government is sovereign and its planning can ultimately involve coercion, the use of its sovereign powers to achieve the results that it desires. Its controls are thus externally oriented, extending their sway over the entire society. If things do not work out as well as expected in public planning, it is the taxpayer and the consumer who bear the main burden.

When we consider the period beyond 1980, the possibility emerges that a fundamental restructuring may occur in the nature of the corporation. Large nationwide corporations—at least in some industries operating in the field of basic natural resources—may be required to obtain federal charters, the rationale being that the individual state governments cannot effectively regulate their total operations. Particularly those companies that receive large federal subsidies may find that the government will appoint one or more members of their boards of directors or require that they be designated by some other group. These "outside" officials may not be responsible to the shareholders, but rather to the public in general or to interests external to the firm, such as labor unions or consumers.

In the early nineteenth century the Congress did grant federal charters to various private enterprises, including railroads, telegraph, canal, and bridge companies. States soon began granting charters to local businesses, usually those residing in the state of incorporation. With the development of the state role in this field, congressional involvement was curtailed sharply.[6] In recent years, the Congress has in general limited itself to incorporating enterprises with special ties to the federal government, notably the Communication Satellite Corporation, Amtrak, and the Corporation for Public Broadcasting.

Of direct concern to American-based multinational corporations are the current efforts of several Western European countries to require local companies to appoint employee representatives to their governing boards. The West German government is considering legislation that would require companies having more than 2,000 employees—including German subsidiaries of United States firms—to give half the seats on their supervisory boards (equivalent to our boards of directors) to representatives of the employees. This is already the case in the coal and iron and steel industries. In those industries, each supervisory board has a neutral member, agreed upon by stockholder and employee representatives, who can break deadlocks.[7]

[6]Willard F. Mueller, "Federal Chartering of Corporations," *American Federationist,* June 1973, p. 18.

[7]"Workers on the Board: The German Debate," *Morgan Guaranty Survey,* November 1974, pp. 10–11.

In Sweden, the government and the Confederation of Trade Unions have proposed a comprehensive set of measures that would alter the traditional relationships between labor and management. The proposals include employees sharing control over the appointment of directors and foremen, pricing policies, and mergers and expansion.[8] Professor George C. Lodge predicts, for the United States, that more use will be made of the corporate chartering power to harmonize corporations with the public interest. He sees the corporate charter increasingly as an instrument for defining the purposes and functions of large corporations.[9]

Efforts are already under way in the United States to extend the antitrust laws to require breaking up large corporations in markets where four or fewer firms hold dominating positions. One pending bill (S. 1284, the Antitrust Improvements Act of 1975 introduced by Senators Philip Hart and Hugh Scott) would require very large corporations to give the government 60-days notice of any merger or acquisition involving a company worth $10 million or more, and would delay the effectiveness of the merger or acquisition if the government files an antitrust action to permit the federal courts to rule on its legality. The bill would also allow the attorney general of any state to file antitrust suits to collect triple damages on behalf of the citizens of that state.

Although such sweeping legislation may not be enacted in its present form, the possibility of some portions being adopted, perhaps substantially modified, should not be ruled out in any realistic appraisal of future prospects. Much will depend on the public's evaluation of the future performance of American business, an evaluation that increasingly is concerned with factors other than profitability. These additional factors range from the basic honesty and integrity of corporate management to its ability to help achieve a variety of social goals. As Professor Lee Preston has noted, the corporation is created out of a public policy process, not from a biological process. Its continued existence depends entirely on public approval.[10] Although the scope of government influence in the operation of business firms in the years ahead is going to increase, it does seem likely that large corporate entities will remain the primary unit of economic activity in the United States for the foreseeable future.[11] Lodge contends that there are no instruments of public management or government entrepreneurship that hold out any promise of better governing the large sector of the economy that historically has been left up to the interplay of market forces.[12]

---

[8] Bernard Weinraub, "Swedes Propose Reform to Widen Worker Role," *New York Times,* October 22, 1975, p. 10.

[9] "Recovery and Beyond," *Saturday Review,* October 22, 1975, p. 24.

[10] See Lee E. Preston, *Socializing the Corporation.* Lecture Presented at Rochester Institute of Technology, March 14, 1974, p. 6.

[11] Ibid, p. 3.

[12] "Recovery and Beyond," p. 26.

PRESSURES FOR REDUCED CONTROLS

Even though most of the changes in government regulation of business are designed to benefit the consuming public, one frequently neglected aspect will surface to an increasing extent as the widening array of controls take their full effect: It is the consumer who ultimately pays the added costs that almost invariably result. Although the manufacturer or distributor initially may bear the expense of destroying products that are banned or revising procedures declared hazardous, much of the increased production costs that result inevitably is passed on to the public in the form of higher prices.

Yet, the key price that the nation may be paying is the attenuation of the risk-bearing and entrepreneurial characteristics of our private enterprise system, which, at least in the past, have contributed so effectively to rapid rates of innovation, productivity, growth, and progress. One hidden cost of federal regulation is the reduced rate of innovation that occurs as the result of governmental restrictions. The longer that it takes for some change to be approved by the federal regulatory agency—a new or improved product, a more efficient production process, and so on—the less likely that the change will be made. In any event, innovation will be delayed. This is clearly seen in the case of the asthma drug beclomethasone dipropionate (let us call it BD). Although this drug has been used by millions of asthma patients in Great Britain, it still has not received the approval of the U.S. Food and Drug Administration.

BD is described as a safe and effective replacement for the drugs now administered to chronic asthma patients, but without the adverse side effects of the drugs in use in the United States. Unlike BD, the steroids currently used in this country, such as prednisone, can stunt growth in children, worsen diabetes, increase weight through water retention, and cause bone softening and rounding of the face. The delaying procedures of the FDA are preventing Americans from switching to BD, the safer product.[13]

Professor William Wardell of the University of Rochester School of Medicine and Dentistry has studied in detail the advantages and disadvantages of the more liberal policy in Great Britain toward the introduction of new drugs. He has concluded that, on balance, Great Britain gained in comparison with the United States from its "permissive" policy toward the marketing of new drugs:

> ... Britain suffered more toxicity due to new drugs than did the United States, as could have been anticipated from the fact that more new drugs were marketed there. However, considering the size of the total burden of

[13] Dr. William Franklin and Dr. Francis Lowell, "Unapproved Drugs in the Practice of Medicine," *New England Journal of Medicine,* May 15, 1975, pp. 1075–77.

drug toxicity, the portion due to new drugs was extremely small, and would in any case be at least partially offset by the adverse effects of older alternative drugs had the latter been used instead. Conversely, Britain experienced clearly discernible gains by introducing useful new drugs, either sooner than the United States or exclusively.[14]

Professor Sam Peltzman of the University of Chicago has estimated some of the costs of the drug lag in the United States. He specifically analyzed the 1962 amendments to the Food and Drug Act, which ostensibly were designed to keep ineffective drugs off the market by extending the process of authorizing new drugs prior to their being available to the public. The main impact of the legislation has been to delay the introduction of effective drugs by about four years and to lead to higher prices for drugs. He estimates the resultant loss to the consumer to be in the neighborhood of $200-$300 million a year. Peltzman also has calculated that if the drugs that combat tuberculosis had been delayed by two years, the average delay now imposed by the Food and Drug Administration, the result would have been approximately 45,000 additional deaths.[15]

The adverse effect of regulation on innovation is likely to be felt more strongly by smaller firms, and thus have an anticompetitive impact. According to Dr. Mitchell Zavon, president of the American Association of Poison Control Centers:

We've got to the point in regulatory action where it's become so costly and risky to bring out products that only the very largest firms can afford to engage in these risky ventures. To bring out a new pesticide you have to figure a cost of $7,000,000 and seven years of time.

Federal regulation has other "costs" to the economy. The impact on the prospects for economic growth and productivity can be seen by examining some recent estimates of the size and composition of investment by manufacturing companies. Lewis Beman has estimated that, in real terms (after eliminating the effects of inflation), total capital spending by American manufacturing companies in 1973 was no higher than the level attained in 1969, about $26 billion.

However, a much larger proportion of the 1973 outlays was devoted to pollution and safety outlays than in 1969. Hence, the effective additions to plant and equipment—the real investment in modernization and new capacity—were lower in 1973, by over $3 billion. This helps to explain why for some substantial period in the economic expansion of 1973, the American economy appeared to lack needed productive capacity, despite what had been very substantial nominal investments in new plant and equipment in recent years.

[14]William M. Wardell, "Therapeutic implications of the drug lag," *Clinical Pharmacology and Therapeutics,* January 1974, p. 73.

[15]Sam Peltzman, "An Evaluation of Consumer Protection Legislation: The 1962 Drug Amendments," *Journal of Political Economy,* September/October 1973, p. 1090.

We can obtain some understanding of the future consequences of pursuing the path on which the nation has embarked by examining that sector of American industry that already has gone down the road of relying upon government leadership and assistance to a substantial degree. Over a period of three decades, the major defense contractors have grown accustomed to the federal government making the basic decisions on which products are to be produced, how the firm is to go about producing them, how capital is to be provided, and in the process assuming a major portion of the risk and the role of the entrepreneur. More Lockheeds and General Dynamics—or more 1011s and TFXs (to cite the well-known products of the two most government-dependent of the large defense contractors)—would hardly be a way of achieving either a rising living standard or a reduced rate of inflation.

As the various costs and other disadvantages of federal controls begin visibly to exceed the apparent benefits, public pressures may mount on government regulators to moderate the now increasingly stringent rules and regulations that they apply. At present, for example, a mislabeled consumer product that is declared an unacceptable hazard often is destroyed. In the future, the producer or seller more likely may be required merely to relabel it correctly—also thus avoiding increasing the environmental problem of disposing of solid and liquid wastes. Rather than dealing with such trivia as lounge facilities for men and evening carfare allowances for women, the equal employment efforts hopefully will focus on rooting out the truly serious discrimination that still exists in hiring, training, and promoting men and women of various racial, religious, and ethnic groups.

Admittedly, the exercise of judgment in regulatory matters can involve striking a balance in some extremely difficult areas, literally of human life. Dr. Alexander M. Schmidt, Commissioner of Food and Drugs, has stated, "In FDA decisions, as in all aspects of human endeavor, we must accept the probability of nonexistence of absolute safety. We usually make our regulatory judgments based on an accommodation between benefits and risks."[16]

Schmidt raises several extremely difficult questions: Just where and when does one draw the line in weighing demonstrable benefit against theoretical risk? Who is to draw the line? Government or industry or the individual consumer? In passing, the commissioner criticizes the anticancer clauses in food safety laws because, literally interpreted, they leave no room for scientific judgment, calling for zero risks from all new food ingredients.[17]

A fundamental change in the regulatory process would come about via the introduction of the requirement to file an economic impact statement before a federal agency could promulgate new regulatory standards. Such action would be in the fashion of the current environmental impact statements. In November

[16]Alexander M. Schmidt, "The Benefit-Risk Equation," *FDA Consumer*, May 1974, p. 1.

[17]Ibid.

1974, President Ford instructed the federal agencies under his jurisdiction to examine the effects of the major regulatory actions that they would be taking on costs, productivity, employment, and other economic factors (Executive Order 11821). Although a useful step forward, there are severe shortcomings in this effort. First of all, many of the key regulatory agencies—ranging from the Consumer Product Safety Commission to the Federal Trade Commission—are so-called independent agencies, which are beyond the president's purview.

Even in the case of the regulatory activities that come within the president's jurisdiction, the new policy is limited to the regulations that, in the issuing agency's own estimation, are "major." In any event, the agencies covered by the executive order are only required to examine the economic aspects of their actions. A broader approach seems warranted.

Society is now supposed to examine the impact on the environment of the various major actions that it takes. Would it not also be appropriate to require each federal, state, and local environmental agency to assess the impacts of its actions on the society as a whole, and particularly on the economy? Surely a cleaner environment is an important national objective. But it is not the *only* national objective. Certainly the nation has no stake in selecting the most expensive or most disruptive ways of achieving its environmental goals.

The same balanced approach could be applied to the other regulatory programs, including product safety, job health, equal employment, energy, and the like. In a sense, public policy would be taking from both the old and the new models of government regulation of business to develop a superior approach.

Prior to the enactment of the wave of new regulatory legislation, the noted free market economist F. A. Hayek provided a theoretical evaluation for the approach suggested here:

> . . .a free market system does not exclude on principle . . . all regulations governing the techniques of production. . . They will normally raise the cost of production, or what amounts to the same thing, reduce overall productivity. But if this effect on cost is fully taken into account and it is still thought worthwhile to incur the cost to achieve a given end, there is little more to be said about it. The appropriateness of such measures must be judged by comparing the overall costs with the gain; it cannot be conclusively determined by appeal to a general principle.[18]

Much would depend on the "teeth" that would be put into the required statement. Merely legislating the performance of some economic analysis by an unsympathetic regulator would primarily delay the regulatory process and make it more costly. But limiting government regulation to those instances where the total benefits to society exceed the cost would be a major departure. It could significantly slow down, if not reverse, the current rising trend of federal regula-

[18]F. A. Hayek, *The Constitution of Liberty* (Chicago: University of Chicago Press, 1960), pp. 224–25.

tion of business. (See appendix at end of this chapter for an example of benefit/cost analysis of federal regulation.)

Getting beyond questions of mathematical measurement of the gains and losses from regulation, there may be a case for "economizing" on the power that the Congress grants to the regulatory agencies. One member of the federal judiciary who encounters a large number of regulatory questions, Judge Carl McGowan, describes the phenomenon whereby the Congress "finesses" hard choices of policy. Instead, the legislature is making broad delegations of authority to heads of government departments or newly created commissions; the latter are required to make policy choices in the form of implementing regulations designed to achieve the general objectives of cleaner air or greater product safety or working conditions less hazardous to health. Judge McGowan notes that the protracted court litigation that results interferes with the traditional judicial functions.[19]

These nonmeasurable impacts of government regulation of business also need to be taken into account when new or expanded applications of the government's regulatory powers are contemplated. At the enforcement level, there may be no effective way of legislating the use of common sense, and thus some restraint in the use of the vast regulatory power available to governmental agencies.

An example of the problem, and one with a happy ending, is provided by the encounter between the city of Canton, Illinois, and the State Environmental Protection Agency. The blasts from a whistle atop the International Harvester plant in that locality apparently had been used for generations by the local residents as a convenient measure of the time of day. The company temporarily shut down the whistle when representatives of the Illinois EPA indicated that they might have to take action to curb the "noise pollution" it was creating.

The state environment agency backed off, and the company resumed blowing the whistle, after angry citizen response ensued, ranging from a petition to letters to state representatives to newspaper editorials.[20]

A NEW APPROACH TO BUSINESS-GOVERNMENT RELATIONS

By and large, the relationships between business and government in the United States can be described as basically adversary in nature. Government probes, inspects, taxes, influences, regulates, and punishes. At least that appears to be the dominant view in many quarters, in both the public and private sectors. In many ways, this unfavorable view does seem to come uncomfortably close to approaching reality.

[19] Carl McGowan, in an unpublished lecture to the University of Chicago Law School Alumni Association, Chicago, April 17, 1975, pp. 12–13 *et ff.*

[20] "A Tale of a Whistle," *Wall Street Journal,* January 16, 1974, p. 12.

The contrast is striking between this situation (or at least this view of it) and what is often taken to be the dominant European and Japanese approach, a "partnership," or at least close cooperation, between business and government. This has lead to suggestions that we import the foreign model of business-government relations. It is often contended that such closer working relations would improve our competitive position abroad as well as enhance productivity at home. However, this approach could result in submerging the public, and especially the consumer, interest.

Yet, the status quo has many undesirable features. It does not seem sensible to expect American business to be successful in waging a two-front war, struggling against increasing governmental encroachment at home and competing against government-supported enterprises abroad.

Hence, a third approach is suggested here, which might be considered a variant of the attitude toward international relations often called "peaceful co-existence." That is, public policy might well explore the possibilities of a sensible division of labor between the public and private sectors in achieving basic national objectives. A short summary may turn out to be more caricature than description, but the following is offered as portraying the current method of decision-making on national priorities, with particular reference to the impacts on business. Subsequently, a new model of national decision-making will be presented.

In practice, decisions on government budgets, particularly on the spending side, are made in the small. Congress acts on a great many individual authorization bills and appropriation statutes. When the bits and pieces are added up, that is done usually on a functional basis—so much for defense, a bit less for welfare, much less for education, and so on. In this approach, business (if it is thought about at all) is regarded as an input, one of a variety of tools or mechanisms that can be drawn upon. In the case of defense spending, business firms are very heavily utilized, although not always in an effective manner. In the case of the rapidly expanding income-maintenance programs, in contrast, they are hardly involved at all.

Thus, a shift in emphasis in budget priorities from warfare to welfare, as indeed has been occurring in recent years, means—perhaps altogether unwittingly—a reduced emphasis on the direct utilization of business firms in carrying out national priorities. The earlier concern about moving toward a "contract state," in which key governmental responsibilities are delegated to private corporations, quite properly has faded away.

Another fiscal development, however, has been occurring, which raises a quite different concern. The desire to exercise a greater degree of control over the size and growth of the federal budget—be that due to the economic concern over inflationary effects of budget deficits or the more philosophical resistance to the growth of the public sector—had led to an effort to "economize" on direct government spending by using government controls.

We need a fundamental rethinking of the tendency for government increasingly to involve itself in what essentially is internal business decision-making. One model that could be followed is one where the process of determining national priorities would be viewed as a two-step affair. The first step should continue, as at present, to focus on determining how much of our resources should be devoted to defense, welfare, education, and so forth, at least to the extent that these basic issues are now decided by design at all.

But this determination should be accompanied by a general and tentative allocation of responsibilities among the major sectors of the economy. This type of indicative planning would recognize that the constant and increasing nibbling away at business prerogatives and entrepreneurial characteristics has a very substantial cost—a reduced effectiveness in achieving some basic national objectives, notably (to use the language of the Employment Act of 1946) "maximum employment, production, and purchasing power." The proposed planning approach would also take account of the different mix of constituencies that the public and private sectors are primarily geared to serve.

In this day when benefit-cost analysis has become fashionable, we should not be oblivious of the very real if not generally measurable effects of converting ostensibly private organizations into involuntary agents of the federal establishment. Rather than pursuing the current course, the nation should determine which of its objectives can be achieved more effectively in the private sector and go about creating an overall environment that is more conducive to the attainment of those objectives.

Without prejudging the results of such an examination, it would appear reasonable to expect that primarily social objectives—such as improved police services—would be the primary province of government. And primarily economic objectives—notably training, motivating, and usefully employing the bulk of the nation's work force—would be viewed as mainly a responsibility of the private sector, and especially of business firms.

The new model of national decision-making envisioned here hardly calls for an abdication of government concern with the substantive issues previously enumerated. Rather, it would require a redirection of the methods selected for achieving these essentially worthy ends. In the environmental area, for example, much of the current dependence on direct controls should be shifted to utilizing the more indirect but powerful incentives available through the price system. Specifically, imaginative use of "sumptuary" excise taxation, as we have grown accustomed to in the cases of tobacco products and alcoholic beverages, can be used to alter basic production and consumption patterns.

The desired results would not be accomplished by fiat, but rather by making the high pollutant product or service more expensive relative to the low pollutant product or service. The basic guiding principle in this area would be that people and institutions do not pollute because they get a positive enjoyment from messing up the environment. Rather, they pollute because it is easier, cheaper, or more profitable to do so. In lieu of a corps of inspectors or regulators, we would use the price system to make polluting harder, more expensive, and less profitable.

Effluent fees encourage extensive efforts to increase pollution abatement by those who can do so at relatively low cost and less antipollution efforts by those for whom the costs would be greater. The objective, often overlooked, is not to punish polluters or to maximize the cost of ecological improvement, but to get a cleaner environment. A study of the Delaware estuary concluded that modest improvements in water quality might cost only half as much if accomplished by effluent fees as they would if done through uniform controls over discharges.[21]

There is a parallel here to the operation of a tariff system. Even a tariff instituted ostensibly only for revenue purposes keeps out some products, to the extent that demand and supply respond at all to price changes. And the higher the tariff, the closer it comes to becoming a "protective" tariff, keeping out the undesirable item entirely.

Similarly, it seems that the current emphasis on putting ever more complicated and costly safety equipment in the automobile is an alternative—a very inflationary alternative—to achieving a higher degree of motor vehicle safety through tougher enforcement of existing laws, especially those relating to drunken driving.

Other areas of the economy could benefit from using alternatives to governmental intervention in business operations. One such area, as we have seen, is the direction over the flow of saving and investment, a basic aspect of a capitalistic or other advanced economy. A result of the expanded use of governmentally sponsored credit agencies, such as the Federal Intermediate Credit Banks, the Export-Import Bank, and a host of others, is that a rising portion—as much as a third in recent years—of all the funds raised in ostensibly private capital markets in the United States now funnels through these federal financial intermediaries. In every period of credit tightness, there is a clamor for setting up additional intermediaries, such as an Aerospace Reconstruction Finance Corporation or an Energy Research and Development Corporation, to assure yet another category of borrowers ready access to capital markets.

Yet none of these federal instrumentalities do anything to add to the available pool of investment funds. In practice, their creation and expansion amounts to robbing Peter to pay or lend to Paul. These instrumentalities simultaneously reduce the tendency of the market to allocate capital resources to the more efficient undertakings, and result in the "unprotected" and truly private borrowers bidding up interest rates to obtain the funds they require. A more positive and fruitful approach to national policy in this area would be to create an overall economic environment that provides more incentive to individuals and

---

[21]Allen V. Kneese and Blair T. Bower, *Managing Water Quality: Economics, Technology, Institutions* (Baltimore: Johns Hopkins Press, 1968), pp. 158–64.

business firms to save, and thus to generate, more investment funds available to the society as a whole.

In the OSHA area the law has lost sight of the basic objective—to achieve a safer working environment. Instead, the current emphasis is on the establishment of bureaucratic procedures and the punishment of violators. An appraisal of the first four years of OSHA by one of its congressional sponsors focused, not on the results that it had achieved, but instead on the "inputs"—the number of officials that had been hired, the comprehensive standards that had been promulgated, and the large number of inspections that had been conducted.[22] As pointed out by Professor James Chelius of Purdue University, the danger for organizations such as OSHA is that its intermediate goals (for example, number of inspectors) become the ultimate goals of the organization. "That danger is, of course, more critical for a government organization because it lacks the ultimate discipline of the marketplace."[23]

In the more positive spirit of the approach suggested here, the basic emphasis of occupational safety and health legislation would be changed from prescribing specific practices to be followed in a company's operations to focusing on reducing the accident and health hazard rate in a given industry or plant. Government policy makers might also give greater weight to Lee Preston's observation that most companies and industries have evolved safety and health systems well above those that could be justified by any strict profit-cost calculation. He attributes that to a variety of factors, including union pressures, industry wide activities, and simple humanitarianism.[24]

It should be recognized that the results of such decentralized decision-making may not necessarily coincide with those of a more centralized system. We would undoubtedly have a different mix of goods and services under the two approaches. That implicit reordering of priorities may be a real price we pay for the reduction of centralized control. Yet, the reordering of priorities may only happen in a relative sense. If our nation's resources are utilized more effectively as a result of reducing the costly burden of government controls, influence, and reporting, the increased national output could yield perhaps the same or even more of the new lower priority items (in absolute terms). In any event, the total level of economic welfare should be enhanced—or, at the minimum, we will have a greater opportunity for enhancing it—as a result of the increased efficiency and productivity that is to be anticipated, and in a less inflationary environment.

The revised division of labor between public and private undertakings envisioned here should not be expected to remain invariant over time. Rather, it should change with underlying circumstances, foreign and domestic, and as ex-

[22]William Steiger, "OSHA: Four Years Later," *Labor Law Journal,* XXV, no. 12 (1974), pp. 723–28.

[23]James R. Chelius, *Expectations for OSHA's Performance: The Lessons of Theory and Empirical Evidence,* March 1975 (processed), pp. 6–7.

[24]Preston, *Socializing the Corporation,* p. 13.

perience is gained from following a strategy of peaceful coexistence between business and government in the United States. Hopefully, that dividing line between public and private responsibilities will shift back and forth in the future, rather than in a predictable single direction as has been the past experience.

It is pertinent that such a strong advocate of the free market as Professor Hayek has made a compelling case for some significant government role in the economy, pointing out that he did not mean "that government should never concern itself with any economic matters." Rather, he points out:

> A functioning market economy presupposes certain activities on the part of the state; there are some other such activities by which its functioning will be assisted; and it can tolerate many more, provided that they are of the kind which are compatible with a functioning market. . . The range and variety of government action that is, at least in principle, reconcilable with a free system is thus considerable.[25]

APPENDIX: BENEFIT-COST ANALYSIS OF TRAFFIC SAFETY STANDARDS*

Congressional concern over the increasing number of motor vehicle deaths led to the enactment of the National Traffic and Motor Vehicle Safety Act of 1966, whose purpose was to reduce motor vehicle accidents and the deaths and injuries resulting from them.

As one means of reducing these deaths and injuries, the act directed the Department of Transportation to establish motor vehicle safety standards. The National Highway Traffic Safety Administration does such work for the Transportation Department. The act required that the standards be reasonable, practicable, and appropriate for the particular type of motor vehicle or item of equipment to which they applied.

In reporting on the proposed legislation that became law, both the Senate Commerce Committee and the House Committee on Interstate and Foreign Commerce stated that safety was to be the overriding consideration in issuing a standard. Both committees pointed out, however, that the motoring public's cost to purchase and maintain safety equipment required by a standard also should be considered. In this regard, the Senate Committee said that, in addition to the technical feasibility of the standard and adequate lead-time for the industry to develop and produce safety equipment, reasonableness of equipment cost

---

[25]Hayek, *Constitution of Liberty*, pp. 222, 231.

*The material in this section is based on Comptroller General of the United States, *Need to Improve Benefit-Cost Analyses in Setting Motor Vehicle Safety Standards*, B-164497(3) (Washington, D.C.: U.S. General Accounting Office, 1974), n. 1–14.

should be considered. The House Committee said that all relevant, including economic, factors should be considered in determining practicality of a standard.

Benefit-Cost Analyses

The National Highway Traffic Safety Administration uses benefit-cost analyses primarily to establish an internal order of priorities among all safety standards. The analyses are considered in evaluating the merits of a proposed safety standard, along with technical feasibility; legislative mandates; congressional, public, and industry views; and legal considerations.

A benefit-cost analysis of a safety standard involves estimating, in dollars, the benefits from establishing the standard and the consumer costs to comply with the standard. Comparing these totals, usually by dividing dollar benefits by dollar costs, gives a benefit-cost ratio. A ratio greater than one indicates that the estimated dollar benefits from establishing a safety standard exceed the estimated cost to comply with the standard. The Safety Administration measures benefits by estimating how much accidents, fatalities, injuries, and property damage cost society and by evaluating a standard's effectiveness in reducing such costs. Costs to comply with the standard include the consumer's cost for the safety equipment.

Comparisons of Estimated Costs of Motor Vehicle Accidents

The U.S. Safety Administration and the private National Safety Council estimated the annual costs of motor vehicle accidents. The Safety Administration's estimates were for use in benefit-cost analyses, and the Council's estimates were for use by state highway officials in requesting appropriations and by research workers and others in the field of safety. The estimates shown in the following table vary widely because of differences in base years, data sources, statistical bases, assumptions, and calculations of future costs.

The Safety Administration and the Safety Council estimates are given in present value terms. Under this method, the current value of future costs is calculated by using a discount rate. Discounting future costs makes them comparable to present costs, that is, the present value of costs. The higher the discount rate used, the lower the value that is placed on future costs. The Safety Administration used a 7 percent discount rate and the Council used a 3.5 percent discount rate.

The Safety Administration measured all costs that directly or indirectly caused a reduction in society's total welfare. It pointed out that each vehicle accident diminished individual and societal welfare. The Safety Administration contended that society's welfare was considerably more than its economic wellbeing and that money could be used only as a proxy measure for estimating

ESTIMATED COSTS OF MOTOR VEHICLE ACCIDENTS IN 1971
(in millions)

Type of cost	Safety Administration	Safety Council
Costs estimated by both:		
Future earnings lost	$18,100	$ 3,700
Medical costs	1,950	1,100
Property damage	7,100	5,000
Insurance administration	6,600	6,000
Total	33,750	15,800
Costs estimated only by Safety Administration:		
Home and family duties	4,500	—
Pain and suffering	3,800	—
Legal and court costs	1,050	—
Service to community	900	—
Time and money losses to others	800	—
Miscellaneous losses	800	—
Asset losses	300	—
Employer losses	50	—
Funeral costs	50	—
Total	12,250	—
Total Costs	$46,000	$15,800

changes in welfare. It further contended that, although the severe shortcomings of measuring welfare in terms of money were obvious, there was no better standard of value useful for public policy decision. Accordingly, the agency attempted to measure and translate identifiable inconvenience and hardship associated with motor vehicle accidents, such as pain and suffering, inability to perform home and family duties, loss of service to community, and similar types of costs, into dollar and cent equivalents.

The Safety Council, in contrast, tried to measure economic costs in what it considered to be the real dollars lost as a result of motor vehicle accidents. Inconvenience and hardship costs were not included in its estimates because it believed that such costs, although very important to the individual who suffered as a result of an accident, did not represent a cost to the rest of society.

Costs estimated by all future earnings lost. The main reasons for the different estimates of earnings lost were the differences in statistical bases, assumptions, and computations used in estimating average annual earnings lost and the number of injuries.

	Safety Administration	Safety Council
	(In billions)	
Fatalities	$ 7.3	$ 2.4
Injuries	10.8	1.3
Total	$18.1	$ 3.7

The Safety Administration estimated that $132,000 in average lifetime earnings would be lost for each of 55,000 traffic fatalities. The estimate was based on assuming that, in the absence of an accident, a person would be productively employed between the ages of 20 and 65 and would earn $9,196 annually at the time of death.

The computation assumed that a child who died in an accident otherwise would have entered the work force at age 20 and remained productively employed for 45 years and that an adult who died in an accident otherwise would have remained productive for an average 20 more years. The Safety Administration separately determined the earnings lost for children and for adults and computed a weighted average wage loss, using the ratio of child to adult fatalities. It based its estimate on gross earnings, adjusted for annual income growth, because it contended that, if a potential accident victim was prevented from dying as a result of some safety investment, society's benefit was equal to the full amount of the person's earnings. In comparison, the Council used net earnings—earnings less the cost of self-maintenance—on the assumption that loss to the family of the deceased more properly measured the economic loss resulting from a traffic fatality.

It estimated that average lifetime earnings of $44,000 would be lost for each of 54,700 traffic fatalities. The Council grouped people by sex, race, and age, and for each group determined motor vehicle fatality rates and net earnings lost, considering annual income growth, unemployment, and mortality rates.

A major cause of variation in the estimate of earnings lost was the difference in estimates of the numbers of injuries and average earnings lost. The Safety Administration estimated that about 3.8 million people suffering injuries of varying severity would lose earnings of about $10.8 billion. It based its estimate of total injuries on a 1969 National Health Survey adjusted to 1971. Its estimates of the severity of injuries—8,000 persons permanently, totally disabled; 250,000 persons permanently partially disabled; and 3,545,000 persons temporarily disabled—were derived from an analysis of a 1970 Department of Transportation study on the automobile personal injury claims. Calculations of average income lost were made under the assumptions established for estimating income lost in fatality cases and were adjusted for the degree of severity of the injuries.

The Safety Council estimated that persons suffering injuries of varying severity would lose about $1.3 billion in earnings. It assumed one-half as many injuries as the Safety Administration used. This difference is attributable to the fact that the Safety Administration included all individuals who have had to restrict their activities or receive medical attention because of injury, whereas the Council did not include less seriously injured individuals in its estimates.

Medical costs.   Major differences in the estimates of medical costs resulted primarily from differences in the Safety Administration's and the Safety Council's estimates of average medical costs for the several classifications of injury severity. The Safety Administration used the same number of fatalities and injuries for estimating medical costs that it had developed for estimating earnings lost. It based its estimates of average costs on a Department of Transportation study on automobile insurance and compensation and on a medical cost study prepared by the Social Security Administration. The average costs ranged from $315 for each of an estimated 3,545,000 persons experiencing temporary disability to $7,900 for each of 8,000 persons suffering permanent, total disability.

The Council's estimate of average medical cost was based on National Center for Health Statistics data and information from state accident reports, social security bulletins, and the *American Hospital Journal.* The average costs ranged from $8 for each person experiencing a nondisabling injury to a high of $1,090 for each person suffering a disabling injury requiring hospitalization.

Property damage.   Differences in the estimates of property damage appear primarily attributable to differences in sources used by the two organizations. The Safety Administration's estimate was partly based on accident cost studies made for Illinois, Ohio, and Washington, D.C. The Council's estimate was based on the consumer price index for auto repairs and maintenance and on data made available by insurance companies.

The Safety Council defined insurance administration costs as the difference between premiums paid to insurance companies and claims paid by them. Insurance claims paid were included in the estimates of earnings lost, medical and hospital expenses, and property damage. Thus, on the assumption that in the absence of accidents there would be no need for automobile insurance, including insurance administration costs has the effect of including all automobile insurance costs in the estimate of automobile accident loss. Insurance administration costs were estimated at $6 billion.

The Safety Administration also included insurance administration expenses as a cost of automobile accidents, although it recognized that there was a problem in trying to determine the extent to which the expenses could be reduced if the number of accidents decreased. It used the Council's data but made several errors in distributing the factor among the various levels of accident severity—fatality, permanent total disability, and so on. As a result, its estimate was $600 million greater. The Safety Administration is now using revised data.

Costs Estimated Only by the Safety Administration

Unlike the National Safety Council, the Safety Administration included in its estimate about $12.3 billion that is associated with the inconvenience and hardships of automobile accidents.

Home and family duties. The Safety Administration has decided that certain nonemployment-related activities, such as housekeeping and home and yard maintenance, contribute to individual and societal welfare, although they are not represented in the gross national product. It assumed that the average person involved in an accident spent about one-fourth of his or her working hours, or 10 hours a week, on home-related productive activities. The Safety Administration placed a value on inability to perform home and family duties equal to about a quarter of the amount computed for income lost. The average losses computed ranged from $50 for each of 3.5 million persons experiencing temporary disability to $35,000 for each of 8,000 persons suffering permanent, total disability. The overall loss was estimated at $4.5 billion.

Pain and suffering. The Safety Administration also decided that society's welfare decreased because of pain and suffering incurred by the victim of a traffic accident, regardless of whether the victim or his or her estate was compensated. On the basis of reviewing a number of court awards for pain and suffering, the Safety Administration computed average amounts for accident victims suffering injuries of varying degrees of severity. These amounts ranged from $100 for each of 3.5 million persons experiencing temporary disability to $50,000 for each of 8,000 persons suffering permanent, total disability. Overall, the Safety Administration estimated the loss associated with pain and suffering at $3.8 billion.

Other estimated costs. The Safety Administration placed dollar values on some additional categories of costs, such as legal and court costs, loss of service to the community, time and money losses to others, and miscellaneous losses, which in total amounted to about $4 billion. Legal and court costs were based on a study by the Travelers Research Corporation, which showed that police and court costs associated with accidents amounted to about $900 million, and was based on the Safety Administration's estimate that the average person spends about two hours a week for volunteer work in the community.

Time and money losses to others were estimated at about $800 million on the basis that the family and friends of accident victims suffered large noncompensated time and money losses. The estimate included travel costs to visit accident victims and attend funerals, costs of time spent visiting and attending funerals, and costs of time spent by members of the family attending accident victims.

Significance of Different Estimating Methods

Estimated costs of motor vehicle accidents form the basis for determining the benefit to be derived from a proposed safety standard. Therefore, reasonable cost estimates must be used to show fairly whether a proposed safety standard is cost effective. As we saw, the specific estimates of the Safety Administration and the Safety Council varied widely. The resulting differences for each motor vehicle accident, fatality, injury, or property damage are shown in the following table:

	Average cost	
	Safety Administration	Safety Council
Typical accident	$ 2,800	$ 960
Typical fatality	200,700	52,000
Typical injury	7,300	3,100
Typical property damage	300	440

For most categories, the federal agency's cost estimates are substantially higher than those of the private organization. The effect of these differences can be seen from the benefit-cost ratios obtained when the Council's average costs for a fatality and injury are substituted for the costs used by the Safety Administration in its benefit-cost analyses for two standards. In the case of the windshield standard, the benefit-cost ratio is reduced substantially but still is extremely favorable. But in the case of the bus standard, substituting the Safety Council's numbers converts a favorable benefit-cost ratio to an unfavorable one.

	Benefit-cost ratio	
Standard	Safety Administration	Safety Council
Windshield zone intrusion	16 to 1	6 to 1
Bus passenger seating and crash protection	2.22 to 1	.88 to 1

Uncertainty In Estimating Effectiveness Of Proposed Safety Standards

The potential effectiveness of a proposed motor vehicle standard is measured by the reduction in fatalities, injuries, and/or accidents that can be expected to result directly from its implementation. The estimate of effectiveness is an integral part of the benefit-cost analysis, because, multiplied by the Safety Administration's average estimated costs of fatalities, injuries, or accidents, it represents the anticipated benefit. For example, if a proposed standard were expected to reduce accidents by 400,000 annually, the estimated benefit would amount to about $1.1 billion (400,000 accidents times the estimated average accident cost of $2,800).

The effectiveness of a proposed standard best can be estimated by using analyses of accident data showing how the vehicle contributed to an accident, injury, or fatality. The Safety Administration spends about $6 million a year to collect accident data and make analyses to evaluate the effectiveness of proposed and existing safety standards. Although it has collected accident data ranging from basic information in police accident reports to in-depth analyses conducted by multidisciplinary accident investigation teams, this information is of limited value for projecting the effectiveness of proposed safety standards because of the lack of sufficient data on the causes of accidents and the problems associated with collecting data.

In the absence of fully usable accident data, the Safety Administration has to rely on judgment in estimating the effectiveness of a proposed standard. Attempting to issue standards in the absence of adequate accident data can be quite difficult. In January 1971, the Safety Administration proposed a revision of Safety Standard No. 111, "Rearview Mirrors," because "Today's standard review mirrors offer the driver inadequate indirect fields of view to the sides of the vehicle and a limited one to the rear." To support this position the Safety Administration reported that:

> Analysis of the statistics published in Accident Facts (1969 ed.) indicates that 22.5 percent of all motor vehicle crashes, or approximately six million crashes per year, occur in the indirect field of view area to the sides and rear. Systems providing broad and clear vision to the rear, in general use, have the potential of reducing this number of accidents by over a million per year.

The Automobile Manufacturers Association, Inc., criticized the Safety Administration's accident statistics, commenting that broad, clear rear vision does not have the potential of eliminating over one million accidents a year. It cited a research study which concluded that lack of rear vision causes less than three percent of all collisions, and this was not a significant contributor. Many motor vehicle manufacturers supported this position and added arguments of their own. One manufacturer said, "In our view, there is insufficient data available to support the proposed indirect visibility system. . ." For this and other reasons, the Safety Administration, in March 1973, decided to do more research before issuing a safety standard. The agency did point out that three percent of all collisions can represent a significant absolute. In 1972, for example, three percent of all collisions accounted for some 510,000 accidents.

Collecting Accident Data

The Safety Administration has developed a national investigation system to collect accident data. Major data sources include summaries of basic police accident reports, investigations in which police data are supplemented by more detailed inquiry into specific topics, and multidisciplinary accident investigation teams, which conduct clinical in-depth studies of selected accidents. The Safety Administration also contracts for "trilevel studies" that use data from all of the three sources.

Police accident reports provide limited causal data on a large volume of accidents. Although the Safety Administration has obtained certain data from police reports on over 15 million accidents since 1968, the reports rarely pinpoint specific vehicle-related factors that contribute to accidents, injuries, and their severity. The reports, therefore, have limited usefulness for evaluating benefits from safety standards.

Accumulating accident data from detailed investigations is extremely slow and time-consuming. Over 88,000 accidents have been investigated at this level. The administrative procedures for requisitioning the work to be done, briefing police or investigators, waiting for the specified type of accident or injury to occur, collecting and summarizing data, and analyzing the data can involve a period of two years or longer. If the investigation is made to evaluate the potential benefit of a proposed safety standard, implementation of the standard could be greatly delayed.

Multidisciplinary accident investigation data are a major source of detailed accident and injury information for a small number of accidents—about 5,500. Team members from various disciplines, including medicine, law, and engineering, are organized by universities, municipalities, and private corporations to make in-depth studies of selected accidents. The teams examine the precrash, crash, and postcrash phases of an accident to determine the involvement of the basic elements of the system—the occupant, the vehicle, and the environment. Findings range from obvious motor vehicle system and component failures to subtle causal factors that cannot be detected by any less sophisticated methods. Careful sorting and analysis of the data can give the Safety Administration insight into specific problem areas. But, because of the limited number of investigations and the selective basis on which samples are chosen, the data gathered have limited usefulness for developing and evaluating standards.

The Safety Administration also obtains trilevel studies, which use the accident data-gathering techniques from all three of the foregoing levels of data collection, to focus on specific problems, such as:

1. Determining the relationship between vehicle defects and crashes.

2. Examining the influence of interior vehicle component modifications on injuries.
3. Evaluating the probability of injury in relation to dissimilar vehicle weights.

Collecting data at all three levels is expensive, and the lead-time to set up alerting systems, collect police reports, and assemble and process data usually requires a year or two. Consequently, it takes two or three years before meaningful results can be obtained.

Bibliography

GENERAL

Bryer, Stephen G., and Paul W. MacAvoy, *Energy Regulation by the Federal Power Commission*. Washington, D.C.: Brookings Institution, 1974.

Clark, John Maurice, "Government Regulation of Industry," *Encyclopedia of the Social Sciences*. New York: Macmillan, 1932.

Cohen, Manuel F., and George J. Stigler, *Can Regulatory Agencies Protect Consumers?* Washington, D.C.: American Enterprise Institute for Public Policy Research, 1971.

Conference Board, *Challenge to Leadership: Managing In A Changing World*. New York: Free Press, 1973.

Jacoby, Neil H., *Corporate Power and Social Responsibility*. New York: Macmillan, 1973.

McKie, James W., *Government Policies to Control and Assist Private Business*. New York: General Learning Press, 1972.

——, ed., *Social Responsibility and the Business Predicament*. Washington, D.C.: Brookings Institution, 1974.

Posner, R. A., "Theories of Economic Regulation," *Bell Journal of Economics and Management Science*, Autumn 1974.

Shepherd, William G., and Thomas G. Gies, eds., *Regulation in Further Perspective*. Cambridge, Mass: Ballinger Publishing Co., 1974.

Weidenbaum, Murray L., *Government-Mandated Price Increases*. Washington, D.C.: American Enterprise Institute for Public Policy Research, 1975.

———, "The High Costs of Government Regulation," *Business Horizons,* August 1975.

———, "The New Wave of Government Regulation of Business," *Business and Society Review,* Fall 1975.

CONSUMER PRODUCT REGULATION

Barksdale, Hiram C., and Warren A. French, "Response to Consumerism: How Change Is Perceived by Both Sides," *MSU Business Topics,* Spring 1975.

Brunk, Max E., "Consumerism and Marketing," in *Issues in Business and Society,* ed. George Steiner. New York: Random House, 1972.

"Controversy Over A Proposed Consumer Protection Agency: Pro and Con," *Congressional Digest,* November 1974.

Goldberg, Victor P., "The Economics of Product Safety and Imperfect Information," *Bell Journal of Economics and Management Science,* Autumn 1974.

Hendon, Donald W., "Toward A Theory of Consumerism," *Business Horizons,* August 1975.

Hopkins, Harold, "A Greater Margin for Food Safety," *FDA Consumer,* September 1974. *The Impact of Government Regulation on General Foods,* General Foods, 1975.

Kelman, Steven, "Regulation by the Numbers—A Report on the Consumer Product Safety Commission," *Public Interest,* Summer 1974.

Magnuson, Warren G., and Edward B. Cohen, "The Role of the Consumer Under the Consumer Product Safety Act," *Journal of Contemporary Business,* Winter 1975.

Miller, William H., "Consumer Product Safety Commission," *Industry Week,* October 29, 1973.

Oi, Walter Y., "The Economics of Product Safety," *Bell Journal of Economics and Management Science,* Spring 1973.

Richardson, Lee, "Consumers in the Federal Decision-Making Process," *California Management Review,* Winter 1973.

U.S. Comptroller General, *Banning of Two Toys and Certain Aerosol Spray Adhesives.* Washington, D.C.: U.S. General Accounting Office, 1975.

———, *A Summary of a Report to the Congress on Food Labeling.* Washington, D.C.: U.S. General Accounting Office, 1975.

U.S. Consumer Product Safety Commission, *Banned Products.* Washington, D.C.: The Commission, various issues.

U.S. Department of Agriculture, *Standards for Meat and Poultry Products,* Animal and Plant Health Inspection Service, 1973.

U.S. Food and Drug Administration, *Inspecting Food Processing Plants,* FDA Fact Sheet, undated.

Weaver, Paul H., "The Hazards of Trying to Make Consumer Products Safer," *Fortune,* July 1975.

Weston, J. Fred, "Economic Aspects of Consumer Product Safety," in

Issues in Business and Society, ed. George Steiner. New York: Random House, 1972.

Winter, Ralph K., Jr., *The Consumer Advocate Versus the Consumer.* Washington, D.C.: American Enterprise Institute for Public Policy Research, 1972.

AUTOMOBILE REGULATION

Duncombe, Henry L., Jr., and H. Paul Root, "Automobiles, Energy and Product Planning Risks," *Journal of Contemporary Business,* March 1975.

General Motors Corporation, *1973 Report on Progress in Areas of Public Concern.* Detroit: The Corporation, 1973.

Glennon, John C., "Priorities for Highway Safety," *MRI Quarterly,* Spring 1975.

Madden, Carl H., *What's Wrong With Consumerism.* Remarks at the Washington Journalism Center, Washington, D.C., December 10, 1973.

Miller, Roger LeRoy, *The Nader Files: An Economic Critique.* A Paper Presented at a Conference on Government and the Consumer, Center for Government Policy and Business, October 22–28, 1973.

JOB SAFETY REGULATION

Brodeur, Paul, "Annals of Industry: Casualties of the Workplace," *New Yorker,* November 19, 1973.

Conn, Harry, "Quieting Ear Pollution, *American Federationist,* October 1975.

Haggland, George, *OSHA: Controlling Noise In Foundries.* Milwaukee: University of Wisconsin, School for Workers, 1975.

———, *OSHA: Coping With Mechanical Hazards.* Milwaukee: University of Wisconsin, School for Workers, 1974.

Moran, Robert D., "Our Job Safety Law Should Say What It Means," *Nation's Business,* April 1974.

"New Job Injury and Illness Survey," *Occupational Safety and Health,* February 1975.

Nicholas, Jack R., Jr., "OSHA, Big Government, and Small Business," *MSU Business Topics,* Winter 1973.

Sheridan, Peter J., "Safety and the Worker," *Management Review,* January 1974.

U.S. Occupational Safety and Health Administration, *Guide for Applying Safety and Health Standards.* Washington, D.C.: U.S. Government Printing Office, 1972.

Weaver, Paul H., "On the Horns of the Vinyl Chloride Dilemma," *Fortune,* October 1974.

ENVIRONMENTAL REGULATION

Action for Environmental Quality. Washington, D.C.: Environmental Protection Agency, 1973.

Commins, James A., and Alfred Stapler, *Reducing Air Pollution In Industry.* Washington, D.C.: U.S. Small Business Administration, 1973.

"Controversy Over Proposed Federal Regulation of Surface Mining of Coal: Pro and Con," *Congressional Digest,* May 1974.

Cremeans, John E., and Frank W. Segel, "National Expenditures for Pollution Abatement and Control, 1972," *Survey of Current Business,* February 1975.

Curran, Robert E., *The Foundry Industry.* Washington, D.C.: U.S. Department of Commerce, Bureau of Domestic Commerce, 1975.

"Environment and Economic Growth," *Environmental Science and Technology,* July 1974.

Henderson, Hazel, "Ecologists Versus Economists," *Harvard Business Review,* July-August 1973.

Lippke, Bruce R., et al, *The Impact of Pollution Standards on Shortages, Inflation, Real Income and Unemployment.* Tacoma, Wash.: Weyerhaeuser Company, 1975.

National Economic Research Associates, *The Inflationary Impact of Federal Pollution Abatement Legislation.* New York: NERA, 1975.

U.S. Council on Environmental Quality, *Environmental Quality.* Washington, D.C.: U.S. Government Printing Office, issued annually.

U.S. Environmental Protection Agency, *Action for Environmental Quality.* Washington, D.C.: U.S. Government Printing Office, 1973.

———, *Clean Air and Your Car.* Washington, D.C.: U.S. Government Printing Office, 1974.

———, *Primer on Waste Water Treatment.* Washington, D.C.: U.S. Government Printing Office, 1971.

———, *Toward A New Environmental Ethic.* Washington, D.C.: U.S. Government Printing Office, 1971.

URS Research Company, *The Economic Impacts on the American Paper Industry of Pollution Control Costs.* San Mateo, Cal.: URS, 1975.

Zavon, Mitchell R., "The Contradictory Impacts of Health and Environmental Regulation on Industry," *Mutation Research,* vol. 26 (1974).

PERSONNEL REGULATION

Bechter, Dan M., "The Elementary Microeconomics of Private Employee Benefits," *Monthly Review of the Federal Reserve Bank of Kansas City,* May 1975.

EEOC At A Glance. Washington, D.C.: U.S. Equal Employment Opportunity Commission, 1974.

Greenwald, Carol, "Maternity Leave Policy," *New England Economic Review,* January/February 1973.

Rosen, Gerald R., "Industry's New Watchdog in Washington, *Dun's Review,* June 1974.

U.S. Department of Labor, *Age Discrimination in Employment Act.* Washington, D.C.: U.S. Government Printing Office, 1971.

——, *Equal Pay.* Washington, D.C.: U.S. Government Printing Office, 1973.

U.S. Equal Employment Opportunity Coordinating Council, *Uniform Guidelines on Employees Selection Procedures.* Washington, D.C.: The Council, 1974.

Zichy, Shoya, "How Small Funds Are Coping With the New Pension Law," *Institutional Investor,* September 1975.

PROCUREMENT REGULATION

Gould, John P., *Davis-Bacon Act.* Washington, D.C.: American Enterprise Institute for Public Policy Research, 1971.

Inderdohnen, John F., *Inspection on Defense Contracts in Small Firms.* Washington, D.C.: U.S. Small Business Administration, 1967.

Kaufman, Richard F., *The War Profiteers.* New York: Bobbs-Merrill, 1970.

Melman, Seymour, *Pentagon Capitalism.* New York: McGraw-Hill, 1970.

Report of the Commission on Government Procurement. Washington, D.C.: U.S. Government Printing Office, 1972.

Thieblot, Armand J., Jr., *The Davis-Bacon Act.* Philadelphia: University of Pennsylvania, The Wharton School, 1975.

U.S. Small Business Administration, *Selling to the U.S. Government.* Washington, D.C.: U.S. Government Printing Office, 1973.

Weidenbaum, Murray L., *Economics of Peacetime Defense.* New York: Praeger Publishers, 1974.

——, *The Modern Public Sector.* New York: Basic Books, 1969.

—— "Social Responsibility Is Closer Than You Think," *Michigan Business Review,* July 1973.

GOVERNMENT CREDIT AND REGULATION

Bowers, Patricia, *Private Choice and Public Welfare.* Hinsdale, Illinois: Dryden Press, 1974.

Break, George F., *Federal Lending and Economic Stability.* Washington, D.C.: Brookings Institution, 1965.

Commission on Money and Credit, *Federal Credit Programs.* Englewood Cliffs, N.J.: Prentice-Hall, 1973.

Federal Reserve Bank of Boston, *Issues in Federal Debt Management.* Boston: The Bank, 1973.

Levy, Michael E., ed., *Containing Inflation in the Environment of the 1970's.* New York: Conference Board, 1971.

Special Analyses, Budget of the United States, Fiscal Year 1974. Washington, D.C.: U.S. Government Printing Office, 1975.

Weidenbaum, Murray L., *Financing the Electric Utility Industry,* publication No. 1. St. Louis: Washington University, Center for the Study of American Business, 1975.

———, *Subsidies in Federal Credit Programs,* working paper 7102. St. Louis: Washington University, Department of Economics, 1971.

THE PAPER WORK BURDEN

Benston, George J., "The Baffling New Numbers Game at the FTC," *Harvard Business Review,* October 1975.

Marik, Robert H., Associate Director for Management and Operations, Office of Management and Budget. *Statement before the House Committee on Government Operations,* 93rd Congress, 2nd session, September 12, 1974.

Mautz, Robert K., and W. G. May, "The FTC Line of Business Reporting Program," *Financial Executive,* January 1975.

Peltzman, Sam, *Regulation of Pharmaceutical Innovation.* Washington, D.C.: American Enterprise Institute for Public Policy Research, 1974.

Scheibla, Shirley, "Illegal Search and Seizure," *Barron's,* February 17, 1975.

U.S. Congress, Senate, Select Committee on Small Business, *Hearings on the Federal Paper Work Burden,* 93rd Congress, 1st session, 1973.

U.S. Congress, Senate, Subcommittee on Budgeting Management, and Expenditures of the Committee on Government Operations, *Hearings on Corporate Disclosure,* 93rd Congress, 2nd session, 1974.

U.S. Department of Labor, *What Every Employer Needs to Know About OSHA Record Keeping,* B.L.S. Report no. 412, 1973.

U.S. General Services Administration, *Federal Register, Document Drafting Handbook.* Washington, D.C.: U.S. Government Printing Office, 1975.

CONFLICT AND OVERLAP IN REGULATION

Benham, Lee, and Alexandra Benham, "Regulating Through the Professions: A Perspective on Information Control," *Journal of Law and Economics,* October, 1975.

Corey, Gordon R., *Central Station Nuclear Electric Power in Meeting the Energy Crisis.* Lecture at the City College of New York, May 14, 1973.

Milk Industry Foundation, *Basics for Consideration by the Milk Industry.* Washington, D.C.: The Foundation, undated.

Neal, Alfred C., *The Business-Government Relationship.* Paper Presented at UCLA, January 24, 1974.

U.S. Department of Health, Education, and Welfare, Food and Drug Administration, *A Study of State and Local Food and Drug Programs,* 1965.

Werner, Robert L., *Antitrust, Social Responsibility, and Changing Times.* Address to the Conference Board's Thirteenth Annual Conference on Antitrust Issues, New York City, March 7, 1974.

IMPACTS ON TOP MANAGEMENT

Clark, C. Spencer, "Management's Perceptions of Corporate Social Responsibility," *Journal of Contemporary Business,* Summer 1975.

Fore, Herbert, "The State of the Art of Technology Assessment," *Astronautics and Aeronautics,* November 1974.

"The Meaning Behind the Words," *Continental System Communicator,* June 1975.

"Producing Safe Products: An Interview With Richard O. Simpson, *ASTM Standardization News,* April 1975.

"The Top Man Becomes Mr. Outside," *Business Week,* May 4, 1974.

U.S. Consumer Product Safety Commission, National Electronic Injury Surveillance System, *NEISS News,* various issues.

U.S. Federal Energy Administration, *Energy Management Case Studies.* Washington, D.C.: U.S. Government Printing Office, 1975.

U.S. Occupational Safety and Health Administration, *Guidelines for Setting Up Job Safety and Health Programs.* Washington, D.C.: U.S. Government Printing Office, 1972.

IMPACTS ON COMPANY OPERATIONS

Brehm, Howard E., "How to Establish a Product Safety Program," *Quality Progress,* February 1975.

Chelius, James R., *Expectations for OSHA's Performance: The Lessons of Theory and Empirical Evidence,* March 1975.

Cooperative Food Distributors of America, et al, *Voluntary Industry Sanitation Guidelines for Food Distribution Centers and Warehouses.* Washington, D.C.: The Associations, 1974.

Day, George S., and William K. Brandt, "Consumer Research and the Evaluation of Information Disclosure Requirements," *Journal of Consumer Research,* June 1974.

Fieleke, Norman S., "The Buy-American Policy of the United States Government," *New England Economic Review,* July/August 1969.

Fisk, George, "Impact of Social Sanctions on Product Strategy," *Journal of Contemporary Business,* Winter 1975.

Gee, Edwin A., "Report on Safety," *Du Pont Context,* no. 1, 1975.

Gibson, Richard F., "Labor Pushing Harder for Safer Work Places," *Industry Week,* December 16, 1974.

Guidelines for Product Recall. Washington, D.C.: Grocery Manufacturers of America, 1974.

Hicks, Lawrence E., "Product Labeling and the Law," *AMA Management Briefing,* 1974.

Jacobs, Richard M., and August B. Mundel, "Quality Tasks in Product Recall," *Quality Progress,* June 1975.

Jankowski, Paul F., "Report on Safety: Du Pont's Long Record," *Du Pont Context,* no. 1, 1975.

Jensen, Michael C., "U.S. Company Payoffs Way of Life Overseas," *New York Times,* May 5, 1975.

Kerin, Roger A., and Michael Harvey, "Contingency Planning for Product Recall," *MSU Business Topics,* Summer 1975.

Kotler, Philip, "What Consumerism Means for Marketers," *Harvard Business Review,* May–June 1972.

Kuhn, James P., "How to Manage Product Safety," *Industry Week,* April 22, 1974.

Mason, J. Barry, and Morris L. Mayer, "Food Industry Sanitary Practices: Guidelines in Regulation," *MSU Business Topics,* Summer 1975.

National Advertising Review Board, *Product Advertising and Consumer Safety.* New York: The Board, 1974.

Oi, Walter Y., *On Evaluating the Effectiveness of the OSHA Inspection Program,* May 15, 1975.

The President's Report on Occupational Safety and Health. Washington, D.C.: U.S. Government Printing Office, 1973.

Shanahan, Eileen, "Federal Rules Aim at Bias in Credit," *New York Times,* April 25, 1975.

Snyder, James D., "Washington's New Watchwords: 'Repair, Replace, or Refund'," *Sales Management,* February 17, 1975.

Spiers, Joseph N., "Workers on the Board: European Experience Intensifies," *Industry Week,* September 23, 1974.

U.S. Consumer Product Safety Commission, *Handbook and Standard for Manufacturing Safer Consumer Products.* Washington, D.C.: The Commission, 1975.

U.S. Federal Trade Commission, *Care Labels,* Buyers Guide No. 10, Washington, D.C., July 1972.

U.S. Food and Drug Administration, *The New Look in Food Labels,* DHEW Publication No. FDA 74–2036, 1974.

U.S. National Business Council for Consumer Affairs, *Safety in the Marketplace.* Washington, D.C.: U.S. Government Printing Office, 1973.

U.S. Occupational Safety and Health Administration, *The Target Health Hazards.* Washington, D.C.: U.S. Government Printing Office, 1972.

"Whither Multinationals?" *European Community,* February 1974.

Wixon, Chuck, "Recycling Engineers for Careers in Safety," *Job Safety and Health*, May 1974.

IMPACTS ON COMPANY STAFFS

Cornell University, "Private Pensions and the Public Interest," *Industrial and Labor Relations Report*, Fall 1974.

Deane, Richard H., "The IE's Role in Accommodating the Handicapped," *Industrial Engineering*, July 1975.

Edwards, James D., and Carl S. Warren, "Management Forecasts: The SEC and Financial Executives," *MSU Business Topics*, Winter 1974.

"From the Thoughtful Executive: Fair Employment," *Harvard Business Review*, March–April 1975.

Hollander, James, "A Step-by-Step Guide to Corporate Affirmative Action," *Business and Society Review*, Fall 1975.

Imberman, Woodruff, "How Expensive Is An NLRB Election?" *MSU Business Topics*, Summer 1975.

Larkin, Timothy, "The Audiometric Assistant: New Recruit in the War Against Noise," *Job Safety and Health*, June 1974.

Lehmann, Phyllis, "Job Stress: Hidden Hazard," *Job Safety and Health*, April 1974.

Purcell, Theodore V., "How GE Measures Managers in Fair Employment," *Harvard Business Review*, November–December 1974.

Research Media, Inc., *Introduction to OSHA: A Complete Training Program*. Hicksville, N.Y.: RMI, 1974.

Shaeffer, Ruth G., *Nondiscrimination in Employment: Changing Perspectives, 1963–1972*. New York: Conference Board, 1973.

"Some Highlights of the New Pension Reform Act," *Taxes and Estates*, December 1974.

U.S. Department of Housing and Urban Development, *Example of Form ECO–1, Parts F and G, Applicant's Environmental Information*. Washington, D.C.: HUD, 1974.

U.S. Equal Employment Opportunity Commission, *Affirmative Action and Equal Employment: A Guidebook for Employers*. Washington, D.C.: U.S. Government Printing Office, 1974.

U.S. Occupational Safety and Health Administration, *Recordkeeping Requirements*. Washington, D.C.: U.S. Government Printing Office, 1973.

———, *Training Requirements of the Occupational Safety and Health Standards*. Washington, D.C.: U.S. Government Printing Office, 1973.

Walker, Michael J., "The Impact of Environmental Impact Statements," *Management Review*, January 1974.

Weston, Frank T., "Prepare for the Financial Accounting Revolution," *Harvard Business Review*, September–October 1974.

IMPACTS ON GOVERNMENT RELATIONS FUNCTIONS

Cherington, Paul, and Ralph Giller, *The Business Representative in Washington.* Washington, D.C.: Brookings Institution, 1962.

Haley, Martin R., and James M. Kiss, "Larger Stakes in State-house Lobbying," *Harvard Business Review,* January–February 1974.

Hoffer, William, "Associations Face Tough State Lobbying Laws," *Association Management,* August 1975.

"How Well Does Industry Communicate With Congress?", *Industry Week,* May 14, 1973.

Murphy, Richard W., "Lobbies As Information Sources for Congress," *Bulletin of the American Society for Information Science,* April 1975.

Webster, George D., "Proposed Lobbying Legislation Raises Constitutional Questions," *Association Management,* July 1975.

Weidenbaum, Murray L., "Private Advisors and Government Policy Making," *Policy Analysis,* January 1975.

TRADE ASSOCIATIONS AND GOVERNMENT

Chamber of Commerce of the United States, *Dialogue With the Agencies and Departments* Washington, D.C.: The Chamber, undated.

——, *Dialogue With the Hill.* Washington, D.C.: The Chamber, undated.

Day, J. Edward, "The Association Executive and the Government," *Association Management,* November 1966.

Elton, Reuel W., *How Trade Associations Help Small Business,* Management Aids No. 32. Washington, D.C.: U.S. Small Business Administration, 1961.

Glass, Andrew J., "NAM's New Look Is Toward Goal of Business Unity," *National Journal Reports,* January 5, 1974.

Goldsmith, S. L., Jr., "What the Aluminum Association Did About the Energy Crisis," *Association Management,* August 1975.

"How Associations Band Together To Achieve Common Goals," *Association Management,* November 1975.

Lyons, Richard D., "Lobbyists Shifting Quarters to Capital," *New York Times,* June 8, 1975.

Medvin, Norman, "How Big Oil Influences Government," *American Federationist,* December 1974.

"New Opportunities for Executive Development," *Association Management,* July 1975.

Shanahan, Eileen, "Antitrust Bill Stopped By a Business Lobby," *New York Times,* November 16, 1975.

BUSINESS IN POLITICS

Blumenthal, W. Michael, "New Business Watchdog Needed," *New York Times,* May 25, 1975.

Committee for Economic Development, *Restoring Confidence in the Political Process.* New York: CED, 1974.

Common Cause, "Integrity in Politics," *Report From Washington,* December 1973–January 1974.

Epstein, Edward M., *The Corporation in American Politics.* Englewood Cliffs, N.J.: Prentice Hall, 1969.

———, "Corporations and the Political Imperative," *Business and Society Review,* Summer 1972.

———, "Dimensions of Corporate Power," *California Management Review,* Winter 1973 and Summer 1974.

Finley, Grace J., *Policies on Leaves for Political and Social Action.* New York: Conference Board, 1972.

"Inside Peter Drucker, *Nation's Business,* March 1974.

"The Question of Federal Financing of National Election Campaigns: Pro and Con," *Congressional Digest,* February 1974.

GOVERNMENT AND BUSINESS DECISION-MAKING

Berle, A. A., and G. C. Means, *The Modern Corporation and Private Property.* New York: Macmillan, 1932.

Burnham, James, *The Managerial Revolution.* Bloomington: Ind. University Press, 1941.

"For a National Economic Planning System," *Challenge,* March–April 1975.

Ford Administration's Efforts to Reform Government Regulation of Business, publication No. 6. St. Louis: Washington University, Center for the Study of American Business, 1975.

Francis, Darryl R., *Public Policy for a Free Economy,* publication No. 3. St. Louis: Washington University Center for the Study of American Business, 1975.

Franklin, William, and Francis Lowell, "Unapproved Drugs in the Practice of Medicine," *New England Journal of Medicine,* May 15, 1975.

Galbraith, John Kenneth, *Economics and the Public Purpose.* Boston: Houghton Mifflin, 1973.

Hayek, F. A., *The Constitution of Liberty.* Chicago: University of Chicago Press, 1960.

Humphrey, Hubert H., "Planning Economic Policy," *Challenge,* March–April 1975.

Jain, Subhasir, and Surendra Singhvi, eds., *Essentials of Corporate Planning.* Oxford, Ohio: Planning Executives Institute, 1973.

Kneese, Allen V., and Blair T. Bower, *Managing Water Quality: Economics, Technology, Institutions.* Baltimore: Johns Hopkins Press, 1968.

Mockler, Robert J., ed., *Readings in Business Planning and Policy Formulation.* New York: Appleton-Century-Crofts, 1972.

Mueller, Willard F., "Federal Chartering of Corporations," *American Federationist,* June 1973.

Peltzman, Sam, "An Evaluation of Consumer Production Legislation: The 1962 Drug Amendments," *Journal of Political Economy,* September/October 1973.

Preston, Lee E., *Socializing the Corporation.* Lecture Presented at Rochester Institute of Technology, March 14, 1974.

———, "The Third Managerial Revolution," *Academy of Management Journal,* September 1974.

Schmidt, Alexander M., "The Benefit-Risk Equation," *FDA Consumer,* May 1974.

Steiger, William, "OSHA: Four Years Later," *Labor Law Journal,* vol. XXV, no. 12 (1974).

Stein, Herbert, *Economic Planning and the Improvement of Economic Policy.* Washington, D.C.: American Enterprise Institute for Public Policy Research, 1975.

Steiner, George A., *Managerial Long-Range Planning.* New York: McGraw-Hill 1963.

United States Congress, Senate, Committee on Interior and Insular Affairs, *Federal Charters for Energy Corporations–Selected Materials,* 93rd Congress, 2nd session, 1974.

Wardell, William M., "Therapeutic Implications of the Drug Lag," *Clinical Pharmacology and Therapeutics,* January 1974.

Index